Kirk Hunsicker

SMALL BUSINESS MANAGEMENT

THIRD EDITION

SMALL BUSINESS MANAGEMENT

THIRD EDITION

William D. Hailes, Jr.
Raymond T. Hubbard

COPYRIGHT © 1983
BY DELMAR PUBLISHERS INC.

All rights reserved. Certain portions of this work copyright © 1965 (Volume 1, Small Business Management), 1967 (Volume 2, Small Business Management), and 1977. No part of this work covered by the copyright hereon may be reproduced or used in any form or by any means — graphic, electronic, or mechanical, including photocopying, recording, taping, or information storage and retrieval systems — without written permission of the publisher.

10 9 8 7 6 5 4 3

LIBRARY OF CONGRESS CATALOG CARD NUMBER: 82-46006
ISBN: 0-8273-2108-2

Printed in the United States of America
Published simultaneously in Canada
by Nelson Canada,
A Division of International Thomson Limited

PREFACE

The economics of our country is sometimes thought of as being dominated by giant corporations with profits in the millions. A characterization such as this one ignores the important role of small business in society. Each year in the United States over half a million new businesses begin operation. Many succeed, while others fail. The purpose of this text is to examine small business practices and to identify those factors which contribute to the success of a small business.

Small Business Management introduces the prospective small business owner to the principles of small business planning and operation. The text explains basic areas of business, ranging from a description of opportunities in a free society to an appraisal of the future for small business. Individuals involved in secondary, vocational, two-year college, and adult education programs, or anyone interested in starting a small business, are given an opportunity to study, discuss, and apply some of the principles and methods successfully used in small business management.

Each unit includes objectives, information, illustrations, and materials which aid the individual in the understanding of the subject. Practical assignments highly relevant to actually starting a small business form the basis of a manual which is completed one assignment at a time. Each unit also contains a unit quiz. The questions are designed to measure the student's comprehension of the material presented. The Instructor's Guide for this text includes model answers to the assignments. However, the emphasis of the assignments is on the results being meaningful to the entrepreneur who hopefully will accomplish most of the planning for a small business while studying this material.

Many persons will be studying this text with the expressed purpose of starting a small business some day or improving a business they may now be involved with. For those persons especially, it is urged that they complete each of the business manual assignments. When the projects are all completed and assembled there will be a comprehensive business guide designed especially for the business chosen, with many of the forms, planning ideas, and problems already worked out. This business manual will greatly simplify the actual process of opening the small business when the time comes. It could also be shown to a prospective employer as evidence of sincerity of purpose in seeking employment for experience, or to a banker in support of a request for a business loan.

Statistical information has been updated in this edition. Two completely new units have been added, one on selecting the right business, and the other on franchises. New information has been included reflecting the constantly changing world of small business. For instance, considerable litigation has ensued recently concerning product liability. This topic is thoroughly discussed, as it will be an important issue for small businesses in the future. Anyone planning to start a small business should be informed about local, state, and federal sources for up-to-date information, rules and regulations, and anything which affects the business. In order to do this, private and public agencies and organizations which can assist the small business owner are mentioned throughout the text.

ABOUT THE AUTHORS

William Hailes and Raymond Hubbard have extensive training and experience in business education and in management. Mr. Hailes is a graduate of Rider College and The University of Rochester. He is a business educator, a small business owner, a public school administrator, a curriculum consultant, and has developed many educational materials.

Dr. Hubbard holds degrees from the State University of New York at Binghamton, Syracuse University, and a doctorate from Rutgers University. He has been an instructor and curriculum coordinator at the secondary level and a professor, business division chairperson, and dean at the two-year college level. He is a management education specialist for a large computer firm. Dr. Hubbard also serves as a small business consultant for employee training and management programs.

ACKNOWLEDGMENTS

Albany *Times-Union:* Figure 9-13

American Express Company: Figure 6-5

Atmospheric Sciences Research Center: Figure 12-7

Camelot: ra group, incorporated: Agency; John Reddish, Copywriter; Pat Nemeroff, Art Director: Figure 9-12

Deluxe Check Printers, Incorporated: Figures 7-26 and 7-29

Digital Equipment Corporation: Figure 12-2

Information supplied by Dun & Bradstreet: Figure 3-1

Forest Park Community College: Figure 2-43

Grand Union Company: Figures 7-5 and 10-4

Hobart Corporation: Figures 2-4 and 12-5

Mark Huth: Figure 2-9

Internal Revenue Service: Figures 7-12, 7-15, 7-18, 7-19, 7-23, 7-24, and 7-25

Jack Lasek: Figures 2-25, 2-27, 2-30, 2-50, 2-53, 4-8, 5-13, 5-15, 5-22, 5-27, 5-28, and 5-29

Lozier Corporation: Figure 2-24

Milwaukee Area Technical College: Figure 10-3

Mutual Publishers: Figure 7-22

Napoleon, Incorporated: Figure 9-2

National Blank Book Company: Figure 7-14

National Cash Register Corporation: Figures 7-2, 7-7, 10-2, 10-5, and 12-4

National Commercial Bank & Trust Company: Figure 7-6

John Nevins: Figure 2-7

Occupational Outlook Quarterly: Figure 9-17

Ohrback's Incorporated: Figure 9-19

Albert Pautler: Figures 2-8 and 2-40

Barbara Schultz: Figures 1-8, 1-9, 2-2, 2-3, 2-6, 2-15, 2-16, 2-17, 2-20, 2-36, 2-38, 2-47, 3-4, 4-1, 4-2, 4-5, 5-3, 5-4, 5-8, 5-10, 5-17, 5-23, 5-25, 5-26, 6-1, 7-4, 7-27, 8-1, 8-6, 8-7, 9-4, 9-5, 9-9, 9-15, 9-16, 9-18, 9-20, and 9-21

Social Security Administration: Figure 7-17

State Bank of Albany: Figures 7-8 and 7-9

Herbert Stemley: Figure 2-44

Sweda International: Figure 12-3

The McDonald's Corporation: Figures 2-22, 4-7, and 11-1

Bert Turner: Figures 1-1, 1-2, 1-4, 1-5, 1-7, 2-1, 2-5, 2-10, 2-11, 2-12, 2-13, 2-14, 2-18, 2-19, 2-21, 2-23, 2-26, 2-28, 2-29, 2-31, 2-32, 2-33, 2-34, 2-35, 2-41, 2-42, 2-45, 2-46, 2-48, 2-49, 2-51, 2-52, 3-3, 4-3, 4-4, 4-6, 5-2, 5-5, 5-7, 5-9, 5-11, 5-14, 5-16, 5-21, 5-24, 6-2, 6-3, 6-4, 6-6, 6-7, 7-1, 8-3, 8-4, 8-5, 10-1, 11-2, 11-3, 11-5, 12-1, and 12-8

United Press International (October, 1981): Figure 1-3

U.S. Small Business Administration: Figure 7-16

CONTENTS

DELMAR PUBLISHERS INC.
2 COMPUTER DRIVE, WEST – BOX 15-015
ALBANY, NEW YORK 12212

UNIT 1

SMALL BUSINESS IN A FREE SOCIETY

OBJECTIVES

After studying this unit, you will be able to

- Describe the free enterprise system.
- Explain the difference between big business and small business.
- Explain the need for rules and regulations in businesses.
- Define the Terms to Know.

WORKING FOR YOURSELF OR OTHERS?

When Sam was in high school, he learned to operate an engine lathe in a vocational machine shop program that his school offered. Even before he was graduated, Sam was working as a beginning machinist in a small shop on a cooperative work-experience program, which helped him learn on the job while still in school. After graduation, Sam stayed on at the machine shop and began an *apprentice* program. After six years Sam became a *journeyman* machinist and eventually a master. Sam was lucky, and worked hard, and was quick to pick up changes in his job. As a result, *technological* changes did not really affect Sam too much. He was able to quickly learn the new machines and procedures as they came along.

The small machine shop grew and became a large manufacturing plant. Sam was offered promotions many times. He refused the promotions on the grounds that he did not want the responsibility. Sam earned good wages over the years. During World War II, he was exempted from military service because the plant was a large defense contractor. After 47 years with the same company, Sam retired. He lives with his wife in Florida on a comfortable pension, and sees his seven grandchildren from time to time.

There are a lot of people like Sam, who want out of life only a steady job, fair wages, and a chance to retire on a decent income. Sam was fortunate. His plant never laid him off, and he was able to save over $5,000 in savings bonds on the payroll savings plan at work. Sam has what many people call *security*.

Take on the other hand, Irving. Irving was a poor student in school, at least academically. In those days, all he was interested in was cars. The school Irving attended did not have a vocational program, so he could not get proper training in auto mechanics. Because of poor attendance, due to staying home to work on his car, Irving finally dropped out of high school. Eventually, Irving had to find work. At the height of the Great Depression, all he could find was a floor-cleaning job at a large auto and truck garage. The job was extremely dirty and hard. The pay was low, but, Irving stayed with the job for five years. During that time, he watched the repairmen and because he was quick to learn, like Sam, they showed him how to repair engines, among other jobs.

One day Irving noticed that they threw out broken parts, usually without trying to repair them. He asked his foreman if he could have the old carburetors, generators, and fuel pumps to work on. He promised not to do the repairs on company time. The foreman agreed, and soon Irving had repaired dozens of engine parts. He began selling the repaired parts on weekends to other garages and shops in town. Irving was a natural repairman. When he repaired a part, it usually worked fine and was inexpensive compared to a new part. His reputation for reconditioned parts earned him much more money for part-time work than his regular job did. Irving soon decided to quit his job with the garage and work full time repairing used auto parts. He rented a shed and traveled to all the garages in town buying their junk parts. In most cases, he got the parts for nothing or for as little as 10 cents apiece. Irving was extremely busy fixing parts. He tried to keep up with the requests for parts from local garages, but decided that he needed help. He hired a person to assist him in fixing the parts and another person to travel to the various garages to pick up the used parts.

About this time, Irving was drafted into the Army during World War II. He wound up in the Engineers working on heavy equipment, trucks, tanks, and half-tracks. When the war ended and Irving was discharged, he had four years of valuable experience working on all sorts of heavy equipment and machinery. Using a GI loan, he started a small parts business. To make a long story short, the business grew rapidly after World War II.

Irving is retired now, living with his wife in Florida. His business grew into a five-state chain of auto parts stores, a manufacturing plant, a reconditioning plant, and several warehouses. Irving incorporated the business in 1950. The last year he was actively engaged in the business, it grossed seven million dollars in sales. Irving gave his two sons complete control of the business, and they appear to be running it well. Irving lives well in the southern climate, draws a six-figure salary as chairman of the board, and still tinkers with automobiles, only this time, just for fun!

If you are more like Irving than Sam, you may want to think about working for yourself, rather than for others. Working for yourself is what this book is all about.

THE FREE ENTERPRISE SYSTEM

Most countries operate within an economic system that provides or attempts to provide its people with necessary *goods* and *services*. Many countries use the capitalist system to fulfill these needs. In the capitalist system, there is much less government interference in the operation of businesses than with other economic systems such as the socialist system. It is important to understand some of the privileges and responsibilities people have in a free enterprise system. These include the right of property, the right of free enterprise, the right of contract, and the right of profit.

Privileges in a Free Enterprise Economy

The *right of property* includes the right to own items that are *intangible* (which you cannot feel or touch) and *tangible* (physical). Copyrights, patents, trademarks, and goodwill or reputation are intangible forms of property. Buildings, machines, and merchandise are tangible forms of property. All of these items owned, both tangible and intangible, are called *assets.*

The *right of free enterprise* allows a person to enter into any business activity that is legal and does not infringe on the rights of others.

The right of profit is the freedom to invest one's own time, labor, and money in an activity in the hope of making a profit. Many people prefer to own a business instead of working for others. If they succeed in business, they feel that their profit and self-satisfaction will be greater than if they worked for others.

An employee works for *wages,* and the business owner works for *profits.* You could say that profits are, in effect, the wages of management. Business owners who undertake the responsibility of risking their assets (capital) in a business are called *entrepreneurs.* From the French, this word means literally "to enter" and "to take" (entre + prenier) presumably, a profit. Profit is what motivates entrepreneurs to risk capital. These risks are sometimes great. Without the *profit motive,* few would risk their money. The free enterprise system is based on this willingness of individuals to risk their accumulated wealth in the hope of making profits. This system is called *capitalism.*

The *right of contract* allows two or more persons to enter into a legal agreement. If one party fails to live up to the contract, the other parties may obtain satisfaction through the court system. Contracts can be enforced by law. If this were not the case, there would be a general lack of confidence among people in business and it would be hard to carry on business.

Responsibilities in a Free Society

When the U.S. was largely unsettled and had a small population, almost any kind of business could be started without the government's permission. Since travel was hard and slow due to poor roads, each community provided many services for itself. Each town had its own local blacksmith shop, barrel maker, cobbler, and furniture maker. Factories and mills employed people from the village and the owner personally knew each worker.

As the country's population grew, the methods of production and transportation improved. Machinery was used to supplement hand labor in manufacturing. Factories employed hundreds of people, and villages and towns became cities. Owners could no longer personally know each person they employed.

It became necessary to hire persons to assist the boss. As a result, managers and supervisors were added to oversee the work of others. The growth of industry lead to a number of practices requiring restraints. In some cases, factories employed children and women who worked long hours at dangerous jobs. Workers were often badly treated and some were injured by moving machinery. People realized that laws were needed to prevent child labor abuses and to improve working conditions.

Laws have been passed to prevent labor abuses and to provide payment for workers injured on the job. Wages and working conditions have also improved. To protect consumers, laws now require businesses to get licenses and permits in order to conduct certain businesses. Various products must be labeled showing ingredients or materials, quantity, and origin of manufacture. Business establishments are now inspected for cleanliness and safety.

Though certain standards are required by law, business owners now realize that it is good business to provide good working conditions for employees. Owners must depend on workers who are treated fairly to provide the high-quality goods and services at a reasonable cost which permit them to compete successfully in the marketplace. This spirit of working together for a common goal is the factor that underlies our democratic free enterprise system.

SMALL BUSINESSES — WHAT ARE THEY?

Numerous definitions of the term *small business* exist. The Small Business Act of 1953 states that a small business is "one which is independently owned and operated and not dominant in its field of operation." The Small Business Administration traditionally uses the following criteria for defining small business:

- Retailing — sales volume
- Service — sales volume
- Wholesaling — sales volume
- Manufacturing — number of employees

The definition varies depending on the government agency. Such agencies as the Small Business Administration, Committee on Economic Development, and Federal Reserve Bank have different definitions. Their size standard for small business continuously changes in order to meet the needs of our changing economy.

If a business is considered small by the appropriate governmental agency, it may qualify for a number of government services. Some of these services include access to federal loans, management assistance, and first chance for certain government contracts.

Measuring Business Size

The following is a list of terms that can be used to describe a business. Each term tells something about the size of a business.

- Total assets — all that a business owns
- Net worth — business assets less what is owed

- Gross profits — money left from sales after all expenses (except taxes) have been paid
- Net profits — what is left from gross profit after business income taxes are paid
- Employees — total number of workers and managers listed on the payroll
- Income — net receipts, the total sales less returns, allowances, and discounts

It is necessary to keep records of a business for tax purposes and as a measure of growth. Some businesses fail because they are improperly expanded. Other businesses are unsuccessful because they expand too quickly and cannot handle the problems that come with rapid growth. Many businesses remain small and provide excellent income throughout their lifetime.

Big business is not bad because it is big. Unethical practices that occur in small or in large businesses must be stopped. Honesty does not depend on size. Some people distrust big business because it is large, complex, and hard to understand. Some small business owners resent the larger companies because they feel they have an unfair advantage. This is not always true. As the size of a business increases, so does its problems. Because government help is available it is easier to operate a small business than a large business. Small business owners who complain that large businesses are giving them unfair competition have not yet found ways to use the advantage of flexibility unique to them.

The Importance of Small Businesses

A great number of kinds of small businesses are possible. It is therefore difficult to decide how you fit into the business world considering your plans, your preferences, and your abilities. Whatever choice is made, it is important that you are fully prepared for it. In Unit 2, several different types and kinds of businesses are explained. Several choices are available, many that you have probably not thought of thus far. So, making a decision, one of the most important in your life, seems most confusing.

Being aware of some of the facts about small businesses and their importance may make you feel better about a decision to own a small business. A few people believe that the contribution of small business to the nation's economy is relatively unimportant. Nothing could be further from the truth, Figure 1-1. According to the Small Business Administration of the U.S.:

- 95% of all businesses in the U.S. are small.
- 43% of the total business volume in the U.S. is done by small businesses.
- 51% of the civilian work force in the U.S. is employed by small businesses.*

*Small Enterprise in the Economy, U.S. Small Business Administration, Office of Advocacy, Planning and Research, Washington, D.C., 20416, March 1975.

FIGURE 1-1
A business does not have to be large to be successful.

Small business plays an important role in our economy. Therefore, the choice that you make is important, for your own sake and also for the country. Several lists of small business possibilities can be found in Unit 2. Study the possibilities carefully, and make sure you understand what each business is. The businesses listed are only suggestions. The list is not intended to be complete, since thousands of choices exist. Since over half a million new small businesses are started every year, there is quite a variety. You should begin now to think of a part-time or full-time business that will challenge your imagination and motivate you to do the planning for it, Figure 1-2. If you are serious about starting a business now or in the future, this project can be the most important one you will ever undertake.

Choosing the right business is an important and difficult task. Many businesses fail because they never should have been started. The person starting a business can either buy an existing business, start a new business similar to ones already operating, or start a completely new kind of business. The buying of an existing business is discussed later in the text. Before a potential proprietor can research a

FIGURE 1-2
Child care services is an excellent example of a small business that can be operated part-time in the home with little outlay in capital. The building must be inspected, and a license is required.

business, however, that person must have an idea of what type of business is desired.

There are a number of steps you can follow in order to choose the right small business. First, analyze your own strengths, weaknesses, and interests. Write down on a piece of paper the work-related experiences you have had in the past. Then identify those experiences you enjoyed most and those you enjoyed least. From this exercise, you should be able to identify types of businesses that are similar to what you like to do.

RESOURCES FOR SMALL BUSINESS IDEAS

Some people know exactly what business they want to start. Others need to search for a business that will be successful. The two basic research activities that follow have worked for several people.

Read the following publications:

- Newspapers. Most daily and all Sunday papers have business opportunity sections.
- Trade papers and periodicals. At least one publication exists for every trade. Most of the publications cover trends and market information for the present and future.
- Economic studies in your area. These studies are usually found at the local chamber of commerce.
- Business journals. These publications discuss trends and opportunities. Many states and large metropolitan areas have their own business publications.

Talk to the following people:

- Bankers, accountants, business consultants and lawyers. These professionals are able to help potential proprietors assess their abilities. They may also know of individuals who have businesses to sell.
- Business brokers, realtors, industrial developers, and chamber of commerce representatives.
- Friends, relatives, and prospective customers. These individuals are able to react to suggested needs that could be met by a potential business.

The prospective new business owner should talk to as many people as possible. Always keep in mind that it is important to choose a field that meets a customer's need and has growth possibilities. Without the possibility of growth, a new business will be short-lived.

RULES AND REGULATIONS

Would a baker living in London 400 years ago have had to obey some of the rules and regulations which exist today? The answer is yes. The baker could not have started a baking business without the permission of the other bakers in town. The size of the loaf, its ingredients, the amount it was sold for, and every other aspect of business would have been subject to very specific regulations. Thousands of years ago in ancient Babylonia, records show that businesses were bound by numerous rules or laws. In many ways, business persons today have more freedom to open a new business or market a new product than their predecessors throughout history.

Nevertheless, the list of regulations grows. More rules are made and more reports are required, and they are getting more complicated. The services of a lawyer, an accountant, or a tax expert are often necessary to fill out forms and meet the requirements of the laws. Some people feel that free enterprise is being restrained by rules, regulations, and reports. Why should there be so many regulations and why should they continue to grow in complexity?

Regulations are Needed

The following example illustrates the need for certain rules and regulations in business operation. Before opening a restaurant, many inspections are made to insure standards in safety. The electrical wiring, refrigeration, water, and sanitation must all conform to current requirements. The proper licenses must be obtained, a minimum wage must be paid, and children who are under age may not be employed.

Business owners might wonder why the government does not trust their good sense and honesty. Unfortunately, some individuals cannot be trusted. A business next door to the restaurant might decide to cut expenses by using defective wiring. If this caused a fire, the restaurant could suffer. Another neighboring business might carelessly dump refuse which would attract animals and insects, creating an odor. Restaurant customers would surely react.

Protection From a Few

As society expands in size and complexity, more rules and regulations are needed. These rules and regulations are necessary if we are to live together in harmony and with maximum individual freedom.

The profit motive results in improvements for society by causing competition, which in turn causes products and services to be improved. Nevertheless, it is also necessary to limit the few people who might make a profit in a harmful way. Most products go through many processes and inspections before reaching the consumer. Federal and state regulations insure that the consumer is protected at various stages of production and distribution. Each state has a consumer protection agency. Consumers can apply to these agencies if they are injured by faulty products, or from malpractice of a service. In the future, it will be necessary to pass even more laws concerning industrial safety, working conditions, retirement pensions, social benefits, product liability, and additional taxes. Laws that limit and direct the disposal of toxic wastes from manufacturing and processing will also be needed.

Regulations originate at various levels of government: local (city, county, town), state, and federal. Trade associations, unions, and companies themselves make rules and regulations, Figure 1-3. A rule or a regulation is often the result of a court decision based on a law which is tested and interpreted by the courts.

City governments pass rules, regulations, and ordinances. The various levels of government issue licenses, permits, and *variances* (exceptions to the general rule). *Codes* are groups of regulations that are classified by governmental departments, such as building codes, sanitary codes, fire regulations, and zoning ordinances.

Wine sellers' war to spill at least into next week

United Press International

NEW YORK—The wine war that New York state retailers have waged since a minimum pricing law was invalidated last week will continue at least until Monday.

State Court of Appeals Judge Jacob Fuchsberg heard oral arguments Friday from the State Liquor Authority, which wants him to grant a temporary stay that would effectively restore minimum prices until the full court meets Oct. 6.

The judge said he will announce on Monday or Tuesday whether he intends to issue the stay. If the temporary stay is granted, it would hold only until the state's highest court could hear the Liquor Authority's appeal.

Fuchsberg warned the authority's attorney, Warren Pesetsky, that he was unlikely to win a reversal. "It would seem to me you don't have very much chance of change," the judge said.

Fuchsberg and the six other members of the court invalidated the law in a unanimous decision Sept. 9. The court cited a U.S. Supreme Court ruling that voided the California statute, similar to New York's.

Since then, liquor stores have slashed their wine prices, and some are selling bottles for as little as a penny above cost. The Liquor Authority attorney noted that 1,895 of 5,000 liquor stores in the state went bankrupt within four years after liquor price controls were repealed in 1964.

The Legislature in 1971 reinstated a minimum liquor price system of 12 percent above cost.

But Fuchsberg defended decontrolling wine prices.

"This is the marketplace," he said. "It's called the free enterprise system."

FIGURE 1-3
Government agencies control business in various ways. One way is by trying to regulate prices, such as in this case.

State governments issue automobile licenses and registration stickers. Many states have passed state laws or statutes controlling wages and working hours, workers' compensation, various factory practices, state speed limits, smoking in theaters and the use of drugs.

The federal government has passed laws which require an employer to withhold income tax from workers' wages and to pay a share of national insurance called *social security*. The federal government has also passed laws to protect the consumer from inferior food, drug, and cosmetic products, mislabeled goods, and unfair trade practices. These laws usually benefit all members of society. The employer is also a consumer who benefits from these controls. Without these controls, chaos would result.

A *rule* is a statement usually preventing a person from performing a certain activity. An example of a rule is a "No Smoking" or "No Fishing" sign, Figure 1-4. To disobey a company rule usually results in a fine, temporary suspension, or dismissal. If the rule is an institutional rule, such as in a school or public library, a warning or a fine can result. However, if the rule is issued by a municipality, such as a town or village, the rule is identified as such, "No Parking, by Order of the Chief of Police". The rule then has the same force as an ordinance, or may actually be an ordinance, and could be enforced with a substantial fine.

A *permit* is temporary permission to perform some activity for a specified period of time. Permits are given for such activities as hunting game, building an addition on a house, or selling specified goods in a given area. A license is a state or federal document, Figure 1-5. A *license* allows an individual to continue the

FIGURE 1-4
A rule usually prevents an individual
from performing a certain activity.

FIGURE 1-5
An individual oftentimes needs a license to practice a profession.

practice of an art, profession, or trade; the right to sell liquor; the right to operate equipment, special machinery, and vehicles; and the right to use explosives or set off fireworks, among other activities. Some people who have licenses to practice a trade or profession have passed a performance test or a state-board examination to prove their competency.

A *regulation* often is a requirement that must be filled, Figure 1-6. The following are examples of regulations: you must be a certain age to vote and you must have the lights on when you are operating a motorcycle. An *ordinance* is a local law, which may also duplicate state and federal laws. State laws are called *statutes* and are applicable where no local ordinance exists. Most ordinances have the same force as statutes and can be enforced by the local justice of the peace.

FIGURE 1-6
Rules and regulations can be quite confusing.

How Can the Small Business Owner Conform to the Law?

If you start a small business, have a lawyer make a list of important laws and regulations that will affect your operation. You are responsible for obeying the law. Knowledge of related rules and regulations is important to business success. By consulting a lawyer and following the procedures outlined in Unit 8, problems in conforming to current laws can be minimized. Mistakes can be made. If a law or regulation is violated unintentionally, the result the first time is usually a warning. If you deliberately break a law, there is a good chance you will be fined or punished as the law provides.

An important part of conforming to laws and regulations is to keep accurate records of all business transactions. Suggestions for keeping accurate records are given in Unit 7. When a business owner is asked for information, the best source is up-to-date records.

By seeking assistance from trade associations, unions, chambers of commerce, better business bureaus, local business organizations, and legislators, business owners may help to change some regulations which are no longer useful. Laws are generally sensible, but occasionally some outlive their usefulness. People who are able to change laws may not know that a particular law has become useless. Since these people depend on business persons like yourself to bring these matters to their attention, they may thank you for it.

Any person who is planning to start a new business has an interest in the laws and regulations that will affect it. This text could not possibly cover all the regulations which apply to each business. Certain general guidelines exist which cover most stores and service establishments. The topics in Unit 8 are not intended to be legal reference, interpretation, or a substitute for legal advice when necessary.

Rules and regulations are imposed upon businesses by local governments. These rules and regulations are in the public interest to protect health, safety, and general welfare. Businesses such as restaurants, taverns, tobacconists, and gasoline service stations must observe special rules. In other parts of this book, topics which apply to specific businesses are described. These topics include regulations for kinds of business organizations, taxes, licenses, and labor practices. The following is a list of agencies that set requirements for small businesses.

- Department of Fire Protection
- Board of Fire Underwriters
- County or City Board of Health
- Department of Labor

Business Operations Subject to Review

Business operations are subject to review by local, state, and federal authorities. These reviews insure that rules and regulations are being obeyed and standards maintained. Some of the operations subject to review are listed here.

Income. Business income must be reported for income tax purposes. Other reasons for reporting business income include providing information for bank loans, attracting investors, making equitable distribution of profits in partnerships, and as a measure of business growth. The records are usually subject to an audit.

Working Conditions. Clean and safe working conditions must be provided for employees and if required, medical and safety equipment must be provided.

Wages and Hours. Work regulations and announcements must be posted where employees can read them, Figure 1-6. Employers must pay at least the minimum wage that applies to their employees. Special requirements must be met if minors are employed.

Advertising, Labeling, and Packaging. Businesses must not be guilty of false advertising, mislabeling, or providing less than the labeled weight in a package, Figure 1-7.

FIGURE 1-7
The ingredients and weight of a product intended for human consumption must be clearly marked on the label.

FIGURE 1-8
Federal and state laws prohibit discrimination against any person because of color, race, sex, religion, or national origin. The employment application must not contain any questions that are discriminatory.

Unfair Practices. Laws prevent business persons from engaging in various unfair practices, such as price fixing and other means of restraining trade.

Discrimination. Federal and state regulations prevent an employee from being discriminated against because of color, race, sex, religion, or national origin, Figure 1-8.

Liability and Compensation. Employers are required to carry insurance and provide adequate compensation for workers injured on the job and customers injured on the business premises.

To find ideas for a possible business of your own, you may want to consult the following sources:

- Newspapers
- Telephone directory (yellow pages)
- Copies of local zoning maps
- Copies of local ordinances
- Local rules and regulations
- Local library
- Brochures from the chamber of commerce
- Recent copy of the *Occupational Outlook Handbook*
- Recent edition of the *Dictionary of Occupational Titles (DOT)*, U.S. Department of Labor
- Magazines and trade journals
- Conversations with local business owners

FIGURE 1-9
This couple seems happy operating their own business. A husband and wife team owning a small business can be a good choice as each can share the work.

BUSINESS MANUAL ASSIGNMENT

For each business manual assignment in this text, you will be preparing materials for a booklet or Business Operations Manual for a small business that you may actually own some day. You may be in school or college now, or you may be working. You may have already started in a business of your own or with a partner. Regardless, this manual will be valuable to you in the following ways.

- Serve as a collection of valuable reference information about your business, organized so you can find the material quickly
- Show others the extent of your planning
- Force you to think out almost every detail of your business before you actually begin
- Greatly reduce your chances of failure by completing all necessary planning before beginning
- Serve as evidence of your commitment to enter business

For the first assignment, write at least two paragraphs to include in your manual explaining why you would prefer to own a business instead of working for others. Give at least three reasons why you favor self-employment. Explain also why it is not possible to do what you want to do in Russia (a communist state) or in England (a socialist state). Entitle your article *Preface* and place it in a folder for manual assignments. At some point in the future, your instructor may want to comment on your work or assist you. When you think you have written the best preface, type it double spaced on a sheet of paper. Center the word *Preface* (use capital letters) at the top of the page.

TERMS TO KNOW

At the end of each unit, a list of Terms to Know can be found. Many of the terms you already know. If you are not familiar with the meaning of a term, the Glossary in the back of the text can be used to find a definition, or you may find the definition in the unit.

capital	right of contract	wages
profit	right of free enterprise	entrepreneur
security	right of profit	apprentice
socialism	communism	permit
law of supply and demand	profit motive	ordinance
rules	regulations	license
master	code	net worth
variance	net profit	intangible
gross profit	liabilities	expense
assets	income	goods
tangible	right of property	trade
employee	capitalism	technological
services		

UNIT QUIZ

In each of the following, select the word or phrase that best completes the statement or answers the question.

1. An economic system which is most favorable to small business is
   a. capitalism.   c. facism.
   b. communism.   d. socialism.

2. A fact that demonstrates the role of small business in the United States is
   a. 95% of the labor force is employed by small businesses.
   b. 20% of the businesses are small.
   c. 43% of the business volume each year is done by small businesses.
   d. 51% of all businesses are small according to the definition of the Small Business Administration.

3. Which statement is not true in relation to business success?
    a. As the population expands, there is a greater need for small businesses.
    b. People with more education and experience usually have a better chance of success.
    c. There is little or no risk in operating a small business if you have adequate capital.
    d. The chances of business failure are reduced if you get sufficient and adequate training.

4. Which one of the following values did Sam (in the illustration) believe was the most important?
    a. Individual freedom   c. Security
    b. Opportunity for promotion   d. Chance to make a lot of money

5. In a socialist society, there is
    a. no government control of small businesses.
    b. considerable control of small businesses.
    c. complete government control of businesses.
    d. only a small amount of control from time to time.

6. The right to enter into any lawful business agreement is called the right of
    a. property.   c. profit.
    b. free enterprise.   d. contract.

7. The right to enter into any legal business you choose is called the right of
    a. property.   c. profit.
    b. free enterprise.   d. contract.

8. All of the following measure business size except
    a. profits.   c. location.
    b. assets.   d. number of employees.

9. Which one of the following would most likely be self-employed?
    a. Teacher   c. Grocery clerk
    b. Barber   d. Minister

10. According to the text, which of the following statements is true?
    a. A need always exists for some rules and regulations to protect others.
    b. Fewer rules and regulations exist today than 20 years ago.
    c. Rules and regulations are not really needed in today's business.
    d. Small business owners are concerned only with local rules and regulations.

11. Irving (in the illustration) was successful in business because he
    a. finished high school.
    b. saw a need and worked hard to fill it.
    c. liked to work on cars.
    d. had a good Army record.

12. Which of the following is not a characteristic of free enterprise?
    a. Individuals have the right to own property.
    b. The government owns most businesses.
    c. Many individuals have their own businesses.
    d. The government regulates some private businesses.

13. Which of the following would be classified as working for someone else?
    a. Physician in private practice   c. Retail sales clerk
    b. Dairy farmer   d. Attorney

14. Small businesses when compared to big businesses,
    a. are more likely to succeed.
    b. employ more workers.
    c. are a greater risk.
    d. usually require less capital to start.

15. Which of the following is the definition of *net profit*?
    a. Income after expenses are paid
    b. Income after all taxes have been paid
    c. Gross income after taxes
    d. Assets minus liabilities

16. Which of the following is not a level of trade proficiency?
    a. Apprentice   c. Foreman
    b. Master   d. Senior

17. It is necessary to keep accurate business records
    a. for tax purposes.   c. to determine earnings.
    b. to determine business size.   d. for all of these reasons.

18. Big business, some people believe,
    a. is unethical.   c. has more political power.
    b. strangles small businesses.   d. does all of these.

19. An advantage of small businesses over big businesses is that small businesses
    a. are more flexible.   c. are less regulated.
    b. have fewer problems.   d. are all of these.

20. According to the Small Business Administration, small businesses account for
    a. 19 out of 20 of all businesses.   c. 4 out of 5 of all businesses.
    b. 9 out of 10 of all businesses.   d. half of all businesses.

21. Which of the following statements is true?
    a. There are more small businesses than large businesses.
    b. There are more people employed in large businesses.
    c. There are more large businesses than small businesses.
    d. None of these statements are true.

22. Which one of the following is likely to be self-employed?
    a. Physician   c. A taxi driver
    b. A cashier   d. Plumber

23. Which of the following would probably not be self-employed?
    a. Attorney   c. Artist
    b. Airline pilot   d. Plumber

24. A wider range of products is available to the public in
    a. a free enterprise society.   c. a dictatorship.
    b. a socialistic state.   d. a communist state.

25. Regulations are necessary because they
    a. help politically powerful big business.
    b. make business practices more equitable and fair.
    c. give government officials power.
    d. create jobs.

UNIT 2

CHOOSING A SMALL BUSINESS

OBJECTIVES

After studying this unit, you will be able to

- Identify and describe the various types and kinds of businesses.
- Explain the difference between public utilities and public service companies.
- Describe in detail a business that you would like to own and operate.
- Choose a name for this business you would like to own and operate and explain why the name was chosen.
- Define the Terms to Know.

CLASSIFYING BUSINESSES

Businesses can be classified in several ways. One way to classify a business is to look at who operates the business, how it is organized, who owns it, and the economic and political environment in which the business operates. When these factors are used to classify a business, the following types exist:

- Sole proprietorships — owned by one person
- Partnerships — owned by two or more persons
- Limited partnerships — owned by two or more persons, having certain restrictions
- Private corporations — owned by one or more persons (frequently physicians, etc.)
- Public corporations — stock companies owned by the stockholders
- Educational corporations — tax-exempt businesses which serve the public
- Cooperatives — nonprofit businesses owned either by producers or consumers
- Government corporations — government owned and operated businesses which serve the public interest
- Public utilities — privately owned businesses, usually closely regulated corporations, which serve the public in a given area
- Public service companies — privately owned corporations which serve the public
- Holding companies — businesses which do nothing more than own other businesses
- Authorities, commissions, and other quasi-public businesses (Explained in Unit 4)

The types of businesses are explained more fully in this unit and in later units. It is only necessary at this point for you to be able to make the distinction between type and kind. *Kind* tells what the business does, as opposed to how it operates. The following is a list of the eight kinds of businesses:

- Production
- Distribution
- Retail
- Personal services
- Communications
- The professions
- Business services
- Trade and technical

KINDS OF BUSINESSES

Two points about small businesses must be made at this time.

- Small businesses can be very small.
- Small businesses do not have to be operated full time.

These two points open many doors to you. You can operate a small business while you are in school or college (if you are not already doing so). If you have a job, you can keep it and start a part-time business. As there are many options for self-employment, it is not necessary to hire any help. You can do all of this with a minimum of capital. There are many ways to go into business for yourself. It is quite possible that you already have some experience in business and may not realize it.

If you had a paper route when you were young, you actually functioned as a commission agent, not as an employee of the paper as you may have thought. You simply collected payment from the customers that you distributed papers to, keeping a small amount of the funds as a commission in exchange for delivering them. If you did deliver papers, you were engaged in a distributive business. When you worked as a babysitter, you were performing a service. If you made cookies for the church bazaar, sold homemade preserves at a county fair or 4-H show, raised a cow as a Future Farmers of America project, or sold Girl Scout cookies, you were engaged in a production and retailing business. If you raised tomatoes or corn in your backyard and sold them to neighbors, or had a lemonade stand on the sidewalk, you were running a small business. You learned quite a bit about business from those experiences. Remember when you made the wrong change for a customer and did not find the error until the end of the day? Remember the problems you had in keeping your friends from drinking lemonade without paying for it? Inventory control, that is what we would call it.

If you stop to think for a moment — a small business is really possible for you or anyone.

Production Businesses

The classification of production businesses includes all businesses which make goods. This includes the production of crops and livestock, mining, forestry, fishing, and inventing. Making paper from wood pulp, making automobiles, and producing maple syrup and sugar are only a few examples of production businesses. There are many other personal and commercial products which we use every day. This country was built on its mass production system. Yet not all the producers in America are big businesses. We shall see that there is an important place for the small business and all its phases in production. Several kinds of production businesses are listed here:

- Cultivating
- Extracting
- Processing and preserving
- Manufacturing

- Refining
- Construction (building)
- Invention

- The creative arts
- The performing arts (entertainment)

Cultivating. *Cultivating* includes the raising of plants, bushes, trees, and vines on the land (*agriculture*), and raising animals and poultry, for the goods they can produce such as milk, wool, eggs, and silk, Figure 2-1. Animals can be raised for food, including beef, lamb, veal, chicken, turkey, and pork. They are also raised for such by-products as leather, pet food, glue, and fertilizer. Animals can be raised for racing, sports, for service as guard dogs and guide dogs, and as pets. The term *animal husbandry* is used to refer to the raising of animals.

More formal cultivation includes many specialties, Figure 2-2. Some of these specialties are *ornamental horticulture* (flower raising), beekeeping (honey making in an apiary or beehive), silk production, thoroughbred breeding, nursery operation (ornamental trees and shrubs) and hydroponic farming (using chemicals instead of soil to grow plants in a greenhouse).

Plants, such as cash crops like grains, vegetables and fodder (food for animals), can be raised in both large and small amounts. Raising of trees for sap production (e.g., maple syrup and turpentine), fruit, fuel, and ornamentation (Christmas trees), suggests many part-time and seasonal money-making projects. Harvesting Christmas trees, collecting pine cones, and making wreaths has brought extra money to ambitious people at holiday time. If you grew up on a farm, you know the many ways you can make money from this and other projects.

FIGURE 2-1
The farmer who runs this roadside stand is a producer. The produce is cultivated and sold directly to the consumer. This is an example of a cultivating kind of business.

Cultivating Activity	Business
From the land Raising of livestock for the production of eggs, milk, meat, wool, leather, and for sport (horse racing) and for pets Raising of crops (agriculture) for the production of grains, vegetables, and fodder Raising of trees for fruit, sap (maple sugar), rubber, landscape shrubbery (nurseries), fuel, ornamentation (Christmas trees) Orchards and vineyards Fiber crops, such as cotton and flax	Farming of all kinds Ranching Tree farming Orchards (orange grove) Vineyards Melon farming Maple sugar grove Rubber plantation Christmas tree lot Cotton farm Horse breeding
From the sea Ocean harvesting — crustaceans (lobsters, crabs), shellfish (clams, oysters, scallops), and fish, such as tuna, swordfish, halibut, and cod Fish hatcheries and aquariums	Fishing of all kinds Lobstering Crabbing Netting Trawling
From the forest Lumbering for construction, fuel, paper pulp, turpentine and resins, and hardwoods for furniture and cabinets Forest as a food source (hunting, fishing, trapping, gathering) and for sport (picnicking, camping, hiking)	Logging Hunting preserves Camping grounds Hunting guide Pine cones and bark (as novelty items)

FIGURE 2-2
This florist shop is a good example of a combination business. Cultivating, retailing, and service are involved. The cultivating of flowers and plants for their beauty is called ornamental horticulture.

When classifying fishing as a business, all deep sea and commercial fishing, along with fish taken from stocked lakes and fish raised in hatcheries (both state and private) are considered *cultivating businesses*. Commercial fishing is usually combined with processing and preserving businesses, since the fish are canned, smoked, or frozen while still fresh. However, fish taken from public waters or for sport, as in deep sea fishing for sailfish, are considered *extracting*, as are hunting and trapping on public lands.

Extracting. *Extracting* means to take out, as in extracting a tooth, or to take out from the ground. Extracting includes drilling, digging, and mining valuable minerals, metal ores, and other items of value in the earth. Articles put in the earth by humans, such as coins and ancient artifacts, are also extracted.

Mining and drilling may not occur to you as a possibility for a small business. However, some people have actually discovered oil or rare minerals in their backyards. More than one enterprising person has polished semiprecious stones they have found and made all types of jewelry with them. Many individuals make popular novelty items from shells, sticks, and foam rubber.

The sale of wild game for food and pelts still occurs. You will probably not start an ore refinery while you are in high school, but the idea of extracting metal, relics, and fossils from the earth is not out of the question. Armed with a metal detector or just a pair of sharp eyes, you could find valuable artifacts, change, or the remains of ancient life forms. Collectors and museums will pay you if the articles are valuable.

Collecting can be a very profitable business. Collectors will pay surprising prices for old beer cans, matchbook covers, old magazines, coins, old stamps, gold and silver jewelry, and bottle caps. Many other possibilities for collecting exist. Returnable bottles discarded along the roadside or in trash cans can amount to quite a large sum for a diligent collector.

There is good money in collecting old newspapers, aluminum containers, and other recyclable materials. These items can be sold to junk dealers and reclamation and salvage companies. You would be surprised what a walk on the beach could produce for you, especially if a metal detector is used. We offer no promises of buried treasure or gold. If you are satisfied with a silver quarter or an antique glass milk bottle, the salvage business may be very rewarding to you. All you need is your hands and determination.

Some people think of a fisherman as a man who gets up early in the morning, gets in his boat, and returns late at night with some wiggly fish in a big box. Fishing, clam digging, crabbing, and netting and trawling, are nice sideline businesses for people who live near the ocean or well-stocked rivers and streams. You can easily sell your fresh catch to local restaurants and seafood markets. It is possible to build a good clientele if you are dependable and the supply of fish is steady.

As long as you get your fish and seafood from public waters, the business is considered *extracting*, Figure 2-3. You are in a sense extracting the fish from their environment (rivers, streams, lakes, bays, and gulfs), unless the water is posted. These waters are considered public domain and the fish you catch is yours to keep. Some states may place restrictions on the number of fish you can catch, just as in hunting. In most places, you are required to have a license to fish and hunt.

FIGURE 2-3
Crustaceans, like this lobster, and fish are brought fresh daily to seafood markets by persons who extract them from the ocean. A license is required in most places to extract seafood and fish from public waters.

Extracting Activity	Business
From the land (mining and drilling)	
Precious ores, such as gold, silver, platinum and uranium	Silver mining
Precious stones, such as diamonds, sapphires, and rubies	Prospecting
Metal ores, such as iron, copper, tin, zinc, and aluminum	Iron mining
Semiprecious stones, such as garnet, zircons, and onyx	Garnet mining
Building stone, such as slate, shale, marble, and granite	Slate quarrying
Fuels — coal, oil, and natural gas	Coal mining
Water — (well drilling, commercial and private use)	Private well drilling
From the sea	
Salt extraction — chemicals and minerals	
Seaweed, kelp, and other matter	
Oil (off-shore drilling)	
Food (see fishing)	
Methods (of extracting)	
Drilling	Wildcatting
Open pit mining	Contract excavating
Quarrying	Blasting
Shaft mining	Contract mining and blasting
Strip mining	Contract excavating
Underground pressure (hydraulic) mining	

FIGURE 2-4
Meat is being wrapped for freezing. This is an example of a preserving kind of business.

Processing and Preserving. Many items can be made on a small scale in the home, including the canning and preserving of homegrown food or purchased food. Homemade items, crafts, and food are in demand by owners of craft and specialty shops, flea markets, and resort stores. Aunt Minnie's old recipe for bread and butter pickles could make you a much sought-after producer.

Process	Product	Business
Processing (processing raw material into product)		
Milk (pasteurization) (milk processing)	Condensed milk, powdered milk	Milk processing plant Cheese factory
	Butter, cheese, evaporated milk	
Grapes (fermentation)	Wine, brandy (distillation)	Winery
Grains (distillation)	Whiskey, liquors, beer, ale	Small distillery — brewery
Fruit (distillation)	Liquors	Small distillery
Iron (heat treating)	Hardened iron	Heat-treating shop
Steel (tempering)	Tempered steel	Tempering shop
Logs, trees (milling)	Construction lumber,	Saw mill
Yarn (weaving, and knitting)	millwork cloth, textiles	Textile mill
Raw metal (extruding)	Extrusions, products	Extruding mill
Raw metal (rolling)	Sheet metal	Rolling
Hides (tanning)	Leather	Tannery
Carcasses (taxidermy)	Ornamental stuffed animals	Taxidermy shop
Raw metal (electroplating)	Protected metal (galvanized)	Plating shop
Painting (painting)	Plated metal	Paint shop (undercoating)
Flour, yeast, and other ingredients (baking)	Bread, rolls, cake, and baked goods	Small bakery
Preserving		
Freezing		Small cold-storage/freezer, locker plant
Drying	Apricots, prunes, figs,	
Freeze-drying (combination)	raisins	Ice plant
Dehydration	Dehydrated fruits	Fruit drying business
Condensation	Condensed soup	Canning
Distilling	Alcoholic beverages	Small distillery
Smoking	Sausage or bacon	Meat packing
Canning	Canned goods	Canning
Bottling	Soft drinks	Bottling
Pickling	Pickles	Pickle making
Salting	Cod fish	Fish packing
Curing	Ham and bacon, sausage	Meat packing
Fermentation	Wines	Winery
Cooking	Maple syrup/maple sugar products	Sugar manufacturing
Cold-pack	Pickles, cheese	Dairy refrigerated locker

Manufacturing. *Manufacturing* is literally the making of goods. The classic definition of manufacturing is the converting of raw materials into finished products. This is done by processing materials, often a separate business, and then assembling the components (various parts). Because the manufacturing activity is oftentimes so complex, manufacturers cannot or choose not to make all of the components. They often elect to have subcontractors make some of the smaller components.

An automobile has hundreds of parts. Most of the components are made in places other than at the assembly plant where the automobile is put together. Everything from fan belts and fuel pumps to carburetors and crankcases must all come from different parts of the world to be assembled. The components are assembled in a plant sequence of production operations called an *assembly line*. Henry Ford, among others, is given credit for establishing this method of making cars. This method uses *standardized parts* (parts which are exactly alike and are therefore interchangeable) and a conveyor belt which advances the partially completed car from stage to stage. As each part is attached and each operation completed, the finished vehicle emerges from the end of the line. Manufacturers inspect their operations to be sure the desired quality is being maintained by the workers. This inspecting is called *quality control*. It is needed to make sure the consumer will be satisfied with the final product.

By using manufacturing techniques such as the assembly line, American producers are able to mass produce the many articles which satisfy the needs

FIGURE 2-5
A manufacturing kind of business

and wants of people. Products are of good quality and much lower in price than if they were handmade one at a time. Manufacturing is obviously a proposition for big businesses due to the complexity and large amounts of money required. But, since so many parts are needed for all of the goods America wants and needs, ample opportunity exists for a small business. Acting as a contractor or subcontractor, it is possible for a small business to become profitable making components of all kinds.

Products	Businesses
Aircraft (commercial and private aircraft, and helicopters)	Aircraft propeller (wooden) manufacturing
Automotive (passenger cars and accessories)	Sun visor manufacturing
Appliances (large and small)	Castors and ball bearing manufacturing
Boats (recreational)	
Building materials	Paneling manufacturing
Clothing and textiles	
Chemicals and plastics	Fertilizer manufacturing
Communications equipment	Radio components (transistors) manufacturing
Computers and software	Components and design manufacturing
Construction equipment	Bulldozer blades manufacturing
Data processing equipment	Printout rack manufacturing
Electronic products and components	Digital calculator manufacturing
Farm machinery and equipment	
Heating, plumbing, and air-conditioning equipment	Brass castings and fittings manufacturing
Industrial goods (machine tools)	
Instruments	Ink stylus markers manufacturing
Machinery and spare parts	Machine screws and parts manufacturing
Medicines, medical equipment and supplies	
Photographic equipment, cameras, and supplies	
Prefabricated products (modular homes)	Metal siding fabrication manufacturing
Printing, publishing equipment, and supplies	
Railroad equipment and supplies	Specialty manufacturing of all kinds
Space exploration equipment and materials	
Toys, games, and sports equipment	
Trucks, construction equipment, and pipelines	
War materials and supplies	

Recent legislation now requires many government agencies to allocate certain percentages of their material needs to small businesses. This gives a small business the chance to bid on government contracts on a fairer basis.

Refining. Resources in the ground are sometimes too bulky or impure to transport to where they are needed. They must therefore be reduced in size and weight, and then purified. This is called *refining,* which literally means to make finer. Iron ore needs to be sifted and smelted (in a blast furnace) into pig iron. Crude oil needs to be refined into its components such as gasoline, kerosene, and fuel oil. Coal needs to be broken into smaller chunks, sized, graded, and the rocks, sand, and gravel removed, as in a coal breaker. Refining differs from processing in that refining makes a raw material pure by removing unwanted material, such as the impurities that are removed from pig iron to make steel. The metal is separated from the ore, oil from the shale, grain from the chaff (threshing), and alcohol from other products by fractional distillation.

A number of small businesses are involved in various phases of refining, including soap making, distillation of wood chips, and the recycling of used oil. The distillation of grain mash, as opposed to the distillation of wood products (producing wood alcohol), produces grain alcohol that is consumable. This type of distillation is generally considered a food process.

Process	Product	Business
Refining (Converting raw material into product)	Kerosene, gasoline, fuel oil, paraffin, coal tar, liquid fuels	Small refinery
Petroleum (crude oil) (cracking)		
Iron ore (smelting)	Iron ingots	
Iron (Bessemer process)	Steel	
Crude rubber (vulcanization)	Hard rubber	Vulcanizing shop
Oils and fats (saponification)	Soap	Specialty soap shop
Grains (distillation)	Industrial alcohol	Small distillery
Bauxite (electrolysis)	Aluminum	
Oil shale (extracting)	Oil	Extracting plant (recycle dirty oil)
Coal	Coal oil	

Construction. Building is a great choice for a small business. In this unit, trades are discussed as service businesses. The plumber who comes to your house to fix a leaky faucet and the carpenter who fixes the roof are both performing repair services. All they are doing is repairing an already existing product. But many of

FIGURE 2-6
Products from the refinery such as gasoline and motor oil are sold in service stations like this one. Gasohol is also sold at this station.

the construction tradespeople, such as carpenters, masons, plumbers, electricians, among others, lend themselves logically to construction businesses, Figure 2-7. If the person is engaged in making a product, such as a new house or an addition to a house then the carpenter becomes a producer.

Most builders are general contractors who get other trades people, also in private business, to help them construct residences, offices, stores, and factories, Figure 2-8. Some builders are large corporations. But, there are many small builders who specialize in private homes, apartment houses, condominiums, and renovations. You may have learned a trade at vocational school, such as sheet metal fabrication. If so, you might want to consider opening your own sheet metal business after completing your apprenticeship. This training will allow you to contract for heating and ducting work in new houses.

FIGURE 2-7
A carpenter/building contractor is reviewing plans with the prospective owner. This tradesperson is self-employed in a construction kind of business.

FIGURE 2-8
A mason contractor laying bricks for a general contractor who is a builder. This mason is a subcontractor and is also in the construction business.

Types of Construction	Business
Building	Structural steel contractor
Dwellings	General contractor — residences
Commercial	General contractor — commercial property
Plant and factories	Heavy construction — contractor
Civil	Paving contractor
Roads and highways	Excavator
Bridges	Subcontractor — plumbing, heating, roofing, and siding
Other	
Stone	Crushed stone/gravel contractor
Foundation	Ready-mix concrete supplier
Sewer and septic tanks	Cinder-cement block maker
	Pipe contractor

Invention. A young man in his California home makes small hedges out of sponge and calls them "Hedges Against Inflation!" They sell like hot cakes. If you can think of an idea equally as creative, you could be off and running with a popular, easy-to-produce product that could make you a fortune. Remember how popular the "frisbee" and the "yo-yo" were and still are today. Who knows, you may wake up in the middle of the night with a really great idea. It has happened to many others.

FIGURE 2-9
Comic strip artists create stories and then draw them in cartoon form. Often, these comic strips are printed in newspapers. Comic strip artists use their art to amuse and entertain other people.

Some examples of inventions include the rubber eraser on the end of a pencil, the three-minute egg timer, the paper clip, the safety pin, the bicycle reflector, the bobby pin, the egg beater, the tie holder, the rear view mirror, and the bumper sticker. Although many people associate manufacturing with automobiles and television sets, there are hundreds of items that can be made by hand or with very little machinery and sold at a good profit. Examples are personal name badges, desk nameplates, rubber stamps, plastic signs, monogrammed items, and almost anything you can think of for which someone else will pay you. You are limited only by your imagination and your resourcefulness. Some unusual items will sell. Remember the recent "pet rock" boom, or the rush to buy "Nerds?"

Creative Arts. People who write plays, songs, poems, and novels are creators. They produce useful and entertaining works from the ideas in their minds. Sculpture, paintings, commercial art, and illustrations and photographs all are beautiful and pleasing creations that seem more tangible than books and plays. If you are talented, you can become self-employed as a creative person, Figure 2-9. It is possible to sell your work. This is usually done through a dealer, as in the case of art, or through an agent, such as a literary agent, if you write. A creator sells works on the open market or may take a *commission* (an order) to produce a specific piece of art or written work. When a creator works this way, they are considered a freelance artist or craftsperson. Freelance work is considered a self-employing production business.

Product	Business
Inventions	Inventor
Sculpture	Sculptor
Portrait painting	Painter
Plays, novels, poetry	Writer/poet
Songs	Songwriter
Art	Cartoonist, illustrator
Photography	Freelance photographer

Performing Arts. The plays, TV scripts (teleplays), and songs others create must be performed to bring out their true value and to give pleasure to others. Actors, musicians, singers, comedians, ventriloquists, and other entertainers all are usually businesses in themselves, Figure 2-10. A successful actress, for instance, could have a business manager, an agent, a publicist, a hairdresser, and a secretary, among others. The actress may even be incorporated as a business.

FIGURE 2-10
A guitar player and singer entertains other people. He is involved in a service kind of business.

Product	Business
Music	Musician — musical group/band
Sports	Professional athlete — free agent
Comedy	Comedian
Theater — Movies — TV	Actor/actress

Distribution

A distribution kind of business is a business that delivers finished goods to the consumer. This kind of business includes packaging, labeling, transporting, refrigeration, storing, and advertising the goods. Any service necessary to prepare the goods for delivery to the eventual consumer can become the basis for a distribution business. Businesses which perform these services include warehouses, wholesalers, cold storage plants, and freezer lockers. Other examples of services include travel agencies, advertising agencies, brokers, jobbers, soft drink bottlers and distributors, and milk processing plants (the packaging part).

A trucking company is an example of a distribution business, Figure 2-11. The people who help get the goods from the producer to the consumer are called *middlemen*. This is an old term that refers to the "middle persons," or those persons who are in between the producer and consumer. Middlemen are necessary to get the job done.

FIGURE 2-11
A trucking company is a distributive kind of business because it transports goods from the producer to the consumer.

Several kinds of distribution businesses exist. Many of them are good opportunities for the small business person. Examples of some distribution businesses are the following:

- Transportation
- Warehousing and storage
- Wholesaling
- Dealerships
- Mail order
- Direct selling
- Route selling
- Vending machines
- Factory outlets
- Wagon wholesaler
- Group buyer

Retailing is also included in this category. Due to the unique nature of retailing, it is discussed in a separate section of this unit.

Transportation. Transportation businesses include any services which move people or freight over land, sea, or in the air. Some obvious transporting choices include charter buses, taxicabs, delivery service, furniture moving, light trucking, and trash and garbage removal, among many others. The young person who delivers prescription drugs for a pharmacy and the child with a paper route are involved in the distribution business.

Warehousing and Storage. Warehousing and storage includes general storage, freezer and cold storage, unit storage (containers), co-op storage, and trailer leasing (old trailers not for use on the road).

Wholesaling. Wholesalers include many middlemen who perform different services in distribution. The distributor claims exclusive territory for the wholesale of brand-name products approved by the manufacturer. All retailers who wish to sell those brands must order from the distributor, not the company. A *broker* shops the market for retailers to help them get the best price. The *broker* then arranges for the goods to be delivered. A commission merchant, a drop shipper, and a central buying agent all operate in a similar manner to this. *Jobbers* are similar to distributors, except they carry many brands within a merchandise classification. Examples include hardware jobbers, grocery jobbers, and sporting goods jobbers. A *manufacturer's representative* is a salesperson who sells products directly from the factory to various businesses. The products they sell are usually in one merchandise classification.

FIGURE 2-12
Goods are stored in a warehouse until they are needed. Warehousing is considered a distributive business because it helps get goods from the producer to the consumer.

FIGURE 2-13
This is a rack of merchandise put in a store by a rack wholesaler (a middleman). The store does not own the merchandise. It was placed in the store on consignment.

Dealerships. A *dealership* is a distribution business which sells such products as new automobiles, snowmobiles, motorcycles, boats, and mobile homes directly to the consumer, Figure 2-14. However, the dealership is required by the manufacturer to perform transportation (delivery and set-up), storage (boat marina), and service to its customers. This requirement takes a dealership out of the realm of conventional retailing.

Mail-order Merchandising. Mail-order merchandising can be a good, small business for a handicapped person, or a person who cannot or prefers not to travel to an office or shop. Products include general merchandise such as magazines, coins and stamps, health, beauty aids, toys and novelties. A glance through any magazine or newspaper shows many examples of mail-order items, Figure 2-15. There are many manufacturers who will set you up in a mail-order business for a modest investment.

Direct Selling and Route Selling. *Direct selling,* known also as door-to-door selling, made the Fuller Brush Company famous and successful, Figure 2-16. Literally hundreds of items are sold at the doorsteps of America. Some of these items include cosmetics, costume jewelry, vacuum cleaners, magazines, and food items. *Route selling* refers to a business operated out of a truck, Figure 2-17. The route seller delivers items like bakery products, milk and dairy products, soft drinks, coffee, ice, laundry and dry-cleaning service, and cheese, just to mention a few. A variation of the route seller is the wagon vendor. A *wagon vendor* sells snack food and ice cream, either along a particular route during the summer or at state and county fairs. Wagon vendors can also be seen at amusement parks, parades, racetracks, and other public gatherings. An early version of the wagon vendor was the fruit peddler who used a pushcart.

FIGURE 2-14
A dealership is a distributive kind of business.

FIGURE 2-15
Mail-order merchandising is a popular form of business.

One type of direct-selling organization is the multilevel direct sales organization. This retailer not only sells products directly to consumers, but also recruits (called *sponsoring*) other individuals to sell direct and acts as a wholesaler for them. This type of direct retailing is called multilevel because there may be many levels of retailers/wholesalers between the producer and consumer. Amway and Mary Kay Cosmetics are examples of this type of organization.

FIGURE 2-16
Door-to-door selling is a form of retailing in which the individual or business owner goes directly to the home of the consumer to sell and distribute products.

FIGURE 2-17
Route selling is a distributive kind of business in which products are sold out of a truck to many different retail outlets along a given route.

Vending Machines. Vending machines can sell both goods and services, Figure 2-18. Machines can dispense everything from health and beauty aids to candy and soda. Wholesalers were the first to explore the possibility of mechanical vending. Therefore, the business is associated more often with a distributive type of business. Sometimes a retailer is approached to permit a vending machine on his or her premises, in exchange for a commission. Vending machines have the advantage of dispensing goods at any time, day or night. They are therefore located in accessible locations in addition to the stores. When vending machines sell a service (an amusement), such as in the case of electronic video games, they are associated with service-type businesses. You may want to consider a group of vending machines or an amusement arcade as a possible business choice.

Factory Outlets. A factory outlet is a distributive business. Since it obviously cannot go door to door directly to its customers, they come to the factory looking for bargains. Bargains are usually available because of the elimination of the middleman. Some examples of factory-outlet businesses include day-old bread and bakery products, textile remnants, and carpet and mill-end shops.

Retailing

Although retailing is frequently considered part of distribution, it is listed as a separate business. This is done because there is an extremely large number of persons employed by retailers. Small businesses account for more than 75% of all retail trade done in the U.S. Retail business represents one of the best opportunities for the potential entrepreneur. Retailing is the last step in the distribution

FIGURE 2-18
Vending machines can be both service and retail businesses, depending on what is sold in them.

FIGURE 2-19
This is a department store that sells a variety of merchandise. This is a retail kind of business.

cycle which deals directly with the consumer. Examples of retail businesses include grocers, florists, drugstore owners, hardware dealers, and vending machine owner-operators.

Retailing is the largest classification of business, since its choices are as numerous as the various products that can be sold. Retail stores sell either one item (*single-line*), a group of related items (*specialty*), or many items (*department or variety*). Depending on the number of stores, retail businesses can be *independent* (one store), *multi-independent* (two or three stores), a *chain* (four or more stores), a *franchise* (owned independently but following the policies of another company), or a *group of stores*, operating independently but as a member of a group of stores of the same kind.

A food business is a retail business if it sells food as "take out" only, such as a Chinese food-to-go store or an ice cream package store. But, if the store has a place for customers to sit and eat the food as well, then the business is considered a service establishment, like any restaurant.

FIGURE 2-20
This ice cream shop is an example of a single-food-item retail business. Since people do not sit down and eat in this type of shop, it is not considered a service business.

FIGURE 2-21
A jewelry store is a specialty (one product line) retail business.

The outlook for retail businesses appears to be good in the next decade. You may want to spend more time learning about this type of business. Many fine programs in high schools and community and four-year colleges are available. These programs offer majors in retail store management or business administration. You could work for a large retailer to get experience, or become a member of a retail management training program offered by many large stores. Once you have gained the experience and knowledge necessary, you might want to open your own store. Many have done this, and are successful at it.

Not all retailing is conducted in a store. Vending machines, route selling, door-to-door selling, and mail-order merchandising are all examples of *nonstore retailing.*

FIGURE 2-22
An early McDonald's hamburger stand. In those days the operation was strictly "takeout," making the business a distributive one.

The following are examples of products that could be sold in a retail business.

Automobiles	Heating and plumbing supplies
Automotive supplies	Jewelry
Boating and marine supplies	Liquor
Books and stationery	Luggage and leather goods
Building materials	Musical instruments
Cards and gifts	Newsstand items
Church and religious supplies	Office supplies
Clothing	Photography supplies
Drug and proprietary items	Records and stereo systems
Flowers, bushes, trees	Sporting goods
Foods	Toys, hobbies, and games
Furniture, floor coverings, and	Used cars
appliances	War surplus, camping,
General merchandise	and outdoor supplies
Hardware	

Service Businesses

A service business primarily offers the skills and abilities of the proprietor, instead of the sale of a product. Supplies and parts are frequently used in performing the service, but it is the training and experience of the person practicing

FIGURE 2-23
This small appliance repair shop owner provides highly skilled repair (trade) services for his customers and also sells appliances, making his business part retail.

the art, trade, or profession for which the customer must pay. There are several kinds of businesses which offer services in addition to retail businesses. Even though retail businesses offer services, usually as part of their sales (sales and service), the main function is to sell goods. The serving of them is often contracted to service businesses. In most cases, the degree of difficulty of each service is the factor that places it in a different category. Generally, the more difficult the service, the more training and experience it requires. Also, more government regulation is usually involved when a service is difficult. The following table explains this concept:

Degree of Difficulty of the Service	Kind of Business	Example
Completely unskilled	Personal service	Car washer/waxer
Little skill	Service	Service station attendant
Partially skilled	Service	Self-service-station owner
Semiskilled	Service	Small service-station owner
Skilled	Service	Small garage
Highly skilled	Trade	Front-end alignment shop
Technical skill	Technical service	Transmission shop
Paraprofessional	Professional service	Engine rebuilding shop
Professional	Professional service	Racing car design shop

If you plan to open a service business, you must plan to educate yourself for that specific business. If you are going to perform the trade or technical service, you must become qualified. However, it is not required that you know a trade or profession in order to operate a business that uses the trade or profession. Many general contractors are not tradespeople. Also, in most states, you do not have to be a pharmacist to open a drugstore. But, if you plan to open a business which uses technically trained people, or people who must be licensed, then you must know all of the legal requirements. You must also know how to select qualified and suitable employees. Most every skilled trade, technical specialty, and profession lends itself very well to self-employment and its benefits. However, many persons who want to open their own service-type business first work for

FIGURE 2-24
You do not have to be a registered pharmacist to own and operate a drugstore. Paid professionals can be employed to fill prescriptions.

others to get experience. Many fine trade schools provide apprenticeship programs and on-the-job training while in school, and after graduation, programs are offered in most of the trades by the various unions, such as the carpenter's union.

Trade and technical schools offer the advantage of speeding up the training, but you must pay tuition to attend. Veterans can get special training funding if they are honorably discharged. Some of the trades and technical specialties are suggested in each section about service and trade businesses. Recently, there has been a growth in the services which offer all kinds of specialized instruction. This specialized instruction ranges from music to martial arts.

FIGURE 2-25
Health spas and figure salons have grown in popularity in recent years.

The quality of this service usually depends on the ability, experience, skill, training, and ethics of the service person. A few examples of service businesses are shoe shine stands, valet services, self-service gasoline stations, restaurants, motels, amusement parks, movie theaters, and bowling alleys. The list that follows contains more examples of possible service businesses. Communication services are put in a separate category and are discussed later in this unit.

Advertising agency	Cleaners: office, home,	Pest control
Audio/video recording	factory	Pet care and training
Automotive car wash	Clerical (temporary)	Physical fitness
Automotive rentals and	Coin-operated services	Parking service
service	Computer services	Restaurant
Babysitting	Costume and tuxedo rental	Roofing and siding
Baking	Interior decorating	Rustproofing
Barber	Landscaping	Shoe repair
Beauty salon	Laundromat	Sign painting
Bridal	Linen supply	Taxi service
Catering	Locksmithing	Tailoring
Chauffeur	Moving and storage	Telephone answering service
Cleaning and dyeing	Notary public	

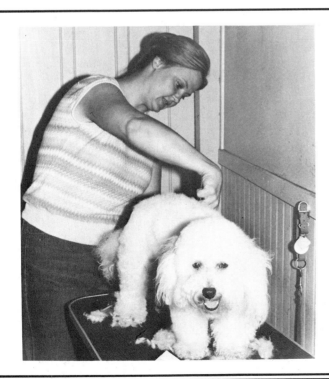

FIGURE 2-26
The quality of a service is dependent upon the ability, experience, skill, and training of the person performing the service.

FIGURE 2-27
Businesses that offer rental items, such as TV sets, are popular with people who have a temporary need for these items.

FIGURE 2-28
Rug cleaners or other do-it-yourself equipment are popular rental items, as consumers today are doing more repair and cleaning services themselves.

FIGURE 2-29
If you are good at a certain sport, there are individuals who will pay you to teach them the sport.

Public schools offer some adult and continuing education courses free or for a very modest fee. However, there are many courses and lessons not offered in schools for which people are willing to pay to obtain information and skills. A list of some of the types of instruction follow, as suggestions for businesses you might consider.

If you are good at a sport, for example, an individual will pay you to teach them the sport, Figure 2-29. Tennis and golf lessons are offered by club pros. Dance studios teach all types of dance, in addition to baton twirling and the skills needed to become a drum majorette, Figure 2-30. Horseback riding lessons are offered by livery stables, and free lessons are usually given when you buy a musical instrument. Due to movies and television, instruction for men and women in karate, judo, and kung-fu is growing in popularity, Figure 2-31. Think about instruction that you might be able to offer. The instruction does not have to be limited to humans. There are schools for dog obedience and equestrian training. It will probably be a long time, however, before lessons in "cat conduct" are available.

FIGURE 2-30
This dance studio, which offers personal instruction, is an example of a service business. The dance supply store (to the right of the studio), however, is a retail business.

FIGURE 2-31
Service businesses offering instruction in the martial arts are very popular as a result of the influence of movies and television, and as a means of self-protection.

Businesses offering instruction are suggested by the following subjects.

Flying lessons (airplane and hang gliding)
Skydiving lessons
Golf and tennis lessons (and other sports)
Baton twirling and drum majorette lessons
Dancing (tap, ballroom, modern, classical)
Musical instrument lessons
Singing lessons (voice)
Martial arts (kung fu, judo, karate, jiujitsu)
Horseback riding
Driver's education (auto lessons)
Art instruction
Knitting instruction
Public speaking
Radio and television broadcasting
Sewing instruction
Speech improvement (voice and diction)
Charm and poise
Modeling
Heavy equipment operation
  (operating engineer)
Electronics, data processing (all trades)
Welding
Chauffeurs training (truck driving)
High-school equivalency
Personality (such as the Dale
  Carnegie course)
Business skills (typing, shorthand,
  machine stenography)

Obedience lessons (for pets)
Animal training for protection (guard
  dogs)
Animal training for assistance
  (seeing-eye dogs)
Lessons in crafts (macrame,
  engraving and ceramics)
Doll making, painting and costuming
Dollhouse construction and other
  miniatures
Chess (and other games)
Swimming and diving lessons (water
  safety)
Archery and marksmanship (rifle range)
Speed-reading
Barber and hairdressing (beauty
  schools)
Meditation instruction
Photography
Reading improvement
Skiing instruction
Tutoring (all subjects)
Yoga

FIGURE 2-32
The number of indoor recreation businesses like this roller skating rink has grown in recent years. With indoor facilities, recreation is possible at any time, regardless of the weather.

Communications

Communications businesses consist of seven kinds. Some of these are based on very recent advances in the technology, which in some cases, created them. This group includes:

- Printing and publishing
- Broadcasting
- Telecommunications
- Wire and cable
- Audio and video recording
- Telegraph and telephones
- Space communications

Printing and Publishing. Many small businesses are successful at printing magazines and local newspapers, not to mention the success of the periodicals themselves. Playboy began in 1955 with a circulation of a few thousand. Its first issues are now collectors' items. Today it has a circulation of over 17 million. There are numerous small-town weekly newspapers published in the United States. Many specialty publications, such as free shopping newspapers and local television program guides, also exist. The number of weekly newspapers and specialty publications, which depend on advertising for funds, has doubled in the last decade.

Many specialty magazines have entered the market with success. They cater to individuals interested in particular subjects. It appears as though there are enough interested people in each category to support the magazines. Some examples of specialty magazines include *Coins, Model Railroader, Money, Sports Illustrated, Miniatures, Soap Digest, Apartment Life, Modern Homes and Gardens,* and *Women's Day.* Perhaps you could think of a hobby, occupation, or part-time activity that appeals to a large enough group to support a special-interest magazine or newsletter. There is one factor that seems common among these specialty magazines. This factor is that although the magazines will never have very large circulations, their readership is very loyal. If you have some printing skills, you can open a print shop and do local job printing. Designing and printing advertising materials, such as brochures, flyers, stuff-ins, broadsides, streamers, and pass-outs, for local advertisers can be lucrative. A growing demand for professionally typed and handwritten resumes and engraved business cards is apparent.

Broadcasting and Telecommunications. Television stations obviously require a lot of capital and the licensing process is a long and costly one. But radio is a different matter. Five-hundred-watt local radio stations broadcasting at assigned

FIGURE 2-33
Numerous small-town weekly newspapers in the U.S. are successful.

times and under power restrictions have increased in number. This is due to the easing of Federal Communications Commission (FCC) regulations. Local advertisers use these stations extensively. In addition to music, radio stations broadcast news, weather, and sports reports. Citizens Band (CB) radio has become very popular, and dealers in equipment, operating procedures, and short-wave ("ham") equipment are successful. Doctors and other people who need to be contacted at all times subscribe to radio paging or beeper services. Frequently, they also lease radio-telephones which are installed in their cars. The maintenance, repair, and sales and service of these somewhat new types of broadcasting suggest many useful and popular business applications, ranging from radio dispatching of delivery vans and taxis to radio-controlled toys and models.

Wire and Cable. Wire and cable technology has made possible, in addition to the historic telegraph, many inventions. A few of these inventions include the "ticker tape," Teletype, Teleprinter, and local TV cable. Many businesses are generated from the need to get better TV reception in many areas. With the increase in popularity of "pay TV," the demand for such services as Home Box Office and Movie Channel continues. Wire services transmit news to local newspapers and radio stations, and can also provide relaxing background music in stores and offices. Although wire tapping is illegal without a court order, the recording of and listening to the various sounds in our world, is becoming more popular.

FIGURE 2-34
Due to the easing of FCC regulations, the number of local radio stations being started is increasing.

FIGURE 2-35
Recording studios are used to tape
performing artists.

Audio and Video Recording. Recording businesses include recording studios for the taping of performing artists and the videotaping of entertainers, among other activities. Manufacturing and releasing of tapes and records has always been popular. It is sure to increase in this decade. The sales and service of recording equipment is another good business choice.

Space Communications. Space communications is just in the early stages. As technology advances, more will be done than just bouncing radio signals off satellites. The future holds many business opportunities in space communications.

Telegraph and Telephones. It would appear that communications businesses are all large corporations. However, consider that American Telephone and Telegraph (AT&T) does not own all of the telephone franchises in the country. There are many small, independent telephone companies, and even long-distance contractors, such as Sprint, and equipment suppliers, such as Radio Shack. Any media service, from the small-town weekly newspaper to the big-city cable service, can be called a communications business. Some excellent business possibilities in communications do exist. Consider the following possibilities: a shoppers guide, a local TV/cable weekly, a radio station, telephone answering service, or a telephone and telegraph controlled security service.

FIGURE 2-36
This privately owned communications business is regulated by a government agency. It provides service to customers within an assigned region.

Professional Services

In order to protect the public, certain types of services require considerable training for those offering the service. Professionals must have a formal education, frequently leading to a baccalaureate degree. Professionals do not generally belong to unions, but rather they join professional societies which have local chapters. Examples of these societies include the American Medical Association (AMA) for doctors and the American Bar Association for lawyers. Professionals must pass certain examinations to get a license to offer their services to the public.

Most people do not think of a doctor or a lawyer as a small business, but they are. Other professionals who generally operate as small businesses include veterinarians who run animal hospitals, pharmacists who operate drugstores, and engineers who operate consulting services. Architectural firms, certified public accounting firms, and law partnerships can also operate as small businesses. Because of the current structure of society, many professionals work for institutions and private companies rather than being self-employed. They include teachers, librarians, pharmacists, engineers, marriage counselors, scientists, nurses, medical technicians, and medical examiners. Other professionals who work for institutions and private companies include pathologists, anesthesiologists, and *roentgenologists* (X-ray doctors).

Within each group of occupations or an industry, there is a hierarchy of ranking of occupations or jobs, depending on the level of difficulty, technology, and amount of training. The table that follows illustrates this point, Figure 2-37.

Degree of Difficulty	Level of Training	Usual Length of Training	License Required?	Kind of Business	Example
Simple	Unskilled	A week or less	No	Personal service	Lawn care (lawn mowing)
Simple	Some skill	A month or less	No	Home services	Home handy person, chopping wood, removing trash, washing windows, etc.
Easy	Semiskilled	A year or less	No	Home services	Maid, practical nurse, painter
Harder	Skilled	Three/four years	Yes	Trade	Carpenter, mason, plumber barber, beautician
Harder	Highly skilled	Five/six years	Yes	Trade	Electrician, cabinetmaker, welder
Technical 1	Technical school	Two/three years	Yes	Technical service	TV repair person, surveyor
Technical 2	Technical college	Four/six years	Yes	Technical service	Funeral director (mortician), optician, dental hygienist, etc.
Paraprofessional	College	Two/four years	Yes	Professional service	X-ray technician, inhalation therapist, medical/surgical assistant, etc.
Professional 1	College/university	Four/six years	Yes	Professional service	Veterinarian, chiropractor, optometrist, etc.
Professional	University/graduate school	Six/ten years +	Yes	Professional service	Physician, dentist, ophthalmologist

† Note: These paraprofessionals would not be self-employed most likely because of the nature of the industry. They might, however, be part owners in a private corporation or partners with a physician in a clinic or medical facility organized as a limited partnership.

FIGURE 2-37 A hierarchy of ranking of occupations

Business and Financial Services

Most people think of financial businesses as mainly banks and loan companies. But, this classification also includes businesses which serve business in many ways. Business services include such activities as data processing services, accounting services, window washing and office cleaning, business printing, stationery and forms, and various kinds of management consulting. Business services can also include repairs to machinery in a plant, repairs to typewriters and other equipment in an office, and repairs to a delivery truck. In short, any service or repair to tools and capital goods used in a business, and repairs, additions, and improvements to the physical plant are considered business services.

In addition to banks, financial businesses include insurance companies, investment firms, property management companies, stockbrokers, and companies which own other companies, called *holding companies.* Also included are credit unions, mints, and foreign exchange banks, and companies which print money, stamps, bank notes and legal paper for foreign governments. The federal government is in the banking business, too. It operates the Federal Reserve System. The federal government also operates a group of banks which serve commercial banks by providing them with money, security services, and other help, somewhat like a wholesaler who supplies many retailers.

Government financial businesses include off-track betting (in some states), lotteries, and legalized gambling, to produce revenue. Insurance and commercial banks, both as business services and as possible business choices, are more fully explained in later units.

FIGURE 2-38
The commercial bank and trust company offers financial assistance to its customers.

Insurance. Insurance is a *business service* when it is used to cover a business and to protect the owner from possible losses. When insurance is used for personal protection, such as fire insurance for your house or life insurance, it is a *personal service*. The agent or broker who sells you the insurance is performing a service. The insurance company, on the other hand, that insures you, or underwrites your possible loss, is a producer, something like the company that makes your car. The insurance company produces your insurance, and the agent acts like a dealer.

Of course, insurance brokers can and do sell insurance to individual people and to businesses. When they do, the use to which the insurance is put determines if the service is one for business or for personal convenience. Take, for example, a partner who insures an associate for $50,000 worth of life insurance. This is considered a business expense, because the partner could suffer a financial loss if the associate were to die. On the other hand, liability insurance to protect you if your dog bites a postal worker is only for your personal protection. This is considered a personal service. Physicians obtain malpractice insurance to protect themselves in case they are sued. They consider this a business expense.

Agents. Agents can be both middlemen and they can also be of service to businesses themselves. If the middleman actually helped get the goods from the producer to the consumer, then a distributive function is being performed, and the service is a distributive business. But, if the middleman was not involved with the merchandise, but just arranged for its delivery, then the middleman performed a business service. Drop shippers, who do not touch the goods, manufacturer's representatives, who sell by sample, and commodity brokers, who buy grains and produce on the exchange, are all providing a business service. They are all serving the business, not the consumer. A real estate agent who finds you a house is providing a personal service. If the agent helps you find a business, this is considered a business service. The distinction is a rather fine one. Do not worry if you cannot figure it out in each case. All that is necessary is your appreciation of such business services as banks, business cleaning and repair services, and property management businesses. Agents who find work for actors are performing a business service, and agents who represent principals in buying property or selling property are serving the business. More about agents is explained in Unit 8.

A definite distinction exists between personal services and business services. Business services are performed for businesses to help them create the goods and services that they sell. Personal services are performed for persons, for their individual use, and not for resale.

The examples show that unskilled and partially skilled occupations within an industry do not lend themselves to independent businesses or to self-employment as easily as do the higher skilled jobs, trades, technical specialties, and the professions. The more skill, experience, and training or education you have, the more likely you are to start and operate a successful business. It is no disgrace to work

Difficulty of Repair	Kind of Repair Business	Example
Personal Repair Services		
Unskilled/semiskilled	Personal service	Changing a tire on a car
Fully skilled	Trade	Unstopping a clogged sink
Technically trained	Technical service	Repairing a color TV
Professionally trained	Profession	Filling a cavity in a tooth
Business Repair Services		
Unskilled/semiskilled	Business service	Changing a fluorescent tube in an office
Fully skilled	Trade	Repairing an office typewriter
Technically trained	Technical service	Repairing a computer
Professionally trained	Profession	Troubleshooting a major power outage (electrical engineer)

for others for ten years before going into business for yourself. Sometimes, it takes that long to assemble the necessary capital, get a good reputation and experience, and develop the required skills to insure your success. For example, in the supermarket industry you could start as a stock boy or bagger and some day become the vice-president, Figure 2-39. This is the way many people have gone up the "ladder of success."

Trade and Technical

Trade and technical businesses have been a part of business endeavor ever since the middle class craftspersons immigrated from Central Europe in the eighteenth and nineteenth centuries. Tradespeople such as the "butcher, baker, and candlestick maker," had belonged to groups called *guilds,* which were the forerunners of unions. Eventually, there was a need for more trades as new inventions were created. As technology developed, more training was required. To learn a trade, a young person could become an apprentice to a master. Apprenticeship training exists today. But, to meet the need of increased technology, there are many fine trade and technical schools which speed up the learning of the needed skills and knowledge. As in the professions, some trades require licensing.

FIGURE 2-39
By acquiring and developing the correct skills, an individual can climb the "ladder of success."

Examples of trades include carpenters, masons, plumbers, electricians, mechanics, body repair persons, welders, practical nurses, landscape gardeners, florists, chefs, and surveyors, Figures 2-40 through 2-43. All of these trades are well adapted to self-employment. Technicals include radio and television repair persons, data processing technicians, inhalation therapists, dental hygienists, ambulance crews, morticians, opticians, hairdressers, stenographers, paraprofessionals, and many more. They are all ideally suited to self-employment, Figure 2-44. Most require two years of college or the equivalent, and an associates level degree, in addition to a license.

FIGURE 2-40
This bricklayer is a skilled tradesperson. He had to serve in a three-year apprenticeship training program before he could become fully qualified as a bricklayer.

FIGURE 2-41
An apprenticeship of at least three years was served by this carpenter. He can work through a union or be self-employed as a small business.

FIGURE 2-42
Surveyors are highly skilled technicians. They can work for contractors and municipalities, or be self-employed.

FIGURE 2-43
This baker is a skilled tradesperson who could easily work for others or operate his own bakeshop.

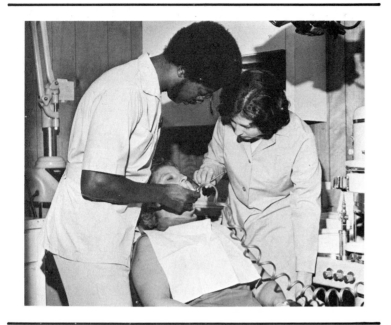

FIGURE 2-44
This dental hygienist is a highly skilled technician working as a para-professional. The dental aide (on the right) who is assisting is technically trained. Both workers must be licensed.

Trades. A carpenter can work for another person or be self-employed as a carpentry contractor. A carpentry contractor provides the carpentry part of a house or building for a general contractor who contracts out some of the other trades, such as electrical, roofing, heating, and plumbing work. A tradesperson can easily be self-employed or be the employer of one or two helpers. An experienced trade contractor could become a general contractor, building houses on either a small basis (one-at-a-time) to limit capital requirements, or in a tract, perhaps with a real estate broker as a developer.

Technical Services/Repair Services. Research and development has created the demand for greater technology, jobs, and technological specialties. Since some people have become dependent on many labor-saving devices, there is a need for individuals who can repair these devices (e.g., can openers, TVs, and personal computers) when they break down. Repair services can be divided into two categories. One category is consumer services for household appliances. The other category is repair services for industrial and business equipment needing maintenance or repair.

The type of repair service is determined by the level of technology required, the nature of the business, and the equipment or machinery to be repaired. Obviously you need to know more to fix a color television set than to change a burned out light bulb.

FIGURE 2-45
A furniture refinisher is an example of a consumer service business.

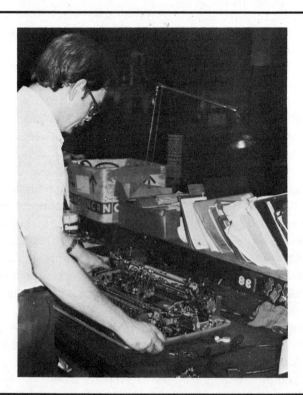

FIGURE 2-46
A repair service business

GOVERNMENT AND BUSINESS

Monopolies have been illegal in this country for many years, as they are considered unfair competition. However, some kinds of businesses either should be allowed to operate as monopolies or should be operated by the government, as indicated by some examples.

In special cases, truly free enterprise would be too confusing for the common good. Some types of businesses are given exclusive territories in which to perform or offer their services. For example, it would serve no useful purpose to have three different telephone companies offering the same service in competition, especially if a person could call only the numbers listed by one company. Some businesses are placed in a special group called public service companies. These companies are allowed to operate in a manner which is similar to a "legal monopoly" under governmental supervision. Public service companies must meet particular standards and treat the public fairly. Examples of public service businesses are electric light and power companies, telephone and telegraph companies, bus lines, taxis, railroads, airlines, radio and television stations, and motor freight lines.

The term *public utility* is similar in meaning to *public service company.* Public utility, however, usually refers to gas and electric companies. Most public utilities and public service companies are privately owned corporations, but their stock is available to the public. In some cases, the government will operate a public utility, such as in the case of the Tennessee Valley Authority (TVA). This was a government dam and generator project built during the Depression to provide low-cost electric power to rural areas in Tennessee. The government has operated businesses and provided services whenever they were necessary and also when there were no private entrepreneurs interested in providing the service.

In the early days as this country expanded, amounts of land were set aside in each township for public use. Usually the land was used for public buildings such as schools, libraries, a town hall, or a courthouse. Soon it became accepted that some activities, land, and services were to be administered by the government in the public interest. As the railroads grew, and moved west, the government gave land grants as an incentive to the privately owned rail lines to expand. They were granted right-of-way to build tracks over land they did not own, so as to provide transportation, a needed service, to the public. When the government uses land and other resources for the common good, it is called the *right of eminent domain.* This gives the government the right to set aside land and other resources for such uses as parks, playgrounds, and other uses, including building land grant colleges in some of the midwestern states.

Right-of-way includes the right to lay gas pipes, water mains, and sewers under sidewalks in cities. It also includes the right to string telegraph, telephone, cable, and power lines on poles from place to place. Water services are frequently

FIGURE 2-47
The Capitol Building of New York State is the center of government where laws and statutes are made. Government operates many businesses.

provided by towns as a public service, but the cost is charged directly to the customer, making this more or less a town- operated water business.

The government operates many businesses. Many goods and services are provided by state and local governments because private enterprise will not or cannot offer them. Police, fire, and emergency health services (ambulance service) are provided as a service supported by taxes in large municipalities, and on a volunteer basis in smaller towns and villages. Agencies of the government offer such services as publications, surplus food, emergency and disaster aid, and all of the equipment and supplies necessary to operate and maintain the vast machinery of our government (at all levels). Government services include the postal service, social security, medicare for the aged, assistance to veterans, and the armed forces. Federal, state, and local governments operate each of the eight kinds of businesses described in this unit, and most of the types of businesses listed, from manufacturing of tanks in wartime, to insurance for bank deposits through the Federal Deposit Insurance Corporation (FDIC)

A government can provide services to the public in several ways. It can form companies such as in the private sector, but there are different types. These types are:

- government corporations
- educational corporations
- authorities
- commissions
- public corporations
- services

FIGURE 2-48
In small towns and villages, police and fire protection are most times provided as a service on a volunteer basis.

FIGURE 2-49
A post office is a government service.

There are many examples of government corporations, such as the FDIC which insures your bank deposit. The FDIC is a corporation which sells stock to the government (itself) and offers protection to banks which private insurance companies do not care to offer. Another corporation that the government operates is the Corporation for Public Broadcasting. This government business gives money to local educational TV stations to help them with programming.

Educational corporations on both the state and federal levels help finance higher education. At the state level, commissions and authorities operate or supervise business activities. The Port Authority of Boston operates bus lines, subways, ferries, and port services including bridges for the city of Boston. The New York State Thruway Authority operates toll roads for the state. At the federal level, the United States Postal Service is a quasi-public corporation. This means that the postal service is partly government, and partly private. The postal service is supposed to be self-supporting; that is, it is supposed to operate at least on a break-even basis. It usually has an annual loss, so the government becomes involved in making up the loss with tax dollars.

Small business owners should be aware that these government agencies are possible customers for goods and services.

NAMING YOUR BUSINESS

What is in a name? Selecting a name for your business is almost as important as the choice of business itself. The name of a business must convey not only the type of business, but also imply the degree of formality and set the tone before a customer enters an establishment. In the retail field, the name can suggest the price range and style of an establishment. For example, a restaurant named "Squat 'n Gobble," suggests informality and speed. On the other hand, a restaurant named "The Altamont Manor," suggests class and quiet graciousness. One would expect formal attire to be worn and the price of the food to be fairly high.

FIGURE 2-50
The name of this business clearly indicates the type of service offered.

If you cannot think of a name for the business, conduct a contest among your customers. Offer a prize if one of the names is selected. If you do not use your name as part of your business name (e.g., "Harold Jones and Son, Hardware"), you must file a DBA (Doing Business As) form with the county clerk's office in your area or with the Secretary of State in your state. This requirement is for the protection of customers and creditors who have the legal right to know the identity of the owners.

Some businesses also have a slogan. A slogan is a phrase describing the business. Try to avoid being too cute when thinking of a possible slogan. If the slogan is too cute or silly, it may turn customers away.

In Unit 5, business signs and exteriors are discussed. Make sure you take into consideration just how your name will be displayed on the front of your business, on your business vehicles, and on your business cards before you finalize the choice. Signs and printing can be expensive, and you should know the limitations.

Your DBA certificate offers you some protection from the abuse or duplication of your business name. If you were the first to use the name in your area, you could probably prevent others from using your name, or at least collect royalties from them for the privilege of using the name. However, even if your legal name should be "McDonald," you would have difficulty in getting the courts to support your right to use the name for a hamburger stand.

Franchises are businesses which legally permit the use of not only the franchise name, but a great deal more, including systems, methods, and merchandise, for which you pay a fee. This fee is called a *franchise fee.* Franchises are discussed more fully in Unit 11.

FIGURE 2-51
A unique business name will attract customers.

The following is a list of some businesses with interesting names and slogans, which serve only as examples.

Type of Business	Business Name	Slogan
Barber/beauty shop	"Hair it is!"	"We need your head in our business!"
Advertising agency	"The Idea Factory"	"We light up your life!" (picture of light bulb)
Cheese shop	"C'est cheeze!"	"A rat's paradise!"
Liquor store	"Cork 'n Bottle"	"Blithe spirits!"

OPPORTUNITIES IN A FREE SOCIETY

In an economic democracy, there is opportunity for profit, recognition, and service for anyone with the imagination, energy, and desire to do a better job or provide a better service than the competition. The essence of the free enterprise system is competition. It is competition that makes a person who is already doing a good job try even harder!

Competition provides a better standard of living for the consumer by providing constantly improving choices. Consumers shop to get the best value and the best quality. When a purchase is made, the dollars paid become "votes" in favor of the product or the service chosen. Those businesses which do not receive sufficient sales in the form of "dollar votes" from customers cannot possibly succeed. Like a politician, a successful business must get enough votes.

It is the job of business to provide a little extra service or a little better product so as to improve its ability to compete. While some businesses fail each year, many others succeed because they perform a service or offer merchandise that satisfies their customers. When a business can no longer satisfy a segment of the population sufficiently large enough to support it, that business will fail.

FIGURE 2-52
A well-stocked produce department will satisfy customers. Businesses which offer products and merchandise that satisfy their customers stand a good chance of being successful.

Each year the number of births, as compared to the number of deaths, in this country increases. With the population growing, there is a need for more business and the goods and services they offer. Existing businesses may not or cannot expand to meet this greater demand for goods and services, and new population centers may arise requiring new business locations.

A business owner does not have to be the best manager or have the biggest inventory to be successful. Success is relative. If an individual sees the need for a new store or service in a growing community and begins that business before anyone else, this business owner can get a head start on competition. If the location is good, other businesses will soon arrive. Other businesses may not be in direct competition with your business if they represent different products and services. They will actually bring more business!

Anyone with imagination and a little courage, and who believes in his or her own ability and ambition, can be successful in business. When education, skills, maturity, and determination combine with a creative business idea, the outlook is good.

Most anyone can start a business. The important factor, however, is to keep it going. The primary requirement for a new venture is to have an item or service which satisfies the public. New businesses must be viewed against the background of the community in which they are located. They must be in keeping with the times. Every day, research and invention produces new products and new services that replace the old products and services. Great opportunity exists for the alert entrepreneur who uses a good business possibility. Your ideas for a business should be thoroughly discussed with bankers, trade association representatives, and departments of commerce. If you have a good idea, and others agree, then by all means go ahead. Good luck!

FIGURE 2-53
If you are ambitious and willing to work hard, you can be successful in a small business of your own. Renting tools and equipment to builders and tradespeople is a good business to be involved in.

BUSINESS MANUAL ASSIGNMENT

Two possible business manual outlines are shown here. Each one generally follows the outline of the text. Look at each outline and pick the one you like most, or make an alternate outline of your own. You may want to check with your instructor for assistance. When you have completed your alternate list, get it approved by your instructor. You must have at least 12 topics in your manual, in addition to the preface, table of contents, and cover pages. Feel free to change the order and to add more material for any of the topics. But, you must follow the assignments more or less as your instructor indicates; otherwise, you will omit valuable material from your manual.

Businesses will of course vary, so not all of the topics will have the same amount of material. The amount of material will depend on the kind of business you choose. In the outline for the Business Manual, the emphasis is on presenting the material mainly for reference purposes so that you can refer back to samples later on. In the outline for Business Operating Manual, the emphasis is on how-to-do it, and each topic reminds you how each task in your company is to be done. You can also use a combination of the two approaches, whichever you like.

Business Manual	Business Operating Manual
Cover	Cover
Title Page	Title Page
Preface	Preface
Table of Contents	Contents
Introduction	Introduction
Purpose of the Business	Business Strategy
Why I Chose the Name	Goals and Objectives
History of the Business	Company Policies
Organization	Organization Chart
Legal Forms	Legal Forms
Kind of Business	Business Classification
Location	Location
Layout	Physical Plant and Facilities
Budget	Capital Planning
Bookkeeping	Records Management
Payroll	Payroll
Sample Forms	Sample Forms
Insurance	Risk Protection
Licenses and Permits	Rules and Regulations
Legal Policies	Legal Checklist
Sales and Service	Sales Promotion and Advertising
Training and Recruiting	Personnel Management
What about Franchises?	Franchise Policies
Future	Future

TERMS TO KNOW

producer	finance	jobber
public utility	public service	wholesaler
distribution	social security	discrimination
distributor	retailing	service
profession	paraprofessional	trade
commission agent	drop shipper	group buyer
vending machine	wagon wholesaler	wagon vendor
peddler	route seller	direct sales
technician	unskilled	semiskilled
franchise	consumer	master
journeyman	apprentice	guild
union	performance test	trade license
variance	apprenticeship program	vocational schools
trade and technical school	college	university
baccalaureate degree	bar	professional society
malpractice	ethics	hierarchy
skilled	technician	trainee
nonstore retailing		

UNIT QUIZ

In each of the following, select the word or phrase that best completes the statement or answers the question.

1. What kind of business listed here is a producer?
   a. Christmas tree farm
   b. TV repair shop
   c. Dentist's office
   d. Theatrical agency

2. Which one of the following persons is probably required to have a license to perform the business suggested?
   a. A barber
   b. A car washer
   c. A retail sales clerk
   d. A paper delivery person

3. Which one of the following does not need a license?
   a. Barber
   b. Electrician
   c. Free-lance artist
   d. Restaurant owner

4. A list of skills in order of difficulty or rank is called
   a. a rank list.
   b. a guild record.
   c. a hierarchy.
   d. a table of skills.

5. Resources in the ground that are too bulky or impure to transport to where they are needed must often times be reduced in size and weight, and then purified. This process is called
   a. extracting.
   b. manufacturing.
   c. refining.
   d. cultivating.

6. If you wanted to learn a trade, you would go to
   a. a vocational school.   c. a community college.
   b. a business college.   d. a technical institute.

7. Which one of the following does not need a license to perform the profession suggested?
   a. Butcher   c. Candlestick maker
   b. Baker   d. Doctor

8. Which one of the following is a performance test?
   a. A driving (road) test   c. A blood test
   b. An IQ test   d. A written drivers' test

9. Which one of the following is not involved in traveling to people's homes to sell them goods?
   a. A drop shipper   c. A route seller
   b. A direct salesperson   d. A wagon peddler

10. Which one of the following probably went to college for four years?
    a. A tree surgeon   c. A marriage counselor
    b. A sign painter   d. A plumber

11. Which business is a public service kind of business?
    a. The telephone company   c. A local private college
    b. The Red Cross   d. The Salvation Army

12. Which of the following products can be sold in vending machines?
    a. Hot soup and sandwiches   c. Insurance policies
    b. Stockings   d. All of these

13. A commission is paid to
    a. a broker.   c. an agent.
    b. a salesperson.   d. all of these.

14. An association of craftspeople dating back to the Middle Ages in Europe was called
    a. a trade union.   c. a guild.
    b. a trade association.   d. a professional society.

15. Which one of the following is the highest level of trade skill?
    a. Master   c. Journeyman
    b. Apprentice   d. Helper

16. Which one of the following is a distributive kind of business?
    a. A radio station   c. A canning factory
    b. An advertising agency   d. A warehouse

17. Which of the following is not a method of preserving?
    a. Distilling   c. Smoking
    b. Pickling   d. Drying

18. Which of the following is a repair business that services businesses?
    a. Watchmaker
    b. TV repair shop
    c. Office machine repair
    d. Dentist

19. Which of the following is not a financial business?
    a. A credit union
    b. An insurance company
    c. An investment banker
    d. A company that prints paper money

20. If you opened a hamburger stand, you would probably need
    a. a license.
    b. a franchise contract.
    c. a variance or permit.
    d. all of these.

21. Which one of the following types of schools would a person attend to become a mortician?
    a. A trade school
    b. A community college
    c. A technical institute
    d. A university

22. What businesses are most people likely to have been involved with while still in school?
    a. Paper route
    b. Lemonade stand
    c. Babysitting
    d. All of these

23. Which of these is not a business service?
    a. Window cleaning
    b. Trash removal
    c. TV repair
    d. Typewriter repair

24. Which one of the following is not considered refining?
    a. Distilling
    b. Drilling
    c. Smelting
    d. Electrolysis

25. Which of the following businesses would the Public Service Commission probably regulate?
    a. The telephone company
    b. The gas company
    c. The electric company
    d. All of these

UNIT 3

STARTING A
SMALL BUSINESS

OBJECTIVES

After studying this unit, you will be able to

- Describe the causes of business failure.
- Explain why it is important for a business owner to acquire and develop good management skills.
- Explain the importance of personality in operating a business.
- Define the Terms to Know.

GUARDING AGAINST BUSINESS FAILURE

A person does not open a business with the intention of failing. Each year, many businesses end in bankruptcy. Why do businesses fail? How can the chances of success be increased? Some causes of business failure are examined in this unit. Understanding these causes and knowing how to avoid them is important.

Management Must Be Good

Dun and Bradstreet, a noted business reporting firm, lists four causes for business failure: poor management, neglect, fraud, and disaster, Figure 3-1. The Small Business Administration estimates that poor management is the most common cause of business failure.

Businesses fail due to incompetence. Therefore, it is important for individuals to put forth their best effort in their first venture. A person is free to enter business, free to succeed, free to fail, and free to try again. These are precious freedoms in our economic democracy.

Management ability does not come automatically. Frequently, some owners who are overly concerned with the present fail to plan for others to take over their positions. There are many businesses that do not have anyone to take over in an emergency. Large companies continually search their employees for talent to meet future needs. These companies choose competent individuals and train them for future management positions. The small business owner must learn to apply good management techniques.

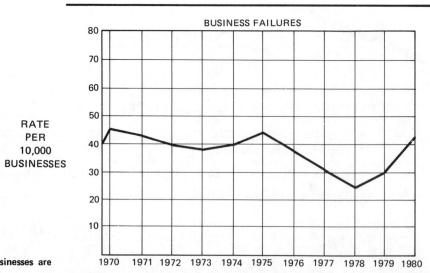

FIGURE 3-1
Each year many new businesses are forced to close.

Poor management, as a cause of business failure, can be divided into the following categories:

- Incompetence (inability to make decisions)
- The wrong kind of experience
- Inexperienced in managing people
- Inexperience with the product or service line
- Extreme overhead costs
- Inadequate sales
- Poor location
- Inventory trouble
- Laziness
- Lack of self-confidence, too cautious

Of these categories, incompetence and the wrong kind of experience account for the majority of failures. The remedy for these is training, experience, and perseverance.

Business Must Not Be Neglected

While poor management is the primary cause of business failure, other causes exist, such as neglect, fraud, and disaster. In each case, the owner can take steps to avoid or lessen the effects of these causes.

Business neglect occurs when an individual either lacks motivation or is so frustrated by the business that he or she literally gives up. An honest and complete examination of your ability, determination, and desire to succeed is necessary before you spend any amount of time and money on a business venture.

Fraud occurs in business when an individual or a company attempts to advance by deceptive and dishonest methods. Inferior products or services that are knowingly offered by a company, advertising that is misleading, or employees who steal from a company are all examples of fraud. There are rules to prevent such practices. However a person or company may succeed for a time without being discovered, causing serious damage to the business.

Natural disasters such as fires, floods, tornadoes, and earthquakes cannot be avoided. A business owner should choose a safe location and obtain adequate insurance for protection against disasters.

MANAGEMENT DECISION MAKING

It may seem obvious to say that the way to avoid failure is to avoid the errors of those who have failed. This is exactly what you must do. Many causes of failure are due to a desire to rush into business without adequate preparation. Without the experience, capital, ability, and personal qualifications such as honesty, self-control, and skill in working with others, entering business is a risky venture. Once you fail in a business, it is harder to start again. Banks and investors are understandably more reluctant to loan money.

All entrepreneurs must:

- recognize their own limitations and get help when it is needed.
- make business decisions on business considerations, not personal considerations.
- understand the business and the factors which affect it.

Personal Factors	What personal qualities account for success in business? Has enough experience been obtained in this particular type of business?
Location	Where should the business be located? What things should be considered in selecting a good location for this business?
Capital	How much money is needed to organize the business? Where might it be obtained: savings, relatives, friends, banks?
Regulations	What laws, regulations, and ordinances affect the business? Are any special permits or licenses necessary?
Records	What kinds of records should be kept? How can the recordkeeping system be started? Who will keep these records and prepare the reports?
Buying	Who will supply the business with the needed items for operation? What goods or services are necessary, and in what quantities? When should they be purchased? What favorable terms are available?
Organization	Should the business be individually owned and operated or would a partnership or corporation be more advantageous?
Layout	Where should the different items of merchandise or equipment be located within the store? How might the available space be put to maximum use?
Building	Can an existing plant or building be rented, bought or leased and then adapted to the business? Should a new structure be built?
Personnel	Where can qualified help be found? What training will the employees need? What benefits should be offered to encourage good workers to stay with the business? What other personnel problems might arise and how will they be resolved?
Expansion	What must be done to expand the business? When would be the best time to expand?

FIGURE 3-2 A summary of questions to help new business owners avoid failure.

Eleven questions that any prospective owner should answer before choosing a business are outlined in Figure 3-2. Larger businesses work with specialists who, by their training and experience, can make decisions about anything from locating a new plant to settling legal questions. These specialists give large businesses what is called *management in-depth.* Even with such talent, mistakes are made. Because of the large size, some of these mistakes can be absorbed and the damage overcome.

Small businesses, however, cannot have such specialized management. The small business owner must make all decisions and is forced to live with them. The small business owner cannot afford to make costly mistakes. More often than not, the business that can best afford an occasional mistake maintains a supply of trained talent to prevent mistakes. While on the other hand, the small business, which cannot afford an error, is almost entirely dependent upon the owner's personal judgment and ability to prevent error.

Four major factors support the sound management of any business:

Training and Experience. The small business owner must be prepared to manage the business. The owner must know when to rely on personal knowledge and foresight and when to get help. Assistance can come from bankers, advisors, government officials, and suppliers who are interested in your success. The small business owner should seek the benefits of management training taught by professionals in evening courses, private business schools, and colleges, Figure 3-3. Excellent service and advice is available from the United States Small Business Administration, Washington, D.C. 20416, which has local offices in most large cities.

FIGURE 3-3
The small business owner can receive good management training by taking courses taught by professionals.

Proper Administration. Administration must be separated from operations. The small business owner must maintain an objective attitude about the business and not let personal considerations affect planning, staffing, and the supervision of operations. Communication among administrators and supervisors and the employees is most important for a successful business.

Effective Planning. Training, experience, and proper administration require that the small business owner be an objective evaluator of the whole enterprise. Such objectivity is the basis of effective planning. The small business owner should not only be interested in operations; but all policies must be set forth concerning every aspect of the business. The owner must constantly evaluate past and present activity in order to plan for the future.

Time Management. One of the constant complaints received from small business owners is the need for more time. They agree that time is one of their valued resources. To be successful, the business owner must learn how to manage time efficiently. The owner must develop a time-use strategy. Part of the strategy is setting priorities and allowing time for unanticipated crises.

Think about some of the mistakes a small business owner makes. Make a list of different errors that could be made and the ways in which they can be prevented. In a larger corporation, what department or company official might be given the responsibility for preventing these mistakes?

KNOWING YOURSELF

The most important asset of a business owner is a personality which lends itself to the success of the business, Figure 3-4. Many kinds of business personalities exist, but good ones evolve from a self-examination necessary for the discovery of your personal strengths and weaknesses, especially as they relate to a business.

In evaluating your personality, the following list may be helpful. Ask yourself how you rate on each of these qualities, noting areas where improvement is needed:

A. Physical Qualities

   1. Appearance
   2. General health
   3. Endurance
   4. Vision
   5. Hearing

FIGURE 3-4
Personality is very important in operating a successful business.

B. **Mental Abilities**

1. General intelligence
2. Knowledge of business
3. Speed of reaction
4. Memory
5. Creativeness
6. Initiative
7. Insight into character

C. **Ethics**

1. Honesty
2. Loyalty
3. Dependability
4. Perseverance

D. **Social Qualities**

1. Courtesy
2. Sympathy
3. Ability to work with others
4. Cheerfulness
5. Self-confidence
6. Adaptability
7. Enthusiasm

E. Executive Qualities

    1. Ability to direct others

    2. Ability to organize

    3. Ability to make decisions

    4. Ability to take responsibility

    5. Ability to accept suggestions or criticism

    6. Ability to deal with stress

FAMILY RESPONSIBILITY

A number of topics relating to business operation have been discussed. One more topic should be mentioned: your responsibility as a business owner (whether single, married, or divorced) to your family, who may depend on you either financially or emotionally.

The financial risks and other problems of a new business affect your family. A business may not show a profit for the first period of operation, frequently not for several months or longer. It takes time to build a reputation and clientele. Your funds (capital) must be sufficient to take care of any family responsibilities, in addition to the business, for as much time as is necessary for the business to get going. When estimating the capital needed to start a business, you should include money to cover family obligations such as food, clothing, shelter, education, medical expenses, and emergencies.

Family and business financial records must be kept strictly apart. You should not dip into the cash register for an extra $5 for family groceries. Once you start the habit, it grows. If you take some inventory items home for personal use, you must record it.

Even when there is no financial problem, family obligations may be present. All businesses demand a great deal of time. This time is usually taken from such family activities as child rearing, household chores, or family recreation. You must be prepared to cope with these demands.

Many businesses are successful because the entire family pitches in. This is likely to occur when the decision to start a business is a family one. If family members are expected to help, they should have a chance to express their opinions. Those family members who might not want to work in the business should also have a chance to discuss problems beforehand.

After reading the following case study, make the management decisions suggested by the questions at the end of the case. You may want to write down your decisions and explain them.

    Sam Robinson is twenty-five years old, married, and has a six-month-old son. He and his wife Cathy rent an apartment for $200 per month. Some day they hope to buy land and build a house.

Cathy was employed for several years after she married Sam, but when their son was born, she left her job to take care of him. Sam earns $280 per week (take home pay) as an assistant traffic manager for a wholesale food distributor. He finished high school, had two years of business college majoring in accounting, and then spent six months in the Army Reserve on active duty as a truck driver. Sam is still in the Reserve and must go for two weeks of summer training each year. Cathy and Sam have managed to save $8,000.

Last month, Sam became interested in opening a small grocery store. He has wanted to own a grocery store ever since working in one in high school. Sam has a chance to lease a new cinder block building in a good location in a growing suburban neighborhood. Ample parking is available and no competition exists nearby.

To get started, Sam estimates that he will need about $30,000 for stock and expenses. In addition to the $8,000 savings, his father will loan him $5,000 without interest for an indefinite period of time. Two different banks have agreed to loan Sam (and Cathy as cosigner) at least $10,000 at 16% interest.

Sam discussed this idea with his present employer. His boss does not want to lose him, but he admitted to Sam that his chances of being promoted to traffic manager would be rather slim unless he obtains a college degree within the next five years.

Sam has been accepted in a grocers' buying group organization that will give him the advantage of mass purchasing, joint advertising, private brands, and sales promotion. The landlord of the new building will give him the first month's rent free and then base future rents on a percent of gross sales, or charge a fixed amount.

Cathy does not oppose her husband in his plans, but states that she cannot work in the store as she must be home to take care of the baby. Sam's brother is a junior in high school and has agreed to help. He has never worked before, but appears willing.

Based on the information provided, what decisions should Sam and Cathy make about starting a business? What factors should they consider? What advantages do they have? What disadvantages would have to be overcome? Should Sam pay a fixed or variable rent?

BUSINESS MANUAL ASSIGNMENT

It is not necessary to have the various parts or pages of your manual in any particular order. You should, however, use a copy of the table of contents or outline as a checklist to keep track of each element of the manual as you complete it. Place the finished work in a folder until you are ready to make a decision on how to bind your manual. In the meantime, think about a cover, a title page, and any introduction you might want to write. The material should be short and to the point.

The topic you will be writing about for this assignment is the strategy or purpose of your business. Explain why you are or would like to be in business, what you hope to accomplish by being in business (in addition to making a profit, of course), and how you intend to go about achieving your purpose. The following is an example:

Purpose — The purpose of my business is to provide high-quality fast food and service at the lowest possible price.

Name — I chose the name "Heap of Hamburgers" because it is an eye-catcher and cute!

History — The hamburger stand business that is being used as an example here has no particular past history. However, you can use the following history as an example.

My father started the business in 1938. When he died, my uncle continued to operate it. I have been working for my uncle for seven years now, and this year he agreed to let me take over the business.

Business strategy — I have studied the fast-food situation in the Capital District area. From conducting extensive research, I have found that there are 3,234 persons for each unit offering hamburgers to the public; however, some of the stands are doing more business than others. I conclude that location and traffic patterns have an effect on the volume of hamburgers sold. I made a diagram of the area and have developed three locations which I believe need to be better covered. Stands located at these places in the next five years should do well. By that time, the projected population ratio should be 4,200 persons per unit.

Goals and objectives — I feel that the area can support more hamburger stands. As long as the unit/population ratio does not drop below 3,000 persons per unit, I feel that the individual units can be profitable. It is our goal to have three units in the area by 1988, in the locations which will best compliment existing units and provide easy access to fast food for persons not currently being served as well.

Policy — The policy of this firm will be to charge the lowest possible price for hamburgers. Every attempt will be made to be at least 5¢ under all competition for each comparable item. Volume, more efficient operation, and high quality will make up for the smaller revenue.

TERMS TO KNOW

fraud	in-depth management	insolvent	inventory
neglect	training	liquidate	competition
disaster	experience	creditor	self-analysis
incompetence	bankrupt	personality	operating funds

In each of the following, select the word or phrase that best completes the statement or answers the question.

1. Henry Forbes could not make his restaurant succeed because there were too many eating establishments in the neighborhood. The reason for the failure of Henry's business was
   a. lack of experience.   c. competitive weakness.
   b. inventory trouble.   d. inadequate sales.

2. Harry Smith did not have accurate inventory records and therefore was often out of merchandise. After three years, his business failed. The reason for failure was
   a. lack of experience.   c. inadequate sales.
   b. inventory trouble.   d. poor collections.

3. Nellie Green has bought enough groceries to think that running a grocery store would be a fairly simple venture. She opens her own store and after six months is forced to close. Which of the following is the main reason for business failure?
   a. incompetence   c. lack of capital
   b. lack of experience in the field   d. disaster

4. Sharon Keeler thought that the property located across from her store would be valuable some day, so she used operating capital to buy it. Within a short time, her business failed. The main reason was
   a. neglect.   c. fraud.
   b. lack of experience.   d. lack of operating funds.

5. In discussing personality of successful entrepreneurs, the authors agree that
   a. there is no connection between success and personality.
   b. family considerations do not affect success.
   c. personality is an important factor in success.
   d. experience does not affect personality.

6. Which one of the following statements is not true when relating it to personality and business success?
   a. A person's physical health does not affect his or her chance for success in business.
   b. A person who is dependable will have a better chance for success in business.
   c. A person's ability to work well with other individuals is important for success in business.
   d. A person's ability to make decisions is important for success in business.

7. The most common cause of business failure is
   a. fraud.   c. disaster.
   b. poor management.   d. business neglect.

8. Which one of the following statements is not true?
   a. A person should seek some management experience before managing a business.
   b. An important aspect of good management is knowing how to manage people.
   c. A person can get too much experience and therefore be a poor manager.
   d. There are people who should never go into business for themselves.

9. Entrepreneurs who hope to survive and prosper must not
   a. base business decisions on personal considerations.
   b. recognize their own strengths and weaknesses.
   c. seek and accept outside help.
   d. understand the factors affecting their business.

10. A comparison of large and small businesses shows that
    a. mistakes made by management in large business are more serious.
    b. business decisions are made differently by small businesses.
    c. more large businesses fail.
    d. large businesses face the problem of doing business with a number of specialists.

11. Which one of the following is not a good idea for a person starting a business?
    a. Starting a business should be a family decision.
    b. Family and business records should be kept together.
    c. Family and business records should be kept separately.
    d. Family expenses should not be paid from business profits.

12. Jerry Black started a hardware business. He let customers charge merchandise and did not try to collect from them. His business failed after 18 months. The reason for the failure most likely was
    a. a poor location.
    b. poor credit management.
    c. lack of experience in the hardware business.
    d. inadequate sales.

13. Which one of the following statements is true?
    a. Small entrepreneurs must concentrate on their strengths and ignore their weaknesses.
    b. Business owners should base business decisions on personal considerations.
    c. Business owners should operate their own business and not seek outside help.
    d. Proprietors must have an understanding of business and the factors that affect it.

14. A firm that analyzes business failure is
    a. Johnson and Johnson.
    b. Dun and Bradstreet.
    c. Standard and Poor.
    d. Merrill Lynch.

15. John Phillips owned a service station. He decided to take a trip to Florida and left his younger brother in charge of the station. When John returned he found he had lost many of his customers and the bills were not paid. The business never recovered and closed five months later. The reason for business failure was
    a. neglect.
    b. lack of experience.
    c. disaster.
    d. top-heavy expenses.

16. Which one of the following statements is not a good business principle?
    a. The small business owner must be prepared to manage the business.
    b. The small business owner should take advantage of business specialists as advisors or consultants.
    c. The small business owner should hire someone else to do most of the work so that he or she has plenty of leisure time.
    d. The small business owner should keep business and private funds separate.

17. Probably one of the most important characteristics of an individual who wants to go into business is that person's
    a. personality.
    b. ability.
    c. education.
    d. experience.

18. When buying a business, the prospective business owner should ask questions about
    a. location.
    b. records.
    c. personnel.
    d. all of these.

19. Sound management of a business includes
    a. training.
    b. experience.
    c. time management.
    d. all of these.

20. In business, when an individual or a company attempts to advance by deceptive and dishonest methods, this is referred to as
    a. stealing.
    b. cheating.
    c. fraud.
    d. shoplifting.

21. When family members are involved in your business, they are likely to work harder for you because
    a. they are related to you.
    b. they have a stake in your success.
    c. they like you.
    d. they are afraid of you.

22. Sound management does not include
    a. anticipating pitfalls.
    b. separating administration from operation.
    c. operational details.
    d. policymaking.

23. Good managers should never
    a. become familiar with their subordinates.
    b. train their employees.
    c. joke with their subordinates.
    d. take their secretaries out to lunch.

24. Which one of the following is not a personal trait?
    a. Race   c. Health
    b. Attitude   d. Aptitude

25. The decision to start a business of your own should be based on
    a. reason.   c. advice of relatives.
    b. location.   d. emotion.

UNIT 4

ORGANIZING YOUR BUSINESS

OBJECTIVES

After studying this unit, you will be able to

- List the advantages and disadvantages of the sole proprietorship, the partnership, the limited partnership, and the corporate forms of business organization.
- Explain the difference between a closed corporation and a public corporation.
- Describe three types of cooperatives and explain the development of each type.
- Explain the three kinds of internal organizations and describe the advantages and disadvantages of each kind.
- Design two organization charts for your business, one in its beginning form, and another showing some organizational growth.
- Define the Terms to Know.

BUSINESS ORGANIZATIONS

A requirement for any business is an organization plan which states the various functions that must be performed. The organization plan defines the relationships and responsibilities of each person involved in the business.

A completely perfect form of organization does not exist. The success of a business organization depends on the attitudes and the contributions of all people involved. Some factors which should be considered when choosing the best form of organization for your business include the following:

- The purpose of the business
- The size of the business
- The capital required
- The degree of government regulation
- The amount of liability that the business owner(s) is willing to incur.

THE SOLE PROPRIETORSHIP

The *sole proprietorship* form of business organization has only one owner. It is a small business which is limited to the owner and usually a small number of employees. The sole proprietorship is the most common form of small business, Figure 4-1. Businesses that can be operated by a small number of persons and that do not require large amounts of capital are best suited to this form of organization. Examples of this type of business include repair shops, small grocery stores, specialty shops, delicatessens, and gasoline service stations, among others.

FIGURE 4-1
An example of the sole proprietorship.

Advantages of the Sole Proprietorship

Ease of Organization and Termination. The sole proprietorship is the simplest type of business organization that can be formed. It is not necessary to obtain special permission from the government to operate this type of business. However, the business may have to be registered with the state or city, depending on the state and local laws.

The owner of a sole proprietorship can terminate the business at any time. It is easier to terminate a sole proprietorship than it is to end other types of business organizations. Creditors must be notified of the plan to terminate, since ending a business does not discharge any debts already owed.

Freedom of Action and Control. The owner of a sole proprietorship is the boss. The owner can operate the business in the way he or she desires. As long as regulations are not disobeyed, the sole proprietor has almost complete freedom to manage the business. The owner sets the policies, hires and fires the employees, and may even make mistakes in learning how to create a successful business, Figure 4-2.

The sole proprietor has control of the business. Decisions may be made without consulting any other people. But, there will be times when the sole proprietor will seek advice from others. A proprietor should not be ashamed to get help in making decisions. Many private and public agencies exist to help the small business owner. When you need help, ask for it.

FIGURE 4-2
Long hours, pressures, and many worries are all a part of being the sole proprietor of a business. Make sure you are willing to take the responsibility for operating a business by yourself.

No Sharing of Profits. All of the profits of a sole proprietorship belong to the owner. The profits need not be shared with any other individual.

Less Government Regulations. There are rules and regulations governing all of the types of businesses. The sole proprietorship has the fewest government regulations to follow.

Smaller Tax Burden. The sole proprietor's profits are taxed as personal income. Compared with other forms of ownership, this is considered an advantage. Sole proprietorships are usually small and tend to pay less tax than other businesses with the exception of cooperatives. Tax advantages are extended to small businesses to encourage and help them stay in business.

Disadvantages of the Sole Proprietorship

Difficulty of Raising Capital. Generally, it is harder for a sole proprietor to borrow money than it is for partners or corporations. When one individual is involved, the risk of a loan is greater. When two or more partners or the officers of a corporation are responsible for a loan, the bank or lending institution is more likely to grant a loan. The limited ability of the sole proprietor to raise capital is critical when the business is being started and when it is being expanded.

Lack of Assistance. The sole owner does not have others to help manage the business. Employees cannot be expected to take the same interest in the business as the proprietor, and when left alone, the employees do not always make the best decisions. This disadvantage is minimized in the partnership and the corporation type of organization.

Unlimited Liability. Even with skill, capital, and other qualities necessary for success, the sole proprietor still takes a chance. There are risks in all business ventures. In a sole proprietorship, however, the risks are not shared with any other people. If the business fails, the owner could lose everything. This loss could include personal possessions. Personal articles which are not actually a part of a business, such as houses and cars, may be repossessed to pay debts. In the case of the sole proprietorship, a creditor's claim is not limited to business property. *Unlimited liability* is the term used to describe the practice of creditors to claim both business and personal property for the satisfaction of debts. Unlimited liability is the major disadvantage of a sole proprietorship.

Limited Life. The life of a sole proprietorship is ended by the death or mental or physical disability of the owner. This can present legal problems if the owner dies suddenly and has not left a will. In other forms of business, it may continue under the control of remaining partners or corporation officers.

THE PARTNERSHIP

A *partnership* is a business consisting of two or more co-owners, Figure 4-3. Sometimes, it is called a *copartnership*. It may be formed when one owner takes on another owner to expand the business, or it may be organized as a partnership from the start.

When several individuals begin to make plans, for example, it may seem easy to them to agree on what they want. They do not feel a lawyer and a written agreement are necessary because they are all honest and friendly people. Salaries are easily decided, and the profits will be shared equally. What happens if a salesperson decides that he or she should get a larger share of the profits? This could be the beginning of troubles for the partnership.

Without a written agreement, the partnership does not really exist. Many circumstances arise which cannot be foreseen and therefore must be anticipated in a written agreement. Partners will save time and money by asking a lawyer to draw up Articles of Copartnership (a partnership agreement).

FIGURE 4-3
A partnership consists of two or more co-owners and is sometimes called a copartnership.

Articles of Copartnership is an agreement among partners describing the duties and responsibilities of each partner in the business. It should include the following:

- Date of the agreement
- Names and addresses of the partners
- Nature of the business
- Name and address of the business
- Duration of the partnership
- Duties of each partner
- Investments of each partner
- How profits and losses will be shared
- Accounting procedures
- Salary or drawing account arrangements of each partner
- Restraints on each partner, if any
- How the partnership will be terminated

The agreement should contain provisions concerning the breakup of the partnership. Reasonable arrangements can be made which are fair to all of the partners. Partners frequently carry life insurance on one another.

Advantages of a Partnership

Additional Abilities, Skills, and Ideas. The more people that are involved in a business, the wider range of abilities, skills, and ideas they can bring to the business.

Division of Responsibilities. The owners of a business have numerous duties that must be performed successfully. If there is more than one owner, the responsibilities can be divided. For example, one partner could be responsible for the bookkeeping, and the other partner could be responsible for sales. In this way, the business could be operated more efficiently.

Increased Sources of Capital. One of the reasons for forming a partnership is to increase the amount of capital, which is needed to start or expand a business.

Ease in Obtaining Credit. A partnership can obtain credit more easily than a sole proprietorship. If necessary, creditors can sue all of the partners in a partnership, whereas in a sole proprietorship, the creditors have a claim only against one person.

FIGURE 4-4
One advantage of a partnership is the division of responsibilities, which often results in a more efficiently operated business.

A partnership has many of the same advantages as a sole proprietorship. The partnership and the sole proprietorship are both easy to organize, and there is little governmental control over either form of business.

Disadvantages of a Partnership

The partnership has disadvantages, and before you search for partners, consider the difficulties of joint ownership.

Unlimited Liability. Like the sole proprietorship, each partner has unlimited liability. Each partner is responsible for the acts of the other partners, since those actions create an obligation for the business.

If one partner sells goods at too low a price or buys at too high a price, the other partners are parties to the agreement. If a partner borrows money for the partnership to buy merchandise, the other partners can be responsible for the debt. Their business investment and their personal property are at stake.

Profit Sharing. The profits of a partnership are shared among the partners. They are shared equally, unless there is some other agreement. Any agreement contrary to equal shares should be stated in the Articles of Copartnership.

Partner's Lack of Effort. The lack of effort on the part of a partner is one problem that exists in some partnerships. Unless all partners contribute their knowledge, ability, and skills, the advantages of this type of organization are greatly reduced.

Limited Life of the Business. A partnership is terminated by the death or mental incompetency of any partner. But, there could be a time when one partner wants to leave the partnership before the time agreed upon. To minimize this problem, an agreement may be included in the Articles of Copartnership stating what will happen if one of these situations occurs.

101

Limited Expansion. A partnership can expand by raising additional money from partners or by adding new partners to the business. If partners who are already part of the business cannot raise the required money, adding partners or forming a corporation may be the answer.

THE CORPORATION

A *corporation* is an association of *stockholders* (part owners), formed with government consent and having the power to transact business in the same manner as if it were one person. A corporation has the same rights as an individual to own property, conduct business, make contracts, sue, and be sued. A corporation is a *single entity* (an individual person) in the eyes of the law.

If you decide to form a corporation, two associates may be needed in states where three or more stockholders are required to start a corporation. These associates then hire a lawyer to apply for a state charter. The application for a charter is called a *Certificate of Incorporation.* It is a document which authorizes individuals to carry on business activities as a corporation, raise funds, and sell stock. The requirements of the certificate vary from state to state, but generally include the following:

- Name of the corporation
- Purpose of the corporation
- Location of the corporation's main office
- Names and addresses of all directors
- Duration of the corporation
- Face value of capital stock which may be issued
- Voting rights of the stockholders

When organizing a corporation, all initial stockholders elect a board of directors and draw up bylaws for the corporation, Figure 4-5. The bylaws describe all rules, regulations, and limits which apply to the corporation.

Corporations are either closed or public. A small business corporation is usually a *closed corporation.* This means that capital stock is not sold to the public. If one of the stockholders decides to sell stock, it is usually sold to one of the other stockholders or to someone of whom they all approve. In this way, the ownership of the business is selective and controlled.

A *public* or *open corporation* offers its stock to the public. This means that its stock is available to anyone who wants to buy it. The principal owner of a public corporation is the majority stockholder.

FIGURE 4-5 The governing body of a corporation is the board of directors. They are elected by the stockholders to operate the business.

Advantages of the Corporation

Limited Liability. A corporation is a limited liability business. In England, instead of using the abbreviation *Inc.* for corporation, the abbreviation *Ltd.* is used to show that it is a limited liability company. This means that only the assets of the corporation can be taken to pay debts, Figure 4-6. If an individual owns stock in a corporation which has unpaid debts, that stock may become worthless, but the stockholder cannot lose more than the value of the stock. Liability is limited to the amount of the purchase price of the stock.

FIGURE 4-6
This hardware store chose the corporation form of business organization probably because of its advantage of limited liability.

103

Variety of Skills, Abilities, and Ideas. The corporation has the advantage of many owners with different skills and talents. In a small corporation, the stockholders may work for the company and divide the responsibilities.

Easy Transfer of Ownership. If a stockholder wishes to leave the corporation, all that the stockholder must do is sell the stock. This is a relatively easy task. Many prospective buyers are available through brokers, the stock exchanges, or over the counter in a private sale.

Ease of Expansion. The corporation can be easily expanded. When more capital is needed, additional stock is sold to the public. Some corporations sell bonds instead of stock to raise capital.

Unlimited Existence. One advantage of the corporation is that the business does not dissolve if a stockholder dies or leaves. The stock goes to the holder's heirs, and the corporation continues operating. In a small corporation where stockholders may take an active part in running the business, changes in assignments may be needed.

Disadvantages of the Corporation

Complexity and High Cost. Incorporation may offer little value for some small businesses. Both state and federal governments tax corporations. Another cost of incorporating includes a lawyer's services to draw up the charter and to handle the papers and reports that must be filed regularly by the corporation.

FIGURE 4-7
A franchise is a business that sells its name and reputation to small business owners who buy the right to use them. The "parent" company of a franchise is usually a corporation, but the local franchise unit can organize in any way.

Lack of Freedom of Action. A corporation can only perform those activities which are stated in its charter. In states where a corporation is not chartered, it can only conduct its activities by paying a registration fee.

Government Regulation. More of the federal and state regulations that exist seem to apply to corporations than to any of the other forms of business. Corporations must be publicly audited each year.

Profit Sharing. Since there is more than one owner in a corporation, profits must be shared among the stockholders. The owners of a corporation share the profits in proportion to the number of shares of stock owned by each individual. The profits are usually in the form of dividends paid annually.

Taxes. The corporate form of business must pay taxes on its earnings. Corporations pay taxes on profits, and stockholders pay taxes on the dividends they received from those profits. Since 1958, the owners of a small business have been able to incorporate and have their corporate earnings taxed as a partnership. This is called a *subchapter S corporation* (named after the subchapter of the Internal Revenue Code that explains it). In order for a corporation to be considered a subchapter S corporation, it must meet certain requirements. A few of the requirements include:

- A limited number of stockholders
- A limited amount of corporate income from investments

THE COOPERATIVE

Another type of business organization which in recent years has received attention is the cooperative, Figure 4-8. The cooperative is important largely as a result of the consumer movement in this country. At least two types of cooperatives exist, the producer co-op and the consumer co-op.

Producer co-ops are not new. In the early part of this century, farmers joined together to form producer co-ops in order to market milk and other farm products. Some of the brand names marketed by producer co-ops include Sunkist, Sun Maid, Welch's, Land o' Lakes and Dairylea. In addition, the Farmer's Federation, the National Grange, and the Dairymen's League banded together to form the Grange League Federation (GLF), a consumer co-op, to provide farm families with goods and services at a savings.

Producer co-ops are owned by the people who provide the raw materials and other items to the co-op for manufacture or processing. Consumer co-ops are owned by the persons who benefit from the goods and services they all work together to share; that is, consumer co-ops are owned by its customers. The

FIGURE 4-8
This is an example of a cooperative which is owned by its customers. It is large enough to afford to pay a manager and some store personnel.

customer/owners benefit in paying lower prices because they perform much of the work voluntarily. The co-op therefore has lower labor costs. At the end of a year, any surplus the co-op has after expenses is distributed back to the members as patronage dividends. As a result, the co-op does not make a profit and therefore does not pay taxes. This is one of the big advantages of a co-op.

Co-ops operate about the same as any other small businesses. Since co-ops are similar in structure to corporations, with their members acting like stockholders, they must be audited annually. Because there are many owners, too many to run the co-op efficiently, the members elect representatives to make decisions for the co-op. This small group is called a board of governors, or a co-op board, and is similar to a board of directors.

Since co-ops are not really small businesses, why are they mentioned? Co-ops, with the exception of their ownership, are operated like any small business. They have become a popular form of business among persons with low or fixed incomes. People have organized co-ops to provide low-cost housing and merchandise. Co-op gas stations and garages, child care centers, and condominiums have also been started. The two main reasons for starting consumer co-ops are to provide goods and services at a large savings to its members, and to permit the members to control their business. For more information about co-ops, write to the Co-op League of the USA, 1828 L Street, NW, Suite 1100, Washington, DC 20036.

The National Co-op Bank in Washington, an agency of the federal government, was formed recently to loan money to co-ops to help them get started. The bank loans have a much lower rate of interest than commercial banks. The bank guarantees the loan to responsible citizen groups whose principal asset is their willingness to work (sweat equity). This encourages inner-city improvements and services for the handicapped and the aging.

INTERNAL ORGANIZATION

Business organizations are made up of people who perform the jobs necessary for business success. *Internal organization* is a plan which outlines how these people work together.

Each person in the business has some authority and responsibility. A shipping clerk has the authority to sign receipts for incoming shipments and the responsibility for keeping records. A sales manager has the authority to direct company salespeople and the responsibility for producing sales as a result of such direction. The principal function of internal organization is the assignment of duties to employees to establish their authority and responsibilities.

Internal organization of a company should establish the following:

- Each employee should have only one boss

- Each employee should know who that boss is

- Each employee should know what his or her duties are

- Each employee should know how much authority he or she has

When a business is small, internal organization is very simple, but not unimportant. Every employee should have or know each of the points just mentioned.

Lack of clear internal organization leads to employee confusion and low morale. Suppose an employee cashes an $80 check for a customer without knowing if he or she has the authority to do so. If the check happens to be bad, the company will take the loss. In cases where employees overstep their authority, as in this case, should the employee be required to take the loss?

Proper organization can reduce such losses. It avoids duplication of effort and eliminates unnecessary functions and friction because each employee knows his or her responsibilities and authority. Improved communications within the business can also reduce costly mistakes.

Small businesses cannot afford to be run inefficiently because competition is too keen. Good internal organization can streamline a business operation and keep it working at a high efficiency rate.

The three different types of internal organization are: line, functional, and line and staff. Each type has advantages and disadvantages.

The Line Organization

The line organization is the simplest form of internal organization. In this type of organization there is a direct line of authority between a superior and a subordinate. As illustrated in Figure 4-9, each employee has only one boss.

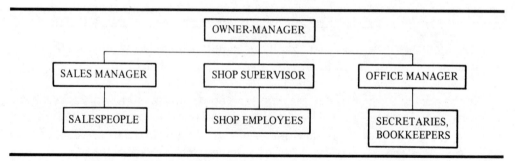

FIGURE 4-9 The simplest form of internal organization is the line organization.

Advantages

- Easy to understand. This is an easy form of organization to understand. A business owner can successfully organize this form without being an expert on business organization. Employees also can easily understand this form of organization.

- Inexpensive to operate. This form of organization does not require specialists for it to operate successfully.

- Direct supervision. The straight line of authority between employer and employees permits a direct and close working relationship between them. It also creates better communication, and decisions can be made quickly.

Disadvantages.

- Responsibility. Each supervisor has a great deal of responsibility. The shop supervisor hires, trains, and supervises shop employees, but also knows production schedules, repair and maintenance of equipment, production processes, and details of shop operation. As the business grows, such responsibility may become too great for one person.

- Lack of specialization. With many duties, a supervisor cannot specialize in any one duty for fear of neglecting the other duties. This lack of specialization can be a handicap as the business grows in size and complexity.

The Functional Organization

The *functional organization* is designed so that there is a specialist for each of the main functions. In this type of organization, each employee may have more than one supervisor, Figure 4-10.

Advantage. The major advantage of the functional form of organization is that it provides for specialization. Each aspect of the operation is grouped into major functional areas, permitting specialists to be developed in each of these areas.

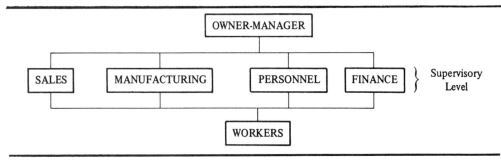

FIGURE 4-10 The functional organization

Disadvantages. With the functional form of organization, some employees may have more than one supervisor. This could lead to a confusing situation in an organization. The functional organization is also too expensive for the small company to operate. The owner most times cannot afford full-time specialists.

The functional organization overcomes the lack of specialization found in the line organization. The line organization works well for the small company. However, neither form is designed for the larger company with problems that are difficult to overcome.

The Line and Staff Organization

The *line and staff organization,* Figure 4-11, combines the advantages of the line organization and the functional organization by adding specialists to help the line supervisors solve problems.

For example, a manufacturer wants to expand and decides to hire and train more employees. The supervisors are too busy to find and train good employees. There are also many personnel problems to be worked out. One solution would

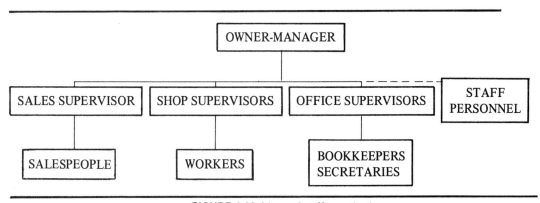

FIGURE 4-11 Line and staff organization

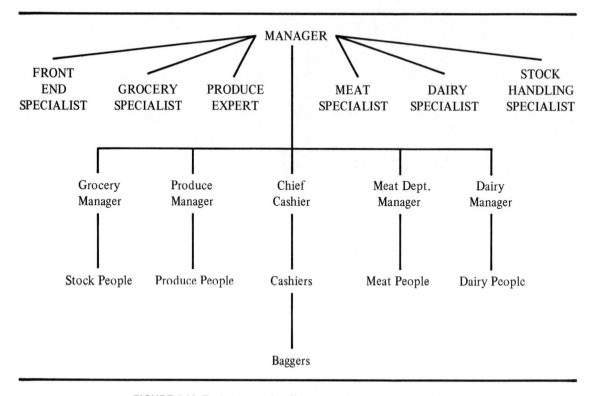

FIGURE 4-12 Typical line and staff organization chart for a supermarket

be to hire a specialist in personnel to help the owner and supervisors. The broken line on the chart in Figure 4-12 indicates that this person is not a supervisor, but an advisor on personnel matters.

Advantages. Line and staff organization allows for a specialist to assist the line supervisors. The personnel staff member would not hire anyone, but would find several applicants. The final choice would be made by the supervisor.

Disadvantages. A business has to be large enough to afford the salaries of specialists. Very small companies cannot usually afford to operate as a line and staff organization.

BUSINESS MANUAL ASSIGNMENT

Decide on the type of organization you will have. Will the type of organization be a line, line and staff, functional, or another combination?

Make up an organization chart for your business. For purposes of discussion, make sure you have at least ten people listed on the chart, even if you will probably not employ that many at first. The idea is to plan for future expansion, and even if you work alone (self-employed) for some time, you will eventually need a chart. Consult the text, references, and talk with local business persons, friends you know who work, and others, to get ideas for your chart. Then draw the chart neatly using a ruler. Print the title in the boxes. You can also use rub-on letters, which are available in most stationery stores.

TERMS TO KNOW

capital	internal organization
sole proprietorship	line organization
partnership	functional organization
corporation	line and staff organization
entity	board of directors
limited life	stockholders
Articles of Copartnership	stocks
profit sharing	bonds
Certificate of Incorporation	shares
closed corporation	investor
public corporation	dividend
cooperative	

UNIT QUIZ

In each of the following, select the word or phrase that best completes the statement or answers the question.

1. One advantage of the sole proprietorship form of business organization is that
   a. it is easy to raise capital.
   b. it has unlimited liability.
   c. there is limited life of the business.
   d. there is no sharing of profits.

2. One disadvantage of the sole proprietorship form of business organization is that
   a. there are fewer government regulations with which the business must comply.
   b. it is easy to raise capital.
   c. there is no sharing of profits.
   d. there is unlimited liability.

3. One advantage of the partnership form of business organization is that
   a. there is a sharing of responsibilities.
   b. there is unlimited liability.
   c. there is a sharing of profits.
   d. it has unlimited life.

4. A corporation obtains the right to operate in a state by obtaining
   a. a franchise.
   b. a license.
   c. a charter.
   d. a Certificate of Incorporation.

5. The legal form of business organization that has only one owner is known as
   a. a sole proprietorship.
   b. a partnership.
   c. a cooperative.
   d. a stock company.

6. The most common form of business organization for a small business is
   a. the corporation.
   b. the cooperative.
   c. the sole proprietorship.
   d. the partnership.

7. One disadvantage of the partnership form of business organization is that there is
   a. a sharing of responsibilities.
   b. unlimited liability.
   c. ease in obtaining credit.
   d. a variety of ideas and abilities from the various partners.

8. Most small businesses that are incorporated are
   a. nonprofit corporations.
   b. private corporations.
   c. public corporations.
   d. closed corporations.

9. One advantage of the corporate form of business organization is that
   a. the number of government regulations is small.
   b. there is unlimited liability.
   c. there is easy transfer of ownership.
   d. taxes are low.

10. One disadvantage of the corporate form of business ownership is that
    a. it has limited liability.
    b. it has unlimited existence.
    c. it requires a sharing of responsibility.
    d. it must comply with a number of government regulations.

11. Which one of the following types of internal organizations is used most by small businesses?
    a. Line
    b. Line and staff
    c. Functional
    d. None of these

12. The type of internal organization that is structured around specialists is known as
    a. line organization.
    b. line and staff organization.
    c. functional organization.
    d. open organization.

13. One of the disadvantages of the line form of internal organization is its
    a. simplicity of structure.
    b. lack of specialization.
    c. number of supervisors for each employee.
    d. expense of operation.

14. One advantage of the line and staff type of internal organization is
    a. the expense of specialists.
    b. its simplicity of structure.
    c. the assistance of specialists.
    d. its lack of control.

15. A corporation that sells stock to the public is known as
    a. a private corporation.
    b. a government corporation.
    c. a nonprofit corporation.
    d. a public corporation.

16. Which of the following businesses could easily be organized as a producer co-op?
    a. A milk processing plant
    b. Grape growers
    c. Orange growers
    d. All of these

17. Which one of the following brand names of products is not produced by a cooperative?
    a. Sun Maid
    b. Land o'Lakes
    c. Sealtest
    d. Dairylea

18. A consumer co-op is organized principally to
    a. save money for the members.
    b. avoid paying taxes.
    c. cut down on government regulations.
    d. make shopping more convenient.

19. A line and staff type of organization is especially useful in
    a. a large food chain.
    b. a small clothing store.
    c. an automobile dealership.
    d. a cooperative.

20. Which one of the following business organizations has in recent years become important largely as a result of the consumer movement in this country?
    a. Corporation
    b. Sole proprietorship
    c. Partnership
    d. Cooperative

21. A law firm might easily be organized as
    a. a partnership.
    b. a sole proprietorship.
    c. a cooperative.
    d. a private corporation.

22. A certified public accounting firm might easily organize as
    a. a partnership.
    b. a sole proprietorship.
    c. a cooperative.
    d. a private corporation.

23. Two partners operating a small amusement park with high-risk rides should consider changing their current partnership to
   a. a sole proprietorship.
   b. a limited partnership.
   c. a private corporation.
   d. a cooperative.

24. When you open a sole proprietorship,
   a. no special forms are needed.
   b. you must get a DBA certificate.
   c. you must register with the sheriff.
   d. you must post a bond.

25. If you have formed a small corporation, you can
   a. sell stock to friends.
   b. list your stock with the New York Stock Exchange.
   c. borrow against your stock.
   d. none of these.

UNIT 5

PLANNING A SMALL BUSINESS

OBJECTIVES

After studying this unit, you will be able to

- Diagram and explain some of the channels of distribution.
- Analyze various business locations and explain the advantages and disadvantages of each.
- Identify the factors to be considered in choosing a business location.
- Design at least one scale layout for your business.
- Design and sketch a sign and a storefront (if appropriate) for your business.
- Define the Terms to Know.

Physical features are an important aspect of planning a business. These include location, physical plant, office, store or shop, and storage areas. Once located, businesses are difficult and expensive to move. The potential owner must therefore take time to plan and carefully research the location of a future business before making a final decision.

Businesses that provide goods and services should be located near their sources and also near their customers. For this reason, you should have a basic understanding of the channels of distribution. A distributive business, as explained in Unit 2, is one that helps get the goods from the producer to the consumer. This can be done in many ways, as the next section of this unit explains.

CHANNELS OF DISTRIBUTION

Businesses which engage in retail, wholesale, and service operations should be concerned with the distribution of goods and services. *Distribution* is defined as all activities which enable a product to flow from the producer to the consumer.

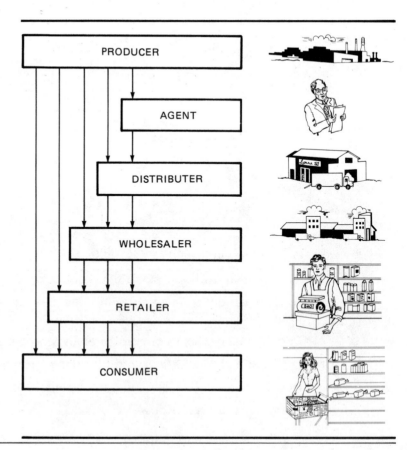

FIGURE 5-1
The channels of distribution

Individuals who perform such services as transporting, packaging, warehousing, packing, wholesaling, and retailing are part of the distribution cycle. The path an article takes on its way from producer to consumer is called a *channel of distribution*. The layout, location, and physical facilities of a business are determined by how the business fits into the distribution cycle. It is important for you to understand the various channels of distribution. Figure 5-1 shows some of the possible routes an article might take on its way to the consumer.

From Producer to Consumer

The simplest and sometimes shortest route a product takes is directly from the manufacturer or producer to the consumer. Because the two must be brought into direct contact with each other, this is not the most common channel of distribution. The purchase of corn, eggs, milk, or garden products directly from a farmer, Figure 5-2, is a good example of what is sometimes called *direct distribution*. For some perishable goods or for custom-made goods, this method is appropriate. The person who buys a tailor-made suit or an artificial limb is dealing directly with the producer and avoids any middlemen in the distribution process.

FIGURE 5-2
This producer sells the products grown on his farm to the consumer via this roadside stand.

From Producer to Retailer to Consumer

As the chart in Figure 5-1 indicates, there is only one *middleman* in this channel of distribution. The middleman (or middlewoman) is in the middle of the distribution cycle. This person performs distributive services which help the product get to the consumer. Middlemen may receive the goods in large quantities and sell them in smaller amounts. Selling in smaller quantities is one of the functions of the retailer. The retailer also performs other tasks such as displaying, advertising, repackaging, delivering, and demonstrating a product.

The retailer who deals only with the producer uses the method of distribution called *direct buying.* This method is helpful in the distribution of such products as cookies and crackers, candy, dairy products, and ice cream. Direct buying is also used often in the fashion industry. The retailer may buy direct to gain an advantage of having newer fashions, lower prices, and manufacturers' discounts.

From Producer to Wholesaler to Retailer to Consumer

This form of distribution adds a second middleman to the cycle. The wholesaler can provide to the retailer the convenience of ordering many items from one source. Other services of the wholesaler include the delivery of goods, credit, and the privilege of returning unsold items. By not delivering goods until they are needed, the wholesaler provides the storage space which the retailer lacks. The wholesaler may also be nearer to the retailer than the manufacturer. Other advantages in buying from a wholesaler include the following:

- Wholesalers may sell in smaller quantities than manufacturers.
- Wholesalers may be nearer than producers and therefore may deliver goods for free.
- Wholesalers may offer prompt delivery on many items.
- Wholesalers may offer better credit terms than producers.
- Placing one order with a wholesaler is simpler than placing orders with many manufacturers.

From Producer to Agent to Wholesaler to Retailer to Consumer

In some cases, such as in the distribution of fish, produce, agricultural products, and similar commodities, the path of goods goes through several "hands" before it reaches the retailer. A middleman called an *agent* or *broker* may enter the cycle. This person represents the producer and may never actually see or handle the goods. *Commission merchants* are agents that bring producer and seller together and receive a commission on the sale. Brokers and agents are common in the sale of real estate, securities, insurance, and in representing theatrical talent.

While it is possible to purchase articles through one channel of distribution, most retailers use more than one. For example, a grocery store owner might buy nonfood items from a manufacturer, grocery items from a wholesaler, and produce directly from a farmer. Specific circumstances determine the channels of distribution that will be used.

The Retailer

The last link in the distribution cycle is the retailer who sells to the consumer. The entire distribution process focuses on the retailer. The needs of customers must be satisfied to complete the distribution cycle. Our system of mass production and consumption depends on mass distribution. Otherwise, adjustments such as reducing production and laying off workers must be made. The retailer is an important part of the distribution process and an excellent choice for a small business. Retailers may be divided into five main categories.

Over the Counter. This is the most common type of retailing. Over-the-counter retailing is found in the typical store situation. It includes all varieties of shops and stores that offer goods and services to the public.

Mail Order. The mail-order retailer reaches customers through the mail with printed brochures and catalogs.

Door to Door (Direct Selling). The direct retailer employs canvassers or door-to-door salespeople who call on the customer at home. A variety of household products, such as brushes, cosmetics, and cookware, are sold door to door.

Automatic Vending Machine. The operator of an automatic vending machine business may place them in a number of locations. Such products as soft drinks, candy, and hot foods are sold in vending machines, Figure 5-3. The refilling and maintenance of the machines is becoming a popular choice for a small business. Electronic games and amusements are a popular variation of the vending machine business, as are coin-operated laundromats.

Route Selling. As mentioned in Unit 2, the route seller follows a schedule in making calls on customers. This is different from direct sales where calls are made once, and sales are a one-shot situation. The route seller may be employed by a producer, such as a driver salesperson who sells bread and rolls for a bakery. Other products sold by the route seller include soft drinks, laundry and dry-cleaning services, milk and dairy products, coffee, tea and spices, and produce.

FIGURE 5-3
Candy, cold drinks, and hot foods are
sold in vending machines.

LOCATING THE SMALL BUSINESS

Determining where a business will fit best into the distribution process is an important first step in choosing a location for the enterprise. Nearness to the market, transportation, communication, personal preference, and community needs should be considered.

The general types of location include the small town, the city, and the suburb. These types can further be divided according to the kinds of shopping areas found within each type.

Types of Locations

The Small Town. In choosing a small town or village for a business, the location is secondary to determining the economic future of the community itself. In small towns, businesses cluster around the main street. Distances between businesses are short and walk-in customers account for much of the trade. Parking facilities, while important, are less of a determining factor than in urban areas. A small town can support a variety of household, food, and service establishments if enough of the citizens in town and in the surrounding area have sufficient buying power. A potential business owner should be careful of one-industry towns, dominated by one company. For example, if the only mill in town closes, the economy of the whole area may be affected. While the trading area of a village has no precise boundaries, some indication of the competitive pulling power of the village or town can be discovered. A village center of 10 or 12 good stores will draw customers from the surrounding area. A shopping center that is at all representative will draw customers from a good-size area. Also, a farm trading area, depending on the topography, can become the center of trading activity for the entire county. A friendliness and spirit of cooperation still exists in the small town, something that is often lost in the high-speed competition of the city. You may never get rich as a small town merchant, but the rural atmosphere provides many other important benefits.

The City. The city (for discussion purposes, a community with a population in excess of 25,000) is a network of interrelated and overlapping communities. Within the city, there are five basic types of business locations. These are the central business district, the secondary business district, string streets and stores, neighborhoods, and shopping centers.

The downtown area is the central district of a city and probably the oldest area. It is the transportation hub and the focal point of the community. In large cities the downtown area, or *central business district*, contains stores carrying both convenience and shopping goods.

In the past, the dominant force of the downtown area was the department store, usually the largest store in the city. The search for suburban sites by department stores is evidence of the declining influence of the downtown department store. Parking problems, changes in customer buying habits, and the movement of people to the suburbs have caused a total change in the character of many downtown areas.

Cities are now engaged in major urban renewal projects to eliminate slums, revitalize downtown shopping areas, and provide more parking for customers. With such improvements, the advantages of downtown shopping to the customer include a larger selection of goods, lower prices, and many businesses in one area. There are some disadvantages. Parking is expensive, traffic is heavy, the area may be crowded and not pleasant or safe for children, and rents and real estate prices are frequently high.

As cities expanded, the amount of retail business done in the central business district lessened. This decentralization of trade is largely a consequence of population growth and improved methods of transportation. The automobile drastically changed marketing by allowing customers to shop in different areas and at greater distances.

Because certain businesses are inconvenient or inefficient in a downtown area, they choose locations in secondary and fringe areas of the city. The *secondary business district* includes such businesses as bakeries, light industry, and automobile repair shops. These enterprises are larger than neighborhood centers and yet less inclusive than the central downtown business district. Geographically, they can be located anywhere in a city other than downtown. In small cities, these secondary business districts are disappearing. In large cities, they tend to form concentric

FIGURE 5-4
Neighborhood stores like this one should have a weekly customer return of at least three or four people.

rings around the downtown core. In general, secondary districts share the strengths and weaknesses of downtown centers.

As the central business district is the focus of the entire city, so the *neighborhood district* is the business core of residential areas. The stores in the neighborhood district draw customers from easy walking or driving distances. These local shops mostly carry convenience goods or offer personal services, Figure 5-4. A neighborhood location is generally suitable for such businesses as food stores that are open 24 hours, shoe repair shops, pharmacies, fruit and vegetable stores, barber shops and beauty salons, and bookstores. Candy stores, dry-cleaning establishments, delicatessens, and radio and television accessory and repair shops are also suitable businesses for the neighborhood district. Each serves the surrounding residential area with convenience goods and services. It is important to note, however, that the shopping plaza offers many of these advantages in addition to later evening hours and ample parking.

Although frequently found in a downtown, secondary or neighborhood shopping district, the *string street* store is a separate type of location as compared to its newer competitor, the plaza. String street stores are located on either side of a street in a row, or in a "string", Figure 5-5. Parking along the street may be parallel or diagonal, and there are usually parking meters.

The choice of which side of the street to put a business on can influence the success of a business. In attempting to increase sales volume, the prospective retailer must be prepared to compete for the customer's dollar not only with other stores selling similar goods, but with stores of all kinds. In order to compete, you will need good merchandising experience and ideas, ample capital, and a knowledge of good buying sources. You will also need a good location and common sense to compete with other merchants.

FIGURE 5-5
String street stores are located on either side of a street in a row.

The Suburb. There has been a vast migration of people out of the inner-city areas into the suburbs. The movement is mainly the result of the automobile. The car allows individuals the freedom of personal transportation. With an automobile, it is possible for workers to live in the suburbs and travel to work in cities and other locations some distance from their homes. People look for less crime and violence, more space, and better schools in the suburbs. It is these middle-class suburban shoppers that make up most of the customers for plazas and shopping centers.

There are many businesses where location might be thought of as secondary to other considerations. Some examples of businesses that consider location secondary include mail order, manufacturing, and processing. If you are going to offer goods or services by mail, delivery or route truck, or service equipment in people's homes, then the accessibility of customers to your business becomes less important. You will need less parking space, and you can afford to take advantage of low-rent districts and quiet, remote areas. When selecting a location, you should ask yourself the following questions:

- How will my customers be served — here or in their homes?
- If customers come to my business, what method of transportation will they use — bus, car, trolley, subway, taxi, or other?

Many businesses which locate in the city are also found in the suburbs. It is sometimes difficult to tell where a secondary business district ends and the suburbs begin. Some suburban communities have become so heavily developed that they have central and secondary business districts of their own. In reality, they are small cities. String streets and neighborhood locations are common.

Probably the most popular business location in the suburbs is some form of the *shopping center* or *plaza.* Plaza comes from the German word *platz* or the French word *place,* which means "place." The plaza idea probably came from a village in central Europe where every Saturday, the farmers and merchants would come from miles around and set up stands and booths on the village square. This has lead to what we know as the farmer's market and the flea market. Many towns still have a village square, usually with bandstand and benches, and it is used mainly as a park. This is a holdover from the marketplaces of central Europe.

A shopping center or plaza is a group of commercial establishments which are planned, developed, and managed as a unit. The shopping plaza has parking provided on the property in direct ratio to the number of stores. These shopping plazas vary in the number of stores and in the size of the parking area. They are usually adjacent to main roads and superhighways. There are six variations of the shopping plaza. Each variation is distinguished by the size and kinds of stores, Figure 5-6.

Type of Center	Number of Stores	Outstanding Characteristics	Enclosed
Neighborhood Shopping Center	6 or less	Mostly service businesses catering to customers within walking distance	Never
Mini-mall	12 or less	In between a neighborhood center and a community center. Draws customers from immediate area.	Not usually
Community Shopping Center	30 or less	Serves larger area. Usually has a large supermarket at one end,	Seldom
Suburban Shopping Center	50 or less	has ample parking, usually on bus line.	
Regional Shopping Center	100 or less	Has at least one "name" department store, and many service and specialty stores. Large parking area.	Frequently
Super Mall	over 100	Has several large department stores, several supermarkets, and well over a hundred other stores of all kinds. Features restaurants and motion picture theaters.	Frequently

FIGURE 5-6 The six variations of the shopping plaza

FIGURE 5-7
This is a mini-mall shopping center. It is larger and a bit more sophisticated in appearance than a neighborhood shopping center.

The *neighborhood shopping center* consists of about five or six small stores. The stores are usually service businesses such as barber shops, shoe repair shops, laundromats, and dry-cleaning stores. The only factor which distinguishes a neighborhood plaza from a string street is that the stores are set back from the main road, which provides for minimum parking off the road. A new type of shopping center is the *mini-mall,* Figure 5-7, which is slightly larger than the neighborhood center. It is a bit more sophisticated than the neighborhood center in appearance and has as many as 12 stores. The focus of the mini-mall is often a boutique or a fancy specialty shop. The mini-mall usually has a pharmacy, take-out food shops or delicatessens, a local bar or pub, and a 24-hour convenience food store. The neighborhood plaza and the mini-mall serve an area of only a few miles in radius. They provide the goods and services needed in heavily populated residential areas, especially in neighborhoods with large apartment houses and condominiums.

FIGURE 5-8
A community shopping center features a supermarket and about 30 other stores.

The focal point of the *community* or *suburban shopping center* is usually the supermarket. It acts as a traffic generator and draws customers to the center for weekly grocery shopping. The 20 or 30 other stores located in the center hope to get the benefit of this shopping traffic, Figure 5-8. They include drug and hardware stores, auto accessory and tire stores, dry- cleaning stores, laundromats, and a variety of specialty stores. In some states, liquor stores are permitted to locate in community and suburban centers. The distinction between a community and a suburban shopping center is somewhat arbitrary. Some experts use the number of stores as the distinguishing factor. Generally, there are less than 30 stores in a community shopping center and over 30 stores in a suburban shopping center, Figure 5-9.

The *regional shopping center* is usually "keyed" to a large discount house, a general merchandise store, or a big department store, which has the reputation of drawing customers. A supermarket may be found at a regional shopping center, but probably only outside of the center. The supporting stores range from sporting goods shops and gift shops to candy stores and ice cream stands. The regional plaza is frequently in the shape of an L or a U. It features at least 50 stores of various kinds. Large parking areas are available, and there are even buses to take customers to their cars in some of the large centers. The layout varies, depending on the location of the department store and its auto accessory and tire store, as this is generally regarded as the traffic generator.

A mall with benches and garden areas is common in many regional centers. Some regional centers are totally enclosed. They are heated in the winter and air-conditioned in the summer, Figure 5-10. Some regional plazas operate buses from the downtown areas of nearby cities to bring in more shoppers. There are

FIGURE 5-9
This suburban shopping area has more than 30 stores. Where parking can be a problem in downtown areas, the suburban shopping area offers a large parking area for customers.

FIGURE 5-10
Many regional shopping malls are enclosed for protection from the weather. They are heated in the winter and air-conditioned in the summer, which makes shopping very pleasant.

regional centers that offer free babysitting service, strollers for children, and game rooms for young people.

A relatively recent development is the super mall. It has over 100 stores and may serve many counties or several states. The super mall is usually located near the intersection of interstate highways, and can easily draw customers from a hundred miles away or farther. The focus of the super mall is a minimum of two large department stores, Figure 5-11. The downtown department stores have had to open suburban branches to survive, and the bigger the center they can find, the better. These stores concentrate on those departments which require large amounts of floor space, for such items as furniture, marine equipment and boats, recreational vehicles and campers, and swimming pools. The super mall may feature such varied services as a medical or dental center, optical services, real estate and insurance offices, figure salons, and health clubs. One might find a landing strip for small airplanes, a motel, and several fine restaurants at a super mall.

FIGURE 5-11
A super mall can easily draw customers from far away. However, for a person just starting out in business, the rents for a store may be extremely high.

For a person just starting out in business, it might be too expensive to locate in a regional shopping center or super mall. Rents are high for a small store. It may also be hard for the new business to achieve a volume of sales that is high enough to succeed in such a competitive environment. At first, it might be better to locate in a suburban or community plaza, provided it is well planned and managed, and the trading area draws from a population base with sufficient buying power.

Choosing a Location

Once you have decided on the town, suburb, or city in which to operate your business, a further evaluation of the locality is needed. A business can only be successful if the community it serves is understood, and if the community is growing. You must understand the community. Its history, population, ethnic makeup, kinds of work the people do, other businesses, schools, and the employment situation must all be considered. It would not be desirable to locate a business in a deteriorating area with high unemployment. Therefore, before moving in, it is a good idea to check state and local population tables, per capita income, and other economic facts for your prospective area. Find out if the community is attracting new businesses, or if businesses are moving out of the area. State departments of commerce and labor can give you all of this information. They will provide you with a file of market surveys, Figure 5-12, business statistics, and a lot of valuable information. Other sources of information include the local library, banks, and chamber of commerce.

County and Community (2,500 population and over)	Apparel, Accessory Stores			Furniture, Home Furnishings, Equipment Stores			Automotive Dealers			Gasoline Service Stations		
	No. of Establish-ments	Sales Total ($000)	Per Capita	No. of Establish-ments	Sales Total ($000)	Per Capita	No. of Establish-ments	Sales Total ($000)	Per Capita	No. of Establish-ments	Sales Total ($000)	Per Capita
New York State	17,205	1,981,640	$123	10,501	1,126,600	$70	5,819	2,385,639	$148	12,484	946,086	$59
Upstate New York[1]	4,709	450,035	77	3,628	323,139	55	3,428	1,213,366	208	6,998	438,863	75
Elmira Area	271	22,683	65	232	17,335	50	252	69,226	198	401	25,122	72
Allegany County	38	1,593	36	33	1,043	24	35	7,751	176	60	2,836	65
Alfred	n.a.	n.a.	.....	n.a.	n.a.	.....	n.a.	n.a.	.....	n.a.	n.a.	.....
Wellsville	20	1,164	192	10	510	84	11	3,681	608	14	746	123
Chemung County	84	8,813	93	63	6,072	64	60	21,739	230			
Elmira	70	7,391	163	39	4,932	109	31	16,677	368			
Elmira Heights	5	*	.....	4	*	.....	1	*				
Horseheads	6	713	110	7	*	.....	10					
Schuyler County	6	284	19	13								
Watkins Glen		99										

FIGURE 5-12 Sample page from a state market survey

FIGURE 5-13
What was once a private home is now a successful pizza business. The location was just right.

Other Businesses in the Area. Other business operations in the area should not be looked upon only as competition. Frequently, the stores in a particular location serve the same class of customers. A women's fashion shop would be misplaced if it were grouped with hardware stores, auto repair shops, and machine shops. An expensive specialty shop would be out of place in a low-income neighborhood. The goods or services provided by a business generally should appeal to the type of customers likely to live or shop in the area.

The Potential Market. One of the most important factors to be considered in choosing a location is the potential market for the business. The business owner should ask a number of questions, including the following:

- What are the specific needs of the community?
- Will customers have any difficulty in reaching the business?
- Are there adequate parking facilities?
- Will the flow of traffic, both pedestrian and automobile, be advantageous?
- Is the business near stores that sell to similar types of customers?
- What is the possibility of an evening or Sunday trade?
- Do potential buyers need, and can they afford, the goods and services offered?

Potential Competition. Assuming that the market looks good, one must determine what the competition for that market will be.

- Are there already too many businesses in the area providing the same goods or services?
- Can a new business be superior enough to capture part of that trade so it can survive?

FIGURE 5-14
The customers operate the pumps at this self-service gasoline station, where no repair work is done. This station is successful in the same location where a full-service gas station and garage failed.

Wholesalers and suppliers are sources of reliable information about competition. The wholesaler deals with some of your potential competition and should be interested in any new businesses coming into the area.

Knowledge of the Community. In evaluating the potential market for a new business, knowledge of the community is essential. When the business is operating, this knowledge is still important. Many small businesses are owned by people who have lived in the community for some time. Their faces are familiar, customers feel at ease, and current community happenings can be discussed. Business people who cater to their customers' needs and understand the community's political, economic, and social background have an advantage. The answers to the following questions are worth knowing:

- What is the religious, racial, and ethnic makeup of the people?
- Are the people generally young, middle aged, or older?
- How do the citizens make a living?
- What do the residents do in their leisure time?

Many more questions should be asked. The answers can provide the potential business owner with important information on which to base many decisions.

Building and Other Costs. When looking at sites, it is wise to make comparisons between the rentals of nearby stores and the property being considered. One of the factors to consider is the building's physical condition.

- Will the property need renovation. If so, how many changes will be needed?
- If many repairs and changes are necessary, will the landlord make these changes, or will the tenant make the renovations? Perhaps the tenant could make the renovations in return for a reduced rental fee.

The amount of rent a retailer can afford to pay will depend on the sales volume. Some rents are based on this volume. There are many factors that enter into the negotiation and the drawing up of a *lease* (rental contract). The length of the lease is important. When starting out, the owner may want to get the shortest lease possible, in case the location is not satisfactory. However, an option for renewal should be included, if the business proves to be successful.

A lawyer should be employed to examine the terms of the lease. The following is a list of questions that should be resolved before you sign a lease.

- What are the restrictions on the merchandise sold?
- Does the building meet fire and building code standards?
- Who provides for insurance, storage space, and security?
- Who suffers a loss if there is a fire or the building is condemned?
- Can the lease be renewed at the same rental fee?
- Who will pay for repairs and renovations?
- Who will pay for the utility costs?

The right to renew a lease, called a *renewal option*, may make possible a short-term lease. This affords a safeguard in the event that the owner wishes to change locations. On the other hand, if the business succeeds, the owner can stay in the same location. At renewal time, if the owner feels that the terms of the lease are excessive, he or she should negotiate with the landlord for more favorable terms.

There is no completely perfect location for a business. An evaluation of all factors provides the potential owner with an excellent checklist for choosing a good location. The advantages and disadvantages of all possible locations should be considered. The location which offers the most advantages should be chosen. It is important to take plenty of time and get advice before selecting a location.

FIGURE 5-15
This Mexican restaurant is popular partly because it is designed for quick take-out food.

LAYOUT AND PHYSICAL FACILITIES

An important consideration in a retail business is customer appeal. When two stores carry the same merchandise at the same price, customers will buy in the store that is more appealing to them. This appeal can be based on the physical facilities, the layout, and the service the store offers. All of these factors add up to a general impression in the shopper's mind. This is frequently called the store's *image*.

The Importance of Good Layout

Customers will shop and return to stores with good lighting, attractive displays, good ventilation, air conditioning, modern design, convenient arrangement, and even music. Each of these factors contributes to customer convenience, customer appeal, and greater business volume. The customer can be impressed by service, efficiency, and quality.

Good layout often means saving money. When a layout is intelligently planned, space is used wisely. Since many retail operations are self-service, merchandise should be arranged so that customers can easily serve themselves. Items should be grouped together in a logical manner. An example of this is a supermarket where several thousand different items are sold, Figure 5-17. The need for grouping is reflected by the various departments. The classification should be more detailed than by department. Customers can usually find the grocery department by themselves, but "Where among all the aisles is the meat sauce?" In this case, a sign that is labeled *Condiments* and hung from the ceiling is a helpful reminder. Especially in food merchandising, customers eventually learn a store's

FIGURE 5-16
The layout of a self-service store's front end is very important. The traffic through the registers must flow smoothly. This is a typical supermarket check-out area.

layout. Some customers know the layout even better than some of the store's employees. Customers will return to stores when they have confidence in their own ability to find items quickly.

All stores are not planned with self-service in mind. There are many stores where product information customer service must be provided. Apparel stores, hardware stores, and personal services are examples of businesses in which the layout must provide each customer with personal attention. For instance, in a hardware store, few customers come in just to look. Most customers have a definite need. They may want a new part for an appliance or paint, but they also want advice and instruction on how to use it. Customers do not want to search shelves and counters looking for something to solve their problem. This does not mean that display is not important. The skillful salesclerk, once aware of the customer's need, uses sales displays to assist in the related or suggestive selling of more products.

Good layout saves space which in turn saves rent, time, and labor. The location of various department divisions, check-out counters, scales, and displays controls traffic and how customers move through the store. Are the aisles large enough for grocery carts? Are the ends of aisles being used efficiently for special promotions? A good business owner constantly evaluates the layout of the store by watching and listening to customers' complaints and suggestions. Adequate stock space should be available, and backup stock for fast-moving items should be near.

FIGURE 5-17
Supermarkets are almost entirely self-service operations. As such, internal layout is extremely important.

Safety and fire prevention are also elements of good layout. Hazards, such as boxes in the aisles where customers might bump into them, should be avoided. A building should have enough exits in case of fire or other emergency.

The purpose of a layout or diagram is to communicate to others the plan for the location of equipment and merchandise in the store. If the drawing does this, it is successful. To just tell a carpenter or decorator what you want is not enough; a sketch or layout is helpful. One may think of a store layout as a map showing location of the various elements in the store.

The layout that is drawn should be to scale, with the length of each line representing actual distance, such as 1/8 inch = 1 foot. This means that a line 5/8 inch long on the drawing actually represents a distance of 5 feet in the store. Scale is important when estimating dimensions for aisles, counters, and doors.

The drawings are much more useful if important features are labeled. Walls and built-in features of the building can be drawn on graph paper with a 1/4-inch grid. Special equipment need not be drawn but just represented as a box with an arrow showing the description. Shelves and counters can be labeled with the appropriate merchandise. When trying to decide on a layout, scale *templates* (cardboard patterns) of fixtures and cases can be cut out. These templates can be moved around on the layout until a pleasing arrangement is found.

Ideas for the layout of a new store can be obtained from existing shops. Distances between various elements of the layout can be measured with a steel tape. There are also certain standard measurements which must be learned. A business owner should also be aware of state laws which require a fixture to be a certain width. Counters vary from 30 to 36 inches in height and from 3 to 12 feet in length. An aisle should be wide enough for three adults to stand in it side by side without touching each other, or the aisle should accommodate at least two grocery carts side by side with room for passing.

Many fixture and display companies will plan stores for owners as a free service. The owner may have to live with the store as it is for sometime, as changes in layout are expensive. The owner should therefore be involved in the store's design.

Types of Layout

The four types of layouts used in retail stores are: self-service or modified self-service, full-service, and special. Many variations of these layouts are possible.

Self-service Layouts. The trend today is towards self-service stores. This type of store reduces the number of salesclerks and allows customers to select merchandise for themselves.

Customers should be induced to move through the store in a way which will expose them to as much display area as possible. Customer flow can be controlled

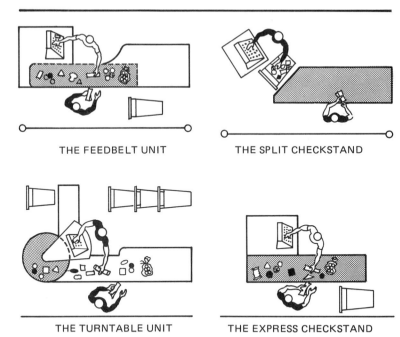

THE FEEDBELT UNIT   THE SPLIT CHECKSTAND

THE TURNTABLE UNIT   THE EXPRESS CHECKSTAND

FIGURE 5-18
Four versions of self-service store
check-out stands

by the layout. The arrangement of aisles and the shape and position of counters, islands, tables, gondolas, and floor displays create various traffic patterns, Figure 5-18. Necessities, convenience goods, and staple items should be placed near the rear of the store. This should be done so that customers pass those goods which must be seen to be sold on their way to the rear of the store.

Traffic may be increased and directed in the following ways:

- Enough aisle width and circulation space should be provided for free movement of customers in the store, especially if shopping carts are used.

- Departments should be easy to find by sign or banner.

- Customers should be able to see large areas of a store at all times. It is difficult to move around if there are high displays cutting off the view.

- There should be no hidden aisles, in order to discourage shoplifting.

- Goods that are in heavy demand should be kept in convenient and popular locations.

- Displays should be streamlined, not cluttered, and restocked frequently.

- Merchandise should be easy to reach and examine.

- Items which are similar or used together should be located in the same part of the store.

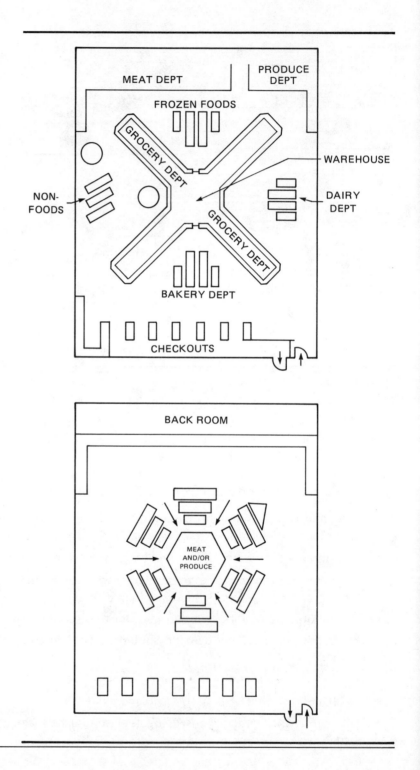

FIGURE 5-19
Two unique supermarket layouts

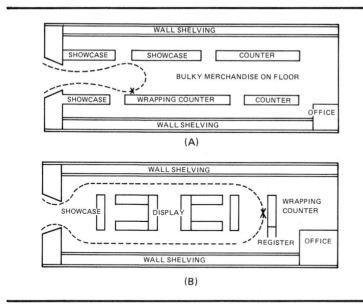

(A)

(B)

FIGURE 5-20
(A) shows an old-style floor arrangement in which long counters separate customers from the merchandise. Selling and wrapping is done in the front part of the store. (B) shows a modern arrangement in which sidewalls are open and the center of activity is moved to the rear. The islands are arranged so that customers can handle all merchandise.

The most valuable part of a store for selling is the front section. Storefront displays and areas around the cash registers are good for selling new items and novelty items, high-profit merchandise, specials, and seasonal items. Customers must pass by these points to leave the store. The use of color and lighting is very important to direct attention to interior displays and to make the most of the store's layout. Floor covering, aisles, ventilation, and displays all contribute to the neat, clean, and attractive appearance of a store.

Full-service Layouts. Many operations cannot be self-service. Specialty stores sell higher priced products to a fewer number of customers. These customers expect sales help, demonstrations, product information, and considerable service. Some examples of products that require time and personal attention to sell them include clothing, office machines, sporting goods, hardware, shoes, jewelry, luggage, furniture, and appliances. A camera shop is also a good example of this point. Cameras and accessories need to be sold. That is, the customer needs information and instruction about the item if a sale is to be made. Full-service layouts provide the areas and equipment necessary in stores where the customer cannot be expected to select merchandise or services without help.

Special Layouts. Some layouts depend on the type of special product or service offered. Laundromats, TV repair shops, fast-food stores, ice cream stores, discount beverage stores, and golf driving ranges are all examples of businesses requiring special designs, Figure 5-21.

FIGURE 5-21
Laundromats require special design in
their layout.

The whole field of amusements, from miniature golf courses to electronic game rooms, demand special layout planning. An entire children's amusement park was set up in a vacant store space near a large shopping center. Another special layout permits empty soda bottles to be returned and new cases loaded in the car by attendants as the customer drives the car by racks stocked with beverages. This type of layout is similar to a car wash. When the market is present, new and unique layout ideas will command attention. Perhaps you can think of a unique layout for your business.

Storefronts

An essential part of any business layout is the storefront. It is the first feature of a business that is seen by customers. The storefront creates impressions for potential customers. These impressions must be to the advantage of the store, and attract the customers to come inside.

Customers generally choose stores that appear attractive, modern, and clean. Stores attract customers for several reasons. They provide needed goods and services, offer luxury items that on occasion are desired by the consumer, and satisfy a curiosity.

Variety stores and supermarkets deal in large quantities of convenience goods. These needed items are normally purchased at stores which are most convenient to the customer. The buyer's major concern for these items is that

FIGURE 5-22
This large general merchandise department store has no windows. It does not depend on window displays to bring customers inside, but rather depends on sales from advertising and a catalog.

they are available, easily found in the store, and reasonably priced. Such stores need not be concerned with a stylish window display, Figure 5-22. Supermarket windows are often covered by price signs, and some stores do not have any display windows. What is important is that the front of the store clearly indicates the store's purpose. Large and lighted signs are effective, especially during the evening hours.

Other types of stores need more attractive fronts because they draw less structured traffic. Many stores attract customers whose original destination was the supermarket. The storefronts of these specialty shops are very appealing. They make use of stone facing, planters and shrubbery, indirect lighting, and exterior music and sound to draw in customers. A restaurant featuring steaks or grill items does well to put its chef and the grill in the window where customers can see the food being prepared. The retail specialty trade in plazas and major shopping centers depends on the food chain stores and the general merchandise or discount stores. A cluster of specialty shops in a plaza surrounds these two key traffic magnets.

Retail stores are usually high volume retail, low volume specialty, or full-service. The specialty shop needs a more appealing design than the other types because it lacks structured traffic. A service station, for instance, may have the advantage of a well-known branch name, a familiar standard exterior, and makes use of customer identification with highly advertised symbols and products, such as the scallop shell, the number 66, or a flying red horse.

Physical Facilities

A *facility* is a physical building, plant, or office that houses a business. The facilities can usually be acquired in the following ways:

- By building the facilities
- By renting existing facilities
- By leasing the facilities for a long period of time with the landlord making the renovations

FIGURE 5-23
Business signs, especially those facing well-traveled roads, must be seen for some distance.

FIGURE 5-24
This sign leaves no question in the minds of people passing by about what type of business is in operation.

FIGURE 5-25
The decision to build your own business facility is a difficult one to make. Here a prospective business owner discusses plans with his builder.

When building a new store, the owner has the advantage of designing exactly what is wanted with the aid of the builder and an architect or designer. A new building can be constructed to fit any layout, rather than fitting a layout to an already existing facility. New buildings are initially more expensive, and much capital may be needed to construct an appropriate facility. It is possible, however, to get financial assistance from manufacturers, wholesalers, and distributors. In the case of franchises, it is possible to get financial assistance from the parent companies.

Existing facilities may be purchased and remodeled to fit your business needs. Remodeling is expensive. In some cases, local regulations may prevent or limit renovation, or the use of the facilities for a different business purpose may be restricted. Remodeling, however, may be considerably less expensive than building from scratch! It is important to get accurate estimates on both and compare. A new building can be financed (mortgaged) for a long period, plus government loan assistance may be available which is not the case with an older building.

Leasing is different than renting because it involves a long-term contract, called a *lease*, to occupy the premises. The advantage of renting existing property for a new business, as compared to building or renovating, is that it requires much less capital. Caution must be exercised in agreeing to a long-term lease. If you are just starting a business, it is better to pay rent on a month-to-month basis, if this is possible. The landlord may not permit remodeling unless the rental period is long enough to justify it, or the landlord may allow you to pay for the remodeling.

FIGURE 5-26
This small-town appliance store was formerly a general store, grocery store, pharmacy, and meat market.

You should plan for changes in your business. If you need more space in the future, a lease could be a problem. The following points should be considered, where they apply, when selecting a physical facility for a business.

PHYSICAL FACILITIES CHECKLIST

Before making a decision about a store, plant or office, you will want to consider each of the following points:

- Age and condition of property
- Location
- Amount of space including storage
- Parking space
- Adequate receiving and shipping facilities
- Local inducements*
- Favorable laws, zoning, and taxes

- Energy requirements (heat, light, and power)
- Special requirements (antipollution, transportation, local supply of labor, and materials)

   *Some communities, anxious for new businesses in their area, will allow tax credits, low-cost loans, and other incentives.

Some states and municipalities are anxious to attract new businesses as they represent more jobs and a larger tax base. They will offer tax incentives, low-cost loans, and other help to entice new businesses. Some of these inducements are discussed in Unit 12.

Adapting an existing property may be an excellent choice for a business. This choice is frequently overlooked. If you own a private residence that happens to be in a business zone, it may be a great location for a restaurant or other service business. You may think of a use for a vacant facility (especially gasoline stations) that would be quite successful. Vacant property does exist, if you look for it. With a little fixing up, you could convert a failing business into a success. Some good examples of this idea are shown in Figures 5-27, 5-28, and 5-29. Each illustration shows a service station that failed, but when converted to a totally different business, each business became successful.

The business which keeps a neat, attractive, and clean appearance both inside and out will continue to draw customers and workers who want to return. People tend to judge a business by appearance. The exterior and interior of a business reflects on the way it is operated. A business may be thoroughly honest and offer good merchandise at fair prices, but if the stockroom is dirty, the shelves dusty, the store in need of painting, the shop or factory dirty or unsafe, and the grounds unkept, it will lose customers.

FIGURE 5-27
What was once a gas station which could not compete with many nearby stations is now a successful fast-food take-out shop.

FIGURE 5-28
A former full-service gas station is now more successful as a business which specializes in installing mufflers and brakes and selling tires.

BUSINESS MANUAL ASSIGNMENT

For your manual, prepare a few of the following as samples. If you cannot sketch or draw, try to find an existing drawing and change it for your needs. You can erase lines with a soft eraser and cover up parts not desired by using white correction fluid. Both are available in any stationery store. But, if you do have an artistic flair, by all means do the artwork yourself.

Store or shop — Lay out (to scale) showing the location of all merchandise and fixtures. You can label or identify the layout with a numbered key, or label each item. Use templates to work out the arrangement. Include the finished layout in your manual. You may want to get advice from your instructor.

Storefront — Sketch an illustration, or adapt one, to show how the exterior of your business will look to customers. Remember that first impressions are very important. Include the illustration in your manual.

FIGURE 5-29
This former service station is now an off-track betting office because its location provided short-term parking at a busy intersection.

Business sign — Design and draw a sign for your business. The type of sign will of course depend a great deal on the kind of business you have. Look at the signs for other businesses similar to yours in the community. See if you can get some ideas from these signs. Include a sketch of your business sign in your manual.

Property layout — Draw a map of your immediate property. Show the location of all buildings, parking areas, driveways, and storage facilities. Locate any railroad tracks, waterways, or other physical features that appear on the property. Try to make your map to scale. Use graph paper if you think this will make it easier to draw. Include your layout map in your manual.

Location — Obtain a county or city map that shows the location of your business in relation to a five-mile-radius area from your business. Show the location of your business on the map in an attractive manner. Write at least two paragraphs explaining why you chose the location and what main features are near the business that you consider assets. Mark your map with a location code, and point out important points on the map using their map references. Include a copy of the location map in your manual.

Contracts — Write a sample lease agreement that might be typical of an actual one for your business. You can get blank lease forms at any good stationery store or from a lawyer. Complete the lease as you would probably want it in an actual situation. Write a paragraph explaining the main points of the lease and why you included them. Include a sample lease in your manual.

Traffic study — Conduct a traffic study of a location you feel would be good for your business. Take vehicle and pedestrian counts at this location in at least three samples of 15 minutes each, and in both directions. Take the samples at different times of the day. Summarize your traffic data and explain your conclusions in one or two paragraphs. Include this report in your manual.

Storage area — Make a separate and enlarged sketch of the layout of your stockroom or supply area. Show the storage facilities to scale, and label the location of each item either directly or with a numbered code. Explain in at least one paragraph the system you have for handling stock, merchandise, and inventory.

Display diorama — Make a model store window, using a shoebox, with scale furniture or merchandise displayed within to simulate an actual window. Your model could consist of a miniature display placed on its side. The size is to be 8 inches high, 15 inches wide and 8 inches deep. The maximum amount each dimension can vary is 1 inch. A description of the type of store should be placed on a 3" x 5" card and attached to the top of the display. No other decorations or protrusions are allowed on the outside of the box. Any type of merchandise can be used and illustrated by cutouts, props, miniatures, and other devices. A clear, plastic material may be used to cover the front of the display to simulate glass.

TERMS TO KNOW

producer	route sales	market
wholesaler	suburb	layout
retailer	string street store	self-service
middleman	neigborhood shopping center	full-service
agent	community shopping center	lease
broker	regional shopping center	renovation
mini-mall	competition	scale
super mall	template	simulate
diorama	display	

UNIT QUIZ

In each of the following, select the word or phrase that best completes the statement or answers the question.

1. Which of the following is not included in the distribution process?
   a. Warehousing
   b. Processing
   c. Packaging
   d. Transporting

2. The most direct channel of distribution is
   a. from the producer to the wholesaler.
   b. from the producer to the retailer.
   c. from the producer to the consumer.
   d. from the producer to the agent.

3. One disadvantage of the retailer buying from a wholesaler instead of directly from the producer is that
   a. it takes longer.
   b. the price is more.
   c. the terms of credit are not so good.
   d. larger quantities are required.

4. When starting a business in a new community, it is important to get information about the community from
   a. the chamber of commerce.
   b. local banks.
   c. state agencies like the Department of Commerce.
   d. all of these sources.

5. The factor least important to consider when selecting a location for a new furniture store is
   a. the weather.
   b. the future.
   c. the competition.
   d. the historical background of the community.

6. Which of the following is usually found in a city's central business district?
   a. Department stores
   b. Motels
   c. Supermarkets
   d. Manufacturers

7. The focal point or traffic magnet of the community or suburban shopping center is usually a large
   a. drugstore.
   b. liquor store.
   c. department store.
   d. supermarket.

8. The business district which depends the least on the automobile as a means of transporting its customers to the area is the
   a. suburban shopping center.
   b. central business district.
   c. string street.
   d. regional mall.

9. The focal point of the regional shopping center is usually a large
   a. supermarket.
   b. gasoline service station.
   c. motion picture theater.
   d. department store.

10. When selecting a location for a business, it is important to
    a. purchase the property.
    b. lease the property.
    c. rent or buy the property to obtain a specific site.
    d. compare buildings and property for sale or rent.

11. The aim of a good self-service layout should be
    a. customer convenience.
    b. stocking merchandise.
    c. the elimination of stockroom space.
    d. appearance.

12. One way to direct customer traffic through the store is
    a. to make merchandise difficult to reach or locate.
    b. to place goods that are in demand in the back of the store.
    c. to place items that are similar or used together in different parts of the store.
    d. to organize the store so that customers do not have a view of the entire department.

13. Which one of the following stores would find the self-service type of layout most convenient?
    a. Jewelry store
    b. Supermarket
    c. Shoe store
    d. Fish market

14. When looking for a location for a gasoline service station, which one of the following factors is most important?
    a. The age of the people in the community
    b. The number of automobiles in the community
    c. The average family income
    d. The vehicular traffic through the community

15. A good store layout will
    a. save money.
    c. need good aisle displays.
    b. save space.
    d. do all of these.

16. Supermarket aisles should be wide enough for
    a. two persons abreast.
    b. three persons abreast.
    c. two persons and one cart abreast.
    d. three carts abreast.

17. The poorest location for a "special" is
    a. a check-out counter.
    c. the end of an aisle counter.
    b. the center of an aisle shelf.
    d. the middle of an aisle.

18. Which one of the following will not minimize shoplifting?
    a. Wider aisles
    c. Larger signs
    b. Lower shelf height
    d. Better lighting

19. Which one of the following will not improve the flow of traffic?
    a. Bigger aisle signs
    b. Wider aisles
    c. Changing the location of staple goods
    d. Grouping items together

20. Which one of the following retail operations requires a special layout?
    a. Delicatessen
    c. Laundromat
    b. Gasoline station
    d. Gift shop

21. A full-service men's apparel shop does not need
    a. a mirror.
    c. a check-out counter.
    b. fitting rooms.
    d. a layaway and service desk.

22. A hardware store would probably not have
    a. a yard goods gage.
    c. a paint-mixing machine.
    b. a key-making machine.
    d. a knife sharpener.

23. A related display for floor waxes might be
    a. waste baskets.
    c. pails.
    b. mops and buffers.
    d. dust cloths.

24. Which one of the following should be located in the rear of a drugstore?
    a. Prescription department
    c. Magazines
    b. Cards and ribbons
    d. Tobacco

25. The following shopping centers are expanding, with the exception of
    a. neighborhood plazas.
    c. regional plazas.
    b. community plazas.
    d. downtown centers.

UNIT 6

RAISING CAPITAL

OBJECTIVES

After studying this unit, you will be able to

- Identify at least five sources of capital for a new business.
- List several types of financial institutions and describe some of the advantages of each.
- Discuss the difference between long-term and short-term credit.
- Explain the advantages and disadvantages of accounts receivable.
- Make a plan for the financing of your business.
- Define the Terms to Know.

The mismanagement of capital is one of the leading causes of business failure. It is therefore important for the potential business owner to have a firm understanding of business finances. What expenses will there be? When must they be met? What sources of capital exist? How difficult is it to borrow money? How might customer financing benefit the business? Equipped with the answers to these questions, potential business persons are more likely to find success.

The capital of a business consists of those funds used to start and run the business. These funds may be either the owner's or creditor's, the latter consisting of borrowed money or something the owner purchased on credit. Capital may be of two types: fixed and working.

Fixed capital refers to items bought once and used for a long period of time. These items include real estate, fixtures, and equipment. With a grocery store, for example, the real estate consists of the store itself and the land on which it is built. The fixtures include such objects as counters, refrigerators, shelves, and showcases. Equipment covers such articles as meat-cutting machines, knives, barrels, and scales.

Working capital refers to the funds used to keep a business working or operating. It pays for merchandise, inventory, and operating expenses such as rent, utilities (light and heat), taxes, and wages. Cash on hand and accounts receivable are also considered working capital. Therefore, working capital is cash, or anything that can easily and quickly be turned into cash.

ESTIMATING CAPITAL

While getting a business started, there will be extra expenses during the first few months which must be met without money coming in. The services of a lawyer are recommended, advertising is needed, and sales help must be paid. It is doubtful that a business, while beginning, will cover the owner's living expenses. Until a business begins to make a profit to cover these and other expenses, they must be paid out of capital.

The business owner must decide just how much money the business will need, and how it is to be spent. The amount of money needed varies according to the type of business proposed. For example, a manufacturing business requires more money invested in raw materials, buildings, equipment, and machinery than a small retail business which invests much of its money in inventory, rent, and advertising. The first question an owner must answer is how much money will be needed for fixed capital. To do this, the owner must first determine if the buildings and land will be bought or rented. Renting avoids an investment in fixed capital, while buying property requires the investment. The owner should develop a list of capital equipment needed to open and operate the business. *Capital equipment* is that equipment needed to produce a product, provide a service, or sell, store, and/or deliver merchandise. The owner should then figure out exactly how much the fixtures, equipment, and machinery will cost. You may not have to pay for all you need at once. It may be possible to mortgage your plant and machinery.

Once an estimate for fixed capital is made, the owner can determine how much working capital is needed. Such operating expenses as materials, inventory, rent, salaries, taxes, telephone, insurance, interest on borrowed money, utilities, advertising, and supplies must be budgeted. The final step is to estimate your living expenses and for how long the expenses must be covered while the business is being established. Living expenses include food, clothing, shelter, taxes, education, and leisure activities.

Estimating Capital for a New Business

When individuals decide to go into business, they may either start a totally new business or they may acquire an established business. This decision should be made very carefully, as each choice has its good points. The following example illustrates this point.

William Evans is considering opening a drugstore. He has heard that new stores are being built near a recently constructed housing project. If he decides to purchase one of these buildings, Mr. Evans would need less money to start the business because he would not be buying the assets or goodwill of an established business. Starting a business from the very beginning, Mr. Evans would be able to invest carefully and consider each move. He would not have to deal with the mistakes of the former owner. Mr. Evans will have a freer choice of location, merchandise, and equipment because he will own the business from the beginning.

Establishing a new business has some disadvantages. Mr. Evans would have to choose a location and organize the business from the start. He would have to be sure that the business complied with local regulations. He would also be responsible for contacting suppliers, keeping the business records, and attracting and keeping customers. Another disadvantage is that the business might not make a profit for some time.

If an established business has a good reputation in the community, it may be well worth the asking price. It may be easier to continue to please an established clientele than to build a new one.

If Mr. Evans bought a drugstore that had been in business for several years, he would discover some advantages. A complete investigation of an established business yields fewer unknowns than does a new business. The location is set and a clientele has been developed. Some of the equipment may also be available. Purchasing an established business also has some drawbacks. The new buyer should find out why the owner wants to sell. Is the owner retiring or is the business losing money? A successful business may cost more than a new one. If the fixtures and equipment are out of date, they may need replacement. Finally, there may not be room for future expansion of the business.

The business must be thoroughly investigated and the advice of experts should be obtained. An accountant should go over the books of the business, and a lawyer should examine any contracts. Caution minimizes the possibility of serious mistakes.

SOURCES OF CAPITAL

One of the most difficult tasks a small business owner faces is obtaining sufficient capital to start and operate the business. The potential business owner should become familiar with the different sources of capital.

Personal Savings. If you are going into business for yourself, one source of money is personal savings. An advantage of using this money is that no interest has to be paid on it. This means one less expense for the business.

Personal savings is not just money that has accumulated in a savings account. It consists of everything of value that an individual has gained. Instead of using personal savings, the potential business owner may want to mortgage property. This is done by obtaining a loan and using the property as security. In this way, the capital is available for a long period of time, and repayment may then be paid from the profits of the business. It may also be desirable and easier to get a loan on life insurance policies. The loan does not always have to be repaid within a set period of time. The money may be used continually with the owner paying only the interest. Of course, by reducing the amount of the loan, the owner also reduces the amount of insurance protection the family has in the event of death.

Banks. The commercial bank is one of the main sources of short-term loans, Figure 6-1. Commercial bank loans are usually for short periods of time (less than one year), but many banks lend money for longer periods. The interest on a commercial bank loan is higher than many other sources. The business owner should establish a credit line with a commercial bank. A credit line means that the bank agrees to lend the business owner an amount of money, to a stated maximum, at any time.

Suppliers. Some suppliers will extend credit to new businesses. They allow the new owner to purchase some inventory and supplies on credit. This can be paid back to suppliers over a period of time from expected profits.

Friends and Relatives. In some instances, friends or relatives may be sources of capital. Certain banks require a friend or relative to cosign loans, and the cosigner thereby accepts responsibility for the loan if it is not repaid. This responsibility is one that families and friends may not want to bear.

FIGURE 6-1
The commercial bank is a common source of financial assistance for the small business.

Private Individuals. There are individuals who are interested in investing their extra capital in a successful business venture. These individuals can sometimes be found through talking with bankers, accountants, and lawyers.

The Small Business Administration. The Small Business Administration (SBA) is a U.S. government agency organized to aid small businesses in many ways. This agency offers small businesses financial aid in the form of guaranteed loans and advice about where financial aid can be obtained. The SBA also offers educational aids and consulting services.

Community Development Corporations. Many communities have associations that are formed to encourage and help businesses start within the community. Many of these organizations can give financial advice and aid, in the form of low-cost loans, to new businesses.

Venture Capital Companies. Venture capital companies are another source of capital funding. These companies specialize in investing in small businesses. Some are licensed by the Small Business Administration. They are called Small Business Investment Corporations (SBIC).

Insurance Companies. Insurance companies sell insurance policies and collect premiums which are then invested in stocks and bonds of large businesses and government, Figure 6-2. Insurance companies are now also investing in small businesses that are good risks. Most insurance company loans are long term.

153

FIGURE 6-2
Insurance companies sometimes extend assistance to small businesses that are good credit risks.

Capital is needed for many items when a business is started. It consists of both fixed and operating capital.

A. List some of the items for which fixed capital is used.

B. List some of the expenses for which operating capital is used.

THE FUNDING PROPOSAL

When applying for a loan the individual should have a prepared business plan to present to the potential source. The plan, or proposal, should consist of the following information.

1. Give a detailed description of the business to be established. This should include:
   a. a description of the business.
   b. the market to be served.
   c. the location of the business.
   d. the number of people originally employed by the business.
   e. the competition the business expects.

2. Explain the background, experiences, and financial conditions of the owner(s).

3. Give an estimate of the amount of money each owner will invest in the business, and also the amount of money which will need to be borrowed.

4. Prepare an estimate of projected expenses and revenue for the business during the first year.

5. List the amount of loan requested and explain the purpose(s) of the loan.

6. List the collateral the owner(s) have to offer as security for the loan.

7. State the length of time the requested loan is for, if possible.

The funding proposal should be personally presented to the potential funding source. Providing other supporting documents such as letters of reference, credit reports, and personal resumes can improve the chances of receiving the loan.

FINANCIAL INSTITUTIONS

Independent business owners are responsibile for managing their finances. It is therefore important that potential business owners become familiar with the types of financial organizations.

The Commercial Bank. When a proprietor starts a business, an account should be opened in a nearby commercial bank. This bank accepts the checks and money deposited, and credits the sums to the business account. This account does not usually collect interest because it is a checking account. The bank may require that a minimum balance be kept in the account, or a service charge is made. With a checking account, the business is then able to pay bills and wages by check. Besides being convenient, the system also provides the proprietor with cancelled checks which are kept as proof of bills paid. Monthly bank statements are sent showing all deposits and withdrawals and the final balance of the account.

Often, a small business needs money for special reasons, over and above regular operating costs. Commercial banks can provide short-term loans for businesses for a variety of purposes.

Small businesses may wish to take advantage of manufacturers' or suppliers' discounts on products. The potential profit on such items may be great. When money is needed to finance such transactions, the commercial bank can prove helpful. When a business has a good credit standing, short-term loans for 30, 60, or 90 days may be easily arranged. The loan is usually in the form of a promissory note. Interest is generally deducted from the total amount of the loan, which must be paid back in one lump sum at the end of its term (at maturity). In some cases, short-term loans may be renewed if necessary for additional periods of time. The extending of such short-term loans to businesses is a major function of commercial banks.

A manufacturer who must buy supplies or materials to make a spring line months before the finished product can be sold often needs a short-term bank credit. The wholesaler or retailer who needs stock for an upcoming holiday may also need such a loan. In fact, such short-term loans are common to small businesses.

FIGURE 6-3
Borrowing money for a business from a finance company is expensive, but convenient.

Most commercial banks have a night depository so that retailers can deposit the day's receipts in a safe place overnight. A proprietor may wish to rent a safe deposit box so that important papers may be kept safe at all times. The services of the commercial bank may also be used for collecting outstanding bills. Since commercial banks are aware of business trends in the community, they are an excellent source of advice on investments and other business matters.

Trust Companies. In the past, trust companies were concerned with arranging trust funds and managing real estate. Today, many trust companies have expanded their activities to include the services of a commercial bank. They are helpful in estate management and in setting up individual retirement accounts (IRA).

Finance Companies. Finance companies lend money to businesses, Figure 6-3. They frequently require security such as accounts receivable (customers' unpaid accounts) or fixtures and equipment. Finance companies make installment loans, as do commercial banks. An installment loan is one which is paid back in equal payments over several years. Though convenient, this is an expensive way to borrow money.

Savings and Loan Associations. These financial institutions originally invested money only in farm and residential housing. Recently, they have expanded their operations to include bill-paying services, investments in local commercial property, and consumer loans, Figure 6-4. Loans and financial advice may therefore be obtained at local savings and loan associations. Some savings and loan associations offer checking accounts.

Sales Finance Companies. The sales finance company aids the business that sells on credit. It buys, at a discount, the customer's sales contracts and then collects from them. In this way, an owner can transfer part of the financial risk of selling goods on credit.

FIGURE 6-4
Savings and loan associations have recently expanded their operations to help small business owners.

CREDIT

Most businesses need credit. They frequently buy merchandise and have it delivered with a promise to pay at a later time. Customers also purchase items with a promise to pay at another time. The *credit* of a business is its ability to buy goods and services when needed with a promise to pay later for the goods and services. This may be done in two ways. The goods or services may be purchased from the seller who is then paid back at a later date, or the money may be borrowed from a bank and the bank may be paid back later. In either case, the proprietor is using credit.

Types of Credit

Short-term Credit. Business owners often use short-term credit. Short-term credit is extended for less than a year, usually for 30, 60, or 90 days. A grocer may wish to place a monthly order for merchandise. In ordering cases of canned goods, soap powders, coffee, and other items, the grocer would no doubt prefer paying for the goods after some of them have been sold. The supplier might permit this by allowing the bill to be paid in 30 or 60 days. Also, discounts can often be obtained if goods are paid for in cash. If the discount were large enough, it might be worthwhile to borrow money from a bank to pay the bill at once and obtain the discount. Either way, short-term credit is useful.

Long-term Credit. Long-term credit is also needed. A business that is doing well may want to buy new equipment, expand, or remodel the storefront. When money is not available from earnings and the owner believes the changes to be necessary, long-term loans may be obtained. These loans are paid back in small amounts over a long period of time. Payments generally are due once a month and may last as long as necessary.

The Credit Rating

Businesses which make regular use of credit must have good credit ratings. The financial institutions that offer credit to businesses must be assured that loans will be repaid on time. Good credit ratings are obtained by paying loans on time. Good financial records will help the business owner to determine just how much the business can afford to borrow. Once a good credit rating is established, suppliers and banks will readily aid a business in financial need. By protecting good credit customers, lending institutions assure themselves of continued business in the future.

In granting loans, bankers need to be cautious. They want to make sure that the loan will be repaid. Bankers are also interested in protecting your business because successful businesses contribute to successful banks.

Before credit is granted to an individual, bankers investigate the applicant's character, capacity, and capital. Prevailing economic conditions are also studied. These four items are often referred to as the *Four C's of Credit.* Providing information to banks and other lending institutions about a person's credit is called *credit reporting.* Firms, such as Dun & Bradstreet, and local credit bureaus sell this service.

Character. Character is an important factor when evaluating a potential borrower. A banker takes into consideration the applicant's attitude towards credit and determination to pay. A record of honesty and integrity in a person's business dealings makes it easier to secure a loan. Such a record must be built up over a period of time and is a most important asset.

Capacity. *Capacity* is the ability to pay back a loan. The established business must show capacity to repay by offering as evidence past profit statements and current balance sheets. In order to borrow money, accurate business records are absolutely necessary. A new business may have difficulty in showing capacity since it can offer only estimates. For this reason, new businesses have more trouble securing loans, and must usually be prepared to provide more collateral than established businesses.

Capital. The banker will want to know an applicant's net worth. What does the individual actually own? What debts does the individual have? The difference between these two is the individual's available *capital* or *net worth.*

Capital can be used as security for a loan. When property is used in this manner, it is referred to as *collateral.* Unless an individual has a good record with the bank, that individual will probably be asked to offer collateral or security for the loan.

Conditions. The banker takes into consideration the economic conditions of the community, state, and nation when deciding whether to grant a loan. For the small business, local conditions are important. Prosperous communities obviously offer a better chance of getting a loan than poorer ones. Unemployment and poor economic conditions can cause interest rates to go up, and it may be too expensive to borrow when this occurs.

Bankers will request an explanation as to how the money will be used. These plans should be definite and should be accompanied by any other document that shows how the money will be used wisely.

Customer Financing

Many businesses find that they become more competitive if they grant credit. It is important, therefore, that the small business owner understand the importance of credit in selling.

All kinds of businesses sell goods on credit. The manufacturer sells goods to the wholesaler on credit. The wholesaler sells goods to the retailer on credit, and the retailer sells goods to the consumer on credit. Credit is also used by such service businesses as restaurants, hotels, and service stations. Most consumers carry at least one of the major credit cards.

The fact that many businesses use credit does not mean that a new owner should rush into a credit policy. Before making a decision, it is important to consider the advantages and disadvantages of granting credit.

Advantages of Credit Sales

Increase in Sales Volume. The main reason businesses sell goods on credit is that it increases sales. Many businesses find that their credit customers buy more goods more often than their cash customers.

FIGURE 6-5
Buying on credit is a convenience greatly appreciated by the customer.

Increase in Steady Customers. When customers buy goods with cash, they can purchase merchandise only when they have the money. If they buy on credit, however, they can purchase goods and pay for them at a later date when the money is available, Figure 6-5. This is an important convenience to most shoppers.

Disadvantages of Credit Sales

Some of the disadvantages of granting credit are discussed here. They should be considered before deciding that you want to grant credit.

Greater Need for Working Capital. When goods are sold on credit, money is not received until a later time. Therefore, extra money is needed to buy more goods and to pay for operating costs.

Increased Operating Costs. Businesses have extra costs if they sell goods on credit. Records of customers' accounts must be kept, and it therefore may be necessary to hire more employees. Not all credit customers pay their bills promptly, so there may be an extra cost of collecting overdue accounts. A few customers never pay their bills. Proprietors should always keep a record of the costs of credit sales. If this cost becomes greater than the increase in sales , improved credit procedures must be developed or a cash policy should be adopted.

In some situations, selling on credit can create poor customer relations. Some customers resent the attempts of owners to collect money from them even though they incurred the bill. Other customers buy on credit in a store until their bill is large, and then trade somewhere else. These credit risks can be reduced by investigating credit customers through the local credit bureau. The credit bureau will give accurate information about a customer if credit has been established.

Types of Customer Credit

Charge Accounts. If a customer wishes to buy such items as food, yard goods, shirts, socks, pillowcases, sheets, and other limited life or perishable goods, that customer is asked to pay on a monthly basis. This is known as selling goods by means of an *open* or *charge account.* The customer says "charge it" and pays the entire bill in 30 or 60 days. Proof of the account is established along with the customer's identity by the use of a *charge card* or *credit card.* A charge card or credit card is issued either nationally by major banks or by the business.

Installment Sales Accounts. If a customer wants goods such as furniture, automobiles, sewing machines, or other items that have a long life and are expensive, sales can be increased by using another type of credit. The customer is asked to make a deposit, or *down payment,* on the goods purchased. The customer then signs a contract promising to pay a certain amount of money each month until the purchase price plus interest is repaid. Such an agreement is called an *installment sales contract.*

The owner may find two other types of credit more useful. A *revolving charge account* permits the customer to buy goods, up to a certain amount (credit limit), and pay for them on a monthly basis. For example, a customer may be granted credit up to the amount of $500. In one month, the customer may buy $80 worth of goods and pay $20 on the account at the end of the month. The balance is $60. The customer is billed the following month for the unpaid balance, plus interest. If the customer reaches the credit limit of $500, no more credit is permitted until part of the account is paid.

The budget account is similar to the charge account except that it covers a longer period of time. An appliance dealer might sell a refrigerator for $300, with the customer agreeing to pay $100 down and $100 a month for two months. This type of agreement is called a *budget account* because it is designed to fit the customer's budget. There may be interest charges.

Credit Cards. In recent years, credit cards have become quite popular, Figure 6-6. The two types of national credit cards available are: the *commercial credit card* and the *bank credit card.* The holder of a commercial credit card pays an

FIGURE 6-6
The commercial credit card and the bank credit card are the two types of national credit cards available.

annual fee. Some examples of commercial credit cards include *Diner's Club, American Express,* or *Carte Blanche.* A bank credit card is issued to the customer and offers the merchant, for a small charge, direct payment through most banks without the usual waiting period. *VISA* and *Mastercard* are examples of bank credit cards.

The retailer discounts credit card sales to the bank or credit company at various rates. In addition, the owner pays initial charges for a sign, an automatic card printing machine, and a supply of forms. In return, the credit card company or bank collects from customers by mail, through the use of monthly statements, and relieves the seller of billing and collecting. A retailer who has sufficient sales volume may choose to accept national credit cards.

Dealing with Credit Customers

For credit selling to be worthwhile, it must be carefully managed. Enough capital should be available to run the business until customers' payments are received. Credit should be extended carefully. Several steps should be taken to reduce the number of unpaid accounts.

Each customer who seeks credit should be carefully examined, Figure 6-7. An application should be obtained including name, address, length of residency,

FIGURE 6-7
If you decide to grant credit to your customers, you may want to consider having a credit manager who can interview customers and check their credit applications to see if they are good credit risks.

and employer's name and address. Important information such as the customer's annual earnings and property owned should be obtained. Bank references and personal savings may also be required. Retail credit bureaus can supply much of this information for a small fee.

When the proprietor is satisfied that the applicant is a good risk, credit may then be extended. This is done by issuing some type of an identification or credit card. The customer must be informed of the exact terms of the credit as required by law.

The proprietor must be sure to keep current records of all credit sales. The cost of this additional record keeping may be included in the price customers pay for credit. This is known as a *carrying charge* or *service charge* and varies according to different businesses. Inadequate records increase the chance of error and loss in collecting money from the customer.

Business owners want to collect money promptly and stay on friendly terms with customers. This may be accomplished by keeping customers informed of their accounts. When customers fall behind on payments, they should be notified. Until the payment is made, follow-up letters should be sent, each one polite, but a bit more forceful than the last. With continued nonpayment, the proprietor may resort to suspending credit, making phone calls or sending out collectors. Understanding the customer's financial situation is important. If the customer is having financial difficulty, extending the period of repayment may be arranged. The business loses less and keeps customers if consideration is shown. On the other hand, the customer just may not want to pay. In these cases, legal action may be necessary. Interest may be charged on overdue accounts.

It is not easy to become familiar with the many aspects of business finance. Lack of knowledge could cause business failure. The prospective business owner should seek counsel in financial affairs. You should ask specialists in law, finance, and government who are willing to offer advice. Common sense and good judgment should be applied to financial decision making.

BUSINESS MANUAL ASSIGNMENT

Look at the operations statement and balance sheet shown in Figures 7-11 and 7-13 in Unit 7. These reports will give you an idea for some of the expenses that you will need to plan for when opening your business. Make up a tentative six-month operating budget. You will have to estimate all the costs you can think of for that six-month period. For the purposes of your manual, use the best estimates you can come up with. If you have some actual figures from talking with persons already in business, then use those figures. Otherwise, allow just a little extra in your planning. Make a trip to a commercial bank and get a loan application. Complete the application and include it in your manual as part of your financial planning.

Using estimated figures, subtract the amount of money you now have on hand, or can obtain, from the total of your six-month budget, and complete the loan application for that amount. You may want to refer to Unit 12 which gives information on assistance for businesses. Unit 12 mentions the names of some agencies which can grant low-cost loans. Consult a local banker for some sample budgets and obtain a list of the information the bank will require when you are applying for a loan.

TERMS TO KNOW

fixed capital	4 C's of credit
working capital	character
commercial banks	capacity
trust companies	capital
finance companies	conditions
savings and loan associations	accounts receivable
sales finance companies	charge accounts
short-term credit	installment sales
long-term credit	revolving charge
credit rating	budget accounts
credit reporting	credit cards
promissory note	layaway plans
credit bureau	budget

In each of the following, select the word or phrase that best completes the statement or answers the question.

1. The funds used to run a business are called
   a. equity.
   b. fixed assets.
   c. operating capital.
   d. current liabilities.

2. If after six months a business shows no profit, it will probably
   a. fail.
   b. succeed.
   c. require a partner.
   d. sell at a profit.

3. Working capital does not include
   a. merchandise.
   b. real estate.
   c. accounts receivable.
   d. cash on hand.

4. One of the fixtures in a bakery is
   a. a refrigerated showcase.
   b. a machine for cutting bread.
   c. the bread and the cake in the store.
   d. the ovens in the back room.

5. Fixed capital includes
   a. money in the bank.
   b. real estate, fixtures, and equipment.
   c. money to pay for repairs.
   d. goods for sale in the store.

6. An example of working capital is
   a. the merchandise in a store and cash on hand.
   b. the display windows in a jewelry store.
   c. the counters and shelves in a grocery store.
   d. the tables and chairs in a restaurant.

7. The financial institution that is the most common source for short-term loans is the
   a. savings bank.
   b. commercial bank.
   c. insurance company.
   d. community development corporation.

8. Long-term credit is usually used for
   a. supplies.
   b. payroll cash.
   c. new equipment.
   d. inventory.

9. Which one of the following is not considered one of the four C's of credit?
   a. Connections
   b. Capital
   c. Character
   d. Capacity

10. The ability to pay back a loan is called the creditor's
    a. character.   c. capital.
    b. capacity.   d. conditions.

11. One of the advantages of a business selling goods on credit is
    a. an increase in working capital.
    b. an increase in operating costs.
    c. a decrease in steady customers.
    d. an increase in sales volume.

12. One of the disadvantages of a business selling goods on credit is
    a. an increase in operating costs.
    b. a decrease in working capital.
    c. an increase in sales volume.
    d. an increase in steady customers.

13. A customer buying a dining room set would most likely use which one of the
    following types of credit?
    a. Charge account   c. Installment sales account
    b. Open account   d. Cash

14. One of the most popular forms of installment credit is the
    a. bank account.   c. open account.
    b. revolving account.   d. charge account.

15. The first step in collecting from credit customers is to
    a. inform them of the amount due.
    b. close the account.
    c. take legal action.
    d. repossess the product.

16. Whatever capital you have to put into a business, be sure you
    a. only put what is necessary into real estate and equipment and save enough
       for operating expenses.
    b. use as much for fixed capital as possible.
    c. own the property, whatever it costs.
    d. worry about buying goods and paying bills when the profits come in.

17. Property that is used as a security for a loan is referred to as
    a. capital.   c. capacity.
    b. collateral.   d. net worth.

18. During the first few months of a new business, expenses will be higher than
    after the business becomes established because of which one of the following?
    a. Telephone service   c. Insurance and licenses
    b. Gas and electricity   d. Rent and salaries

19. A person's net worth is
   a. the debts a person owes.
   b. what a person has left after paying all debts.
   c. all the assets a person owns.
   d. the total sales of the business.

20. Credit is sometimes extended to a business by a supplier in the form of
   a. credit.
   b. cash.
   c. a bank note.
   d. all of these.

21. The ability of a business to buy goods and services when needed with a promise to pay later for the goods and services is called
   a. capacity.
   b. credit.
   c. capital.
   d. income.

22. Working capital includes
   a. merchandise.
   b. real estate.
   c. equipment.
   d. cash on hand.

23. You might do better to rent rather than buy a certain store because
   a. you would not have to worry about an unpleasant landlord.
   b. you would be able to do whatever you pleased with the store.
   c. you could save capital for operating expenses and not have too much money invested in real property.
   d. you would be sure of a permanent place in the neighborhood.

24. Working capital is used to
   a. buy real estate.
   b. pay salaries to your employees.
   c. buy equipment and fixtures for your store.
   d. all of these.

25. Which one of the following services is not provided by a bank?
   a. Loans
   b. Assessments
   c. Savings accounts
   d. Protection against bankruptcy

UNIT 7

KEEPING RECORDS OF THE BUSINESS

OBJECTIVES

After studying this unit, you will be able to

- Set up financial records and personnel records for your business.
- Compute discounts, and markup and markdown on both cost and selling price.
- Record a series of daily business transactions.
- Complete simple tax forms.
- Explain the balance sheet and the operations statement.
- Figure and prepare a simple payroll with employee wages and deductions using time cards, payroll data sheets, and tax tables.
- Design inexpensive business forms for your business.
- Design a good inventory control system and make samples of the forms.
- Define the Terms to Know.

The success of any business organization depends on the owner's ability and determination to fully understand the enterprise. Complete records of the business give an owner a clear picture of exactly how well the business is doing.

BUSINESS RECORDS

Good record keeping by a business is not only wise, but is required by many laws. Legal and financial questions may be raised by various agencies, banks, and employees. These questions can be accurately answered when written records of business proceedings are kept.

By recording daily transactions, the owner can learn from mistakes and avoid errors in the future. A record of all the events that occur in a business permits evaluation, improvement, and a good chance for personal and financial success.

Answering Outsiders' Questions

Many people will want to know about the conditions of a particular business. Bankers may be interested because the owner applied for a loan, state and federal tax agencies are interested in business income, and relatives and friends who may have loaned the business money are interested in its progress. The business owner should be able to answer the following questions:

- How much does the business own, how much does it owe, and how much is it worth?
- What was the total business income last year?
- What part of sales is cash and what part of sales is owed?
- Are receivables collected promptly?
- What is the overhead, and what part of gross sales is the overhead?
- What expenses does the business have?
- What is the value of the building, equipment, vehicles, fixtures, and other assets of the business?
- What items of inventory are the best and worst sellers?
- What are the most profitable and least profitable departments?
- Does the owner take full advantage of cash discounts, trade discounts, and advertising and merchandising allowances?
- What is the normal size of inventory and what is the cost to carry it?

Answering One's Own Questions

In addition to the questions asked by outsiders, the individual owner will have personal questions, some of which follow:

- Is my business making a profit? How much?
- Can my profit be increased and, if so, how?
- Should I trade in old equipment and buy new?
- Should any merchandise or service be cut down or new ones added?
- Should the business reorganize as a corporation or partnership?

It is your responsibility to get the answers to these questions. They are largely a matter of judgment. However, you should have the facts available on which to base your decisions. Accurate information of the sales of a department or an item makes the decision easier. Guesswork may cause wrong decisions to be made. The wrong department may be expanded and a profitable one closed.

When the owner chooses to keep the records of the business, a bookkeeper or an accountant may be needed. These people are specialists in their field, and they should know what information is needed. Their job is to set up the records for your business and maintain them, or train others to do so.

The owner needs a record of cash receipts and payments, Figure 7-1. This may be done in several ways, depending on the type of business. In a business that deals strictly in cash transactions, such as a grocery store, the owner can use a good cash register. In businesses that permit charge sales, accounts receivable records must be kept to show how much each customer owes.

The bookkeeping system that a business owner sets up should be as simple as the bank, government regulations, and individual requirements permit. The owner should not try to get information that will not be used or which is too time consuming to obtain. Remember that the time business owners spend on keeping records takes the owners away from other aspects of their business.

FIGURE 7-1
A good cash register is an excellent means of keeping records of cash receipts and payments.

For a typical small business, it is suggested that the following records be kept.

- Cash receipts and cash payments journal
- Record of credit sales (sales journal)
- Record of purchases (purchases journal)
- Record of wages (payroll)
- Operations statement
- Balance sheet

Handling Business Records

Depending on the owner's educational background and the size of the business, record keeping can be handled in several ways.

Individual Owner May Keep the Records. If the business is small and you have some background in bookkeeping, you may want to keep the records for your business. By taking on this job, you may be prevented from doing some other task for the business, perhaps one that you are good at. Plan to delegate the record-keeping job as soon as you can afford to, but always be sure you understand the system so you can step in at any moment if necessary.

Record Keeping May Be Assigned to Another Employee. If you employ other workers, the task of keeping all or some of the records may be given to a qualified employee. All employees should understand that they have some record-keeping responsibility since they make out sales slips, operate cash registers, and in many ways, perform record-keeping tasks during the course of a business day. You must train and instruct your employees and periodically evaluate their performance.

A Full-time or Part-time Bookkeeper May Be Hired. When your business is large enough to afford one, you should hire a competent part-time or full-time bookkeeper. The bookkeeping job may be a difficult one for you to delegate. You may feel that you must keep your eye on the books. Your wishes and requirements should be explained, and the bookkeeper should then be left to work independently.

Owner May Contract for the Service. There are many firms which sell various record-keeping services. These services range from an annual audit with the preparation of an operations statement and a balance sheet to weekly payrolls, daily sales analysis, and inventory control and analysis.

Owner May Establish an Accounting Department. Eventually, if size warrants, you could form an accounting department. The department maintains a set of books, including accounts receivable, accounts payable, and general ledger accounts. Data processing equipment may be feasible, depending on the volume of information needed, or a terminal can be installed for the use of shared services.

If you plan to keep your own records and have no experience or training in bookkeeping, you can buy several good account books especially designed for a small business. A good stationery store has these account books, and some of them are designed especially for your type of business. Trade associations, manufacturers, and suppliers may be able to supply the materials and forms needed. Manufacturers of cash registers and other office machines also supply forms. The forms may already have column headings, but with some thought, they can be adapted to your particular business needs.

TYPES OF RECORDS

The most important records of a business are those kept each day. These must show cash received, sales, and purchases. From cash records, you will know how much cash you have on hand at any given time. You also will know the amount of money needed to handle a typical day's transactions. Sales records can be as detailed as desired. They can show the kinds of merchandise or services most in demand. Purchasing records show the business expenses and the amount spent for equipment, supplies, and merchandise.

Financial Records

Most businesses use a cash register. It can show the amount obtained from each sale, the department in which the sale was made, the clerk who made the sale, and other information. This is done automatically on most cash registers by using special keys parallel to the cash keys. Figure 7-2 shows the information provided on a typical cash register tape.

Some cash registers have separate totals for each department. If this is the case, it is possible to get a reading from the register when the machine is cleared at the end of the day. The totals of each department are then posted on a daily sales sheet under the proper headings. Cash registers can also provide an accurate check on the money in the cash drawer, if operated properly, a customer count, and the amount of sales tax collected.

Sales records must show credit sales or charges if this privilege is granted to your customers. These sales can be posted on the daily sales sheet from the day's charge slips, as well as on individual customers' monthly billing. The cash register daily detail tape and the charge slips provide enough information to keep an accurate account of sales. You should know how much has been recorded on the register each day, making sure that the cash drawer is reconciled. Errors should not be allowed to go uncorrected. Posting should be done daily. With good record-keeping habits, the work is more accurate and less time consuming.

THESE VALUABLE FEATURES SERVE
THE CUSTOMER, MANAGEMENT, AND THE CHECKER-CASHIER

The register indicates the amount charged for each item, tax amounts, and totals. Visual indication makes checking faster, since the customer sees the amount charged and does not delay the checking procedure by asking questions.

The receipt issued by the register shows the price of each item, the department it was purchased in, amount of tax (if any), total amount of purchase, date, name of store, courtesy "Thank You" message and transaction number.

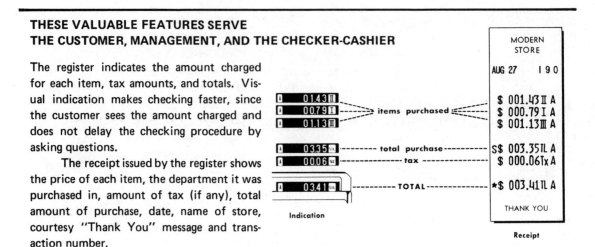

FIGURE 7-2 A typical cash register tape

One set of books is all that is necessary to satisfy requirements of the business and the government. Photocopies of documents can be made if duplicates are needed.

No matter how carefully records are kept, they are at best only a tool of management. They can achieve nothing by themselves. If misused, they can do much harm and slow down the business operation. Good business judgment and industriousness are ingredients in the success of a business. Although necessary, records are no substitute for good judgment and common sense.

Personnel Records

In addition to the regular payroll card kept for each employee, you should have a record of personnel information for each individual. How detailed the personnel files are depends on the number of people employed and how important you believe the information is.

Obviously you must have the name, address, and phone number of each employee. Increasingly, some owners believe they need more information in order to know and utilize their employees fully. When a business is small, an owner may know all employees individually. The hobbies, interests, and personal facts about employees' families can be remembered, thus enhancing the relationship between employer and employee.

As a business expands, it may be impossible for an employer to know all employees by name or to remember personal facts about them. There are many reasons for keeping up-to-date and complete files on all employees. It is important

to watch the progress of individuals. Those who are loyal and work hard should be rewarded or promoted. The record of an employee's progress with the company — successive earnings, and jobs performed, among other facts — should be considered an important document.

The Application Blank. When interviewing prospective employees, the application form is an important tool, Figure 7-3. It provides information in writing while the interviewer speaks with the applicant, Figure 7-4. Whether or not an individual is hired, it is good practice to keep all applications on file.

Interviewers often talk with many individuals who, for various reasons, do not come to work immediately. When a particular individual is needed for a job quickly, one can refer to the application forms on file of candidates who may still be interested in employment.

Testing. Tests on various subjects may be purchased from commercial firms that specialize in them, Figure 7-5. For instance, before a secretary is hired, you may want to test typing, shorthand, and transcription skills. The skill of a bookkeeper may be judged by giving a short bookkeeping test, or a prospective advertising clerk might be asked to submit some sample ads.

Sometimes, applicants who are eager to impress an employer quite innocently expand on their abilities and experience in their resume. If certain skills are important, testing these individuals is a much safer and fairer way to screen candidates.

FIGURE 7-4
After reviewing the application form, the employer interviews the applicant to clarify necessary details.

NEW EMPLOYEE TEST — SOLVE EACH PROBLEM.
WRITE THE ANSWER IN THE SPACE PROVIDED.
USE SCRATCH PAPER WHERE NECESSARY.

ADD	ADD	SUBTRACT	Answer Column
1) $ 1.29	2) $ 247.41	3) $821.88	1) $39.43
2.36	389.73	679.91	
27.88	265.52		
3.63	1,829.99		2) $3813.20
4.27	846.67		
	233.88		
			3) $141.97

MULTIPLY	DIVIDE	
4) $.38	5) 37)1813	4) $1.14
3		

6) If oranges cost $1.20 per dozen, how much will 7 oranges cost?

5) 49¢

7) If 3 units sell for 35¢, how much does 1 unit cost?

6) .84¢

8) Beets are priced at 2 bunches for 59¢. A customer buys 6 bunches. How much is the customer charged?

7) .11¢

9) If 20 bags of potatoes weigh 110 lb, and each bag when empty weighs 1/2 lb, what is the total weight of the potatoes?

8) $1.77

10) A case of 24 cans of peaches costs $14.40 by the case, or wholesale. If sold separately, each can costs 69¢. How much does a customer save on each can if they are purchased by the case?

9) 100 lbs.

10) .09¢

FIGURE 7-5
Before hiring a new employee, the employer may wish to test certain skills. This is a sample math test. (Adapted from a test used by Grand Union Company)

Job Performance Review. After a person has been hired, a record of progress with the company should be maintained. The rating sheet shown in Figure 7-6 is used to evaluate employee performance. Promotions or raises may be considered on the basis of these ratings.

The rating sheet is useful if the subject of a raise is brought up by the employee. The individual may feel entitled to a raise, but records of his or her progress may not justify it. Keeping records in this way protects an employer from unfair demands from dissatisfied employees. Employees respect fair treatment. When accurate records of your employees are kept and established policies are always followed, everyone's morale is likely to be higher.

KEY

1 — **Poor** — generally below minimum level
2 — **Below average** — generally below expected level
3 — **Average** — generally at expected level, occasionally above
4 — **Good** — generally above expected level, occasionally outstanding
5 — **Excellent** — consistently above expected level

		1	2	3	4	5
QUALITY OF WORK:	Consider care and exactness on work performed; freedom from error; thoroughness.		✓			
QUANTITY OF WORK:	Consider speed and amount of work accomplished; promptness in completing work.		✓			
KNOWLEDGE OF WORK:	Consider knowledge of own and related work; experience; adaptability; versatility.			✓		
JUDGMENT:	Consider the wisdom of decisions in the absence of detailed instructions; judgment in unusual situations.			✓		
DEPENDABILITY:	Consider the manner in which the worker approaches the job; amount of supervision required to get desired results; punctuality and attendance.			✓		
ATTITUDE:	Consider attitude toward job and bank and the acceptance of policies and procedures; cooperation with associates; pleasantness in contact with customers and others; sales personality.			✓		
Considering all job factors and conditions, indicate appraisal of all-around performance.			✓			

REMARKS: Elaborate on the above judgments. Comment on special or outstanding ability, potential, desirable or undesirable traits, and circumstances or conditions not covered in this appraisal.

FIGURE 7-6 Job performance review

PRACTICE EXERCISE

A fundamental knowledge of arithmetic is essential for the future business owner. The following problems provide an opportunity to evaluate your basic skills in addition, subtraction, multiplication, division, decimal equivalents, and common fractions.

1. If a customer buys a blouse for $14.89 and pays for it with a $20.00 bill, how much change should the customer receive?

   $5.11

2. How much should a customer be charged for 2 1/2 yards of dress material which sells for $4.98 a yard?

   X $11.45

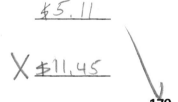

3. How much should a customer be charged for the
    following purchases?
    a. 2 pairs hosiery at $1.19 a pair
    b. 1 handbag at $14.98
    c. 2 handkerchiefs at $1.25 each

    a. $2.38
    b. 14.98
    c. 2.50
    Total 19.86

4. Add the following:

a. $ .14	b. $ 2.64	c. $10.16	d. $ .03
1.91	10.98	.04	3.31
+5.38	+13.04	+ 1.23	4.01
10.43	26.66	11.43	9.50
			+12.69
			29.54

    a. $10.43
    b. $26.66
    c. $11.43
    d. $29.54

5. Multiply the following:
    a. 4 1/2 X $1.20
    b. 5 1/2 X $2.14
    c. 2 3/4 X $1.10

    a. $5.40
    b. $11.77
    c. $3.02

6. Subtract the following:

a. $20.00	b. $462.81	c. $9.50
- 1.98	- 31.89	-1.37
		8.13

    a. $18.02
    b. $430.92
    c. $8.13

7. If oranges cost $.90 per dozen, how much do 7 oranges
    cost?

    .56¢

8. If 3 pairs of socks sell for $5.98, how much does 1 pair
    cost?

    $1.99

9. Beets are priced at 2 bunches for $.49. The customer
    buys 6 bunches. What is the total cost?

    $1.47

10. If 20 bags of potatoes weigh 110 lb, and each bag when
    empty weighs 1/2 lb, what is the total weight of the
    potatoes?

    $100

KEEPING RECORDS OF DISCOUNTS

Cash Discounts

Business owners find that they can save money if they pay bills on time.
Most wholesalers want to be paid as soon as possible after they have delivered the

merchandise. To encourage prompt payment, suppliers offer *cash discounts* when bills are paid. A proprietor may order $100 worth of merchandise and receive an invoice or bill marked *2/10, n/30.* This means that if the bill is paid within ten days, there would be a 2% discount on the items purchased. The cost of the items would then be $98. If the proprietor paid after the ten-day period, the normal price of the goods, $100, would be due.

Two or three percent may not seem like much of a savings, but an owner should take advantage of all discounts offered. In the course of a year, an owner can realize quite a savings. Prompt payment of bills also gives the owner an excellent credit rating. Wholesalers offer special prices and other advantages to get and keep cash customers. Cash payment actually means payment within ten days, so the owner does have a little time to get the discount.

PRACTICE EXERCISE

Compute the cash discount in each of the following cases.

Amount of Invoice	Terms	Amount Saved	Net Amount of Invoice
$ 90.00	2/10,n/30	$ 1.80	$ 88.20
120.00	2/10,n/30	2.40	$117.60
140.50	3/10,n/30	4.21	$136.28
240.00	1/10,n/60	2.40	$37.60
160.00	2/10,n/45	3.20	$156.80

Determine if the following invoices qualify for discounts. In each case, what is the final cost to the proprietor?

Amount	Terms	Date of Invoice	Date Paid	Value of Discount	Net Cost
$ 20.00	2/10,n/30	Apr. 6	Apr. 15	$ .40	$ 19.60
35.00	2/10,n/30	May 8	May 10	.70	34.30
90.00	1/10,n/30	Jan. 7	Jan. 10	.90	89.10
115.50	3/10,n/60	Feb. 11	Feb. 20	3.47	112.03

Trade Discounts

A *trade discount* is usually a larger discount than a cash discount. On purchases of larger quantities of goods, manufacturers offer trade discounts of 5%, 10%, 20%, and even more. These trade discounts are offered to people in the trade who buy regularly, and in wholesale quantities.

Series of Discounts

Usually trade discounts are given as a series of discounts. A proprietor might find merchandise offered at a discount of 20%, 10%, and 5%. Why wouldn't the manufacturer just give a 35% discount? The following example illustrates that the two discounts are not the same.

A. List price: $10.00
   Less 35%   −3.50
              $ 6.50

B. List price: $10.00
   Less 20%   −2.00 = $8.00
   Less 10%   −.80 = $7.20
   Less 5%   −.36
                            $6.84

The series of discounts is used by manufacturers in order to keep up with price fluctuations. Instead of going to the expense of publishing new catalogs to keep up with price changes, the manufacturer simply changes or adds percentage discounts. When prices go up, the same manufacturer may not offer discounts.

Quantity Discounts

Many wholesalers offer even larger discounts when a proprietor buys in carload quantities. It is important to remember, however, that the best policy is to buy only what can be sold profitably and quickly. Losses can occur when large stocks of merchandise are purchased at bargain prices and then cannot be sold.

DETERMINING THE PRICE OF GOODS AND SERVICES

When a business owner decides what price to charge for different items and services offered, some kind of method should be used. Poor pricing may end up costing the owner customers and profits. Two basic questions must be answered:

- Are prices high enough to cover expenses and assure a fair profit?
- Are prices low enough to meet or undersell the competition and attract customers?

Markup

The term *markup* refers to the amount which a proprietor adds to the cost of an item in order to arrive at a selling price. The selling price may be expressed in a simple formula: cost price plus markup equals selling price.

If a particular product costs a proprietor $1.00, it may be sold to the customer for $1.50. The markup on the item is $.50 based on the cost.

COST PRICE   +   MARKUP   =   SELLING PRICE
    $1.00 $.50 $1.50

Because most businesses deal in a large number of different items, an owner should not have to decide on a markup every time new merchandise arrives. A standard markup system should therefore be adapted. The owner finds, for instance, that a 30% markup is enough to cover expenses and get a fair profit. This means that the owner charges 30% more than was paid for each item.

Many businesses, however, fail to make expected profits because the owners figure their percentage of margin on the cost of goods. The owners assume that percentages of margin and markup on cost are the same. This confusion is understandable because margin and markup in dollars are identical. Both represent the difference between cost of merchandise and selling price. The percentages, however, are different.

Selling price covers the cost of merchandise plus all expenses of operation and expected profit. When figuring percentage of margin, the selling price is considered to be 100% because it is the total amount of money derived from the sale. Margin is always figured on the selling price. *Example:* Suppose an article is purchased for $1.20 and sold for $1.60. The margin is $.40, which is 1/4 or 25% of the selling price. Therefore, the margin on this article is 25%.

Markup may be computed as either a percentage of cost or a percentage of selling price. Many people consider markup to be a percentage of the selling price. However, retailing authorities point out that figuring markup on the cost price is easier and less confusing in everyday pricing. The important point to keep in mind is that when markup is figured on the selling price, a different markup percentage must be used than when figuring the markup on the cost price. Otherwise, the anticipated markup will not be the same.

Example: Suppose an article is purchased for $1.20 and you wish to sell it for a markup of 25%. What must the selling price be? The markup of 25% times the cost, $1.20, equals $.30. By adding $.30 to the cost price of $1.20, a selling price of $1.50 is reached with a margin of $.30, or 20%. However, if you want to mark up the article so that a 25% margin is obtained, first determine the percentage that will yield the desired margin when applied to the cost price. By consulting the Markup Table in Figure 7-7, you will see that a 25% margin is equivalent to a 33 1/3% markup on cost. Multiplying 33 1/3% by the cost, $1.20, equals $.40. Adding $.40 to the cost price provides a selling price of $1.60 and a margin of $.40, or 25%.

It is obvious from the previous examples that on an item costing $1.20, a margin of 25% gives a selling price of $1.60, but a markup on cost of 25% gives a selling price of $1.50. If it is necessary to have a margin of 25% to cover the cost of operations and net profit, a merchant would be losing money by pricing merchandise on the basis of a 25% markup on cost. To realize a 25% margin, the merchant would need a markup of 33 1/3% on the cost.

There are two ways of figuring markup. One method is based on the cost price. The other more modern method is based on the selling price:

1. Markup based on cost price:

    COST PRICE + 50% MARKUP = SELLING PRICE

    $1.00 $.50 $1.50

2. Markup based on selling price:

    SELLING PRICE – 33 1/3% MARKUP = COST PRICE

    $1.50 $.50 $1.00

In theory, for every dollar taken in over the counter, the merchant should know how much is clear profits, how much goes for merchandise, and how much goes for expenses. When a customer gives a merchant $1 for an item, that sales dollar might look like this:

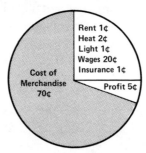

Of course, a merchant does not actually analyze every dollar. But when $1 is multiplied by 10,000 at the end of a six-month business period, the effects are important.

Sales Dollars

10,000 × $1.00		$10,000.00

Business Expenses

Rent	10,000 × $.01	$ 100.00
Heat	10,000 × .02	200.00
Light	10,000 × .01	100.00
Wages	10,000 × .20	2,000.00
Insurance	10,000 × .01	100.00
	Total Expenses	$ 2,500.00

Cost of Merchandise

	10,000 × .70	$ 7,000.00

Total Expenses $ 9,500.00

Profit

	Sales Dollars	$10,000.00
	– Total Expenses	9,500.00
	Profit	$ 500.00

The sales figures indicate that a markup of 30% of the selling price is needed in this case in order to achieve a 5% profit.

Suppose that a merchant has an item which costs $3.50 and wants to sell it at a markup of 30% of the selling price. What should the selling price be?

Solution:

Let selling price (x) = 100%
Markup = 30%
Therefore, cost price = 70%
  = $3.50

$$\frac{3.50}{x} = \frac{70}{100}$$

$$70x = 350$$

$$x = \frac{350}{70} = 5$$

Selling cost x = $5.00

Rather than doing these computations, many merchants use markup tables. These tables make the job of figuring markups on selling price easy, Figure 7-7.

Margin Percent of Selling Price	Markup Percent of Cost	Margin Percent of Selling Price	Markup Percent of Cost	Margin Percent of Selling Price	Markup Percent of Cost	Margin Percent of Selling Price	Markup Percent of Cost
4.8	5.0	15.0	17.7	24.0	31.6	36.0	56.3
5.0	5.3	16.0	19.1	25.0	33.3	37.0	58.8
6.0	6.4	16.7	20.0	26.0	35.0	37.5	60.0
7.0	7.5	17.0	20.5	27.0	37.0	38.0	61.3
8.0	8.7	17.5	21.2	27.3	37.5	39.0	64.0
9.0	10.0	18.0	22.0	28.0	39.0	39.5	65.5
10.0	11.1	18.5	22.7	28.5	40.0	40.0	66.7
10.7	12.0	19.0	23.5	29.0	40.9	41.0	70.0
11.0	12.4	20.0	25.0	30.0	42.9	42.0	72.4
11.1	12.5	21.0	26.6	31.0	45.0	42.8	75.0
12.0	13.6	22.0	28.2	32.0	47.1	44.4	80.0
12.5	14.3	22.5	29.0	33.3	50.0	46.1	85.0
13.0	15.0	23.0	29.9	34.0	51.5	47.5	90.0
14.0	16.3	23.1	30.0	35.0	53.9	48.7	95.0
				35.5	55.0	50.0	100.0

FIGURE 7-7 Markup table

Merchants rarely price all store items on the same markup. Certain goods may be priced lower than others to attract buyers. Other items may have been purchased from a manufacturer at good discounts and can be sold at competitive prices.

It is important to remember that a standard markup should be used as a guide and not as a fixed rule. The idea is to establish the markup at a point where the largest overall dollar profit can be earned. The amount of actual markup may be different for each item sold.

Markdown

Markdown is not as difficult to figure as markup. *Markdown* is simply an amount or percentage cut from the original selling price. For example, if men's shirts are not selling at $16.95, they might sell for $14.95. The dollar value of the markdown is $2.00 and the percentage, found by dividing the markdown by the selling price, is 11.8%. To mark down an item 25%, simply multiply the selling price by 25%, or divide the selling price by 4 and subtract to find the new selling price.

PRACTICE EXERCISE

Complete the following table.

	Cost	Selling Price	Margin	Markup	Gross Profit
1.	$ 3.00	4.29	30%	42.9	1.29
2.	5.00	6.67	25%	33.3	1.67
3.	6.00	6.67	10%	11.1	67
4.	27.00	35.99	25%	33.3	8.99
5.	40.00	50.00	20%	25.0	10.00
6.	40.00	$ 50.00	16 2/3%	20.	10.00
7.	32.68	49.00	25%	33.3	16.32
8.	26.25	35.00	20%	25.0	8.75
9.	47.99	56.00	12 1/2%	14.3	8.01
10.	35.00	42.00	17%	25 %	$ 7.00
11.	60.00	75.00	20%	20%	15.00
12.	360.00	400.00	10%	11%	40.00
13.	35.00	50.00	23.1%	30%	15.00
14.	31.50	42.00	20.0%	25%	10.50
15.	60.00	75.00	16.7%	20%	15.00
16.	65.00				20.00
17.	80.00				12.00
18.	36.00				9.00

BANK RECORDS

When a person starts a business, an account should be opened at a nearby commercial bank. This bank accepts the checks and money the business owner deposits each day and credits that amount to the business account. A commercial bank does not pay interest, as a savings bank would. A minimum balance must be kept in the account to avoid paying a service fee. With this type of account, the business owner can write checks to pay business bills. Checks must never be written in excess of the amount on deposit. Every month the owner will receive those checks which have been paid by the bank (called *cancelled checks*) and a bank statement. The cancelled checks should be kept since they are proof of payment. The bank statement lists the sums which have been deposited during the month and the amounts of all checks paid. The owner compares the business account with the bank statement each month to reconcile the statement.

Sometimes bills are paid by certified check. The bank certifies that there is money in the account to pay the check and stamps the check *certified.* The amount of the check is then subtracted immediately from the account. On other occasions, a cashier's check may be used. Such a check is drawn on the bank itself and is preferred by manufacturers and wholesalers because it is backed directly by the bank. Records of such transactions should be maintained.

To open a bank account, it is necessary to talk to an officer of the bank, who will want certain information about you and your business. How much is going to be deposited? How often will deposits be made? How often will checks be written? How large are the checks going to be? With what other banks do you do business?

The Signature Card

If the bank accepts you as a depositor, it is then necessary to fill out a signature card. The *signature card* bears your name and legal signature, address, and telephone number, Figure 7-8. The card should be signed with the exact signature that will be used when signing your business checks. This signature card is kept on file at the bank. When checks come in, the signature on the card is compared with your signature on the checks.

When the signature card is completed and the first deposit is made, you are given a passbook (bankbook) with the amount of the first deposit recorded in it. A checkbook is also issued, usually a week or ten days later. Temporary checks are issued right away.

The Deposit Slip

Whenever money is deposited in the bank, a deposit slip must be completed. This is a list of the bills, coins, and checks that are to be deposited in your account, Figure 7-9.

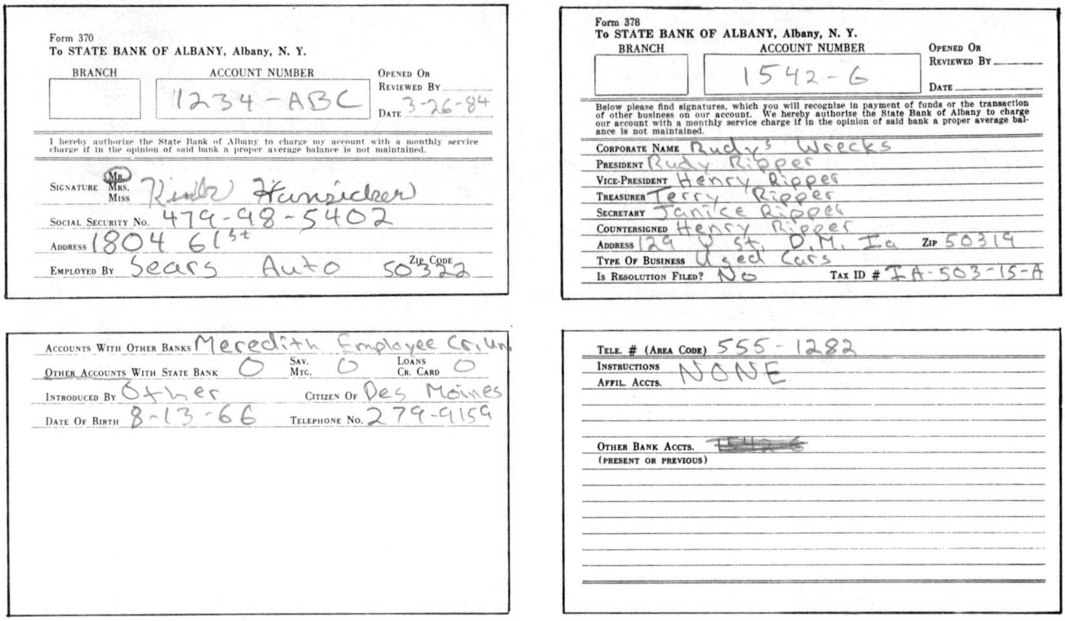

Form 370
To STATE BANK OF ALBANY, Albany, N. Y.

BRANCH	ACCOUNT NUMBER	OPENED OR REVIEWED BY
	1234-ABC	DATE 3-26-84

I hereby authorize the State Bank of Albany to charge my account with a monthly service charge if in the opinion of said bank a proper average balance is not maintained.

SIGNATURE MR. MRS. MISS Rudy Hunsicker
SOCIAL SECURITY NO. 479-48-5402
ADDRESS 1804 61st
EMPLOYED BY Sears Auto ZIP CODE 50322

ACCOUNTS WITH OTHER BANKS Meredith Employee Cr. Un.
OTHER ACCOUNTS WITH STATE BANK 0 SAV. MTG. 0 LOANS CR. CARD 0
INTRODUCED BY Other CITIZEN OF Des Moines
DATE OF BIRTH 8-13-66 TELEPHONE NO. 279-9159

A

Form 378
To STATE BANK OF ALBANY, Albany, N. Y.

BRANCH	ACCOUNT NUMBER	OPENED OR REVIEWED BY
	1542-G	DATE

Below please find signatures, which you will recognize in payment of funds or the transaction of other business on our account. We hereby authorize the State Bank of Albany to charge our account with a monthly service charge if in the opinion of said bank a proper average balance is not maintained.

CORPORATE NAME Rudy's Wrecks
PRESIDENT Rudy Ripper
VICE-PRESIDENT Henry Ripper
TREASURER Terry Ripper
SECRETARY Janice Ripper
COUNTERSIGNED Henry Ripper
ADDRESS 129 U St. D.M. Ia ZIP 50319
TYPE OF BUSINESS Used Cars
IS RESOLUTION FILED? No TAX ID # IA-503-15-A

TELE. # (AREA CODE) 555-1282
INSTRUCTIONS
AFFIL. ACCTS. NONE

OTHER BANK ACCTS.
(PRESENT OR PREVIOUS)

B

FIGURE 7-8 Bank signature cards for an individual (A) and for a corporation (B)

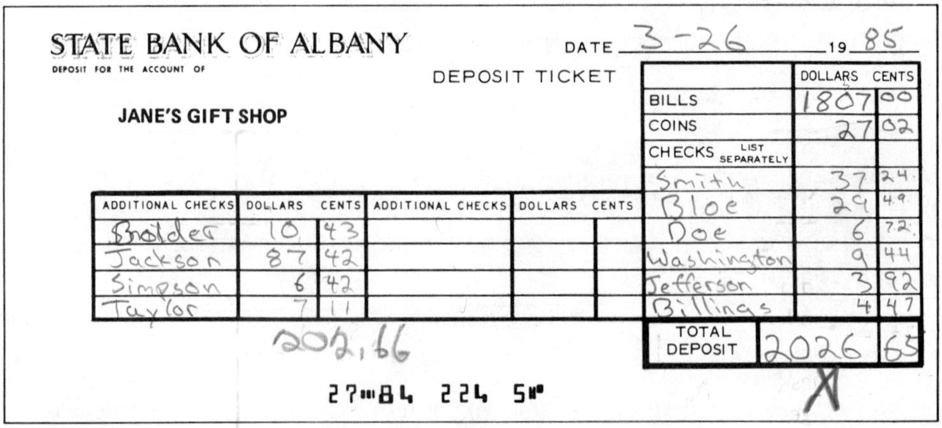

STATE BANK OF ALBANY
DEPOSIT FOR THE ACCOUNT OF
JANE'S GIFT SHOP
DEPOSIT TICKET
DATE 3-26 19 85

	DOLLARS	CENTS
BILLS	1807	00
COINS	27	02
CHECKS LIST SEPARATELY		
Smith	37	24
Bloe	29	49
Doe	6	72
Washington	9	44
Jefferson	3	92
Billings	4	47
TOTAL DEPOSIT	2026	65

ADDITIONAL CHECKS	DOLLARS	CENTS	ADDITIONAL CHECKS	DOLLARS	CENTS
Brolder	10	43			
Jackson	87	42			
Simpson	6	42			
Taylor	7	11			

202.66

27⑈84 224 5⑈

FIGURE 7-9 A sample deposit slip

When you make a deposit, the teller counts the money to be sure that the amount received and the amount on the deposit slip are the same. Checks are examined to see they are endorsed properly. The teller then enters the amount of the deposit in your bankbook, or issues a receipt.

BOOKKEEPING

As a business grows, more detailed records may be needed. A system of recording business transactions daily permits the owner to have control of the business. Information from these daily records helps to correct any weak areas of the business.

It is very important to keep receipts. The following example illustrates this point.

Fourteen-year-old Tommy sells newspapers. He starts out one day with 30¢ in his pocket and 25 papers under his arm. At the end of a few hours, he has sold all his papers at 15¢ each. He adds up his cash receipts and finds he has $4.05 in his pocket. Whether he realizes it or not, Tommy has kept a mental record of his cash receipts. He does not need a book in which to write down the amounts he has taken in.

Some small business owners try to run their businesses the way Tommy does. They usually become highly frustrated. It is impossible to remember every transaction that takes place in a store. Money is being taken in and paid out for different purposes. Written records are obviously necessary.

The Cash Book or Cash Receipts/Payments Journal

The cash book is a simple means of showing what happens to every business dollar, Figure 7-10.

Date	Explanation	Receipts	Payments	Merchandise Purchased	Salaries & Wages	Other Payments
May 1	Sales (cash)	$1,000.00				
2	Radio tubes		$500.00	$500.00		
3	Fire Ins.		15.00			$15.00
4	Sales (cash)	800.00				
5	Sales (cash)	350.00				
5	Wages		80.00		$80.00	

FIGURE 7-10 A sample cash book

This simplified version of one page of a cash book gives the following facts about cash received and cash paid out:

May 1 $1,000 cash is taken in (sales)
May 2 $500 is paid out for merchandise (tubes)
May 3 $15 is paid out for fire insurance
May 4 $800 cash is received (sales)
May 5 $350 cash is received (sales)
May 5 $80 cash is paid out in wages

The columns to the right of the receipt and payment columns give details as to where the cash payments are going. If more information is desired, extra columns may be added.

The Ledger

Although the cash book records in chronological order all receipts and payments of money, it does not give a cumulative summary of transactions with individual suppliers or customers. The ledger provides this summary. Each page of the ledger is reserved for one account.

The sample ledger that follows indicates that a merchant bought television sets valued at $1520.00 from the Esser Television Corporation on April 20. The cash book shows that the sets were paid for on May 4. The ledger includes the transactions as follows:

		Debit	Credit	Balance
Esser Television Corporation				
April 20	April 20–30 days		$1520.00	$1520.00
May 4	Cash	$1520		0.00

The ledger contains as many accounts as necessary. For the suppliers, a separate accounts payable ledger should be set up. When a business sells merchandise to customers on credit, information about what is owed and by whom is recorded in an accounts receivable ledger. One page (or card) is reserved for each customer.

PRACTICE EXERCISE

The following are 30 transactions similar to those that may be encountered in business. Simplified forms make it easy to record these daily transactions. Either the owner or one of the employees keeps records similar to these. It is therefore important for future business owners to understand this exercise. The first transaction for May 3, public utilities, is already recorded as check number 62. Continue recording the transactions on the ledger sheets provided by your instructor.

Paid		To	Amount	Account #
May	3	National Gas & Electric Co. ($20 gas, $10 elec.)	$ 30.00	8&, 11
	3	United Parcel for delivery expense	18.00	7
	4	Yourself, for travel expense	20.00	30
	4	American Red Cross, donation by your business	25.00	6&
	4	Postmaster for postage meter reading (April)	31.00	19
	4	Smith Realty for rent on building	310.00	20
	4	F. Norris (lawyer) for monthly retainer	10.00	15
	4	Adams Bag & Paper Co. for supplies for month	20.75	5
	4	Elm Street Laundry, bill for April	40.00	14
	4	First National Bank, interest due on note	60.00	13
	5	State sales tax due for month	19.00	25
	5	Local #94, union (trade) dues	2.50	29
	5	Jones Insurance Agency, insurance premium	30.00	12
	5	Harry Sims for repairing door to stockroom	20.00	21
	5	Central City Clerk, license fee, freight elevator	40.00	16
	6	Wm. Jones, employee, wages for week:		
		(Gross $184; SS $13.13; Fed Tax $21.87)	149.00	31
	6	Ajax Office Supply for used file cabinet	40.00	18
	6	Nancy Allen, employee, wages for week:		
		(Gross $127.26; SS $9.26; Fed Tax $18.00)	100.00	31
	6	New York Telephone Co. for May bill	13.13	28
	6	Weekly Courier for Thursday's ad	18.00	3
	6	Sam Ginsberg for filing quarterly tax return	29.41	2
	6	Apex Forwarding Co. for freight bill due	32.77	10
	7	Eastern Oil Co. for April fuel bill	50.00	4&
	7	John's Mobil Station for repairs company car	30.00	4
	7	Central City Clerk for water bill for month	5.33	32
	7	Petty Cash for month (charge to Misc. Expense)	11.20	17
	7	Drawn to self for week	40.00	55
	7	Yourself, for travel expense in advance	50.00	33 &
	7	State Dept. of Taxation, Unemploy. Ins. Tax	30.00	24
	7	United Parcel for delivery expense	9.00	7

The Operations Statement

The main purpose for keeping records is to know clearly what is happening to the business and if a profit is being made. How does a business owner know whether a profit has been made within the past month or accounting period?

Most business owners frequently want a periodic *statement of operations* (also referred to as an *operations statement* or a *profit and loss statement*). This statement is a summary of the income and expenses of the business. The operations statement summarizes these facts for any period of time. The heading of the operations statement in Figure 7-11 indicates that this statement covers a one-year period ending December 31.

Although many items appear on the operations statement, the basic idea is very simple. The same principle applies here as in the sale of Tommy's newspapers (previously mentioned). The formula is:

NET SALES minus COST OF GOODS equals PROFIT
Amount taken in minus Amount paid out equals Profit

Not Enough Lines ↓

DETAIL OF WEEKLY EXPENDITURES

	EXPENDITURES BY CHECKS AND CASH					EXPENDITURES BY CHECKS AND CASH			
DAY	TO WHOM PAID	CHECK NO.	ACCT. NO.	AMOUNT	DAY	TO WHOM PAID	CHECK NO.	ACCT. NO.	AMOUNT
3	Gas & Electric Co	62	8,11	30 00	6	Wage	77	31	149 00
3	United Parcel	63	7	18 00	6	Office Supply	78	18	40 00
4	Yourself	64	30	20 00	6	N. Allen Wages	79	31	100 00
4	Redcross	65	6	25 00	6	Phone Co.	80	28	13 13
4	Postmaster	66	19	31 00	6	Courrier	81	3	18 00
4	F. Norriss	67	15	10 00	6	Figured Tax	82	2	29 41
4,	Bag & Paper Co	68	5	20 75	6	Apex Co.	83	10	32 77
4	Laundry	69	14	40 00	7	Eastern Oil	84	4	50 00
4	Smith Realty	70	20	310 00	7	Johns Mobil	85	4	30 00
4	Bank	71	13	60 00	7	City Clerk	86	32	5 33
5	State Tax	72	25	19 00	7	Petty Cash	87	17	11 20
5	Union Dues	73	29	2 50	7	Drawn	88	55	40 00
5	Insurance	74	12	30 00	7	Yourself, Travel	89	33	50 00
5	TOTAL THIS WEEK	75	21	20 00	7	TOTAL THIS WEEK State Dept.	90	24	30 00
5	City Clerk	76	16	40 00	7	UPS	91	7	9 00
5	Total the Wk			676 25		Total			607 84

short lines

Total – 1284.59

WEEK ENDED   **19**

TOTAL RECEIPTS FROM BUSINESS OR PROFESSION			
DAY			**AMOUNT**
SUN.			
MON.			
TUES.			
WED.			
THUR.			
FRI.			
SAT.			
TOTAL THIS WEEK			
TOTAL UP TO LAST WEEK			
TOTAL TO DATE			

MEMO

	EXPENDITURES			
ACCT. NO.	**ACCOUNT**	**TOTAL THIS WEEK**	**TOTAL UP TO LAST WEEK**	**TOTAL TO DATE**
	DEDUCTIBLE			
1	MDSE.-MATERIALS			
2	ACCOUNTING	29 41		29 41
3	ADVERTISING	18 00		18 00
4	AUTO EXPENSE	80 00		80 00
5	CARTONS, ETC.	20 75		20 75
6	CONTRIBUTIONS	25 00		25 00
7	DELIVERY EXP.	27 00		27 00
8	ELECTRICITY	10 00		10 00
9	ENTERTAINMENT			
10	FREIGHT & EXPR.	32 77		32 77
11	HEAT	20 00		20 00
12	INSURANCE	30 00		30 00
13	INTEREST	60 00		60 00
14	LAUNDRY	40 00		40 00
15	LEGAL EXPENSE	10 00		10 00
16	LICENSES	40 00		40 00
17	MISC. EXP.	11 20		11 20
18	OFFICE EXP.	40 00		40 00
19	POSTAGE	31 00		31 00
20	RENT	310 00		310 00
21	REPAIRS	20 00		20 00
22	SHOP EXP.			
23	TAX — SOC. SEC.			
24	TAX — STATE U. I.	30 00		30 00
25	TAX — OTHER	19 00		19 00
26	SELLING EXP.			
27	SUPPLIES			
28	TELEPHONE	13 13		13 13
29	TRADE DUES, ETC.	2 50		2 50
30	TRAVELING EXP.	20 00		20 00
31	WAGES & COMM.	249 00		249 00
32	WATER	5 33		5 33
33		50 00		50 00
34				
35				
	SUB-TOTAL	✗ 1244.09		
	NON-DEDUCTIBLE			
51	NOTES PAYABLE			
52	FEDERAL INC. TAX			
53	LOANS PAYABLE			
54	LOANS RECEIV.			
55	PERSONAL	40 00		40 00
56	FIXED ASSETS			
57				
	TOTAL THIS WEEK	1284 09		
	TOT. UP TO LAST WK.			
	TOTAL TO DATE			1284 09

COPYRIGHT DOME ENTERPRISES

PAYROLL

EMPLOYEE	TOTAL WAGES	DEDUCTIONS			NET PAID
		SOC. SEC.	**FED. INC. TAX**		
Wm. Jones	184 00	13 13	21 87		149 00
Ney Allen	127 26	9 26	18 00		100 00
	311 26	22 39	39 87		249 00

(Courtesy Dome Publishing Co., Inc.)

With a larger business, expenses change the formula somewhat:

NET SALES minus COST OF GOODS SOLD equals GROSS PROFIT
GROSS PROFIT minus EXPENSES (RENT, LIGHT, PHONE) equals NET PROFIT

In business, there are two kinds of profit: **Gross profit** is net sales less the cost of goods sold.   **Net profit** is gross Profit less expenses.

NET SALES minus COST OF GOODS SOLD equals GROSS PROFIT
GROSS PROFIT minus OPERATING EXPENSES equals NET PROFIT

Consider newsboy Tommy again as an example. He had $.30 in cash and 25 newspapers which cost $3.75. He owes his father $.50. It is possible to construct a balance sheet from this information:

NEWSPAPER ROUTE
Balance Sheet
May 1

ASSETS

Cash	$ .30	Debts Payable	$ .50
Papers	3.75	Net Worth (Capital)	3.55
Total Assets	4.05	Net Worth and Liabilities	4.05

The operations statement in Figure 7-11 is a summary of facts which have been recorded daily in the books of the business. No matter how complicated it may look, it is based on the following simple formulas:

GROSS PROFIT equals SALES minus COST OF GOODS
NET PROFIT equals SALES minus COST OF GOODS AND EXPENSES

The operations statement is a summary of what has taken place during a specific period. The various sections of the statement provide information for decision making. The final figure, net profit, is of the greatest importance.

The operations statement might be compared to a "moving picture." It describes the business in action. It summarizes the results of past activities and gives hints of what the future holds. One might find, for instance, that even though sales had increased since last year, profits were less. The operations statement might show that expenses were too high. It might also show that the utilities increased or there was too much loss on bad debts. Once a problem area is identified, steps can be taken to correct it.

The operations statement provides tax, loan, and operating information. Income tax returns are based on the operations statements, Figure 7-12. State and local taxing agencies also require information provided by the statement. When applying for a loan, the bank may want to examine several operations statements.

THOMAS PARKER

Operations Statement
For Year Ending December 31, 19—

Total Sales for the Year	$21,458.00	
Less Returns and Allowances on Sales	350.00	
Net Sales		$21,108.00
Total Sales for the Year	$21,458.00	
Merchandise Inventory, January 1, 19—	$ 2,560.00	
Total Merchandise Purchases		
During the Year $14,952.65		
Less Returns and Allowances		
On Purchases 121.88		
Net Merchandise Purchases	14,830.77	
Total Merchandise Handled During the Year	$17,390.77	
Less Merchandise Inventory, December 31, 19—	3,250.00	
Cost of Goods Sold		14,140.77
Gross Profits on Sales		$ 6,967.23
Less Operating Expenses:		
Wages and Commissions	$ 2,590.00	
Freight, Drayage and Express	84.72	
Printing and Stationery Supplies	25.00	
Heat, Light and Power	305.00	
Rent.	600.00	
Insurance	15.00	
Property Taxes	165.00	
Telephone and Telegraph	45.60	
Depreciation	650.00	
Loss on Bad Debts	50.00	
Total Operating Expenses		4,530.32
Operating Profit		$ 2,436.91
Add Financial Income:		
Interest Received . . . . $ 19.02		
Discounts Allowed Us 125.50		
	144.52	
Interest Paid . . . . $ 60.00		
Discounts Allowed Customers 32.09		
	92.09	
Net Financial Income		52.43
Net Profit		$ 2,489.34
Less Withdrawals During the Year		2,142.19
Net Profit After Withdrawals, Available for Distribution		$ 347.15

FIGURE 7-11 The operations statement is a summary of daily transactions over a period of time.

V = Variable
F = Fixed

SCHEDULE C (Form 1040) Department of the Treasury Internal Revenue Service (O)	**Profit or (Loss) From Business or Profession** (Sole Proprietorship) Partnerships, Joint Ventures, etc., Must File Form 1065. ▶ Attach to Form 1040 or Form 1041. ▶ See Instructions for Schedule C (Form 1040).	OMB. No. 1545-0074 **1981** 08

Name of proprietor **MARY + ROBERT DOE**

Social security number of proprietor **56 00 0100**

A Main business activity (see Instructions) ▶ **DRESS SHOP** ; product ▶ **WOMEN'S APPAREL**

B Business name ▶ **MARY'S DRESS SHOP**

C Employer identification number

D Business address (number and street) ▶ **12 MAPLE STREET**
City, State and ZIP Code ▶ **ANYTOWN, USA 01210**

E Accounting method: (1) ☒ Cash   (2) ☐ Accrual   (3) ☐ Other (specify) ▶ _____

F Method(s) used to value closing inventory:
(1) ☐ Cost   (2) ☐ Lower of cost or market   (3) ☐ Other (if other, attach explanation)

	Yes	No
G Was there any major change in determining quantities, costs, or valuations between opening and closing inventory? . . If "Yes," attach explanation.		✓
H Did you deduct expenses for an office in your home?		✓

Part I   Income

1 a Gross receipts or sales	1a	51,210	
b Returns and allowances	1b	1,940	
c Balance (subtract line 1b from line 1a)	1c	49,270	
2 Cost of goods sold and/or operations (Schedule C-1, line 8)	2	30,251	
3 Gross profit (subtract line 2 from line 1c)	3	19,019	
4 a Windfall Profit Tax Credit or Refund received in 1981 (see Instructions)	4a		
b Other income (attach schedule)	4b		
5 Total income (add lines 3, 4a, and 4b) . . . . ▶	5	19,019	

Part II   Deductions

6 Advertising V	860 —	29 a Wages V	1,800 —	
7 Amortization		b Jobs credit		
8 Bad debts from sales or services V	200 —	c WIN credit		
9 Bank service charges		d Total credits		
10 Car and truck expenses V . .	710 —	e Subtract line 29d from 29a .		
11 Commissions V	1,200 —	30 Windfall Profit Tax withheld in 1981		
12 Depletion		31 Other expenses (specify):		
13 Depreciation (see Instructions) .		a		
14 Dues and publications . . .		b		
15 Employee benefit programs . .		c		
16 Freight (not included on Schedule C-1) .		d		
17 Insurance F	250 —	e		
18 Interest on business indebtedness		f		
19 Laundry and cleaning . . .		g		
20 Legal and professional services F	50 —	h		
21 Office supplies and postage . .		i		
22 Pension and profit-sharing plans .		j		
23 Rent on business property . .		k		
24 Repairs		l		
25 Supplies (not included on Schedule C-1) V	61 —	m		
26 Taxes (do not include Windfall Profit Tax, see line 30) V	2,400 —	n		
27 Travel and entertainment . .		o		
28 Utilities and telephone V	1,105 —	p		

32 Total deductions (add amounts in columns for lines 6 through 31p) . . . . . . ▶	32	8,636	—
33 Net profit or (loss) (subtract line 32 from line 5). If a profit, enter on Form 1040, line 11, and on Schedule SE, Part II, line 5a (or Form 1041, line 6). If a loss, go on to line 34	33	10,393	—

34 If you have a loss, do you have amounts for which you are not "at risk" in this business (see Instructions)? . . ☐ Yes ☒ No
If you checked "No," enter the loss on Form 1040, line 11, and on Schedule SE, Part II, line 5a (or Form 1041, line 6).

For Paperwork Reduction Act Notice, see Form 1040 Instructions.

FIGURE 7-12 Income tax returns are based on the operations statement.

Schedule C (Form 1040) 1981   Page **2**

SCHEDULE C–1.—Cost of Goods Sold and/or Operations (See Schedule C Instructions for Part I, line 2)

1 Inventory at beginning of year (if different from last year's closing inventory, attach explanation) .		1	*10,291* —
2 a Purchases	2a *30,450* —		
b Cost of items withdrawn for personal use	2b *1,110* —		
c Balance (subtract line 2b from line 2a)		2c	*29,340* —
3 Cost of labor (do not include salary paid to yourself)		3	*5,120* —
4 Materials and supplies		4	*810* —
5 Other costs (attach schedule)		5	
6 Add lines 1, 2c, and 3 through 5		6	*46,191* —
7 Inventory at end of year		7	*15,940* —
8 Cost of goods sold and/or operations (subtract line 7 from line 6). Enter here and on Part I, line 2 . ▶		8	*30,251* —

SCHEDULE C–2.—Depreciation (See Schedule C Instructions for line 13)

Complete Schedule C–2 if you claim depreciation ONLY for assets placed in service before January 1, 1981. If you need more space, use Form 4562. If you claim a deduction for any assets placed in service after December 31, 1980, use Form 4562 to figure your total deduction for all assets; do NOT complete Schedule C–2.

Description of property (a)	Date acquired (b)	Cost or other basis (c)	Depreciation allowed or allowable in prior years (d)	Method of computing depreciation (e)	Life or rate (f)	Depreciation for this year (g)
1 Depreciation (see Instructions):						
2 Totals				2		
3 Depreciation claimed in Schedule C–1				3		
4 **Balance** (subtract line 3 from line 2). Enter here and on Part II, line 13 . . . . ▶				4		

SCHEDULE C–3.—Expense Account Information (See Schedule C Instructions for Schedule C–3)

Enter information for yourself and your five highest paid employees. In determining the five highest paid employees, add expense account allowances to the salaries and wages. However, you don't have to provide the information for any employee for whom the combined amount is less than $50,000, or for yourself if your expense account allowance plus line 33, page 1, is less than $50,000.

Name (a)	Expense account (b)	Salaries and wages (c)
Owner		
1		
2		
3		
4		
5		

Did you claim a deduction for expenses connected with:	Yes	No
A Entertainment facility (boat, resort, ranch, etc.)?		
B Living accommodations (except employees on business)?		
C Conventions or meetings you or your employees attended outside the North American area? (see Instructions) . . .		
D Employees' families at conventions or meetings?		
If "Yes," were any of these conventions or meetings outside the North American area?		
E Vacations for employees or their families not reported on Form W–2?		

☆ U.S. GOVERNMENT PRINTING OFFICE : 1981—O–343 409 13 5606244

FIGURE 7-12 (Continued)

The bank is interested in how sales compare with expenses, how much inventory is carried, and credit which is extended by the business. The owner is provided with information about the business from the operations statement. Profits earned over a period of time, department performance, inventory size, overhead costs, and many other items are shown on the statement. Proper use of the operations statement gives owners an understanding of their businesses. Past and present conditions may be easily observed and the necessary improvements made.

The Balance Sheet

In contrast to the operations statement, the balance sheet is a "still picture" of the business. Assets on one side are balanced against liabilities on the other. *Assets* include everything that is owned by the business. *Liabilities* are those amounts which the business owes.

The principle is the same regardless of the size of the business. It is expressed in the formula:

ASSETS minus LIABILITIES equals NET WORTH
or
ASSETS equal LIABILITIES plus NET WORTH

When Tommy, the newspaper boy, subtracted his liabilities ($.50) from his assets ($4.05), he found that the net worth of the business was $3.55. That was the status of his business on May 1. On any other day, the net worth might have been entirely different. Assets and liabilities in any business change. But a business owner can stop and make up a balance sheet at any time.

Examine the balance sheet in Figure 7-13 for the Cambridge Television and Appliance Store. Note that, despite the large number of items, the sheet is based on the same formula.

ASSETS equal LIABILITIES plus NET WORTH

The figures for the balance sheet come from the records kept by the business. Each item on the balance sheet is based on facts that have been recorded daily in different ledger accounts. The records used for the operations statement are also used in preparing a balance sheet.

TAX RECORDS

The tax responsibilities of a small business owner are not easily determined. You must spend a good deal of time to be fully informed about taxes and the forms that must be filed with federal, state, and city governments. In addition to the taxes that must be paid to the federal government, there are sales and property taxes and license fees that differ for each type of business. Theaters, bowling

CAMBRIDGE TELEVISION AND APPLIANCE STORE

Balance Sheet
December 31, 19___

Assets

Current Assets
Cash on Hand		$ 60.00
Cash in Bank		540.00
Merchandise Inventory		6,700.00
Accounts Receivable		300.00
		$ 7,600.00

Fixed Assets
Real Estate – Land		1,000.00	
Real Estate – Buildings			
Original Cost	$5,000.00		
Less Depreciation	1,000.00		
		4,000.00	
Furniture and Fixtures			
Original Cost	600.00		
Less Depreciation	100.00		
		500.00	
Delivery Truck			
Original Cost	800.00		
Less Depreciation	200.00		
		600.00	
			6,100.00

Total Assets	$13,700.00

Liabilities

Current Liabilities
Accounts Payable	$ 2,000.00	
Notes Payable	1,000.00	
		$ 3,000.00

Total Liabilities
Capital or Net Worth		
Capital, Jan. 1, 1975	10,200.00	
Profit after withdrawals		
Jan. 1, 1975 – Dec. 31, 1975	500.00	
		10,700.00

Total Liabilities and Capital	$13,700.00

FIGURE 7-13 A balance sheet summarizes the assets and liabilities of a business.

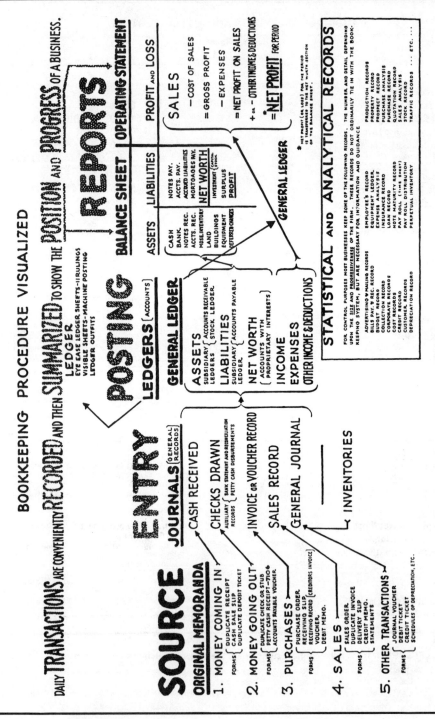

FIGURE 7-14 Bookkeeping procedure visualized

alleys, and places of amusement pay special taxes. Luxury taxes must be paid on jewelry, luggage, and gift items. In many places, sales taxes must be collected by the retailer and paid quarterly to the government. The taxes discussed here are general. Tax structures vary from state to state. Before starting a business, you should investigate your state's tax requirements.

Tax rates and regulations constantly change. By employing a qualified tax accountant to file your tax returns, you will keep up to date on tax information. Tax accountants are specialists who devote a great deal of time to handling tax matters. Their work is accurate and can save money for you and your business.

The Internal Revenue Service is another source of tax information. The IRS publishes *The Employer's Tax Guide,* which contains a calendar of employer's duties (Circular E) as they relate to federal taxes, Figure 7-15. The booklet is revised whenever there are changes in tax requirements.

Calendar

If any date shown falls on a Saturday, Sunday, or legal holiday, use the next regular workday.

By January 31 or When Employment Ends

Give each employee a completed Form W-2, Wage and Tax Statement. Give each annuitant a completed Form W-2P, Statement for Recipients of Periodic Annuities, Pensions, Retired Pay, or IRA Payments, by January 31.

By January 31

Federal Unemployment (FUTA) Tax.—File Form 940, Employer's Annual Federal Unemployment Tax Return. If you deposited all the tax when due, you have 10 more days to file the return.

By February 28

Income Tax Withholding.—File Form W-3, Transmittal of Income and Tax Statements, with the Social Security Administration and include Copy A of all Forms W-2 and W-2P you gave employees or annuitants for the year before. (See section 15.)

By April 30, July 31, October 31, and January 31

Deposit Federal unemployment tax due if it is more than $100. File Form 941, Employer's Quarterly Federal Tax Return, or Form 941E, Quarterly Return of Withheld Federal Income Tax, and pay any undeposited income and FICA taxes. If you deposited all the taxes when due, you have 10 more days to file the return.

File Form 942, Employer's Quarterly Tax Return for Household Employees, if you have such employees, and pay the tax due. (See section 13.)

Before December 1

Income Tax Withholding.—Ask for a new Form W-4, Employee's Withholding Allowance Certificate, from each employee whose withholding allowances will change for the next year.

On December 31

Form W-5, Earned Income Credit Advance Payment Certificate, expires. Eligible employees who want to continue receiving advance payments of the earned income credit for the next year must file a new Form W-5.

By May 1

Ask for a new Form W-4 from each employee who claimed the exemption from withholding during the prior year.

On May 1

Stop the exemption from withholding for each employee who has not given you a new Form W-4 for the current year. (See section 10(g).)

Reminders

When Hiring New Employees

Income Tax Withholding.—Ask each new employee to complete Form W-4.

FICA Taxes.—Record each new employee's name and number from his or her social security card. Any employee who does not have a number should apply for one. (See section 5.)

When Paying Wages or Annuities

Income Tax Withholding.—Withhold tax from each wage payment or supplemental unemployment compensation plan benefit payment according to the employee's Form W-4 and the correct withholding rate. If requested on Form W-4P, Pension, Annuity, or Sick Pay Recipient's Request for Federal Income Tax Withholding, withhold tax from annuity payments, or sick pay, if applicable. (See sections 6 and 11.)

FICA Taxes.—Withhold 6.70% from each wage payment in 1982. (If the employee reported tips, see section 7.)

Unresolved Problems

IRS has a Problem Resolution Program for taxpayers who have been unable to resolve their problems with IRS. If you have a tax problem you have been unable to resolve through normal channels, call the toll-free telephone number for your area and ask for the Problem Resolution Office. This office will take responsibility for your problem and insure that it receives proper attention. Although the Problem Resolution Office cannot change the tax law or technical decisions, it can frequently clear up misunderstandings that resulted from previous contacts.

FIGURE 7-15 An excerpt from Circular E of *The Employer's Tax Guide,* published by the Internal Revenue Service. Circular E contains a calendar of employer's duties as they relate to federal taxes.

This worksheet is designed to help you meet your tax obligations. You may want an accountant or bookkeeper to prepare the worksheet so you can use it as a reminder in preparing for and paying the various taxes.

Kind of Tax	Due Date	Amount Due	Pay to	Date for Writing the Check
FEDERAL TAXES				
Employee Income Tax and Social Security Tax				
Excise Tax				
Owner-Manager's and/or corporation's income tax				
Unemployment Tax				
STATE TAXES				
Unemployment Taxes				
Income Taxes				
Sales Taxes				
Franchise Tax				
Other				
LOCAL TAXES				
Sales Tax				
Real Estate Tax				
Personal Property Tax				
Licenses (retail, vending machine, etc.)				
Other				

FIGURE 7-16 Worksheet for meeting tax obligations

Employers are responsible for the following taxes payable to the federal government:

- Income tax withheld from employees' wages
  (See W-4 form in Figure 7-18.)
- Employee and employer taxes under the Federal Insurance Contributions Act (Social Security)
- Employer tax under the Federal Unemployment Tax Act (Unemployment Insurance)

Owners who are sole proprietors must complete and file federal and state personal income tax forms. This also applies to partners. Income from a business must be reported on Schedule C of the 1040 form. The income of self-employed individuals is subject to social security taxes. Some states have unincorporated business tax on income earned within the state. Exemptions and certain allowable deductions are provided.

If a business is a corporation, the corporation itself pays federal or state corporate income taxes. The stockholders and employees of the corporation report income they receive from the corporation on their individual tax returns. A corporation is a form of business that, in most states, must pay an annual franchise tax. This tax is imposed on a percentage of entire net income, after certain inclusions and deductions, and is figured only on that portion actually earned within the state. Corporations pay corporate income tax, taxes on certain surpluses, personal holdings, regulated investments, and foreign corporations tax. They also pay estate and gift taxes, excise tax, import and export duties, license fees, and special occupational taxes. All of these taxes are not usually related to small businesses. Business owners should be aware of these taxes, should their businesses get larger or incorporate.

Income tax forms and laws change, so advice will be needed from time to time. A general understanding of taxes and forms should be acquired by any prospective entrepreneur.

The Social Security Tax

The Federal Social Security Administration provides old-age pensions and some income to dependents of disabled or deceased workers. This old-age and survivor's insurance system is paid for by employees and employers. Most employers must file an application for an employer's identification number on Form SS-4. This form is obtainable from the nearest office of the District Director of Internal Revenue where federal personal income tax forms are also available. The employer pays a tax on wages each year for each employee and the employee pays a similar share. For example, the maximum individual employee social security tax in 1982 was 6.7% of $32,400 in earnings, or a tax of $2,170.80.

Any excess over that amount would be a tax credit. A chart of the contribution rates is shown in Figure 7-17. The employee's share is deducted from earnings each pay period. The *Employer's Tax Guide* previously mentioned explains the tax law and is helpful when preparing the necessary withholding forms. The booklet is available at no cost from your local IRS office.

Application for a social security account number may have to be made for an employee who is being hired for the very first time. Most people will have a social security number, but it is a good idea to have application forms on hand. The forms are available from the local office of the Social Security Administration. The details of deducting social security tax from wages are explained in the payroll section of this unit. The social security tax tables are shown in Figure 7-25.

Tax Rate for Employees and Employers (each)

| | Percent of Covered Earnings | | |
Years	For Cash Benefits	For Hospital Insurance	Total
1981	5.35	1.30	6.65
1982–84	5.40	1.30	6.70
1985	5.70	1.35	7.05
1986–89	5.70	1.45	7.15
1990 and after	6.20	1.45	7.65

Tax Rate for Self-employed People

| | Percent of Covered Earnings | | |
Years	For Cash Benefits	For Hospital Insurance	Total
1981	8.00	1.30	9.30
1982–84	8.05	1.30	9.35
1985	8.55	1.35	9.90
1986–89	8.55	1.45	10.00
1990 and after	9.30	1.45	10.75

FIGURE 7-17
The contribution rate schedules for the social security tax

Unemployment Insurance

Another form of tax seeks to provide aid for the unemployed. This unemployment insurance tax is on a cooperative state-federal basis. The contributions are collected from employers only and paid to employees if they become unemployed. The tax is based on the employee's gross annual wages. Details concerning unemployment insurance taxes may be obtained by writing state and federal authorities.

Unemployment insurance laws provide merit systems for contributing employers. Individual accounts are set up for employers and they are rated according to benefits paid, length of time they have been members of the plan, and the relative stability of their payrolls. These ratings govern the extent to which the employers are entitled to a reduction in contribution rates for each year.

Unemployment insurance is complicated and subject to change. It is described very briefly here. When organizing a business, you should contact the appropriate tax sources in your area for current requirements.

Worker's Compensation

Worker's compensation insurance must be carried by every employer whose work is listed as hazardous in Section 3 of the Worker's Compensation Law. In addition to this, the insurance must be carried by every employer of three or more workers. Hazardous occupations include manufacturing, construction and repairwork, canning and food processing, distribution, storage, transportation, communications, janitorial services, installation, and service occupations. Retail businesses are not usually considered hazardous, with the exception of hardware and paint stores, automobile repair and service stations, and dry-cleaning plants and laundromats. Meat-cutting operations in grocery stores, some stock operations with conveyor belts, and other similar operations are also classified as hazardous.

A business owner has an obligation to provide for employees who are injured on the job. Good relations between employer and employee are built on the belief that an employee will be treated fairly, protected from financial loss due to injury on the job, and provided with safe and pleasant working conditions. Worker's compensation insurance can be purchased from private insurance companies authorized to transact business in the state or from the insurance pools. This insurance must be secured before any employees can work. As soon as you take out this kind of insurance, a notice stating that you have complied with the rules governing worker's compensation must be posted in a conspicuous place. Notices are furnished by the insurance company. You or your partners, except salaried officers of a corporation, are not covered by worker's compensation. It is therefore advisable for the business owner to carry accident and health insurance.

205

The individual who starts a small business may have, in the course of time, one or more employees. An owner must know the state and federal regulations concerning safe working conditions, the minimum wage, hours, worker's compensation, unemployment insurance, disability insurance, social security, and fair employment practices. By writing to the Department of Labor in your state, you can get information on all of these subjects. You can also obtain information from many of the sources discussed in Unit 10.

Estimated Income

When a person has an annual income of $200 or more from sources other than regular wages, a declaration of Estimated Income Tax, Federal Form 1040-ES, must be filed in addition to a regular income tax return. There are some exceptions to this, but self-employed persons and part-time owners of small businesses must report estimated income to the government. The reason for this is that some income is not subject to payroll deductions. Because some withholding tax tables are not accurate after a certain point, enough withholding tax may not be deducted from wages. The taxpayer then has to pay additional taxes when the return is filed in April. To prevent this, taxpayers who have part-time businesses spread the payments in quarterly payments over the tax year. For example, while you have a full-time job in a factory, you may also operate a small landscaping business during the summer. From the landscaping business in the summer, you made a $400 profit. In this case, Form 1040-ES must be filed to show this additional source of income. Regulations explaining estimated returns are covered fully in income tax guides. These are available at newsstands, stationery stores, and local offices of the IRS.

State and Local Retail Sales Taxes

Many businesses are located in cities or states that have local retail sales tax. A business owner must collect this tax at the point-of-sale and then pay it to local tax authorities, usually quarterly. Retail sales taxes range from 3% to 8% and will probably increase in the future. Such establishments as churches, charities, nonprofit organizations, hospitals, community-supported agencies (the Red Cross), and schools and colleges are exempt from taxes. Each business or individual must have a certificate of exemption or collection from the sales tax agency showing the tax exemption number. When business owners report their sales taxes, these exemption numbers must be included for all goods that were untaxed due to an exemption. Sales tax is not paid on goods you use in your store. You must have an exemption number to avoid paying the tax.

Proprietors should understand local regulations and mark price tags accordingly. Cash registers can be ordered with special sales tax keys and subtotals of tax. Tax tables should be kept near the cash register. You must know how to report sales tax, based on a percent of taxable sales. It is important for a business owner to know the system and the necessary records so that the correct tax is paid. If the tax is not paid, your business can be closed. You can be fined and/or sent to jail.

Excise and Other Taxes

Special federal and state taxes are imposed on some retail items. Some taxes are collected from the manufacturer or importer and passed on to the retailer. Federal excise and luxury taxes on retail purchases of jewelry, furs, tires, gasoline, cosmetics, luggage, handbags, and other items are added to the retail price. Such taxes should be shown or listed on items separately so that customers can see the tax they are paying. Some taxes are hidden in the retail price of an article. For example, federal taxes on liquor, tobacco, and playing cards are included in the price. Federal taxes on gasoline, oil, and automobile tires together with state and local taxes are sometimes hard to distinguish. The gasoline tank meter records the amount of purchase based on the number of gallons pumped, thus making it hard to figure the actual price of the gasoline.

Accurate records of untaxable items sold must be kept separate so that tax is not paid on them. Items returned as unsalable, such as a damaged chair, are not taxable. Since tax is payable only when sold, the retailer does not pay taxes in advance on merchandise not yet sold.

Other examples of state and federal taxes imposed at the point-of-sale include amusement taxes, taxes on telephone calls, taxes on telegrams and cables, transportation taxes (air, rail, and ship), and customs or import duties.

Real Estate Taxes

If the physical facilities of a business are owned, the proprietor pays real estate or property taxes annually or as a part of the mortgage payment, just the same as a homeowner does. If the site is rented, the taxes are included in the rent.

PAYROLL RECORDS

The Minimum Wage

The law requires that wages in manufacturing and many other industries be paid weekly, within six days following the close of the workweek. The wages must be paid in cash unless special permission to use checks is obtained in writing from the state Industrial Commissioner. Discrimination in the rate of pay because of sex, race, color, or creed is forbidden. On public works, wages must not be less than those prevailing in similar jobs in private industry. Details concerning federal minimum wages in various job classifications may be obtained from the Federal Fair Labor Standards Bureau and the department of labor in your state.

Minimum wages have been established by each state and are equal to or exceed the federal minimum wage. The rates may be obtained by contacting the labor relations agencies in your state.

State departments of labor advise businesses about the working hours for men, women and minors, and the restrictions in some industries. When women and minors are employed in factories or mercantile establishments, the schedule of hours for their employment must be approved by the state. Employees must have one full day off in each week, plus at least one hour per day for lunch in factories, or 45 minutes in stores and offices. In those industries for which minimum wage standards have been fixed for women and minors, no male workers age 21 or over may be employed at wages below such standards.

The Federal Fair Labor Standards Act in the U.S. sets a minimum wage for all employees engaged in interstate commerce. This federal law also provides for overtime payment at the rate of time and a half for all time in excess of 40 hours per workweek. The number of hours worked per day is not covered by this legislation. There may be, however, local, union or state regulations in effect which govern the wages the employer must pay. Furthermore, there may be accepted trade practices. For example, employees in food service establishments are usually granted a meal during each workday, and an allowance is usually made for uniforms. You will need to decide on all of these matters if you employ workers. The policies you make for your business must be known by the workers in order to avoid confusion and discontent.

Payroll Deductions

The total earnings due an employee who is paid hourly wages is called *gross wages*. Total earnings are found by multiplying the number of hours worked times the hourly rate. Regular wages are computed at this regular rate and are added to any overtime wages figured at time and a half the regular rate. There are several deductions which the employer must subtract from the gross wages. The amount remaining is called the *net wages*, or sometimes called the *take-home pay*.

Required payroll deductions include federal and state income taxes, social security taxes, and disability insurance. Other deductions required by law include worker's compensation and unemployment insurance. Employers must account for these deductions in a separate account and make tax payments quarterly for their employees. State and federal taxes are held in reserve for each employee until the end of each quarter, and the owner then files a tax return (Form 914) to deposit the taxes. The amount of tax withheld from an employee's wages depends on the number of dependents that employee claims on Form W-4. The employer must keep a copy of this form for each employee, Figure 7-18. This form shows the number of withholding exemptions or dependents that the employee claims. The employee can change the number of exemptions at any time and, if preferred, may specify the actual amount deducted.

At the end of each calendar year (January 31), an employer must prepare Federal Form W-2 for each employee, Figure 7-19. This form tells employees exactly how much tax (federal, state, city, and social security) the employer has paid for them during the year. This form is needed by employees so that they can complete a personal income tax return.

Some payroll deductions are optional and include such items as payroll savings, hospitalization, medical plans, life insurance plans, and retirement plans. Other optional deductions include union dues, contributions to charities, company savings, profit-sharing plans, payroll savings bonds plans, and tax sheltered annuities. An employee who has been careless about the use of credit may, as the result of a judgment in court, suffer attachment or garnishment of wages for an amount stipulated by the court. This means that the employer must deduct an amount each week from the employee's wages and pay it directly to a bank or other designated collection agency for the purpose of paying off the employee's debts.

Form **W-4**	Department of the Treasury—Internal Revenue Service	OMB No. 1545–0010
(Rev. January 1982)	**Employee's Withholding Allowance Certificate**	Expires 4–30–83

1 Type or print your full name: Kirk Alan Hunsicker

2 Your social security number: 479-98-5402

Home address (number and street or rural route): 1804 61st

City or town, State, and ZIP code: Des Moines Iowa 50322

3 Marital Status: ☑ Single ☐ Married ☐ Married, but withhold at higher Single rate

Note: If married, but legally separated, or spouse is a nonresident alien, check the Single box.

4 Total number of allowances you are claiming (from line F of the worksheet on page 2) . . . .

5 Additional amount, if any, you want deducted from each pay . . . . $ 0

6 I claim exemption from withholding because (see instructions and check boxes below that apply):

  a ☐ Last year I did not owe any Federal income tax and had a right to a full refund of **ALL** income tax withheld, **AND**

  b ☐ This year I do not expect to owe any Federal income tax and expect to have a right to a full refund of **ALL** income tax withheld. If both a and b apply, enter "EXEMPT" here . . . . ▶

  c If you entered "EXEMPT" on line 6b, are you a full-time student? . . . . ☑ Yes ☐ No

Under the penalties of perjury, I certify that I am entitled to the number of withholding allowances claimed on this certificate, or if claiming exemption from withholding, that I am entitled to claim the exempt status.

Employee's signature ▶ Kirk Hunsicker Date ▶ 3-26-85 , 19 85

7 Employer's name and address (including ZIP code) (FOR EMPLOYER'S USE ONLY)

8 Office code

9 Employer identification number

-------------------------------- Detach along this line --------------------------------

FIGURE 7-18 Federal Form W-4. This form is filled out by an employee when hired so that the employer can determine how much tax to withhold from the employee's wages. The amount of tax withheld depends on the number of dependents claimed.

1 Control number	22222	OMB No. 1545–0008		

2 Employer's name, address, and ZIP code	3 Employer's identification number	4 Employer's State number
Your Business Name Here Street Address City, State Zip 09123	123456	NY

5 Stat. em- ployee ☐	De- ceased ☐	Pension plan ☐	Legal rep. ☐	942 emp. ☐	Sub- total ☐	Cor- rection ☐	Void ☐

6	7 Advance EIC payment

8 Employee's social security number	9 Federal income tax withheld	10 Wages, tips, other compensation	11 FICA tax withheld

12 Employee's name, address, and ZIP code	13 FICA wages	14 FICA tips
Employee's Name Goes Here Address City & State Zip	16 Employer's use	

17 State income tax	18 State wages, tips, etc.	19 Name of State
20 Local income tax	21 Local wages, tips, etc.	22 Name of locality

Wage and Tax Statement 1982   Copy 1 For State, City, or Local Tax Department ☐
Employee's and employer's copy compared.

FIGURE 7-19 Federal Form W-2. The employer fills out this form for each employee at the end of the year. The form shows the total wages earned and the taxes paid on behalf of the employee.

Payroll Data Cards

A business owner should make up payroll data cards. These cards contain information needed to complete each week's payroll and can be updated when necessary, Figure 7-20. Payroll data cards are used in addition to time cards. The form is a sample to indicate one of the ways payroll cards can be made up. There are many commercial versions on the market. Some of these forms use NCR (no carbon required) paper and are easy to use.

Time Cards

Most employers require that each individual employee complete a time card each day. The card becomes the individual's record of hours worked. Most time cards are marked by an electric time clock which prints in the appropriate boxes on the card the time and date when the employee arrives at work and leaves work. In very small businesses, the time can be written on the time card by the supervisor or by the employee.

The time card bears the employee's payroll number as well as other data. The time card shows totals at the end of each day and at the end of the week. These cards are used for making out the hourly payroll and must be accurate.

Payroll Data Card	Payroll Data Card
Name: _____ No. __	Name: _____ No. __
Address: _____	Address: _____
City: _____ State: _____ Zip: _____	City: _____ State: _____ Zip: _____
Social Security Number: _____	Social Security Number: _____
Exemptions Claimed on W-4: _____	Exemptions Claimed on W-4: _____
Job Title: _____	Job Title: _____
Hourly Rate: _____ __ Married __ Widowed	Hourly Rate: _____ __ Married __ Widowed
Date Hired: _____ __ Single __ Divorced	Date Hired: _____ __ Single __ Divorced

FIGURE 7-20 Payroll data cards summarize the information needed to complete the weekly or biweekly payroll.

Two sample time cards are shown in Figure 7-21. The partially completed cards indicate the hours each individual worked and also include other important data. Complete the time cards by making the necessary additions and extensions. The cards will then be used to complete a sample payroll in the Practice Exercise.

Most time is figured in quarters of an hour (15 minutes). An employee who works 8 minutes (which is the major part of 15) is paid for 15 minutes. For example, an employee who punches in at 8:07 AM for the 8 o'clock shift would not lose any wages. An employee, however, who comes in at 8:08 AM would lose one-quarter of an hour (15 minutes) and would actually be paid for 45 minutes. The following information explains this point. (Reporting time is 8:00 AM)

Time In	% of Hourly Rate Due		
7:53*	100%	ALL	60 min
8:07	100%	ALL	60 min
8:08	75%	3/4	45 min
8:22	75%	3/4	45 min
8:23	50%	1/2	30 min
8:37	50%	1/2	30 min
8:38	25%	1/4	15 min
8:52	25%	1/4	15 min
8:53 or later	0%	—	0 min

*An employee reporting earlier than 7:53 AM would either be entitled to an additional one-quarter hour wages or not be allowed to punch in.

211

PAYROLL TIME CARD							No. 3			PAYROLL TIME CARD							No. 4	

NAME: _Nancy Allen_   NAME: _William Jones_

For Pay Period Ending: _Jan. 6_ 19 _85_   For Pay Period Ending: _Jan. 6_ 19 ____

Social Security Number: _550-03-2197_   Social Security Number: _107-00-1040_

Hourly Rate: $ _3.75_ Dept: _Cashier_   Hourly Rate: $ _4.40_ Dept: _Grocery_

☐ Male ☒ Female ☒ Part-time ☐ Full-time   ☒ Male ☐ Female ☐ Part-time ☒ Full-time

☐ Married ☒ Single   WE. _1_   ☒ Married ☐ Single   WE. _4_

Card No. 3 — Nancy Allen

	Mon	Tues	Wed	Thurs	Fri	Sat	Sun	
In						8:04		01
Out								02
In								03
Out						12:02		04
In								05
Out								06
In	4:01	3:59	3:58	3:57	3:59	1:01		07
Out								08
In								09
Out	8:03	8:04	8:00	7:59	8:01	5:02		10
In								11
Out								12
	4	4	4	4	4	8		13
T	X	X	X	X	X	X		

Date: _1-6_   Signature: _Nancy Allen_

Card No. 4 — William Jones

	Mon	Tues	Wed	Thurs	Fri	Sat	Sun	
In								01
Out								02
In	9:01	8:05	7:59	8:00	9:02	8:59		03
Out								04
In								05
Out	12:02	12:01	11:58	12:01	1:03	12:02		06
In								07
Out								08
In	1:03	1:01	1:02	12:59	2:01	12:59		09
Out								10
In								11
Out	6:04	5:02	5:00	4:59	6:03	5:04		12
								13
T	8	8	8	8	8	7		

Date: _1-6_   Signature: _William Jones_

FIGURE 7-21 Sample time cards

PRACTICE EXERCISE

This exercise allows you to complete a sample payroll for the employees of a store. The hourly rates, number of hours worked, and other pertinent information that you will need to complete the payroll register is shown in the following chart.

Using the payroll register shown in Figure 7-22, complete the payroll for as many employees as you wish. The necessary information for federal and state income tax deductions and social security tax is given in Figures 7-23, 7-24, and 7-25.

Name of Employee	Line No.	Hours Worked							Hourly Rate	Marital Status	Sickness Disability	Savings	W.E.*
		M	T	W	T	F	S	S					
† Smith, John	1.	8	8	8	8	8			$4.00	M	$5.00	$1.00	3
† Doe, Joseph	2.	8	8	8	8	8	4		4.50	S	2.50	.50	1
Donnelly, Mary	3.	8	8	8	8	8			3.95	D	4.00	1.50	2
Robinson, June	4.	8		8	8	8		8	4.10	S	2.50	4.00	1
Stone, Charles	5.	8	8	8	8	8	8	4	5.30	M	5.00	2.00	6
Gonzales, Pedro	6.	8	8	8	8	8	8		4.25	M	5.00	1.00	7
Lovell, Mary	7.	8	8	8		8			3.95	S	2.50	2.50	0
** Allen, Nancy	8.	4	4	4	4	4	8		3.75	S	2.50	2.00	1
** Jones, William	9.	8	8	8	8	8	7		4.40	M	5.00	/	4
Harrison, John	10.	8	8	8	8	8			6.19	M	5.00	8.00	3
Smythe, Henrietta	11.	8	9	8	9	8	4		5.17	S	2.50	5.00	1
Millsap, George	12.	7	9	7	9	7	4		6.00	M	5.00	2.50	4
Winston, Henry	13.	8	8	8	8	8			5.00	M	5.00	1.00	2
Gregson, Marcy	14.	8	8	9	9	9	5		5.10	M	2.50	2.00	0
Fredrickson, John	15.	8	8	8	8	8	4		5.90	M	5.00	5.00	5

†These first two employees have been completed on the payroll register in Figure 7-22.

*W.E. stands for withholding exemptions (the number of dependents claimed by the worker)

**Time cards for these two employees appear in Figure 7-21. Obtain the hours worked for these two employees by extending the two cards.

13

SAMPLE PAYROLL

PAYROLL WEEK ENDING JAN. 6 19 85

FIGURE 7-22 Payroll register

NAME OF EMPLOYEE	M	T	W	T	F	S	S	TOTAL REG. TIME	TOTAL OVERTIME	WAGE RATE	REGULAR WAGES	OVERTIME WAGES	TOTAL	FED. OLD AGE	FED. WITH-HOLD. TAX	STATE WITH-HOLD. TAX	SICKNESS DISABY	SAVINGS	TOTAL	NET PAY
1 Smith, John	8	8	8	8	8	-	-	40		4⁰⁰	160	-		160	10.72	5 70	4.30	5.-	1.-	34 73	135 28
2 Doe, Joseph	8	8	8	8	8	4	-	40	4	4⁵⁰	180	-	27 -	207	13.87	24 60	7.60	2.50	.50	49 07	157 93
3 Donelly, Mary	8	8	8	8	8			40	0	3.95	158	-		158	10.59	13 -	4.30	4.00	1.50	33 39	124 61
4 Robinson, June	8		8		8	8		32		4.10	131 20			131 20	8.79	12 40	4.-	2.50	4.-	31 69	99 51
5 Stone, Charles	8	8	8	8	8	8	4	40	12	5.30	212	-	95 40	307 40	20.60	20	10	9.70	5.-	2.-	57 40	250 -
6 Gonzoles, Pedro	8	8	8	8	8			40	8	4.25	170	-	51 04	221 04	14.81	5 30	4.20	5.-	1.-	30 31	190 70
7 Lovell, Mary	8	8		8				32		3.95	126 40			126 40	8.47	14 70	4.40	2.50	2.50	32 57	93 83
8 Allen, Nancy	4	4	4	4	4	8		28		3.75	105	-		105 -	7.04	8 40	2.80	2.50	2.-	22 74	82 26
9 Jones, William	8	8	8	8	8	7		40	7	4.40	176	-	46 20	222 20	14.89	13 50	6.30	5.-		39 69	182 57
10 Harrison, John	8	8	8	8	8			40		6.19	247 60			247 60	16.59	19 80	8.20	5.-	8.-	57 59	190 01
11 Smythe, Henrietta	8	9	8	9	8	4		40	6	5.17	206 80		46 56	253 36	16.98	34 60	10.70	2.50	5.-	69 78	183 56
12 Millsap, George	7	9	7	9	7	4		40	3	6.00	240	-	27 -	267 -	17.89	19 40	8.60		2.50	53 89	213 11
13 Winston, Henry	8	8	8	8	8			40		5.00	200	-		200 -	13.40	16 40	6.80	5.-	1.-	42 60	157 40
14 Gregson, Mary	8	8	9	9	9	5		40	8	5.10	204	-	61 20	265 20	17.77	33 20	12.50	2.50	2.-	67 97	197 23
15 Frederick, John	8	8	8	8	8	4		40	4	5.90	236	-	35 40	271 40	18.18	18 40	8.50	5.-	5.-	55 08	216 32
• TOTAL								71, 56			2753 00		389 73	3142 73	210, 57	261 60	102, 59	58 00	671 87	2470 86

Add up the number of hours the employee worked Monday through Sunday and enter no more than 40 in the column *Total Reg. Time.* Enter any hours over 40 in the column *Total Overtime.* To find gross wages, multiply 40 hours times the hourly rate, and the overtime hours times 11/2 times the hourly rate. In the case of Joseph Doe, who worked 44 hours, multiply 40 X $4.50 to get $180 (*Regular Wages*), and multiply 4 X 11/2 X $4.50, or 6 X $4.50, to get $27 (*Overtime Wages*). These figures ($180 + $27) give a total (*Gross Wages*) of $207.

Fed. Old Age (FICA) or social security is 6.70% of the gross wages. The table in Figure 7-25 only goes to $100. But, if you look at the multiples of $100, you will see that $200 is $13.40 at 6.70%. The gross wages are $207, so multiply the $7 X .067, and the result is .467. Add this to $13.40 for the first $200 of wages and you get a social security deduction of $13.87. Notice that this amount is entered in the column *Fed. Old Age.* If you wish, when figuring social security deductions, you can simply multiply the gross wages by .067 if a table is not available.

Federal income tax for Joseph Doe is $24.60. On the *Single Persons* table in Figure 7-23, weekly deductions for at least $200 but less than $210 under the

214

SINGLE Persons — WEEKLY Payroll Period
(For Wages Paid After June 1982 and Before July 1983)

And the wages are—		And the number of withholding allowances claimed is—										
At least	But less than	0	1	2	3	4	5	6	7	8	9	10 or more
		The amount of income tax to be withheld shall be—										
92	94	9.20	6.10	3.30	1.00	0	0	0	0	0	0	0
94	96	9.50	6.40	3.60	1.20	0	0	0	0	0	0	0
96	98	9.80	6.80	3.80	1.50	0	0	0	0	0	0	0
98	100	10.10	7.10	4.00	1.70	0	0	0	0	0	0	0
100	105	10.70	7.60	4.60	2.10	0	0	0	0	0	0	0
105	110	11.50	8.40	5.40	2.70	.40	0	0	0	0	0	0
110	115	12.30	9.20	6.20	3.30	1.00	0	0	0	0	0	0
115	120	13.10	10.00	7.00	3.90	1.60	0	0	0	0	0	0
120	125	13.90	10.80	7.80	4.70	2.20	0	0	0	0	0	0
125	130	14.70	11.60	8.60	5.50	2.80	.50	0	0	0	0	0
130	135	15.50	12.40	9.40	6.30	3.40	1.10	0	0	0	0	0
135	140	16.30	13.20	10.20	7.10	4.00	1.70	0	0	0	0	0
140	145	17.10	14.00	11.00	7.90	4.80	2.30	0	0	0	0	0
145	150	17.90	14.80	11.80	8.70	5.60	2.90	.60	0	0	0	0
150	160	19.10	16.00	13.00	9.90	6.80	3.80	1.50	0	0	0	0
160	170	20.70	17.60	14.60	11.50	8.40	5.30	2.70	.40	0	0	0
170	180	22.50	19.20	16.20	13.10	10.00	6.90	3.90	1.60	0	0	0
180	190	24.50	20.80	17.80	14.70	11.60	8.50	5.40	2.80	.50	0	0
190	200	26.50	22.60	19.40	16.30	13.20	10.10	7.00	4.00	1.70	0	0
200	210	28.50	24.60	21.00	17.90	14.80	11.70	8.60	5.60	2.90	.60	0
210	220	30.50	26.60	22.80	19.50	16.40	13.30	10.20	7.20	4.10	1.80	0
220	230	32.50	28.60	24.80	21.10	18.00	14.90	11.80	8.80	5.70	3.00	.70
230	240	34.50	30.60	26.80	22.90	19.60	16.50	13.40	10.40	7.30	4.20	1.90
240	250	36.60	32.60	28.80	24.90	21.20	18.10	15.00	12.00	8.90	5.80	3.10
250	260	39.00	34.60	30.80	26.90	23.10	19.70	16.60	13.60	10.50	7.40	4.30

MARRIED Persons — WEEKLY Payroll Period
(For Wages Paid After June 1982 and Before July 1983)

And the wages are—		And the number of withholding allowances claimed is—										
At least	But less than	0	1	2	3	4	5	6	7	8	9	10 or more
		The amount of income tax to be withheld shall be—										
130	135	11.00	8.10	5.70	3.40	1.10	0	0	0	0	0	0
135	140	11.80	8.70	6.30	4.00	1.70	0	0	0	0	0	0
140	145	12.60	9.50	6.90	4.60	2.30	0	0	0	0	0	0
145	150	13.40	10.30	7.50	5.20	2.90	.60	0	0	0	0	0
150	160	14.60	11.50	8.40	6.10	3.80	1.50	0	0	0	0	0
160	170	16.20	13.10	10.00	7.30	5.00	2.70	.40	0	0	0	0
170	180	17.80	14.70	11.60	8.60	6.20	3.90	1.60	0	0	0	0
180	190	19.40	16.30	13.20	10.20	7.40	5.10	2.80	.50	0	0	0
190	200	21.00	17.90	14.80	11.80	8.70	6.30	4.00	1.70	0	0	0
200	210	22.60	19.50	16.40	13.40	10.30	7.50	5.20	2.90	.60	0	0
210	220	24.20	21.10	18.00	15.00	11.90	8.80	6.40	4.10	1.80	0	0
220	230	25.80	22.70	19.60	16.60	13.50	10.40	7.60	5.30	3.00	.70	0
230	240	27.50	24.30	21.20	18.20	15.10	12.00	8.90	6.50	4.20	1.90	0
240	250	29.40	25.90	22.80	19.80	16.70	13.60	10.50	7.70	5.40	3.10	.80
250	260	31.30	27.70	24.40	21.40	18.30	15.20	12.10	9.10	6.60	4.30	2.00
260	270	33.20	29.60	26.00	23.00	19.90	16.80	13.70	10.70	7.80	5.50	3.20
270	280	35.10	31.50	27.80	24.60	21.50	18.40	15.30	12.30	9.20	6.70	4.40
280	290	37.00	33.40	29.70	26.20	23.10	20.00	16.90	13.90	10.80	7.90	5.60
290	300	38.90	35.30	31.60	28.00	24.70	21.60	18.50	15.50	12.40	9.30	6.80
300	310	40.80	37.20	33.50	29.90	26.30	23.20	20.10	17.10	14.00	10.90	8.00

FIGURE 7-23 Excerpts from federal tax tables

WEEKLY PAYROLL - Sample State Tax Table

WAGES		EXEMPTIONS CLAIMED										
At Least	Less Than	0	1	2	3	4	5	6	7	8	9	10 or more
		TAX TO BE WITHHELD										
38	39	.80	.40	.10								
39	40	.80	.40	.20								
40	41	.80	.50	.20								
41	42	.90	.50	.20								
42	43	.90	.50	.20								
43	44	.90	.50	.20								
44	45	1.00	.60	.30								
45	46	1.00	.60	.30								
46	47	1.00	.60	.30								
47	48	1.10	.70	.30	.10							
48	49	1.10	.70	.30	.10							
49	50	1.10	.70	.40	.10							
50	51	1.10	.80	.40	.10							
51	52	1.20	.80	.40	.10							
52	53	1.20	.80	.40	.20							
53	54	1.20	.90	.50	.20							
54	55	1.30	.90	.50	.20							
55	56	1.30	.90	.50	.20							
56	57	1.30	.90	.60	.30							
57	58	1.40	1.00	.60	.30							
58	59	1.40	1.00	.60	.30							
59	60	1.40	1.00	.70	.30	.10						
60	62	1.50	1.10	.70	.30	.10						
62	64	1.50	1.10	.80	.40	.10						
64	66	1.60	1.20	.80	.40	.20						
66	68	1.70	1.30	.90	.50	.20						
68	70	1.80	1.30	.90	.60	.30						
70	72	1.80	1.40	1.00	.60	.30						
72	74	1.90	1.50	1.10	.70	.30	.10					
74	76	2.00	1.50	1.10	.70	.40	.10					
76	78	2.10	1.60	1.20	.80	.40	.20					
78	80	2.20	1.70	1.30	.90	.50	.20					
80	82	2.30	1.70	1.30	.90	.50	.20					
82	84	2.30	1.80	1.40	1.00	.60	.30					
84	86	2.40	1.90	1.40	1.10	.70	.30	.10				
$ 86	$ 88	$ 2.50	$ 2.00	$ 1.50	$ 1.10	$ .70	$ .40	$ .10				
88	90	2.60	2.10	1.60	1.20	.80	.40	.10				
90	92	2.70	2.20	1.60	1.20	.90	.50	.20				
92	94	2.70	2.20	1.70	1.30	.90	.50	.20				
94	96	2.80	2.30	1.80	1.40	1.00	.60	.30				
96	98	2.90	2.40	1.90	1.40	1.00	.70	.30	.10			
98	100	3.00	2.50	2.00	1.50	1.10	.70	.40	.10			
100	105	3.10	2.60	2.10	1.60	1.20	.80	.40	.20			
105	110	3.40	2.80	2.30	1.80	1.40	1.00	.60	.30			
110	115	3.60	3.00	2.50	2.00	1.50	1.10	.70	.40	.10		
115	120	3.90	3.30	2.70	2.20	1.70	1.30	.90	.50	.20		
120	125	4.20	3.50	2.90	2.40	1.90	1.40	1.10	.70	.30	.10	
125	130	4.40	3.80	3.10	2.60	2.10	1.60	1.20	.80	.40	.20	
130	135	4.60	4.00	3.40	2.80	2.30	1.80	1.30	1.00	.60	.30	
135	140	4.90	4.20	3.60	3.00	2.50	2.00	1.50	1.10	.70	.30	.10
140	145	5.10	4.40	3.80	3.20	2.60	2.10	1.60	1.20	.80	.50	.20
145	150	5.30	4.70	4.00	3.40	2.80	2.30	1.80	1.40	1.00	.60	.30
150	160	5.70	5.00	4.30	3.70	3.10	2.60	2.10	1.50	1.20	.80	.40
160	170	6.20	5.50	4.80	4.10	3.50	2.90	2.40	1.90	1.40	1.00	.70
170	180	6.80	6.00	5.20	4.60	3.90	3.30	2.70	2.20	1.70	1.30	.90
180	190	7.30	6.50	5.70	5.00	4.40	3.70	3.10	2.60	2.10	1.60	1.20
190	200	7.90	7.00	6.30	5.50	4.80	4.20	3.50	2.90	2.40	1.90	1.40
200	210	8.50	7.60	6.80	6.00	5.30	4.60	4.00	3.30	2.80	2.30	1.70
210	220	9.10	8.20	7.30	6.50	5.80	5.00	4.40	3.70	3.10	2.60	2.10
220	230	9.70	8.80	7.90	7.10	6.30	5.50	4.80	4.20	3.50	3.00	2.40
230	240	10.30	9.40	8.50	7.60	6.80	6.10	5.30	4.60	4.00	3.30	2.80
240	250	11.00	10.00	9.10	8.20	7.30	6.60	5.80	5.10	4.40	3.80	3.10
250	260	11.70	10.70	9.70	8.80	7.90	7.10	6.30	5.60	4.90	4.20	3.60
260	270	12.50	11.50	10.50	9.50	8.60	7.70	6.90	6.20	5.40	4.70	4.10
270	280	13.30	12.30	11.30	10.30	9.40	8.50	7.60	6.80	6.00	5.20	4.60
280	290	14.20	13.10	12.10	11.10	10.10	9.20	8.30	7.40	6.60	5.90	5.10
290	300	15.20	14.00	12.90	11.90	10.90	9.90	9.00	8.10	7.20	6.50	5.70
300	310	16.10	14.90	13.80	12.70	11.70	10.70	9.70	8.80	7.90	7.10	6.30
310	320	17.00	15.90	14.70	13.50	12.50	11.50	10.50	9.50	8.60	7.70	6.90
320	330	18.00	16.80	15.60	14.50	13.30	12.30	11.30	10.30	9.40	8.50	7.60
330	340	19.10	17.80	16.50	15.40	14.20	13.10	12.10	11.10	10.10	9.20	8.30
340	350	20.10	18.80	17.50	16.30	15.20	14.00	12.90	11.90	10.90	9.90	9.00
350	360	21.10	19.80	18.50	17.30	16.10	14.90	13.80	12.70	11.70	10.70	9.70
360	370	22.30	20.90	19.60	18.30	17.00	15.90	14.70	13.50	12.50	11.50	10.50
370	380	23.40	22.00	20.60	19.30	18.00	16.80	15.60	14.50	13.30	12.30	11.30

FIGURE 7-24
Excerpt from typical state withholding tax tables

Social Security Employee Tax Table for 1982 and 1983—

6.70% employee tax deductions

Wages at least	But less than	Tax to be withheld
$53.66	$53.81	$3.60
53.81	53.96	3.61
53.96	54.11	3.62
54.11	54.26	3.63
54.26	54.41	3.64
54.41	54.56	3.65
54.56	54.71	3.66
54.71	54.86	3.67
54.86	55.00	3.68
55.00	55.15	3.69
55.15	55.30	3.70
55.30	55.45	3.71
55.45	55.60	3.72
55.60	55.75	3.73
55.75	55.90	3.74
55.90	56.05	3.75
56.05	56.20	3.76
56.20	56.35	3.77
56.35	56.50	3.78
56.50	56.65	3.79
56.65	56.80	3.80
56.80	56.95	3.81
56.95	57.09	3.82
57.09	57.24	3.83
57.24	57.39	3.84
57.39	57.54	3.85
57.54	57.69	3.86
57.69	57.84	3.87
57.84	57.99	3.88
57.99	58.14	3.89
58.14	58.29	3.90
58.29	58.44	3.91
58.44	58.59	3.92
58.59	58.74	3.93
58.74	58.89	3.94
58.89	59.03	3.95
59.03	59.18	3.96
59.18	59.33	3.97
59.33	59.48	3.98
59.48	59.63	3.99
59.63	59.78	4.00
59.78	59.93	4.01
59.93	60.08	4.02
60.08	60.23	4.03
60.23	60.38	4.04
60.38	60.53	4.05
60.53	60.68	4.06
60.68	60.83	4.07
60.83	60.98	4.08
60.98	61.12	4.09
61.12	61.27	4.10
61.27	61.42	4.11
61.42	61.57	4.12
61.57	61.72	4.13
61.72	61.87	4.14
61.87	62.02	4.15
62.02	62.17	4.16
62.17	62.32	4.17
62.32	62.47	4.18
62.47	62.62	4.19
62.62	62.77	4.20
62.77	62.92	4.21
62.92	63.06	4.22
63.06	63.21	4.23
63.21	63.36	4.24
63.36	63.51	4.25
63.51	63.66	4.26
63.66	63.81	4.27
63.81	63.96	4.28
63.96	64.11	4.29
64.11	64.26	4.30
64.26	64.41	4.31
64.41	64.56	4.32
64.56	64.71	4.33
64.71	64.86	4.34
64.86	65.00	4.35
65.00	65.15	4.36
65.15	65.30	4.37
65.30	65.45	4.38
65.45	65.60	4.39
65.60	65.75	4.40
65.75	65.90	4.41
65.90	66.05	4.42
66.05	66.20	4.43
66.20	66.35	4.44
66.35	66.50	4.45
66.50	66.65	4.46
66.65	66.80	4.47
66.80	66.95	4.48
66.95	67.09	4.49
67.09	67.24	4.50
67.24	67.39	4.51
67.39	67.54	4.52
67.54	67.69	4.53
67.69	67.84	4.54
67.84	67.99	4.55
67.99	68.14	4.56
68.14	68.29	4.57
68.29	68.44	4.58
68.44	68.59	4.59
68.59	68.74	4.60
68.74	68.89	4.61
68.89	69.03	4.62
69.03	69.18	4.63
69.18	69.33	4.64
69.33	69.48	4.65
69.48	69.63	4.66
69.63	69.78	4.67
69.78	69.93	4.68
69.93	70.08	4.69
70.08	70.23	4.70
70.23	70.38	4.71
70.38	70.53	4.72
70.53	70.68	4.73
70.68	70.83	4.74
70.83	70.98	4.75
70.98	71.12	4.76
71.12	71.27	4.77
71.27	71.42	4.78
71.42	71.57	4.79
71.57	71.72	4.80
71.72	71.87	4.81
71.87	72.02	4.82
72.02	72.17	4.83
72.17	72.32	4.84
72.32	72.47	4.85
72.47	72.62	4.86
72.62	72.77	4.87
72.77	72.92	4.88
72.92	73.06	4.89
73.06	73.21	4.90
73.21	73.36	4.91
73.36	73.51	4.92
73.51	73.66	4.93
73.66	73.81	4.94
73.81	73.96	4.95
73.96	74.11	4.96
74.11	74.26	4.97
74.26	74.41	4.98
74.41	74.56	4.99
74.56	74.71	5.00
74.71	74.86	5.01
74.86	75.00	5.02
75.00	75.15	5.03
75.15	75.30	5.04
75.30	75.45	5.05
75.45	75.60	5.06
75.60	75.75	5.07
75.75	75.90	5.08
75.90	76.05	5.09
76.05	76.20	5.10
76.20	76.35	5.11
76.35	76.50	5.12
76.50	76.65	5.13
76.65	76.80	5.14
76.80	76.95	5.15
76.95	77.09	5.16
77.09	77.24	5.17
77.24	77.39	5.18
77.39	77.54	5.19
77.54	77.69	5.20
77.69	77.84	5.21
77.84	77.99	5.22
77.99	78.14	5.23
78.14	78.29	5.24
78.29	78.44	5.25
78.44	78.59	5.26
78.59	78.74	5.27
78.74	78.89	5.28
78.89	79.03	5.29
79.03	79.18	5.30
79.18	79.33	5.31
79.33	79.48	5.32
79.48	79.63	5.33
79.63	79.78	5.34
79.78	79.93	5.35
79.93	80.08	5.36
80.08	80.23	5.37
80.23	80.38	5.38
80.38	80.53	5.39
80.53	80.68	5.40
80.68	80.83	5.41
80.83	80.98	5.42
80.98	81.12	5.43
81.12	81.27	5.44
81.27	81.42	5.45
81.42	81.57	5.46
81.57	81.72	5.47
81.72	81.87	5.48
81.87	82.02	5.49
82.02	82.17	5.50
82.17	82.32	5.51
82.32	82.47	5.52
82.47	82.62	5.53
82.62	82.77	5.54
82.77	82.92	5.55
82.92	83.06	5.56
83.06	83.21	5.57
83.21	83.36	5.58
83.36	83.51	5.59
83.51	83.66	5.60
83.66	83.81	5.61
83.81	83.96	5.62
83.96	84.11	5.63
84.11	84.26	5.64
84.26	84.41	5.65
84.41	84.56	5.66
84.56	84.71	5.67
84.71	84.86	5.68
84.86	85.00	5.69
85.00	85.15	5.70
85.15	85.30	5.71
85.30	85.45	5.72
85.45	85.60	5.73
85.60	85.75	5.74
85.75	85.90	5.75
85.90	86.05	5.76
86.05	86.20	5.77
86.20	86.35	5.78
86.35	86.50	5.79
86.50	86.65	5.80
86.65	86.80	5.81
86.80	86.95	5.82
86.95	87.09	5.83
87.09	87.24	5.84
87.24	87.39	5.85
87.39	87.54	5.86
87.54	87.69	5.87
87.69	87.84	5.88
87.84	87.99	5.89
87.99	88.14	5.90
88.14	88.29	5.91
88.29	88.44	5.92
88.44	88.59	5.93
88.59	88.74	5.94
88.74	88.89	5.95
88.89	89.03	5.96
89.03	89.18	5.97
89.18	89.33	5.98
89.33	89.48	5.99
89.48	89.63	6.00
89.63	89.78	6.01
89.78	89.93	6.02
89.93	90.08	6.03
90.08	90.23	6.04
90.23	90.38	6.05
90.38	90.53	6.06
90.53	90.68	6.07
90.68	90.83	6.08
90.83	90.98	6.09
90.98	91.12	6.10
91.12	91.27	6.11
91.27	91.42	6.12
91.42	91.57	6.13
91.57	91.72	6.14
91.72	91.87	6.15
91.87	92.02	6.16
92.02	92.17	6.17
92.17	92.32	6.18
92.32	92.47	6.19
92.47	92.62	6.20
92.62	92.77	6.21
92.77	92.92	6.22
92.92	93.06	6.23
93.06	93.21	6.24
93.21	93.36	6.25
93.36	93.51	6.26
93.51	93.66	6.27
93.66	93.81	6.28
93.81	93.96	6.29
93.96	94.11	6.30
94.11	94.26	6.31
94.26	94.41	6.32
94.41	94.56	6.33
94.56	94.71	6.34
94.71	94.86	6.35
94.86	95.00	6.36
95.00	95.15	6.37
95.15	95.30	6.38
95.30	95.45	6.39
95.45	95.60	6.40
95.60	95.75	6.41
95.75	95.90	6.42
95.90	96.05	6.43
96.05	96.20	6.44
96.20	96.35	6.45
96.35	96.50	6.46
96.50	96.65	6.47
96.65	96.80	6.48
96.80	96.95	6.49
96.95	97.09	6.50
97.09	97.24	6.51
97.24	97.39	6.52
97.39	97.54	6.53
97.54	97.69	6.54
97.69	97.84	6.55
97.84	97.99	6.56
97.99	98.14	6.57
98.14	98.29	6.58
98.29	98.44	6.59
98.44	98.59	6.60
98.59	98.74	6.61
98.74	98.89	6.62
98.89	99.03	6.63
99.03	99.18	6.64
99.18	99.33	6.65
99.33	99.48	6.66
99.48	99.63	6.67
99.63	99.78	6.68
99.78	99.93	6.69
99.93	100.00	6.70

The multiples of the withholding for FICA on $100 are

Wage	Tax to be withheld
$100	$6.70
200	13.40
300	20.10
400	26.80
500	33.50
600	40.20
700	46.90
800	53.60
900	60.30
1,000	67.00

FIGURE 7-25 Excerpt from social security tax tables

PAID TO John Smith
STATEMENT OF EARNINGS AND PAYMENTS FOR EMPLOYEE'S RECORD — DETACH BEFORE CASHING CHECK

PERIOD ENDING	HOURS	RATE	AMOUNT EARNED AT REGULAR RATE	OVERTIME AND OTHER	TOTAL EARNINGS	S.S.	Fed.	State	Sick	Save	TOTAL PAID TO YOUR ACCOUNTS	BALANCE OF EARNINGS
1-6	40	4.00	160	0	160.	10.72	7.30	4.10	5.-	1.-	28.12	131.88

PAY ROLL CHECK

Jan. 6 19 85

PAY TO THE ORDER OF John Smith $131.88

One Hundred Thirty One and 88/100 DOLLARS

THIS SAMPLE FORM PX PAYROLL CHECK ILLUSTRATES THE CHECK IN BLANK FORM BEFORE IMPRINTING. ANY OF THE PAYMENT CAPTIONS DESIRED MAY BE SPECIFIED FOR IMPRINTING IN THE SPACES PROVIDED.

SPECIMEN

Kirk Hunsicker

PAY ROLL CHECK

PAID TO Joeseph Doe
STATEMENT OF EARNINGS AND PAYMENTS FOR EMPLOYEE'S RECORD — DETACH BEFORE CASHING CHECK

PERIOD ENDING	HOURS	RATE	AMOUNT EARNED AT REGULAR RATE	OVERTIME AND OTHER	TOTAL EARNINGS	S.S.	Fed.	State	Sick	Save	TOTAL PAID TO YOUR ACCOUNTS	BALANCE OF EARNINGS
1-6	44	4.50	180.-	27.-	207.-	13.87	24.60	7.60	2.50	.50	49.07	157.93

PAY ROLL CHECK

Jan. 6 19 85

PAY TO THE ORDER OF Joeseph Doe $157.93

One Hundred Fifty Seven and 93/100 DOLLARS

THIS SAMPLE FORM PX PAYROLL CHECK ILLUSTRATES THE CHECK IN BLANK FORM BEFORE IMPRINTING. ANY OF THE PAYMENT CAPTIONS DESIRED MAY BE SPECIFIED FOR IMPRINTING IN THE SPACES PROVIDED.

SPECIMEN

Kirk Hunsicker

PAY ROLL CHECK

PAID TO Mary Donnelly
STATEMENT OF EARNINGS AND PAYMENTS FOR EMPLOYEE'S RECORD — DETACH BEFORE CASHING CHECK

PERIOD ENDING	HOURS	RATE	AMOUNT EARNED AT REGULAR RATE	OVERTIME AND OTHER	TOTAL EARNINGS	S.S.	Fed.	State	Sick	Save	TOTAL PAID TO YOUR ACCOUNTS	BALANCE OF EARNINGS
1-6	40	3.95	X	0	158.00	10.59	13.00	4.30	4.00	1.50	33.39	124.61

PAY ROLL CHECK

Jan. 6 19 85

PAY TO THE ORDER OF Mary Donnelly $124.61

One Hundred Twenty Four and 61/100 DOLLARS

THIS SAMPLE FORM PX PAYROLL CHECK ILLUSTRATES THE CHECK IN BLANK FORM BEFORE IMPRINTING. ANY OF THE PAYMENT CAPTIONS DESIRED MAY BE SPECIFIED FOR IMPRINTING IN THE SPACES PROVIDED.

SPECIMEN

Kirk Hunsicker

PAY ROLL CHECK

FIGURE 7-26
Payroll check forms

column for 1 dependent are shown as $24.60. This amount is entered in the column *Fed. With-hold Tax.* State tax is found in a similar manner using the table in Figure 7-24. With 1 exemption, the tax is $7.60. Sickness/disability and savings deductions are given in the first chart that was presented. The total deductions for Joseph Doe are $49.07. When this amount is subtracted from $207 (gross wages), net pay amounts to $157.93.

When you feel that you can complete this payroll register comfortably without any errors, you are probably qualified to do your own payrolls. The last step in this exercise is to complete individual payroll checks for any three employees using the blank payroll forms in Figure 7-26.

When employees are paid, they must be informed of the various deductions from their pay. There are several ways an employer can do this. One way is to work with your bank to design a check which has a place for each payroll deduction on a detachable stub. In this way, the employee has a permanent record of deductions and the tax which was withheld from the gross wages. If your employees are paid in cash, you should have them sign a pay receipt. You may want to make up small envelopes with the cash inside. Written on the outside of the envelope is the pay data for the individual. As previously mentioned, some states require written authorization to pay workers by check.

INVENTORY RECORDS

Inventory is all the merchandise you have on hand for sale. Since many businesses sell hundreds of different items, it is important to keep records of everything that is bought and sold. Bills, receipts, and invoices for purchases must be saved for at least one year. Taking an inventory includes counting all of the items on the shelves and in the stockroom, and making a record of all of these goods. Different businesses require different inventories. For example, a variety store at a summer resort would take an inventory at the end of the season. When many small items are sold, such as in a grocery store or hardware store, an inventory should be taken more often. Such items as automobiles or furniture are less difficult to keep track of because individual records of each unit sold are kept. This method of inventory is called *perpetual inventory,* and the number of units on hand is always easily found.

If a grocer ordered six cases of canned peas the previous month and found half of a case left at inventory time, more peas should be ordered. If, on the other hand, the grocer found five-and-a-half cases left, then the number of cases of canned peas must be allowed to reduce in number. In this case, the grocer would try to find out whether peas were no longer popular or if too many cases had been ordered. The cases of peas should be sold because the longer they are kept the less profit is made since capital and shelf space are tied up. To sell them quickly, the grocer might lower the price and take less margin. This is called *marking down* the items.

Inventory control is the setting up of balanced stocks of merchandise in relation to the demand for items and in the correct quantities, sizes, and colors. To stay in business, merchandise must be sold to your customers for more than you paid for it, and it must satisfy them.

A good system of inventory control keeps you informed of when and what to buy. It also serves as a barometer of consumer preference as to the type and quality of goods, Figure 7-27. Slow-moving items of inventory must be discovered so that you can determine if prices are too high or if the items are just not in demand. You should avoid stocking more than is necessary of any item. Inventory represents your major capital investment, but does not earn you a profit until the merchandise is sold. Stock depreciates in value, costs a certain amount to store, has limited shelf life (may spoil), or may go out of style.

The owner must compromise between the extremes of buying. When buying in very small amounts, quantity discounts are lost. When buying in very large amounts, more capital is tied up. Also, goods may become obsolete before they

FIGURE 7-27
Business owners should take complete and accurate inventory of all store merchandise at least once a year.

are sold, and storage space is greater than needed. It is impossible to stock every item for which customers might ask. You cannot afford to buy an item that does not sell at a profit within a reasonable time. Profit comes from the turnover of investment. You must therefore know which items sell.

Once a year a complete inventory must be taken. Some preparation is necessary before taking inventory. Items of merchandise should be tagged with the price and a counting slip should be placed with each type of merchandise. Slips of paper or codes can be placed on all stock items to show how old they are. When all stock is checked and written down on counting slips, the totals from the counting slips are transferred to the inventory listing sheets.

With these listing sheets, you know how much inventory is old or sells slowly. Adding the listing sheets by department results in inventory for specific departments. The totals of all departments give a total inventory for cost and retail pricing purposes.

Invite a small business owner to speak to the class on methods of taking inventory. The student might ask the following questions.

1. How often is physical inventory taken? Why?
2. What happens to goods that are out of style, obsolete, or overstocked?
3. What methods are used to take physical inventory? How are these methods suited to the merchandise stocked by the business?

Turnover

The term *turnover* describes the number of times an entire inventory is sold in a given period. To find the turnover, total sales is divided by the average retail value of inventory at any given moment.

Example: Beginning inventory (1st of month) .... $ 8,000
Closing inventory (last day of month)............. $ 6,000
$14,000

$14,000 ÷ 2 = $7,000 Average inventory per month
Estimated sales per month $5,000 X 12 months = $60,000 Estimated annual sales
Annual sales $60,000 ÷ $7,000 Average monthly inventory = 8.5714 Turnover
Turnover is about 8 1/2 times per year.

Want Slips

To carry as many items as your customers want, when they want them, you must record information that your salespeople obtain. To predict the demand for an item, you must know how many units were sold during a given period. Sales volume, seasonal fluctuations, and competition are all things your salespeople, if asked, can report. When a customer requests an item not in stock, the salesperson should try to sell a substitute item. If this fails, an order should be taken for the item. A list of these items should be made on a *want slip*. If enough want slips indicate a demand for the item, it should be added to the regular inventory. Items not requested should be dropped from the inventory when the current supply is sold.

Overstocks

It is important to recognize early the presence of overstocks on an item. No merchant, no matter how clever or experienced, can be right every time. It may be unwise for you to keep merchandise over until the next selling season. Capital needed to buy current items may be tied up and the stock would no longer be fresh. If you think it is necessary to reduce an item, you should reduce the selling price by taking a markdown.

Markdowns

If a price must be reduced, the reduction should be made while the item is still in its selling season, if possible. A small early price reduction prevents a larger loss later on. In the long run, to keep your stock moving will save you money.

Date Codes

In determining the age of merchandise, some type of receiving date code should be established so that salespeople will know which items are older. Most merchants use the FIFO (First in, First out) method of selling stock. With this method, the newest items should be placed behind the older items which are brought forward. Both manufacturers and retailers have systems for coding merchandise. You can develop your own. A simple system is to let any letter of the alphabet represent a month: for example, A for January, B for February, and so on. If weekly control is desired, the weeks can be numbered. The second week in February would be 2. For example, an item received during the second week of February would have a code of B-2. Date codes can be combined with price codes.

A popular code used is the Julian calendar which simply takes into account that there are either 365 or 366 (leap year) days in a year. Each day of the year, beginning with January 1, is assigned a number in consecutive order. By placing the last digit of the year, 2 for 1982, in front of the number of the day regardless of the month, a four-digit code results that can be easily translated into the month, day, and year. For example: 2029 is January 29, 1982, and 2116 is April 26, 1982 (31 + 28 + 31 + 26 = 116).

The Checklist

The checklist can be used for small items. A list of the basic stock carried in a store or shop is called a *catalog*. The lists are grouped according to shelves, counters, or departments. When needed, each counter or department is checked. In this way, every counter or department is checked easily when desired. The edges of shelves and counters can be labeled with descriptions of items stored in that place.

The Unit Control Board

Some items of stock may be kept up to date by the unit control method. This method provides perpetual inventory cards which are always current because entries are continually made. This is a very good method for a limited number of items, when volume is not too high. Separate cards for each item are made, Figure 7-28. Every time an item is ordered, received, sold, or marked down, a record is made on the card.

Item: Spark Plugs   **Cost:** 86¢   **Minimum**
Stock Number: ARF-42   **Retail Price:** $1.27   **Stock:** 100

Ordered			Received		Sold		On Hand	
Date	Quantity	Wholesaler	Date	Quantity	Date	Quantity	Date	Quantity
1-4-85	250	R.G. Wright	1-5	187	1-2-85	52	1-1-85	105
			1-6	63	1-3	48		
	X							

FIGURE 7-28 Sample card

Cost Codes

Sometimes it is desirable to show the cost or the wholesale price of an article. This is done using cost codes. The cost of each article is marked on the article or on a tag attached to it. The cost is written in a code so that it is hidden from the customer. A letter representing a number through ten (zero) is needed, and a one-word or two-word code phrase is used. In the phrase BLACKHORSE, for example, each letter stands for a number.

$$\begin{array}{ll} \text{B L A C K H O R S E} & \$27.98 = \text{LOSR} \\ \text{1 2 3 4 5 6 7 8 9 0} & \$\ 2.49 = \text{LCS} \end{array}$$

To become familiar with price codes, practice changing the following prices into codes as indicated:

Price	Code Word (Blackhorse) 1234567890	Code Word (Come and Buy) 1234 567 890	Code Word (Lemon Syrup) 12345 67890	Code Word (Money Talks) 12345 67890
Example				
$ 4.50	CKE	EAY	ONP	EYS
1. $ 7.95	OSK	OUA	YUO X	AKE X
2. 11.65	BBHO X	CCNA	LLSN	MMTY
3. 7.90	OSE	DUY	YUP	AKS
4. 2.35	LAK	OMA	EMO X	ONY
5. 18.00	BREE	CBYY	LRPP	MLSS
6. 27.50	LOKE	ODAY	EYOP X	OAES X
7. 117.72	BBOOL	CCDDO	LLYYE	MMAAO
8. .56	KH	AN	NS	YT

A Word about Forms

When you first open a sales type of business, simple sales slips with two copies are needed. These forms can be inexpensively made. Most stationery departments carry blank sales forms in pads. Using a custom-made rubber stamp for your company, each slip can be stamped with the business name. Carbon paper can then be cut and inserted in the sales pads. A number of business forms can be made at a nominal cost. When such forms are simply but intelligently designed, the task of record keeping becomes much easier.

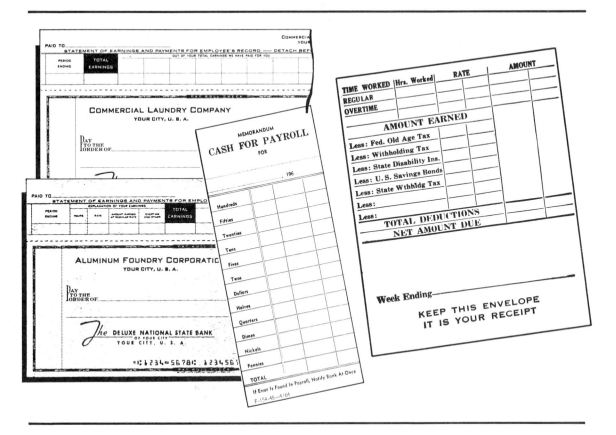

FIGURE 7-29 Commonly used business forms

The types of business forms you will need are determined by the kind of business, size, number of employees, and other factors. Whatever forms you choose, they are useful only when prepared accurately and consistently. Most instant copy centers have catalogs of business forms which can be copied inexpensively with your company's name, address, and phone number appearing at the top of the form. Some samples are shown in Figure 7-29.

BUSINESS MANUAL ASSIGNMENT

A great deal of paper work is involved with operating a business of your own. The following is a list of some of the forms you may need in your business. Go through the list and pick out the forms which you think you will need and make some samples. Include at least five samples in your manual, with a short explanation for each one.

Business Forms

application form
employee personnel record
payroll data card
simple arithmetic test
simple typing test
sample bookkeeping test
rating sheet (for evaluating employees)
suggestion blank (for employee suggestions)
interviewing guide
rating sheet (for interviews)
time card
payroll record (record of earnings)
employee infraction (warning)
employee infraction (action)
sales slip
invoice
billhead
statement
credit memo

want slip
interoffice memo
purchase order
company check
receipt
ledger card
cash refund slip
supply requisition
request for credit memo
packing slip
inventory check sheet
agenda (for a meeting)
purchase requisition
petty cash slip
receiving slip
layaway ticket
work order
payroll worksheet

Samples of these forms are easily obtained from local businesses, from your own family's mail, and from print shops. Adapt an existing form or redesign it, and put your company's name at the top. You can make up copies of forms, not previously listed, that you think you might need in your business.

Also make a sample of the following for your business:

- A balance sheet
- An operating statement

TERMS TO KNOW

balance sheet
bank deposit slip
blank check
cash book
W-4 form
W-2 form
performance review sheets
rating sheets
personnel data cards

cash refund slip
cash receipt
delivery ticket
layaway ticket
credit sales
employee discount slip
inventory counting forms
inventory ticket
job application

ledger account
ledger card
operations statement
payroll register
service record
service work orders
receiving tickets
suggestion blanks
time cards

want slips	invoice	packing slip
purchase orders	statement	shipping order
supply requisition	bill of lading	petty cash slip

UNIT QUIZ

In each of the following, select the word or phrase that best completes the statement or answers the question.

1. When business owners pay their bills early, they are usually entitled to a
   a. dividend.
   b. profit.
   c. cash discount.
   d. trade discount.

2. When business owners purchase large quantities of goods from a seller, they are usually entitled to a
   a. trade discount.
   b. cash discount.
   c. markdown.
   d. dividend.

3. The difference between the cost of an article and its selling price is
   a. profit.
   b. markup.
   c. expense.
   d. margin.

4. The form used to record daily transactions is called
   a. a ledger.
   b. a statement of operations.
   c. a balance sheet.
   d. a journal.

5. FICA is a payroll withholding deduction for which one of the following?
   a. Federal tax
   b. Social security
   c. State tax
   d. Unemployment insurance

6. The purpose of the balance sheet is
   a. to give a clear financial picture of the business.
   b. to avoid paying taxes.
   c. to attract investors.
   d. to meet federal regulations.

7. An amount of money or a percentage that is cut from the original selling price of an article is referred to as
   a. markup.
   b. markdown.
   c. profit.
   d. margin.

8. Which one of the following terms is used to refer to merchandise that is kept on hand for sale?
   a. Fixed assets
   b. Stock
   c. Supplies
   d. Inventory

9. An employee is normally entitled to overtime pay for work in excess of
   a. 35 hours in one week.   c. 40 hours in one week.
   b. 37 1/2 hours in one week.   d. 44 hours in one week.

10. Assessments for unemployment insurance are levied on an employer based on the
    a. total payroll.   c. layoff history.
    b. number of employees.   d. employee turnover.

11. Worker's compensation is paid for by
    a. the employer.   c. the employer and the employee.
    b. the employee.   d. the federal government.

12. The federal minimum wage applies to most employees except
    a. those not engaged in interstate commerce.
    b. females.
    c. minorities.
    d. part-time employees.

13. Which one of the following forms describes the number of withholding exemptions claimed by an employee?
    a. Form 941   c. W-3 form
    b. W-2 form   d. W-4 form

14. The total earnings due an employee who is paid hourly wages is called
    a. net wages.   c. take-home pay.
    b. gross wages.   d. overtime pay.

15. An employee who punches in at 8:22 AM for the 8 o'clock shift would be paid for how many minutes of that hour?
    a. 30 minutes   c. 60 minutes
    b. 15 minutes   d. 45 minutes

16. A cost code is used to
    a. simplify records.
    b. show the date of purchase of an article.
    c. conceal the wholesale cost of the article.
    d. take a markdown.

17. The Julian calendar is used in business to show
    a. the age of the merchandise.
    b. the shipping date.
    c. the date merchandise was sold.
    d. the last date merchandise can be sold.

18. The number of times an inventory is sold in a given period is referred to as
    a. perpetual inventory.   c. turnover.
    b. overstock.   d. sales.

19. A rating sheet is used for which one of the following?
    a. To figure tax rates for a business
    b. To evaluate employee performance
    c. To determine the prices for goods being sold
    d. To take an inventory

20. Which one of the following records in chronological order all receipts and payments of money for a business?
    a. Cash book   c. Balance sheet
    b. Ledger   d. Operations statement

21. When considering an applicant for a job, you should
    a. interview the applicant.   c. check the applicant's references.
    b. test the applicant.   d. all of these.

22. A margin percent of 37 1/2% is equivalent to a cost markup of
    a. 40%   c. 60%
    b. 50%   d. 70%

23. Which one of the following is the net amount due on an invoice of $100 discounted at 20% and 10%?
    a. $80   c. $88
    b. $72   d. $70

24. An invoice shipped on terms of 2/10, n/30 on March 27 would be due in full on or after
    a. April 26.   c. April 28.
    b. April 27.   d. April 6.

25. Which one of the following is not a financial record?
    a. Operations statement c. Balance sheet
    b. Dosier   d. Time card

UNIT 8

LAW AND INSURANCE

OBJECTIVES

After studying this unit, you will be able to

- Determine the different types of insurance you will need for your business.
- List and explain the various kinds of commercial paper.
- Write out each kind of check endorsement and explain how each is used.
- Discuss the conditions of a contract which make it legal.
- List the terms that may be found in a lease.
- Determine when you should consult a lawyer.
- Define the Terms to Know.

FIGURE 8-1
It is always wise to obtain the service of a good lawyer if you need one.

Understanding business law takes many years. No one expects a small business owner to get a law degree or to have a complete understanding of legal concepts related to business ownership and operation. Because you will deal with numerous people, products and companies, you should be aware of your rights and responsibilities. You are a creditor and a debtor, and a user of negotiable instruments, checks, notes, and bills of exchange. You will function as an employer, a taxpayer, a user of real property, and a shipper and receiver of transported goods. Each of these roles is accompanied by certain legal and ethical responsibilities.

You should be familiar with some business law and current insurance practices to protect your enterprise and the people you serve. When there is a question of legality or wisdom of a specific act, you should have a base on which to make a judgment or seek competent advice. Common sense and caution are essential in business. A general understanding of business law and insurance go hand in hand with good business management.

CONTRACTS

Agreements which a business owner makes in the course of carrying on a business may be called contracts. A *contract* is a legal agreement between two or more parties in which each has rights and obligations. Contracts may be enforced by the courts if they meet certain requirements. Suppose that a car dealer made an agreement to sell you an automobile for $10,000. You have the right to possess and use the car and an obligation to pay for it. So that both parties know exactly what is agreed upon, there should be written copies. A contract must have the following characteristics to be legal: mutual agreement, consideration, form, competency, and legal subject matter.

Owners and workers enter into contracts every day. When merchandise is bought and sold, buyers and sellers enter into contracts. Business owners are involved with contracts when merchandise is sold, employees are hired, insurance is purchased, money is put in the bank, and when property is rented, bought, or sold. When agreements are simple and the amount of money involved is small, business persons often handle these matters themselves. When the agreement is more complicated or involves more money, the parties usually hire a lawyer.

Since contracts can be enforced by law, it is important that people understand them. When an individual fails to honor a contract, the other parties to the contract can legally require that the contract be fulfilled or a satisfactory remedy be provided. Consider the following situations.

Customers who shop at a furniture store have asked for chairs upholstered in nylon fabrics. The proprietor purchased ten chairs for $150 each from a manufacturer who said that the fabric was 100% nylon. After the chairs were delivered, the proprietor discovered that the fabric contained only 20% nylon. The proprietor refused to pay the manufacturer for the chairs. The manufacturer insisted that the fabric was just fine according to the contract and that the chairs must be paid for. Was there a valid contract? Explain what could be done.

A dealer quoted a price to a customer of $200 for an antique table. The customer said she would think about it. Another customer offered $250 for the table and the dealer sold it. The first customer came back to buy the table. When she found that it had been sold, she claimed that the dealer had an obligation to her and had no right to sell the table to someone else. She said that unless the table was delivered to her promptly, a law suit would be filed against the dealer. Was there a valid contract? Explain what might happen.

The courts decide questions such as these. Their decisions are based on the following five elements essential to every legal contract. Without these elements, the courts will not enforce contracts.

Mutual Agreement. For an agreement to be mutual, there must be a clear, definite, and serious offer and an unqualified acceptance. For example, in the previously mentioned case the customer who decided that she wanted the antique table for $200 could not show that there was a contract. She made no unqualified acceptance when the dealer made the offer. "Thinking about it" does not constitute acceptance. However, if she had put down a deposit, then matters would have been different.

If there is to be mutual agreement, there is no need for a true meeting of the minds. This means that the parties involved need not be thinking of the same thing. Outward manifestations legally mean more than secret intentions. If a merchant offers to sell some goods for $55 and a customer accepts the offer, it does not really matter that the merchant intended to say $75. There is a binding contract at $55 if the party can prove the offer was made and accepted. This can be done by producing witnesses and documents. The subject matter of a contract must be stated in definite terms. If an individual owns two cars of the same type and offers to sell one of them to a customer who accepts, a valid contract does not exist unless it can be proved that both parties were thinking of the same car. Proving such situations by oral testimony alone is difficult. This is why contracts should be written.

Consideration. Parties to a contract must receive something of value and give something of value in return. This something of value is called *consideration.* The consideration may be cash, goods or a service, or it may even be a particular action.

If a man offers to give a friend a car and two days later changes his mind, he cannot legally be forced to give up the car. The contract cannot be enforced because there was no consideration at the time of the original offer. The friend did not give, or agree to give, anything of value in exchange for the car. If the friend had given the man $1 and had obtained a receipt for it, then the offer could be enforced.

Form. A contract is made if there is an offer and acceptance, consideration, competent parties, and legal subject matter. The contract may be written or oral. However, the law in various states has modified this general rule. In New York State, a contract for the sale of goods worth $50 or more must be shown by a written agreement, by partial payment, or by partial acceptance of the goods for it to be legally enforceable. A contract for the sale or transfer of land or real property must be in writing. Contracts which take more than one year to perform usually must be in writing. This includes leases of more than one year.

Competency and Legality. A *competent party* is one who has the legal capacity to enter into a contract. A person must be of legal age and sane in order to be considered competent.

In order for a contract to be enforceable, it must be a legal agreement. Gambling debts cannot be collected through the courts because gambling is illegal in most states. If a person makes a worker promise not to join a union while working for a particular company, the person cannot legally force the worker to obey the agreement. Such contracts infringe on the workers' right not to join the union. A contract is not enforceable if the subject of the agreement is not, in itself, legal, or infringes on one's civil rights.

REAL PROPERTY

The difference between real property and personal property is based on the legal action needed to recover property from someone who has taken it from the owner. If the property can be compensated for by money, it is *personal property.* If the property cannot be compensated for by money, it is considered *real property.* For example, a car can be bought for a certain sum (personal property), but land cannot be replaced (real property).

Real property includes the land and everything on it, often referred to as *appurtenances.* When an individual owns a farm, the real property includes the land, the crops growing on the land, the farmhouse and outbuildings, and anything attached to the farmhouse, outbuildings, or the land. Personal property is everything else, usually movable, which is owned. You should understand the distinction between real property and personal property. Many disputes between landlords and tenants involve this distinction.

Advantages and Disadvantages of Owning Property

One advantage of buying property is that the original investment may increase (appreciate) with time. Suppose that an individual purchases property worth $60,000. After paying for the property, the individual will have gained on the original $60,000. *Appreciation* is this increase in value of property. Other advantages of owning property are satisfaction and freedom. The property may be used and enjoyed as long as it is owned. As long as you own property, you are free to manage it in any manner that you wish not contrary to law.

Disadvantages of owning business property also exist. More capital may be needed to start the business with purchased property than if a building was rented. However, when money is invested in a business, there is always a risk of loss. If you purchase a building for $60,000 and the business fails, the $60,000 could be lost. To get back an investment in real property, you would need to operate the business for a long time. It may also be difficult to relocate a business if you own the property. If a store is located in the center of town, for example, and most of your customers move to the suburbs, the business could lose money if you tried to sell the property to permit a move.

When purchasing property for your business, you may select the property yourself or go through a real estate broker. Sometimes it is necessary to hire a lawyer to make sure the title to the property is clear.

Owning Real Property

If you have found that the advantages to owning property outweigh the disadvantages for your type of business, go ahead and purchase property. Whether you acquire property on your own or with the advice of a broker, the services of a lawyer should be obtained.

The Sales Contract. The first step is to make an agreement with the person selling the property. According to law, this contract of sale must be in writing and must be signed by all parties involved. The *sales contract* for real property should include a description of the property, the purchase price, terms of payment including any unpaid debts, and the method of financing. The buyer should be advised of all covenants, easements, restrictions, or liens against the property. Liens include, for example, water charges, back taxes, and insurance payments. Any parts of the property that can be removed or any restraint of trade clauses should be fully explained.

Before the sale is closed, the buyer usually gives the seller a deposit as evidence of intention to buy. Whether this transaction is totally enforceable as a sales contract depends upon the wording of the receipt given for the deposit. The receipt may contain phrases such as "subject to the execution of sales contract," "subject to approval by owners," or "by owner's attorney." These phrases require the return of the deposit in the event the owner decides not to sell the property to the buyer.

The Title Search. Before purchasing property, a survey of the land should be made. This shows the location of the exact boundaries of the property. A title search should also be conducted. A *title search* provides the continuous history of ownership of the property. The search is important to assure the buyer that there are no liens against the property. A lawyer or a title abstract company can accomplish the search to make sure there is a clear title.

Deeds. The buyer of real property should obtain a deed from the *grantor* (present holder of the title) who has an obligation to prove the validity of title. The following are the three common types of deeds.

- Quit-claim deed. This deed surrenders to the buyer (grantee) the real property of the grantor.
- Bargain-and-sale deed. This deed contains a description of the real property being transferred. It usually includes a clause stating that the grantor has done nothing to impair the title to this property. This clause is called a *covenant against the grantor.*
- Full-covenant-and-warranty deed. With this deed, the grantor affirms that the title is good and that there are no defects in it.

The grantor of a quit-claim deed or a bargain-and-sale deed without covenant against grantor does not assume responsibility for the validity of the title. The grantor of a bargain-and-sale deed with covenant against grantor is responsible only for holding of the title. The grantor of a full-covenant-and-warranty deed is responsible for the actions of all past title holders of the property. The bargain-and-sale deed is the most common type. However, if it is possible, a full-covenant-and-warranty deed is preferred.

All documents pertaining to the sale of the property (contract, deed, title policy, mortgage) should describe the property. The description should be worded the same in each document. The description may be obtained from the present owner's deed or from a title search.

Prior to making arrangements for the purchase of real property, the prospective buyer should carefully examine the owner's survey. The survey shows whether there are encroachments upon the property from adjoining property. The survey also shows whether driveways, fences, or walls are shared with adjoining properties.

The Closing. All persons concerned with the sale meet to close the sale. These people include the seller, buyer, attorneys, bank representative if the property is to be mortgaged, and attorney for the insurance company if the title is to be insured. Everyone examines each document carefully. Insurance policies are transferred to the buyer. Any adjustments are brought up to date. Documents settling any defects found on the title are inspected by the attorney representing the title insurance company. Tax stamps are affixed to the deed and mortgage. The purchase price is paid in cash or by certified or bank check. If payment is made by check, it is wise to make the check payable to the buyer and endorsed to the seller. The check can then be deposited to the buyer's account if the closing should be delayed. The check must be endorsed by the seller to make a record of receipt of payment.

The last step is to record the deed in the county clerk's office of the county in which the property is located. With this final act, the purchaser is now the owner of the property and has all of the rights and responsibilities that go with it.

THE LEASE

Because of the greater capital required to own real property, most small business owners start out by renting or leasing business space. When an owner decides to rent, an agreement is made with the landlord specifying the amount of rent to be paid and other conditions. The conditions agreed upon, when put into written form and signed by both tenant and landlord, make up the lease.

A *lease* is a contract to rent land and/or buildings for a specified time for a consideration. A lease is usually written and states the tenants' rights and obligations. A written lease is common business practice. When the term is for more than one year, it is required to be in writing in most states.

Tenants, of course, try to keep the rent as low as possible and should not agree to pay more than they think the income from the business will permit. The lease should contain the following information:

- The names of the parties to the lease
- The duration of the agreement
- A complete description of the property

- All repairs, painting, decorating, and altering which the landlord agrees to do .
- The amount of rent to be paid, and the date or day of the month on which it is due
- Provisions for late penalties, security, or deposits

Tenants are not legally responsible for paying rent until it is due. When tenants move out before their leases expire, they must pay rent to the end of the lease, if an agreement to break the lease cannot be arranged. The landlord can obtain a judgment against the tenant for payment of rent.

The lease usually states the term of the tenancy in months or years. However, sometimes in unwritten agreements nothing is said about the length of time the property is to be rented to the tenant. This type of tenancy is known as *tenancy at will.* When the landlord wants the tenant to move, 30 days written notice must be given. The tenant, on the other hand, does not have to give the landlord any notice. If the lease is for a term of one year or more and the tenant stays longer than the time specified, then the landlord may consider the tenancy to be continued for another year on the same terms.

The length of the lease is an important consideration. You may not want a long lease, especially if your business is not successful. On the other hand, an owner does not want an increase in rent if the business does well. It may be desirable to have a short-term lease with the option of renewing at the same rent. This is known as an *optional term lease.*

Leases may be classified according to the manner in which rent is paid. The *term lease* is a popular type of lease. It states the amount of rent to be paid for a specified time. Other types give the landlord a percentage of business income instead of a rent. This is called a *percentage lease.* Sometimes the rental agreement is a combination of the term lease and the percentage lease. With this agreement, the landlord receives a fixed rent in addition to a percentage of business income.

FORMS OF CASH

Business law is concerned with the everyday transfer of cash. Most business transactions are not made in actual cash, but in various forms of "business paper" called drafts. A *draft* is a signed order in writing, directing payment of an amount of money, on demand or at a future time, to the bearer or to the order of a specified person. Drafts serve as substitutes for money and have certain advantages. It is important that you know the types of drafts commonly used in business and the laws which govern them.

Checks

The most common type of draft is a check. A *check* is an order drawn against a deposit of funds in a bank. The person who writes the check is known as the *drawer.* The person to whom the check is payable is known as the *payee.* The bank on which the check is drawn is known as the *drawee.* The check is payable on demand and should be presented or deposited within a reasonable period of time after it has been drawn.

When writing a check, it is important to protect against alteration. Any blank spaces should be filled in with a wavy line to prevent the insertion of words or numbers. Words and figures should be written close to the dollar sign to prevent the amount from being raised. When possible, you should use a check writer.

Checks should be used to pay bills and can serve as proof of payment. They are more convenient and safer than cash. Checks may be sent through the mail since special endorsements make them safer than money.

NEGOTIABLE INSTRUMENTS

In early times, business people transferred gold and silver to complete business transactions or traded items. This was called *bartering.* As more business was done, this method of transacting business became burdensome. Eventually, various substitutes for money such as salt, pebbles, and shells, took the place of actual gold and silver. Today, almost all business transactions are completed by using commercial paper. These are called *negotiable instruments* because they can be negotiated (transferred) to another person just as though they were money. Any contract in writing that is transferable by endorsement or delivery to a third party is a negotiable instrument. Negotiable instruments can be classified as either *drafts* or *promissory notes.*

Endorsements

If a customer owes a business $50 and sends the proprietor a check, could that check then be transferred to a wholesaler to whom the business also owed $50? The answer is yes. In order to transfer the check to the wholesaler, it can be endorsed. The proprietor's name is signed on the back of the check. Most checks are endorsed this way. However, signing a check on the back is not the only way to transfer it and this may be the most risky method. In business, checks and cash should be deposited in the bank whenever possible to reduce theft and to protect against fraud and forgery. There are five different kinds of endorsements, Figure 8-2.

Endorsement in Blank. This is the type of endorsement just mentioned which involves a signature on the back of a check. If the check is lost after it has been endorsed, it may be cashed by anyone who happens to find it.

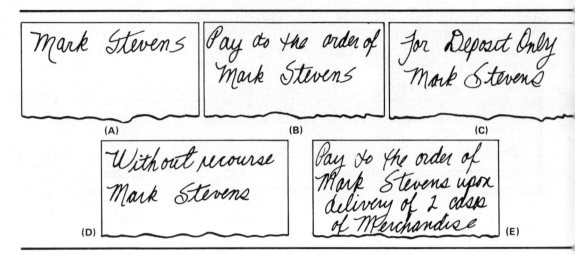

FIGURE 8-2 Five kinds of endorsement: (A) endorsement in blank, (B) special endorsement, (C) restrictive endorsement (D) qualified endorsement, and (E) conditional endorsement

Special Endorsement. With this type of endorsement, "pay to the order of _____" is written on the back of the check. Only this person may cash the check. A check with a special endorsement is safely sent through the mails since only the person to whom it is endorsed may use it.

Restrictive Endorsement. Often, people wish to deposit checks by mailing them to the bank. In such cases, "for deposit only" should be written on the back of the check. The check can only be deposited in the holder's account and cannot be transferred to someone else.

Qualified endorsement. When an individual wishes to transfer a check to a third party but does not want to be liable if the first party has insufficient funds to cover the check, the words "without recourse" should be written before signing the back.

Conditional Endorsement. In some instances, the person writing the check does not want payment to be made until the person receiving the check has completed that for which he or she is being paid. In this case, the person issuing the check writes "Pay to the order of _____ upon delivery of _____ merchandise" on the back of the check.

Cashing Checks

It is difficult to be strict about check cashing policies since customers and your own employees will put pressure on you to be lenient for certain people. You

FIGURE 8-3
For the good of their businesses, proprietors must establish standard check cashing procedures.

can buy insurance to protect yourself, but it is expensive and does not cover all situations. Insurance is available with various amounts of deductible coverage. That is, the first $100 or $200 of loss in bad checks in any period is not covered by the insurance. For this reason, insurance protection is questionable unless you have very big losses. If you do have big losses, it would be wise to examine the reasons for this situation.

If customers are required to show two forms of identification you are safer, since it is harder to steal two items of identification along with checks. Be careful about social security and other government checks as they can be stolen easily. Cash these checks only for people you know. If you do not take out-of-town checks your problems in seeking recourse will be considerably easier if you have to deal only with local authorities.

Some of your best customers will make mistakes in their checkbooks. It happens to many people. To fail to make an exception for one of these customers will most certainly cost you any further business. Knowing when to make an exception takes experience, good judgment, and common sense. A year or more handling cash and cashing checks for an employer is almost a requirement for owning your own business. If you have never done this, you would be well advised to get this experience. You would be amazed by the sometimes careless manner in which customers and clerks handle checks and cash and commercial paper.

In spite of the laws that govern negotiable instruments, you will come in contact with bad paper consisting of fraudulent, forged or stolen checks, overdrafts, checks returned for insufficient funds, and counterfeit money. For this reason, you should be careful who you let cash checks for customers in your store or shop. All personnel who you trust to do this must be bonded and thoroughly trained to handle the responsibility. They must know and strictly follow your policies.

If you are careful, you can reduce the amount of bad paper you hold at any one time. It is not uncommon, however, for the average merchant to be carrying several hundred dollars of returned items. You may be able to collect some of the bad paper by resorting to the courts and prosecuting for criminal action.

CASHING CHECKS

Do . . . require two forms of identification.
use photo identification equipment.
require state driver's license if possible.
require good photo identification.
compare signatures on identification with that on check.
avoid cashing personal checks.
avoid cashing two-party checks.
limit the amount of check to the amount of purchase.
take a credit card for sales in preference to a personal check.
require check to be presented at office — do not pay from register.
check name against bad check file.
keep a current list of bad check passers, and use it.

Do not . . . cash two-party checks (checks that are not made out to you or your business).
cash out-of-town checks.
cash checks made out to *cash*.
cash checks drawn on anyone you do not know.
let employees cash checks.
cash checks from the register.
cash checks for strangers.
cash checks for more than the purchase.

Very strict check cashing policies will cause customers to go elsewhere. You must use good judgment so that potentially good customers are not lost. Most good customers are embarrassed about writing a bad check and usually make good on the check. Business owners want to allow customers the time to make good on bad checks before they write them off as bad debts. Doing this for a large number of customers, however, can easily result in losses of several hundred dollars a month.

SALES LAW

The Sales Contract

Business owners enter into agreements to buy and sell goods. These agreements are called sales contracts. A *sales contract* is an agreement to transfer title (ownership) to personal property from one person to another for a consideration. The transfer of title is between the seller and the buyer.

Suppose a wholesaler agrees to sell the owner of a radio and television shop six radios at $30 per radio. The wholesaler has agreed to transfer title of the radios to the shop owner. In return, the shop owner has agreed to give the wholesaler consideration of $180 ($30 X 6 radios).

Because the sale of goods is so common in the business world, each state has its own laws on this subject. For example, each state has a law (*statute of frauds*) stating that for a sales contract over a certain amount to be enforceable, it must be in writing, partial payment must be made, or part of the merchandise must be delivered. Many states have set the amount at $500, but because this amount varies from state to state, you should check the sales laws of the state in which you live.

The passing of title depends on the agreement between the seller and the buyer. The general rule is that title passes when the agreement has been carried out.

Why is it important to know when title to goods passes? If the goods are damaged or destroyed, the person having title to the goods usually bears the loss. Suppose after purchasing the radios (mentioned earlier) the shop owner leaves all but one of them at the wholesaler's warehouse. If the warehouse burns down, who must legally bear the loss for the radios? Whoever has title to the radios at the time of the fire takes the loss. In this case, the shop owner would suffer the loss, since the radios became the shop owner's possession when partial delivery was accepted.

The law states that only the owner, or someone authorized by the owner, has the right to pass title to personal property. It would be impossible for the owner of a large department store to serve all of the customers, so salespeople are hired and given permission to sell and to pass title to the customer.

An *agent* is a person who is given the authority to enter into a sales contract as a representative for someone else (the *principal*). Agents were discussed in Unit

2 in connection with distribution businesses. An example of an agent is an insurance company representative who is given authority by the insurance company (the principal) to sell insurance contracts.

As a business owner you will be continually involved with credit, both as a user (borrower) and as an extender (creditor) of credit to your customers. You may find that selling on credit will bring in many new customers. These credit customers may buy more than cash customers. When you make up an account for a credit customer who will presumably pay you in the future, you are creating what is called an *account receivable.* Accounts receivable make up the bulk of the assets of many credit businesses. They are deferred sales, in the sense that you will get paid eventually, but at that moment the customer owes you, and you have delivered the merchandise. More operating capital is needed in a credit business, but in some fields it is normally the custom to grant credit, and your competitors grant credit, so must you. Appliance stores, clothing stores, and department stores commonly have charge accounts. All credit businesses have collection problems, but most customers can and do pay faithfully and on time. Experience has shown, however, that some customers cannot or will not pay. The *conditional sales contract* is your protection against this type of customer.

Installment Selling

Installment selling is a method of selling in which the customer makes a small deposit or down payment on specific merchandise. The balance is then financed, usually by a bank, for payment in regular monthly (usually) amounts over a specified period of time. An *installment contract* is legally binding even if it is not filed in the county clerk's office. If possible, the contract should be filed. Filing protects you, the seller, from persons who do not know about the sale, should the purchaser try to dispose of unpaid goods.

For example, Mrs. Evans purchased a sofa from your furniture store on an installment plan. She failed to make payments and you then learned that she had moved out of town. A neighbor told you that Mrs. Evans had sold the sofa to Mrs. Johnson before she left town. When you called Mrs. Johnson, she had the sofa. If the conditional sales contract was properly recorded, you can repossess the sofa, and there is nothing that Mrs. Johnson can do. Mrs. Johnson can, of course, try to locate Mrs. Evans, but since Mrs. Evans did not have clear title to the sofa, she could not sell the title to anyone else. The sofa, as far as Mrs. Johnson was concerned, was the same as stolen goods. The title (ownership) does not pass on a conditional sales from seller to buyer until the last payment has been made. That is why the word *conditional* is used, that is, on the condition it is paid for.

Whenever an item is sold under the installment plan, the customer must sign a conditional sales contract. The seller allows the customer the use of the merchandise on the condition that the payments will be paid on time. If the buyer does not meet the conditions of the contract, the seller has the right to *repossess* (take back) the merchandise and resell it to satisfy the remainder of the debt.

Warranties

Any business owner who sells merchandise should be familiar with warranties. A *warranty* is a promise or guarantee that a certain fact or statement about an article is true or correct. This statement, if relied on by the buyer, must be fact and not opinion. For example, an automobile salesperson who sells you a used car makes the statement that the car has been driven only 15,000 miles. If this statement happens to be untrue, that the speedometer was tampered with, then the customer has a legal claim against the seller. The sales clerk also stated that the car is "the best looking sports car in town." This is the salesperson's opinion, however, and it has no legal significance as a warranty.

A warranty is either expressed (spoken or written) or implied (understood). *Expressed warranties* are statements made by the seller which the buyer relies on when making a purchase. These are statements of fact. If later they are proved to be false, the seller has committed a *breach of warranty* for which the buyer can claim damages. *Implied warranties* are not statements, but are true facts which are understood to apply in each case as a result of fair and established business practice. It is not necessary for the seller to tell the buyer that he or she owns the goods and has a *right to sell* the merchandise. It is a store, and goods obviously are for sale. Customers have the right to assume (rely) proper title exists. The seller has the right to sell the property. The buyer can expect because of an implied warranty of title that the goods can be legally sold. If the seller does not legally own the property, as in the case of Mrs. Evans and Mrs. Johnson, the buyer can sue for breach of an implied warranty of good title.

The *property is fit for use* is another implied warranty. Both the buyer and the seller must agree on the purpose for which the property will be used. If they do agree, but the item is not or cannot be used, then the seller must replace the item or return the purchase price. For example, Mrs. Jones comes into your hardware store and requests a screwdriver to install some screws. She does not specify the type of screw and you sell her a standard screwdriver. She comes back later and says the screwdriver will not fit. It turns out that the screws are Phillips type screws. Since the regular screwdriver which you sold her will not fit a Phillips head screw, you must either replace the item (give her a Phillips screwdriver) or refund her money.

Another implied warranty is that the *quality of the goods meets generally acceptable standards.* If the goods are substandard, it must be agreed upon by both seller and buyer that the goods are sold *as is.* The buyer now has the responsibility for inspecting the goods before accepting delivery. If the buyer does accept delivery and inspects the goods, the buyer cannot thereafter claim breach of warranty for quality.

In order to sell products, a manufacturer promises additional guarantees or promises to refund the purchase price if the customer is not satisfied. Usually the unused portion of the product is returned. The customer is often required to show proof of purchase with a sales slip. The manufacturer then reimburses the retailer for the refund. Oral warranties such as *satisfaction guaranteed* are difficult to enforce. It becomes a case of one person's word against another's. As a customer, it is better to get a guarantee in writing.

If you offer merchandise for sale to the public in your store, you should advertise or guarantee only those products warrantied that you are prepared to make good on or that are backed by your suppliers. Examples of implied warranties include the following:

- Fit for a particular purpose. The buyer relies on the seller's judgment to select goods suited to a particular use.
- Good title. The seller owns the item and can rightfully transfer title to the buyer.

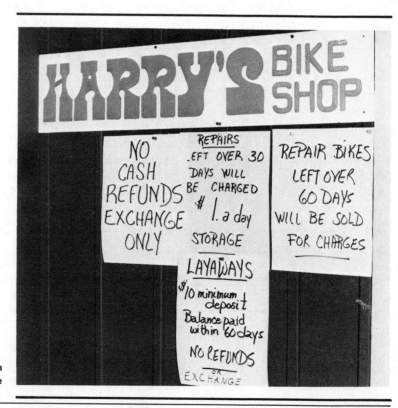

FIGURE 8-4
A business owner usually posts a sign stating the refund or exchange policy for the business.

- Standard quality. In particular situations, products must meet standards required by law.
- Fit for human consumption. It is required by law that food sold for that purpose be fit for consumption.

Returns and Allowances

The law of warranties also applies to returns and allowances. Most owners agree that it is good business practice to refund or make an adjustment to keep a satisfied customer. Usually the only conditions for return are that the merchandise was purchased at the store and that the actual price paid by the customer can be determined. A sales slip can establish these facts. Frequently, your wholesaler or manufacturer will make good on merchandise that you return. For instance, if you take back a can of spoiled peas, the food processor usually allows you credit on your next purchase.

Generally speaking, only the buyer can benefit from a warranty. There must be a contractual relationship between the person claiming the warranty, either expressed or implied, and the seller. This principle is called *privity of contract*. For example, if a person buys a product which is unfit for use, that person can, in most cases, sue only the merchant from whom the item was bought. The merchant, in turn, can sue the manufacturer of the product.

Product Liability

If you as an individual suffer injury or loss from the use or consumption of a product warranted for the purpose, you are entitled to fair compensation through the courts for any damages that you can prove you sustained. Establishing who in the chain of distribution must make good on your claim is known as *fixing product liability*. Normally, the party responsible is the manufacturer or producer of the product, if it can be shown that no one tampered with or changed the contents of the item.

Mrs. Jones bought a hair conditioner in your store. The chemical in the product was too harsh for her, and she lost most of her hair. Mrs. Jones attempts to sue you since you sold her the product and she did use it for the purpose intended. However, if you can show that the product was sealed at purchase time and there was no way that you could have changed its contents, then the manufacturer can be held responsible under current product liability laws. Retailers and others who simply pass on products to the consumer would be reluctant to sell them if they could not claim protection under the law. The principle is that the middleman in most cases is held "safe-harmless" if it can be shown that the products were transmitted as is to the consumer.

The Uniform Commercial Code

The Uniform Commercial Code is in effect in most states. The code governs the handling of checks, notes, bank deposits, drafts, and other written and set standards which business persons must follow in everyday transactions. Much of the Uniform Commercial Code is lengthy and difficult to understand. In fact, many lawyers and bankers are not in agreement about all the provisions. Article 2 of the code is directed toward business owners who often enter into contracts for the purchase or sale of goods. The code defines rights and liabilities which apply only to merchants and small business owners. A business owner should understand the special rules contained in the code which govern the sale of goods.

For example, the code states that goods must be delivered if this term is not included in the sales contract. The code defines such terms as FOB which means freight on board. These provisions and more should be understood by anyone who hopes to be successful in business. You should get a copy and study the provisions of Article 2 of the Uniform Commercial Code. A condensed version of Article 2 appears in the appendix.

Every sale, whether written or oral, is a contract because it is an agreement in which the seller transfers property to the buyer for compensation. An *executory sale* is an agreement to make a sale at some future time. A sale at the time the agreement is made is known as an *executed sale.* The definitions of these two terms depend on when the title to the property is transferred, not when the price is paid for the property. If the property is not transferred (delivered), the sale is incomplete and parties return as before.

Because of the previous definitions of a sale, the owner of the property to be sold is responsible for all risks until the title is transferred to the buyer. Therefore, if goods are damaged before title is transferred, the seller must bear the loss. For example, Mrs. Parks puts a winter coat on layaway at your store. The next day, the coat is damaged by flooding in your stockroom. You must therefore take the loss for the coat. If, however, Mrs. Parks charges the coat and takes it home, she bears any loss for the coat because she has assumed possession. When the title is transferred, in this case on delivery, the risk of loss is transferred with it.

The time for transfer of title is agreed upon by the seller and buyer. If they do not specifically state in their agreement when title passes, their intentions are determined from the available evidence. This evidence includes such facts as the type of merchandise, the type of sale, the terms of delivery, the kind of transportation, who pays for the transportation, and the customs of general business practice. The transfer of title depends on the accumulation of certain acts, not on one specific characteristic of the transaction.

If a buyer will not pay for goods purchased, your alternatives depend on who has physical possession of the property at the time. It is said that possession is nine-tenths of the law. If you hold the property, you can refuse to make delivery until it is paid for. Or, you may sell the goods below the agreed upon price to someone else and charge the buyer the difference. You may also cancel the sale. If you have already delivered the merchandise, you may sue the buyer. You cannot repossess the property unless delivery was made according to a conditional sales agreement.

LICENSES AND PERMITS

There are licensing requirements for various businesses which usually include the payment of a small fee and proof that standards have been met. You should consult local authorities to see if any local licenses or permits apply to your particular business.

Operations Which Require Licenses

Generally, a license or permit is needed to conduct any of the following activities or to provide any of the following services.

- Group One. Auctioneers, employment agencies, pawnbrokers, junk dealers, dating services, secondhand dealers, operators of any public vehicles (cabs, buses, driving service), solicitors for hotels and motels, boats for hire which carry passengers, lodging houses, riding academies, and garages and wagon or street peddlers must have permits in resort localities.

- Group Two. Retail businesses need permits if they are involved in the sale of goods of any description within the limits of a town from canal boats, in the canals or from the lands by the side of such canals and within the boundary lines thereof, or from boats on a lake or river.

- Group Three. Circuses, theaters, motion picture houses, drive-in theaters, shows and other exhibits, billiard and pool rooms, bowling alleys, shooting galleries, skating rinks, amusement parks, and certain public gatherings and parades must all have special, locally issued permits.

- Group Four. The use of any public hall and only if it is rated for a safe capacity, satisfactory and suitable exits appropriately marked, and fire regulations enforced, requires a license.

- Group Five. Restaurants, eating places, lunch counters, soft drink counters, drive-in food stores, frozen custard stands, take-out food businesses and similar places for the sale or consumption on or off the premises of beverages of any class or description must have licenses.

- Group Six. The use of any hall or public place for dancing, whether or not such dancing is open to the general public, requires a permit.

- Group Seven. Persons offering plumbing, heating, ventilation, automotive, mechanical, electrical work, and refrigeration services to the public in the home or in a garage or shop must be licensed.
- Group Eight. The operation of hotels, motels, inns, boarding houses, rooming and lodging houses, nursing homes, associations, and clubs furnishing food or lodging services or facilities must be licensed.
- Group Nine. The operation of trailer camps, tourist camps, mobile home parks, camping grounds, public pools, and similar facilities must be licensed.
- Group Ten. The operation and use of any lands or premises for the excavation of sand, gravel, stone, or other minerals and the accompanying stripping of topsoil requires a license.

In addition to local licensing ordinances, there are many licensing provisions in state laws. An important group includes persons and establishments offering for sale to the public, food and drink. Restaurants, bars, catering establishments, clubs, and other places selling alcoholic beverages are licensed and subject to state inspection. Bakeries must obtain sanitary certificates, and restaurants are subject to state health inspection. Regulations also apply to canneries, commission merchants, net return dealers, and cold storage plants. This type of control applies to dairy products, milk stations, and the manufacture, processing and distribution of ice cream, milk, and dairy products. The taking of lobsters and commercial fisheries are also licensed.

Other Businesses Requiring Licenses

A second group of licenses under state regulations applies to professionals in business for themselves. These individuals include doctors, lawyers, teachers, engineers, nurses, architects, accountants, shorthand reporters, and many others. Licenses are also necessary to operate the following businesses:

- Private trade schools
- Insurance agencies
- Licensed lenders and cashiers of checks
- Dealers in securities and mutual funds
- Funeral directors, embalmers, and undertakers
- Social workers (public practice)
- Firms furnishing character and credit information
- Private detectives and investigators
- Agencies furnishing police or security services

FIGURE 8-5
A hairdresser is required to have a license.

- Taxidermists
- Slaughterhouses
- Food-processing plants

In addition, those persons who have close business dealings affecting public health, welfare, safety, or morals are subject to licensing, Figure 8-5. These include the following:

- Auctioneers
- Chauffeurs
- Driver-training instructors
- Handlers of explosives

- Dealers in feed and fertilizer
- Ticket agents
- Guides
- Operators of kennels and pet shops
- Real estate brokers
- Persons offering nursing and child care services
- Barbers
- Hairdressers
- Cosmetologists
- Blood donors
- Midwives
- Maternity and nursing homes
- Manufacturers and distributors of medicines, alcoholic beverages, firearms, and explosives
- Weight-masters in coal yards
- Well drillers.

Any occupation can be subject to license by a state legislature or a local town council. In most states, licensing and regulations governing trade and commerce are enacted to protect the public's health, safety, morals, and welfare. Occasionally a law is passed which requires the effort of business owners to point out that the controls are unnecessary, that the law is unenforceable, or that the purpose is defeated for which the law was enacted. Business organizations can sometimes persuade reasonable legislators to change the mistake.

The list of individuals who need licenses is not intended to be complete. Be sure you check with local authorities for licensing and regulation requirements which apply to your particular business.

INSURANCE

Basic Insurance

In ancient times, merchant ships were sometimes captured by pirates and held for ransom. Merchants began to contribute to a common fund which was used to pay the ransom. After a time, the merchants saw the advantage of extending this system of sharing risks to take care of the loss of cargo from fires and storms, in addition to piracy.

When a person takes out insurance, these same principles of sharing losses are followed. Perhaps one in a thousand merchants will have a serious fire. If each storekeeper pays $5 a year to a common fund, it will provide the one owner who has a fire with $5,000 to buy new goods or establish a new business. This is the principle of insurance funds.

Insurance Risks. In our system of free enterprise there are many risks. Competition is a risk to the business owner and can be met by ability, knowledge, and imagination. There are other risks that are not insurable. These include the effects of a business depression, changes in styles and public tastes, and population changes from one part of the city or country to another.

There are risks that are insurable, and a business owner can guard against them. There is always the possibility of financial loss due to fire, breakage, theft, and claims against you because of personal injury, Figure 8-6. Property damage of various types and liability for damage occurring on property are examples of insurable risks. These are risks for which the possible great financial loss can be transferred all or in part to an insurance company pool. It should be noted that only the financial loss can be transferred. The annoyance and inconvenience caused by damage, loss of property, or personal injury still remains.

FIGURE 8-6
Insurance may be purchased to cover losses due to burglary, robbery, theft, or shoplifting.

Insurance Companies. If 1,000 merchants each give $5 as a contribution to insurance against fire, who collects and handles the money? Some organization must do the job. Whoever does this should know, from previous occurrences, what the possibility of a fire is in a certain area so that the proper amount to cover the risk is being charged. This is the business of an insurance company.

There are two types of insurance companies: stock and mutual. A *stock insurance company* is owned by stockholders, but anyone can be a policyholder. If there is a profit, only the stockholders receive dividends. In a *mutual insurance company,* the policyholders are the owners. If there is a profit, the policyholders receive the dividends.

Basic Insurance Terms

There are several insurance terms which you should know. You must have an *insurable interest* in something in order to insure it. A financial loss must occur, and only property or relationships which are valuable to the insurer can constitute an insurable interest. For instance, you could not insure the life of your competitor. You must be able to prove a loss or the insurance company will become suspicious.

The *policy* is a contract between the insured and the company. It gives the exact details of the property to be insured, terms of the policy, amount of premiums, and other specific information.

The *premium* is the amount of money which is paid to keep the policy in force. If the period covered by the policy passes and another policy is not issued, the policy is said to *lapse.* Policies insure for only a specified period of time and losses which occur only during that period are covered.

Expiration of Insurance

A policy that is not renewed is said to have *expired.* A policy that is no longer in force because the premiums have not been paid on time is said to have *lapsed.* A policy is not cancelled for nonpayment of premiums until the expiration of a grace period. The grace period is usually 15 or 30 days after the due date of the premium. The *face value* is the amount of the insurance policy, that is, the maximum amount that the insurance company will pay out in the event of a claim.

Dividends are sometimes paid to policyholders. Part of the net profit of a company may be returned to stockholders or policyholders in the form of dividends. This actually means that the next premium could be reduced by the amount of dividend. Companies paying dividends are called *mutual companies.*

Types of Insurance

Insurance for your business can be divided into six classes. These classes include liability insurance, property insurance, business interruption insurance, fidelity bonds, business life insurance, and special insurance.

Liability Insurance. Suppose a customer slips on the floor of your store and is injured. For how much can you be sued? You should carry insurance which will cover your business for any suit a customer brings against you for personal injury caused in the store or by the products or services you offer.

Public liability insurance protects you from financial loss due to claims for the injury of people on your property or the premises you rent. It is important that you carry this type of insurance because such claims can be large. The premiums you will pay for this type of insurance are reasonable.

Product liability insurance protects businesses from financial loss due to claims by people injured from the use of products which are sold. A comprehensive liability insurance policy includes many public and product liability situations. Many insurance firms offer this type of policy.

It is also important that businesses carry *automobile liability insurance.* This type covers claims for personal injury or death caused by a motor vehicle owned or operated by the business. Furthermore, it is wise to carry property damage insurance, in addition to liability insurance. Property damage insurance covers claims made against your employees for damage they may have done to the property of others while operating company owned vehicles. If you operate a delivery service you must have this type of insurance coverage.

The individuals who are involved in the many professional services previously listed are required to pass exams and obtain licenses in most states. Persons who are self-employed and offer personal services to the public not only need licenses but should also have *malpractice insurance.* This type of insurance protects, to the limit of the policy, the practitioner against loss from suit should an accident occur, or a mistake injuring a client or his property.

Property Insurance. Fire, burglary, robbery, and theft insurance are all examples of insurance needed by business firms. There are two types of property-fire insurance. *Real property insurance* is one type that covers buildings. *Personal property insurance* is the other type that covers furniture, equipment, and inventory. It is possible to cover both buildings and personal property in one policy. However, lower premiums are sometimes available when separate policies are issued or different insurance carriers are used.

Although most all businesses carry some kind of fire insurance, especially if the business is mortgaged, not all owners invest their insurance money wisely. It is important to carry enough insurance to get adequate protection from losses,

Figure 8-7. Many fire insurance policies have a clause which states that you have to insure a percentage (usually 80%) of the value of your property. If you do not insure that amount, the policy will pay you for a proportion of the loss. The amount paid is based on the percent of the property insured to its full value. This is called a *coinsurance clause.*

Let us say that you take out a $5,000 policy on your store which is valued at $15,000 because you feel that even a big fire would not destroy it. With a co-insurance clause, the company would pay only one-third of the loss. If your loss was $3,000, the insurance company would pay you only $1,000 regardless of the amount of the insurance policy (face). If you had insured the store for at least $12,000, which is 80% of $15,000, the company would have to pay damages up to the $12,000 face limit. In this case, the insurance company would have to pay the full amount of loss, which was $3,000. Not all policies have this clause. It depends on the company and the state in which the insurance policy is issued. Because many states have standard fire insurance contracts determining the language of their policies, state and local insurance laws should be examined. It is also important that you read the entire policy in order to determine the exact terms of the insurance. You may want a lawyer to help you with this.

FIGURE 8-7
Business loss due to fire can be devastating. Adequate fire insurance for real and personal property protection is necessary.

The rate paid for fire insurance usually depends on the degree of danger of fire which exists. This is affected by such factors as type of building construction, location and condition of neighboring buildings, location of a fire station or hydrant, and previous occurrences in the area. Installation of a sprinkler system or removal of trash and certain hazards may reduce the rate considerably.

The combination *fire and extended coverage policy* is desirable for small businesses. Fire insurance companies usually offer extra coverage for a slightly higher premium. This extends the policy to include damage resulting from riots, windstorms, explosions, water, and smoke. While the risks included under this extended coverage are not common, they could easily destroy a business. It may be wise to pay the slightly greater amount to get this protection.

You always run the risk of having goods or money stolen. Therefore, it is wise to purchase insurance to cover loss due to theft or robbery. There are many types of policies available which differ for industries, stores, and offices.

Business Interruption Insurance. If a business is damaged by a severe fire, the owner may collect the value of the goods and fixtures damaged, but may suffer considerable loss because the business is closed for repairs. Purchasing *business interruption insurance* will protect you against this loss.

Fidelity Bonds and Forgery Bonds. Loss is not always due to an outsider's dishonesty as in the case of theft. There are also dishonest employees. A *fidelity bond* is a type of insurance that protects you against financial loss due to dishonest employees. This insurance may be purchased to cover any and all of your employees. *Forgery bonds* protect you against financial loss due to forged or altered checks, or commercial paper.

Business Life Insurance. Personal life insurance can be used in business situations also. It can protect against the loss to a business as a result of the death of the owner or a business associate (partner or employee). If the business has a mortgage for $25,000, for example, insurance can be purchased to pay the $25,000 mortgage in the event of the owner's or partner's death. Life insurance may also be provided by employee group life insurance, usually at a shared cost.

Special Types of Insurance. Specific types of business insurance may be purchased to cover specific losses.

- It is possible to purchase insurance that covers loss due to glass breakage. *Plate glass insurance* is important for modern stores with large windows. A type of glass insurance which covers neon signs is also available.

- If a business depends on the weather for its income, such as the case with a sports team, it is possible to purchase insurance to cover loss of income due to inclement weather.

- A separate policy can cover loss due to water damage. Types of insurance include *flood insurance, water sprinkler leakage insurance,* and *sprinkler damage.*

- A business that transports goods frequently can protect itself against loss due to goods damaged while in transit by carrying *inland marine insurance.*

- Some businesses lose money because customers do not pay their bills. *Credit insurance* protects these businesses against loss when customers cannot meet their obligations.

- *A blanket insurance policy* covers a group of risks. An example of a blanket policy is comprehensive liability covering several risks.

- It is possible to insure certain contents of a building or store especially in cases where the insured rents or leases the property. Such a policy is called a *floater* because it covers only listed items and insures them wherever they are.

Buying Insurance

Insurance is a service which businesses purchase from either an *insurance broker* or an *insurance agent* by paying premiums. An *insurance broker* is an independent business owner who sells insurance for several different insurance companies. An *insurance agent* is a representative of usually one insurance company and sells only that company's insurance. Both of these business persons must meet certain standards before they are licensed to sell insurance. As a rule, they can be counted on to give you good service and advice on the types and amounts of insurance needed for your particular business. Insurance companies must be approved by each state in which they sell policies. Information about the companies can be obtained from the state insurance department.

When insurance is purchased, it is important that you get the best protection for the money paid. The best value is not always the policy with the lowest premium. Usually, the longer the term of the policy, the lower the premium is each year. A policy for five years would have a lower annual premium than a policy for one year. Businesses save money by purchasing a blanket policy instead of individual policies. However, these are money-saving practices only if they provide needed insurance.

Most owners of small businesses do not have extra money to cover emergencies. If adequately insured, the proprietor of a small business cannot be forced out of business by a fire or large liability claim. Adequate insurance is important because many business owners are underinsured.

One factor to be considered when evaluating your insurance program is the replacement cost of property. Because a plate glass window was purchased for $50 many years ago does not mean that it can be replaced for that price today. In order to keep insurance coverage in line with property value, it is important to have your agent evaluate insurance programs periodically.

The insurance policy is a contract between the insured and the insurance company. Therefore, it is important that the buyer read, understand, and fulfill the obligations of the agreement. One of the obligations in an agreement is to report any damage or claim against the insured property to the insurance company promptly and within the reporting requirements of the agreement. If this is not done, the insurance company may not cover the loss.

Small business owners need not be experts in law and insurance. With a working knowledge of their rights and responsibilities in dealing with the public, business owners can protect themselves, their businesses, and individuals related to the enterprise.

In this and other units throughout the text, the business owner is urged to seek legal advice for business problems. You may feel that getting a lawyer is too expensive. If you make a mistake that a lawyer could have prevented, however, the loss could easily cost you a great deal more than the lawyer would have charged you. Whether it is buying insurance, getting an accountant, seeking legal aid, or buying merchandise, you should never be ashamed of asking for help. All business owners need help in making decisions. Oftentimes you can get help from government agencies and private organizations. Some communities have legal aid societies, chambers of commerce, and better business bureaus, which can help you. In any event, when you think you need professional advice, it is best to get it.

BUSINESS MANUAL ASSIGNMENT

Prepare for your business an insurance program and budget. Explain in a paragraph or two what business risks you expect and how you plan to protect yourself against any loss. Make out a budget for insurance for one year. Obtain actual quotes of premiums from local insurance agents or brokers. Decide if you want to use coinsurance as a way of reducing costs. Type up your budget and include it in your manual.

Prepare a list of at least three local attorneys who you might consult for legal advice. Determine what legal costs you will have in your business, for example if you incorporate or form a partnership, and make out a budget for legal expense. Investigate what it would cost to retain a lawyer. Type up your summary of legal expense and include it in your manual.

TERMS TO KNOW

casualty	lease	tenant
dividend	insurable interest	landlord
mutual	arson	negotiable instrument
contract	face	conditional
parties	malicious mischief	vandalism

flood	draft	premium
collision	check	money order
payee	grace period	postal money order
drawer	theft	certified check
drawee	appreciation	coinsurance clause

UNIT QUIZ

In each of the following, select the word or phrase that best completes the statement or answers the question.

1. The seller of an article sometimes promises or guarantees that a certain fact about the article is true. This is considered a
   a. contract.
   b. promise.
   c. convenant.
   d. warranty.

2. A buyer owns the goods purchased in an installment sales contract when
   a. the sales contract is signed by both parties.
   b. the goods are delivered.
   c. the last payment is made.
   d. the sale is recorded in the county clerk's office.

3. Which one of the following items would be classified as real property?
   a. An automobile
   b. A garage
   c. A sailboat
   d. A valuable art collection

4. Which one of the following is the advantage of owning the building in which your business is located?
   a. An appreciation on the investment is possible.
   b. There is less chance of financial loss.
   c. It is easier to relocate the business.
   d. Less money is needed to start the business.

5. When depositing a check by mail in a savings account, the safest endorsement is the
   a. endorsement in blank.
   b. restrictive endorsement.
   c. conditional endorsement.
   d. qualified endorsement.

6. Which one of the following statements is unwise advice for potential insurance buyers?
   a. You should always be sure that the insurance company is state approved.
   b. You should always purchase the policy which has the lowest premium.
   c. You should consider the replacement cost of insured property when buying insurance.
   d. You should contact your insurance company promptly in the event of a claim.

7. The type of lease best suited for a new business is a
   a. percentage lease.
   b. long-term lease.
   c. renewable short-term lease.
   d. combination fixed rent and percentage lease.

8. An insurance dividend is
   a. the amount paid by the policy holder for the policy.
   b. a part of the profit that a stock company returns to its policyholders.
   c. the amount an insurance company pays when there is a loss.
   d. a part of the profit that a mutual company returns to its policyholders.

9. Insurance that protects the policyholder from loss due to claims of individuals injured on that policyholder's property is referred to as
   a. public liability insurance.   c. fidelity insurance.
   b. product liability insurance.   d. accident and health insurance.

10. A contract between the insured and the insurance company is called a
    a. premium.   c. dividend.
    b. policy.   d. lease.

11. Which one of the following is an insurable risk?
    a. Style changes   c. Competition
    b. Theft   d. Economic depression

12. The amount paid regularly to keep an insurance policy in force is called a
    a. binder.   c. dividend.
    b. premium.   d. commission.

13. A policy lapses when
    a. it is not renewed.   c. the premium is not paid on time.
    b. it is extended temporarily.   d. it is terminated by the company.

14. The best advice for a person cashing checks is to
    a. cash out-of-town checks.
    b. avoid cashing personal checks.
    c. cash all checks from the cash register.
    d. let employees cash their own checks.

15. Which one of the following best describes the philosophy of insurance?
    a. Gambling   c. Protection against loss
    b. The sharing of risks   d. Everyone for themselves

16. An insurable risk is
    a. your partner.   c. your spouse.
    b. your merchandise.   d. all of these.

17. The maximum amount that an insurance company will pay out in the event of a claim is called the

a. rate.   c. dividend.

b. premium.   d. face value.

18. An insurance company that pays dividends to policyholders is

a. a mutual company.   c. a stock company.

b. a family company.   d. a premium company.

19. When a person wishes to transfer a check to a third party but wants to protect himself or herself from the first party having insufficient funds to cover the check, the best endorsement to use is

a. an endorsement in blank.   c. a restrictive endorsement.

b. a special endorsement.   d. a qualified endorsement.

20. A type of insurance that protects a business owner against financial loss due to dishonest employees is

a. business interruption insurance.

b. malpractice insurance.

c. a fidelity bond.

d. customer insurance.

21. Which one of the following is not tangible?

a. A store   c. A written contract

b. Good will   d. Merchandise

22. It is not possible to insure the life of which one of the following?

a. Your partner   c. A friend

b. Your spouse   d. Your parents

23. An insurance policy that covers the contents of a building, but not the building, is called a

a. floater.   c. binder.

b. rider.   d. premium.

24. Insurance that protects the business owner from financial loss due to claims for the injury incurred from products sold is called

a. product liability insurance.   c. public liability insurance.

b. malpractice insurance.   d. customer insurance.

25. In a conditional sales contract that has not been paid off, a TV set which is destroyed by fire in the buyer's home becomes the loss of the

a. buyer.   c. insurance company.

b. seller.   d. buyer and seller split the loss.

UNIT 9

MARKETING

OBJECTIVES

After studying this unit, you will be able to

- Demonstrate good selling by presenting a product or service to an individual in a role-playing sales demonstration in front of a group of people.
- Describe in detail at least four advertising media available to the small business and give advantages of each.
- Design and sketch (rough draft) for your store or business a newspaper ad layout and write the copy for the ad.
- Prepare an outline for a complete advertising campaign for your business.
- Demonstrate a basic knowledge of interior design by constructing a model window display, aisle display, or counter display.
- List some of the factors that must be taken into consideration when selecting an advertising agency.
- Define the Terms to Know.

263

Many references to sales oriented kinds of businesses have been made throughout the text. There is no intention to neglect service businesses, but when it comes to a final selection of a business, it is likely that your choice will involve selling of some kind. Even service businesses require some selling. You must sell yourself and your skills in order to stay in business. Just as in merchandise businesses, the customer must be satisfied. Selling techniques are easy to acquire with practice and dedication. These techniques are just as important to the garage mechanic or the hairdresser as they are to the butcher or the jeweler.

Marketing includes all the activities that are needed to get a product or service from the producer to the consumer. These activities consist of selling, advertising, merchandising, customer relations, public relations, storage, and sales promotion. The main objective of these activities is to increase the sales of goods and services.

CUSTOMER RELATIONS

Establishing a pleasant environment for the buyer is the key to an effective sales promotion. This involves appearance of the store, cleanliness, arrangement of the stock, background music if available, and especially the personalities of all the store personnel who come in contact with customers. The manner in which a customer is treated reflects on the reputation of the store. Credit customers must be treated just as politely as cash customers.

Discrimination must be avoided. In recent years, the civil rights movement has brought about vast changes in the manner in which minorities are treated. This is especially true in the business community. Some of your salespersons may still however have prejudices against certain people because of various reasons. The salespeople may insult or harrass them or refuse to serve them. As a business owner, you

Across-the-counter sales

In-store relations

Sales promotions

Credit extensions

Merchandise adjustments

Business ethics

Store security

Outside-the-store activities (parking and loading, for example)

FIGURE 9-1
In dealings with customers, such as those listed here, fair and courteous treatment should be employed.

cannot allow this to happen. Rude salespeople should be dismissed as quickly as possible. Your personnel should be allowed to discuss this important matter openly so that your policies are fully understood. Everyone will know the action you intend to take if your wishes in these matters are not followed. Many small businesses employ minority group members, and some small business owners are minority group members. Obviously, they cannot afford to discriminate either. Nothing will ruin a business more quickly than a reputation for unfair treatment toward any individual or group.

Advertising and window displays must be in good taste and in keeping with the image the store wishes to convey to the public. It is equally as important for a stock clerk or cashier to treat the customer as a guest in the store as it is for the salesperson. Some store personnel may not be engaged in selling to customers, but they still affect the sales of the store. Discourteous stock persons and impolite cashiers can erase the good effects of even the best selling.

When customers return merchandise, they judge the store also. They will without a doubt tell friends of the kind of service they received. Even a potential shoplifter must be treated politely. Caution must be used so that a customer is not falsely accused of shoplifting. Out-of-store customer relations are just as important. Many stores employ parking-lot personnel, and the conduct of these people reflects on the store just as much as the conduct of the people within the store. Another area of customer contact is the telephone. When customers call the business for information they will be talking to people who represent the business. The personalities of these people are very important to the positive image of the business.

The Value of Personality

One of the most obvious and least expensive promotional assets is usually found within your store. This asset is the positive sales ability of your employees. *Selling* is the ability of an individual to sell merchandise. Good selling depends on personality which appeals to all kinds of customers in all situations, Figure 9-2. Honesty, sensitivity, courtesy, and flexibility are probably the most important elements of selling.

Appearance. Salespeople should be clean, neat, and well groomed. Clothing should be clean, well pressed, and in good repair. Good posture should be exercised, and a smile is greatly appreciated by customers.

Attitude. Salespeople should be willing to do the work required. They should be friendly, helpful, courteous, and businesslike. Salespeople should demonstrate self-control and handle customers with tact and diplomacy. They should display enthusiasm for the job and for the goods and services they offer.

FIGURE 9-2
The importance of a pleasant personality as a sales technique cannot be
overemphasized.

Habits. Salespeople should use soft, pleasant voices and the words they use should be well chosen. Money and stock counts should be handled accurately.

Each of the items may not seem important by itself. But together they make up a selling personality that affects customers. Good selling means more sales and more income. Owners and employees alike are respected and trusted by customers who, after a time, will become loyal and satisfied shoppers. Customers rely on the judgments, opinions, and advice of the salespeople they respect.

Six Steps to Good Selling

Good selling involves six important steps: approach, determining needs, presenting merchandise, overcoming objections, closing the sale, and suggesting purchases.

The Approach to the Sale is Important. Salespeople must remember that they are there to serve the customer. The names and personal preferences of regular customers should be known. Personnel should be pleasant, agreeable, and alert to customer needs. Sales should not be forced. Customers should feel that they are choosing and buying themselves without pressure.

Customer Types	Customers Who Are	Require
NERVOUS CUSTOMERS	Tired and cross Fussy and nervous Excitable Impatient Unreasonable	Patience Consideration Quiet manner Dispatch Calmness
DEPENDENT CUSTOMERS	Timid and sensitive Undecided Old and deaf people Children Foreigners	Gentleness Decisiveness Sympathy Power to think for them Helpfulness
DISAGREEABLE CUSTOMERS	Skeptical Inquisitive Talkative Insulting	Candid manner Knowledge Courteous brevity Self-control
TRYING CUSTOMERS	Critical Indifferent Silent Bargain hunters	Knowledge of goods Tact Perseverance Convincing manner
COMMONSENSE CUSTOMERS	Pleasant Intelligent	Goods they expect Efficient service

FIGURE 9-3 Salespeople should be prepared for all types of customers.

Customer Needs Must Be Recognized. It is important to understand customer types, Figure 9-3. Definite customers know what they want and require little assistance, if any. Uncertain shoppers want help and should be carefully guided with good suggestions from salespeople familiar with what the store offers. Casual shoppers like to look around and may leave if sales are forced on them. Some customers like to talk; others say nothing. Some are shy; others are suspicious. Some may be irritable or do not feel well. Some are pleasant and others have bad manners. Salespeople must be able to spot these differences quickly and change their behavior to suit the particular customer.

Merchandise Should Be Presented Promptly and Intelligently. Customers usually want to know the contents of an item and why it is better than another item. They want to know how it meets their needs and how much wear or service can be expected. Guarantees, cost, value, and special features are all important to the customer and should be explained. Salespeople should be prompt in showing customers what they ask to see. They should also show interest in the customers and the merchandise.

Customer Objections Must Be Understood and Overcome. Customers may object to the items that a salesperson tries to sell them. The salesperson must try to understand the reasons for the objections. Refusal to purchase an item may be due to the price, yet the customer offers other reasons instead. In this type of situation, the salesperson's sensitivity is important. Sometimes customers simply cannot afford an item. Trying to convince them that they can will embarrass them. Customers may object to an item because they do not understand its use or it may not fit their needs. An intelligent explanation and suggestion can sometimes overcome these objections.

Closing the Sale May Be Done in Several Ways. Salespeople sometimes pressure customers into taking merchandise they do not want. It is much better to have customers feel satisfied with what they bought because they really wanted the merchandise. Good closings make customers satisfied with their goods and will therefore lessen the number of returns of unwanted items.

Further Purchases May Be Suggested. Suggestions may be made to a customer who has just purchased an article, and sales may be increased with a little effort. Articles related to one another (a tie and socks to go with a shirt), new products, and special sales should always be mentioned.

After the sale is completed, the salesperson should follow up to make sure the item satisfied the customer's need. This is especially important with expensive items. The follow-up is also a good opportunity to encourage customers to buy other goods and services from your business.

FIGURE 9-4
Salespersons must be adequately trained and retrained and periodically informed about new products and store policies.

Training

Frequently owners and managers do not have enough experienced or trained salespeople. Good employees leave and replacements must be trained. New products are constantly entering the market and even experienced salespeople must learn about them. Therefore, employees must be continually trained and retrained, Figure 9-4.

Sales Demonstrations

Experience has shown that the best way to teach selling is to practice the *sales demonstration,* Figure 9-5. This is a role-playing exercise in which one person plays the part of the customer and the other person tries to sell the product or service to the customer. Informal comments from those watching often improve the sale. A rating sheet should be used. The people making the sale should keep the rating sheets as a record of their progress, Figure 9-6. Sales demonstrations in front of a group can help an individual overcome nervousness and develop a sense of confidence.

FIGURE 9-5
Sales demonstrations are a necessity. Customers must understand how a product works or how it will benefit them before a decision to buy can be expected. This is especially true of machinery and electrical products.

SALES DEMONSTRATION RATING SHEET

Note: This form may be used ten times for the same individual to be rated.

Name: _____   Class: _____

Grade: _____   Date: _____

Item Sold: _____

THE SALESPERSON						PRESENTATIONS									
						1	2	3	4	5	6	7	8	9	10
Approached the customer correctly for the selling situation	5	4	3	2	1										
Used an appropriate greeting	5	4	3	2	1										
Was groomed properly	5	4	3	2	1										
Spoke distinctly	5	4	3	2	1										
Determined customer needs	5	4	3	2	1										
Showed the merchandise effectively	10	8	6	4	2										
Was interested in customer's problem	5	4	3	2	1										
Met objections tactfully	10	8	6	4	2										
Used sufficient merchandise information	10	8	6	4	2										
Demonstrated merchandise effectively	10	8	6	4	2										
Used suggestive selling	10	8	6	4	2										
Closed the sale effectively	10	8	6	4	2										
Change making, wrapping, and sales slip procedure	10	8	6	4	2										
TOTAL POINTS	100														

FIGURE 9-6 Sales demonstration rating sheet

Sales Force Management

Many small businesses, especially retailers and wholesalers, have their own sales force. This means that they have to recruit, select, train, motivate, and sometimes fire the salespersons. Most of these functions are covered in Unit 10. Many small manufacturing firms sell their products through manufacturer's representatives. These are middlemen who represent a number of small manufacturers. Manufacturer's representatives usually sell goods on a commission basis.

ADVERTISING

Advertising refers to the use of various media to inform the public of a business, product, or service offered. A specific method of advertising is called a *medium* (plural is *media*). Advertising is distinguished from other selling techniques because it spreads information, is nonpersonal in imparting information, and it delivers a message to a group.

Advertising serves several purposes, but it is mainly designed to increase sales. As a source of information, advertisements tell people about a business. Advertisements explain the types of goods or services which are available. They also give people other information, such as seasonal sales, new products, and reasons for buying. Advertising can create a business image. It can build confidence in the quality of merchandise, service, and honesty of a business.

Because of the power and expense of advertising, care should be used in the planning of its activities.

Planning Advertising

Several points should be considered in planning advertising. A business owner should know how much advertising costs and if the increase in business is worth the cost. Items of advertising must be chosen carefully. Ads should be timely; seasons, weather, holidays, parades, conventions, and paydays should all be highlighted. Advertising should be planned according to the habits and tastes of the customers. Prices stated in an ad must be accurate. Good advertising policies result in increased patronage and greater sales.

Each type of store will have special needs in planning advertising. Certain values should be emphasized in the advertising for each type. For example:

- Department stores should stress complete assortments, moderate prices, buying sources, purchasing power, "name brands," convenient locations, and convenient credit.

- Specialty shops should point out that they excel in a particular line and that they have the latest goods in their shops. These shops should also emphasize that they have specially trained salespersons interested in the customer.

- Chain stores should emphasize that they carry quality merchandise, are centrally located, and are known for prompt and courteous service. These stores should also point out that their goods are priced as low as their volume permits.
- Small independent stores should emphasize residential neighborhood connections, stock of selected merchandise, and personal, friendly service especially for their customers.
- Service retailers should emphasize quality, dependability, and economy of service.

Advertising Media

Several ranges of advertising exist, such as national, retail, mail order, trade and industrial, and professional. Figure 9-7 provides a further breakdown of media available for most of these categories. The small merchant can use all types of advertising.

National advertising is that type of advertising which covers large areas. It is usually used by manufacturers and chain stores making use of mass media such as television and large-circulation magazines. *Retail advertising* is the most familiar type for the small business because this type may best serve its needs. The most frequently used medium for retail advertising is the local newspaper.

Mail-order advertising centers around the catalog. Catalogs list the items offered for sale together with an illustration, a description, the price, and the catalog number of each item. Many small business owners have used mail-order advertising very effectively. Catalogs of special products do not have to be large or expensive.

PUBLICATIONS	SIGNS	DIRECT	BROADCASTING	IN-THE-STORE
Newspapers	Posters	Direct mail (letters, envelope enclosures, postcards, self-mailing folders, broadsides, booklets and catalogs)	Television	Handouts
Shopping publications (merchant owned and independent)	Bulletins		Radio	Samples and demonstrations
	Electric spectaculars			Merchandise attachments
Local and community publications	Billboards	Package inserts		Catalogs
College and school publications	Cards (car cards, bus cards, station posters)	Gift novelties		Sales checks
Directories (telephone yellow pages, etc.)	Truck posters	Wrapping supplies		Signs
	Street banners	Telephone selling		Public address system
Programs	Skywriting			Trading stamps, merchandise certificates, coupons
National magazines	Kites and balloons			

FIGURE 9-7 The media available for advertising are diverse and vary in effectiveness and cost.

Trade and industrial advertising appears in trade journals. These are professional magazines circulated to particular trade and industrial customers. The messages they carry are aimed at a specialized and limited audience. For instance, a manufacturer of heavy steel punch presses would not advertise in the magazines *Better Homes and Gardens* or the *Saturday Evening Post.* The ad would not reach the people who would be interested in the product. Such an ad would be more effective in such magazines as *Mill and Factory* or *Machine Design.*

Business owners must examine the available media and decide what methods of reaching their customers are best for a product or their stores, Figure 9-8. Advertising costs should show results. Manufacturers of major merchandise lines will help with the cost of local advertising. They may grant a discount called an *advertising allowance* to store owners who run ads in local papers advertising their products at the store. There are advantages in accepting help from large manufacturers. After all, they are just as interested in selling their product as you are. Large producers can afford to maintain a professional advertising department with artists, specialists, and layout experts not available to small merchants. In this way, small business owners get a great deal of personalized advertising they could not otherwise afford. The danger, however, is that these producers are interested in their own merchandise.

For the most part, business owners advertise in the local newspaper. It is relatively inexpensive for the market it reaches and can be controlled easily by the owner. Many consumers read the newspapers to plan their shopping. However, for some small retailers, city-wide newspapers are too expensive and wasteful. They

1. Does the medium reach the largest number of prospects at the lowest cost per prospect?

2. Does the medium provide an opportunity for an adequate selling message or does it make possible only the briefest of copy?

3. Does the medium provide opportunity to illustrate the products or service being sold?

4. Does advertising in the medium present any difficult, time-consuming or creative problems?

5. Does the medium actually sell products or service, or merely announce them?

6. What is the medium's flexibility — can the copy message be changed easily?

7. Does the medium provide opportunity to repeat the selling message?

8. Does the medium provide excitement for special promotions?

9. Does the medium fit the type of store in prestige and distinction?

10. Does the medium cover the entire market area?

FIGURE 9-8 When thinking about advertising media, business owners should consider certain questions.

should instead use leaflets, handbills, direct mail, or supplementary media. Many retailers also find radio an effective advertising medium. Despite its superb qualities, television is often out of reach for the small advertiser. For large stores and manufacturers, television can supplement newspapers as a retail advertising medium.

Local *shopping newspapers* that are free to customers have low advertising rates and large circulations. Since they are free, these newspapers reach a lot of people and are a good advertising bargain for the merchant on a tight advertising budget.

Advertising Agencies

Many owners of small businesses do not have the time or talent to plan, design, or implement their business' advertising campaign. Therefore, many small business owners hire advertising agencies.

Advertising agencies employ many specialists. These people research the market, plan the advertising campaign (including the theme, media, and follow-up), and design and place the advertisements. The business owner must decide if this service is worth the cost. One question to ask when making the decision should be, "Is my time more valuable doing other work and allowing an agency to do my business' advertising?"

FIGURE 9-9
It is much easier than you think to do your own layouts. You can also get help from printers and ad agencies.

When choosing an agency, the business person should consider the suggestions that follow:

- Contact at least three agencies.
- Have selection criteria before you start.
- Select agencies that have done work for small businesses.

The following are some criteria the business person should use when selecting an advertising agency:

- The agency should understand your business or be willing to learn it.
- The people working on your account should be people you can easily work with.
- The agency should share with you examples of their work. It should be the quality that you feel comfortable with.
- The agency should provide you with all the costs you will encounter.
- The agency should have a good credit rating.
- The agency's advertisements should reflect creativity.

Some businesses start working with an agency by hiring the agency to work on one project. This way the business owner has a chance to see how the agency produces for their business.

Advertising Layouts

A *layout* is to the advertiser what a blueprint is to an architect. It tells the newspaper where advertising eléments should be placed. Although department stores usually prepare their own layouts, small business owners often allow the newspaper to handle this job for them. They provide the newspaper with a rough layout and may supply the copy.

Mat services can provide owners with illustrations and *logos* (distinctively designed name or trademark). Other ideas can be adapted from old ads. Layouts are supplied by manufacturers and suppliers of goods on request. You can also create your own layouts. No matter what specific idea you use, there are several points which should be followed:

- The headline should be big enough to compete with other advertising on the page.
- If prices are included in the ad, the figures and dollar sign ($) should be large enough to attract attention.
- There should be at least one central idea in each ad and it should be obvious to the viewer.

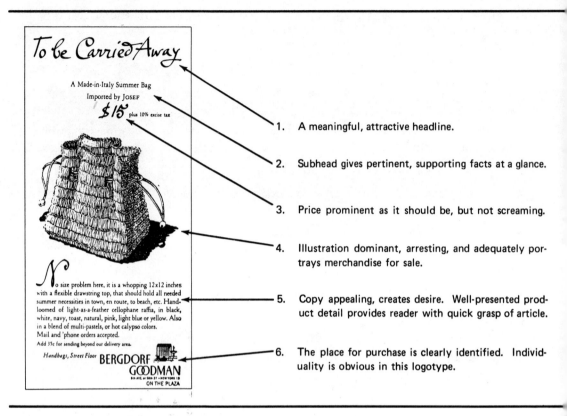

The ad shows, with numbered arrows pointing to elements:

To be Carried Away

A Made-in-Italy Summer Bag
Imported by JOSEF
$15 plus 10% excise tax

No size problem here, it is a whopping 12x12 inches with a flexible drawstring top, that should hold all needed summer necessities in town, en route, to beach, etc. Hand-loomed of light-as-a-feather cellophane raffia, in black, white, navy, toast, natural, pink, light blue or yellow. Also in a blend of multi-pastels, or hot calypso colors. Mail and 'phone orders accepted.

Add 35c for sending beyond our delivery area.

Handbags, Street Floor **BERGDORF GOODMAN**
5th AVE. at 58th ST • NEW YORK 19
ON THE PLAZA

1. A meaningful, attractive headline.

2. Subhead gives pertinent, supporting facts at a glance.

3. Price prominent as it should be, but not screaming.

4. Illustration dominant, arresting, and adequately portrays merchandise for sale.

5. Copy appealing, creates desire. Well-presented product detail provides reader with quick grasp of article.

6. The place for purchase is clearly identified. Individuality is obvious in this logotype.

FIGURE 9-10 Good advertising principles are exemplified in this neat, orderly ad. The eye follows naturally from head line to logotype. Typeface is well selected. The entire ad reflects the character of the merchandise and store.

- The product should be shown in sufficient detail to arouse interest and attract the customer.
- The layout should have a flowing design, not just a collection of unrelated elements thrown together. The elements should draw the eye along in a regular pattern. The letters S, C, and Z and their reversals provide good eye movement.
- Layouts should be planned for easy reading. Headlines should be prominent and brief. Copy should be short and in a typeface that is easy to read. One good-size illustration is usually better than many little ones.
- Layouts should have sensible proportions, such as three to five (five units deep to three units wide).
- If coupons are used, they should be noticeable and easy to use. There should be ample room for name and address on the coupon.

FIGURE 9-11
Anyone who likes seafood, particularly lobster, is bound to be influenced
by this ad. This small, two-column-
wide offering (approximately 3 5/8''
x 3 1/8'') should be effective in almost
any spot in the newspaper.

Preparing a layout for a small store is not difficult. It is simply a guide for the newspaper for placing the elements in the finished advertisement. Owners who create layouts themselves should make them as simple as possible.

The element in a layout that causes the biggest problem is the illustration. Unless an owner has special artistic talent, illustrations are obtained in other ways. Illustrations should be traced and duplicated or mounted directly on the layout. Mats and photographs may also be used. A *mat* or *matrix* is a papier-mâché or composition impression of an ad used in molding a stereotype plate for printing in newspapers. They are easily obtained from various sources.

When the layout is finished, it is placed on a page of the newspaper that has other advertisements on it. If the following questions can be answered positively, the layout is a good one.

- Does the ad stand out from the other advertisements?
- Is the headline large enough?
- Does the logotype stand out?
- Does the advertisement need a border?
- Is the illustration big enough?

SALES PROMOTION

Sales promotion refers to a variety of activities intended to increase sales. Sales promotion techniques increase store traffic and therefore increase your clientele. Businesses must create a positive identity or image for the store and its products, or customers may not return.

Leave your car in our castle...

park FREE!

That's right! FREE PARKING after 5:00 p.m. at Cy & Ellie's New Camelot, Nikusake of Tokyo, Camelot Lounge and for private parties and banquets à la Camelot.

Cy & Ellie's New

camelot

Reservations: 449-1160
Twin Towers Albany, New York

FIGURE 9-12
Another two-column ad takes advantage of graphic eye appeal. The graphics of this ad are eye appealing and therefore effective in various sections of the newspaper.

Promotion techniques are informative devices. They tell customers about new products and their uses and introduce new styles and methods. When these techniques are planned and properly used, they create demand and goodwill. The result is a business that succeeds for its customers and owner.

Visual Merchandising

In merchandising, one method of communicating to the buyer is by visual means. Most people respond better to visual stimuli than to other senses. The best way to tell customers about a product is to visualize it for them. Visual merchandising is a sales promotion device which, by displaying a product to its full advantage, allows products to "sell" themselves.

Window Displays

The window of a store is its "face." No one will ever know how many customers have turned away because a store had a dirty or unattractive face. The exterior

FIGURE 9-13
The border in this ad separates the ad from surrounding material by suggesting an attractive theme, the elements of nature in a certain season.

Your turkey will be as fresh and as plump as though you raised it yourself.

It will be dressed to your liking — what we call "oven ready" — ready to stuff and roast. We clean it that way, so that you won't have to give it a lot of going over at a busy time.

So for less kitchen work and for a truly fine bird, phone us — or stop in and place your order right now.

(Just ask for Jack or Herb.)

GREEN'S QUALITY MARKET

WA 7-1775   1615 Home Boulevard

FIGURE 9-14 A short, appropriate message can be sent on a postcard. A simple illustration adds to its effectiveness. Retailers will find the postcard an excellent and inexpensive advertising medium that can be used in many cases.

of a business can be an asset. Many store locations are selected and high rents paid because owners hope that there will be many potential customers going by the store and noticing the windows. When attractive windows are exposed to traffic, potential buyers are encouraged to enter the store, Figure 9-15.

You should be aware of the appearance of your business, whether you display merchandise or not. First impressions are always important. Garages, filling stations, laundromats, and barber shops are all businesses not normally associated with displaying merchandise. They can all increase their business by intelligent and imaginative use of window displays and nice exterior appearance. No one wants to eat in a restaurant with unkept grounds and a dirty exterior.

The artistic ability of a business owner or an employee is always a great asset in creating displays. However, anyone can produce satisfactory displays by using common sense and listening to the suggestions of your customers, sales representatives, and employees.

The display should be simple and not crowded. A window display which offers too many points of interest is distracting. It is also a good idea to drape windows when they are being changed. When possible, a professional window trimmer should be hired to design and construct your window displays. These individuals may work on a freelance basis and periodically redesign store displays. The obvious advantage here is that a first-rate job is done. It may well be worth the cost. It is a good idea if you have a window to let a professional do the display once or twice a year, especially for a holiday or a sale.

FIGURE 9-15
Creative window displays are an effective technique in visual merchandising, and hopefully will make customers want to come into the store.

Interior Displays

In arranging the inside of a store, many display arrangements are possible. Displays can be located on counters, aisle tables, floor stands, ledges, niches, and shadow boxes. A store should not be crowded, but good display locations should not be overlooked. A well-lighted and well-ventilated interior, with modern fixtures and arrangements which allow shopping comfort and convenience, increases sales. The types of displays that are used in a grocery store are different from those used in a women's clothing shop. Nevertheless, displays must show imagination and be attractive, Figure 9-16. Wholesalers and suppliers usually have many good ideas to pass on.

FIGURE 9-16
Good displays allow customers to examine merchandise, something they must be able to do if they are expected to buy.

FIGURE 9-17
Showcases and counters create interest and traffic.

The main object of a store layout is to encourage movement of customers through the entire store. Goods cannot be confined solely to shelves along walls or behind counters. Islands, aisle tables, showcases, and counters create interest, affect traffic, and produce sales, Figure 9-17.

Displays should increase the sales of merchandise. For example, one merchant created a unique display to sell a large inventory of handbags. The merchant spray-painted an ordinary grocery cart, fastened a clip-on parasol to the top of the cart, and filled it with handbags. This display not only stopped traffic, but sold handbags. Most consumers are familiar with the use of carts and displays of "impulse" merchandise near check-out counters and cash registers. There are many variations of this idea. Displays which are attractive and from which customers may serve themselves will increase sales.

FIGURE 9-18
Displays vary from store to store; the products sold determine the nature of the display.

FIGURE 9-19
Displays should encourage customers to examine the merchandise.

Merchandise should be displayed where customers can examine it and read the price tags easily. There should be nothing hidden between the customer and the merchandise. Customers should feel comfortable with displays and should be encouraged to examine the merchandise, especially in self-service or partially self-service stores.

Salespeople are an important part of displays, Figure 9-20. They can maintain displays and provide ideas and suggestions to improve them. Ideas may be obtained from your competition and from other stores with good displays selling completely different merchandise. Trade magazines can be helpful in providing ideas for new displays.

FIGURE 9-20
Even though a display may be easily inspected, sometimes you need the help of a salesperson. This salesperson is using a color chart to show the actual color of the paint.

People like to come into stores which look attractive and pleasant, and which offer a free choice. Customers do not like to be pressured into making purchases. If allowed to browse, they usually buy more. When shopping is easy and pleasant, customers buy.

OTHER PROMOTION TECHNIQUES

Public Relations

Public relations, sometimes called *publicity,* is public information about a store or an organization which has news value. In some ways, publicity may be viewed as free advertising. A store performs some worthwhile community service and the event is described in the local newspapers. The store is entitled to credit for supporting community activities such as a Red Cross Blood Drive or a United Fund Appeal. When these activities are described in news media, the store gets valuable publicity. The store's name is mentioned and this type of publicity helps to build goodwill.

Because good public relations do not just happen, many stores hire a public relations person. This person may be professionally trained and skilled in public relation techniques. A less-expensive approach would be to give an employee some public relations duties in addition to that employee's regular activities.

If the store is large enough, it may have a public relations department. Businesses often organize a number of activities to improve their public image. Some of these include the following:

- Organized field trips of an educational nature to the store for schools and other groups
- News releases distributed to local papers about noteworthy events in the store and achievements of employees
- A store newspaper or magazine for the employees
- Support of community organizations, such as the Chamber of Commerce, Board of Trade, Kiwanis, Rotary, and Lions
- Sponsorship of various community activities, such as bowling teams, local contests, and softball clubs
- The planning and staging of fashion shows if the store carries apparel lines
- Development of publicity releases about new personnel, promotions of employees, new products and services, and store improvements and additions

The potential for good public relations is dependent upon the nature of the community itself. Knowledge of the community is important to the success of a business. Public relations is a prime example of this fact. When a business supports a community, it is appreciated and also patronized. Business owners who serve the community in an honest, courteous, and dignified manner are promoting good public relations and creating a firm place for their business in the community. They are least likely to fail. Some businesses are so popular that they have actually become community institutions.

Sales Promotion Campaigns

A sales promotion campaign is usually built around a central idea or theme. The campaign may last a day, a week, or even several months. It may be seasonal or associated with a store opening or anniversary, a new product, or the introduction of a new service. The opening of a new department, a new location, or a national or historic commemoration can also be the basis for a campaign.

When the theme is chosen, the campaign itself must be carefully planned. The list that follows outlines a number of important campaign elements:

- A basic promotion idea or philosophy must be developed.
- Store objectives should be defined.
- A tentative budget should be drawn up.
- Various elements of the campaign — advertising, display, and public relations should be studied.
- Responsibilities should be assigned to employees.
- The program of activities should be scheduled, using a calendar and a timetable.
- Individual promotions should be reviewed after the campaign. Critiques should be written and filed for future reference.

Campaign Elements

Radio and television spots	Giveaways
Window displays	Outdoor advertising (billboards)
Interior displays	Contests
Direct mail postcards, brochures, (broadsides, stuff-ins)	Free samples
	Coupons
Newspaper ads	News releases
Point-of-sale displays	Special store decorations
In-store demonstrations	Special sound (music)
Store bulletins	Special lighting
Posters	Search lights
Carnival rides and celebrity personalities	Balloons and free food
	Specialty advertising

Trading Stamps

Trading stamps tend to increase and decrease in use depending on many factors. In recent years, the value of trading stamps as an attraction to customers has decreased. Some stores still give trading stamps. But many stores have discontinued the practice since they are unable to justify the costs in terms of increased sales. This is not to say that trading stamps should not be considered for your business. In such areas as the Midwest and the South, stamps are still in demand by shoppers. It is important for business owners to know the buying habits of their customers. If other merchants are giving stamps, then you may have to in order to meet the competition. This unit describes other methods of sales promotion which may prove more effective for your business.

The first trading stamps were given by Schuster's Department Store in Milwaukee, Wisconsin in 1891. However, Thomas Sperry established the first trading stamp company in 1896. The company provided stamps, catalogs, stamp books, and merchandise to a group of New England retailers to give to their customers. One stamp for each 10¢ purchase was the rule then and still remains the most popular ratio today.

The idea behind stamp plans is that if customers get in the habit of saving stamps, they return to your store instead of shopping at a competitor's store where stamps are not given. However, since there are many stamp plans on the market today, this argument has lost some of its point.

Coupons

In recent years, retailers, manufacturers, and wholesalers have discontinued the use of trading stamps as an incentive for customers. Instead, discount coupons for specific items have grown in popularity as a sales builder. In this way, the retailer and the manufacturer can share in the promotional expense, and the campaign can be selective. Coupons are issued for specific items. A manufacturer will often introduce new products with coupons. Coupons can be inexpensively distributed either by direct mail or by printing them in local newspapers. Since the customer is appraised of a specific savings, for example, 10¢ off, sales for that item are stimulated. Retailers simply collect the coupons from customers. They can either claim a credit against purchases plus a small handling fee, or seek a cash refund from their suppliers. Many retailers use coupons as traffic builders, especially on slow days. For instance, they may advertise "double coupons on Wednesdays" in an attempt to increase the number of shoppers who come to buy discounted items, but purchases as well.

Samples

Manufacturers, especially of food products, and food processors have found that free samples of consumer products are effective in two ways. They can either introduce a new product or stimulate an already established one in a given market area. Tied in usually with intensive radio and television advertising, products are given out door-to-door either through the mail or by agencies who offer this as a business service. If the product is found satisfactory by customers, the presumption is that they will ask for it by brand name or select it from a shelf in a retail store. Samples can be offered in the retail store. Food processors may conduct promotions for the retailer on the premises. This is usually done at no additional cost. Food items such as sausages or egg substitutes can be prepared by a salesperson and then offered to shoppers as they pass by. Demonstrations are usually located near the counter where the particular item being promoted is stocked.

Rain Checks

Storewide sales are an excellent sale promotion device. Oftentimes, however, items on sale are sold out because of a very successful promotion. To treat all customers fairly and to prevent customer complaints, stores issue *rain checks*. These are tickets which the customer can redeem in the future for a sale item when supplies have been restocked. This method also builds goodwill for the store. It is always a good idea, however, to make sure that you have a large enough quantity on hand of the item to be promoted before you start such a sale.

Miscellaneous Promotion Techniques

Contests. Supermarkets and fast-food chains have recently been spending promotional dollars on various types of contests. Usually the customer receives some type of card or slip of paper which represents a chance. Since gambling is illegal in most states, the chance is given for free, whether the customer makes a purchase or not. By matching various combinations, playing a game, or "betting" on a race, a customer can qualify for various cash and merchandise awards.

Cash Register Tapes. Some promotions use cash register tapes instead of trading stamps. The customer saves the tapes until the total purchases correspond to the amount required for a desired premium. The customer then redeems the tapes for the gift at the store.

Catalogs. Many stores publish catalogs describing their merchandise and then mail the catalogs to their customers. Specialty stores and those stores which buy through a central buying office can get preprinted merchandise catalogs listing many standard items. These catalogs are printed in large quantities, with the name of the individual store omitted from the front of the catalog. When a local merchant decides this would be a good promotional item for the store, the business name can be printed on the catalog at a greatly reduced price.

Merchandise Certificates. These certificates are similar to trading stamps in that they are saved by the customer and redeemed for merchandise. However, merchandise certificates are usually sold at 5¢ each at the time of purchase and at the rate of one 5¢ certificate for each 50¢ worth of merchandise. The advantage to the customer is that it takes fewer merchandise certificates to purchase (or redeem) a given item than it does with stamps. Merchandise certificates, however, are declining in popularity.

Decorations. Store decorations in preparation for holidays are expected by owners themselves and their customers. In contributing to holiday festivity, decorations also help to increase sales. Merchants' associations or groups of stores, particularly in a mall or plaza, contribute to a joint fund to trim the surrounding area with lights and flowers, or whatever decorations the occasion calls for.

Holiday Promotions. Often a store or a group of stores will hire a person to pose as Santa Claus or as the Easter Bunny to speak with children while parents shop. Employees can easily be trained for these jobs. Promotions are frequently tied in with the sale of photographs, and samples, such as jelly beans, are distributed.

Special Sound and Lighting. Stores are increasingly making use of piped-in music and special lighting effects. Music relaxes customers so that they move more slowly through the store and buy more merchandise. Lighting accents various merchandise,

FIGURE 9-21
Decorations can announce store-wide promotions and sales, such as holidays and special events, and give a festive atmosphere to the store.

and may also be used outside of the store to help identify the store and encourage customers to enter.

Other forms of promotion involve combinations of techniques. Some shopping plazas have made effective use of old-fashioned trolleys to transport customers from store to store, or from a downtown area to a mall location. Celebrities make public appearances to promote sales. Parades, fireworks, and amusements may be used in a successful sales promotion campaign.

One way to plan a sales promotion is to allow promotion companies which specialize in this type of advertising to do the work. Ad agencies sometimes will plan entire campaigns. Public relations agencies handle publicity and provide clipping service. Visual merchandising can be turned over to an agency, and a contract can be signed to have windows trimmed professionally. Functions turned over to an agency must be paid for. The size of the store, the talent of its personnel, and the initiative of the owner all determine whether the business needs outside help.

No matter who takes care of a sales promotion, it must be carefully planned. Mistakes will be made. For instance, an ad may attract only a few customers, or customers may object to the music selection. Measuring the effectiveness of various techniques is difficult. Experience will provide many of the answers. At first, you should make use only of those promotions which do not cost too much. Taking advantage of manufacturer and supplier assistance and local newspapers whenever possible is a good idea. The creativity of owners and their employees should be examined and developed. With a little imagination, sales promotion can be one of the most enjoyable aspects of small business ownership.

BUSINESS MANUAL ASSIGNMENT

Prepare for your business at least five of the following items as samples and include them in your manual. Include also in your manual an appropriate statement concerning your advertising policies.

30-second radio spot — Write out the copy for a radio ad for your business. Type the copy for the announcer to read over a local radio station. Visit local stations to get an idea of how they want copy submitted. Try to make the ad a "grabber" so that people will know about and patronize your business. Have another individual read the finished copy to see if it fits into the time slot. Include the ad in your manual.

Ad layout — Design and draw an ad for a local weekly shopping newspaper to fit in a one-half-page or larger space. You can feature a sale or a specific product. Write the copy, do the artwork or cut out illustrations if you cannot draw, and paste-up the ad. Call a local paper to find out how much the space would cost to run the ad. Include the sample ad in your manual.

Matchbook cover — Design a matchbook cover for your business. This is a good item for restaurants and lounges. Trace a real matchbook to get the correct size. Sketch the design on the matchbook, making sure the printer will know what you want. Remember that you can use both sides. Include the sample in your manual.

Napkin — Design a napkin for your business (a restaurant, for example), if appropriate. Show exactly what you want printed on the napkin. Call local suppliers for cost estimates. Include the design in your manual.

Business card — Go to a printer and get some sample business cards. Then design one for yourself and your business. Try to use imagination in your design. Include the designs in your manual. Obtain prices from local printers.

Brochure — Design and write the copy for a brochure describing your business and/or service. This is a good item for a travel agency, employment agency, or a business that offers a range of services such as a caterer, a lawn-care specialist, or a dentist. (It is now legal for professionals to advertise in some states.) Include the sample brochure in your manual.

Pencil or pen — Design a novelty pen or pencil as a giveaway for your business, or design a similar novelty item. For ideas, get a catalog from an advertising service that supplies novelties. Key chains, flashlights, name tags, calendars, memo pads, and rulers are just a few suggestions. Include the design in your manual.

Contest — Think of a contest, giveaway, or drawing that will increase the sales of your business. Outline in detail the contest. Write out the rules, list the prizes, and explain how you intend to promote the contest. Figure the total cost for the contest. Include the outline in your manual.

TERMS TO KNOW

marketing	mat
selling	sales promotion
role playing	store displays
advertising	publicity
medium	public relations
national advertising	sales promotion campaigns
retail advertising	coupons
industrial advertising	samples
advertising allowance	merchandise certificates
layout	public relations agency
logo	

_____ **UNIT QUIZ**

In each of the following, select the word or phrase that best completes the sentence or answers the question.

1. Which one of the following actions would not increase sales?
   a. Providing more space for display
   b. Training salespersons
   c. Increasing product information on sales tickets
   d. Improving departmental displays

2. Good selling cannot
   a. increase business income.
   b. compensate for poor management.
   c. increase customer loyalty.
   d. improve the company image.

3. Which of the following statements is not good advice for a new or beginning salesperson?
   a. You should sell the customer merchandise no matter what.
   b. The casual shopper should be left alone.
   c. Most customers respond to a smile.
   d. A customer does not always reveal true objections.

4. The small retailer will usually use all of the following media except
   a. local radio.　　　　　　　　c. local newspapers.
   b. national TV.　　　　　　　 d. local telephone directories.

5. When designing an advertising layout, you should use
   a. large headlines since big print is easy to read.
   b. as many ideas as possible since space is expensive.
   c. a series of elements which draw attention to a regular pattern.
   d. startling proportions so that the advertising attracts attention.

6. Which one of the following departments usually has the responsibility in a company for the development of a favorable community image for the business?
   a. The advertising department　　c. The public relations department
   b. The personnel department　　 d. The purchasing department

7. The most important advertising layout element is the
   a. illustration.　　　　　　　　c. headline.
   b. copy.　　　　　　　　　　　 d. logo.

8. Which one of the following media is usually the most expensive?
   a. Radio　　　　　　　　　　　c. Television
   b. Newspapers　　　　　　　　d. Outdoor advertising (billboards)

9. Which form of media carrying print ads does not cost the reader anything?
   a. Newspaper
   c. Direct mail
   b. Magazine
   d. Shoppers' guide

10. Window displays (storefront windows) are being used less
    a. because they are expensive to change and maintain.
    b. because customers generally do not look at them.
    c. because it cannot be proved that window displays increase store traffic.
    d. for all of these reasons.

11. One way to cut down on advertising expense and still reach customers is to
    a. join a merchants association which shares the cost of advertising.
    b. take advantage of cash credits given by manufacturers for giving premium space to their products.
    c. advertise national brands in local papers where an allowance is provided by the national company.
    d. take advantage of all of these opportunities.

12. Which one of the following elements of an advertising layout would be a problem for you if you could not draw or sketch?
    a. Headline
    c. Illustration
    b. Copy
    d. Media

13. When you design a window display for a small business, you should
    a. place as much merchandise in the window as possible.
    b. leave the display in the window for a long period of time to create an image.
    c. always use the most expensive equipment and products, and hire a professional window trimmer at least six times a year.
    d. make sure your display is simple and visually appealing.

14. Which one of the following statements is not an accepted principle of interior display?
    a. Displays should show imagination.
    b. Impulse items should be displayed in the rear of the store to draw customers to them.
    c. Some displays prepared by manufacturers should be used.
    d. Merchandise should be displayed where customers can examine it.

15. Which one of the following policy recommendations offers poor advertising advice?
    a. The advertiser should spend as much as the budget will allow.
    b. The advertiser should periodically evaluate the advertising dollar for effectiveness.
    c. The advertiser should vary media from time to time to reach different markets.
    d. The advertiser should read the results of research and polls of buying habits in the area.

16. Customers frequently judge a store by the
    a. sales personnel.
    c. physical layout.
    b. exterior store windows.
    d. all of these.

17. Which one of the following is the term which refers to the greatest number of marketing activities?
    a. Advertising
    c. Sales promotion
    b. Sales promotion campaign
    d. Visual merchandising

18. A method of sales promotion used in supermarkets is
    a. trading stamps.
    c. coupons.
    b. games of chance.
    d. all of these.

19. Dependent customers are usually
    a. impatient.
    c. nervous.
    b. skeptical.
    d. undecided.

20. The first step in planning a sales promotion campaign is to
    a. draw up a budget.
    b. hire an advertising agency.
    c. assign jobs to various employees.
    d. develop a schedule with dates and times.

21. Which one of the following terms is used to refer to all of the activities that are needed to get a product from the producer to the consumer?
    a. Advertising
    c. Selling
    b. Marketing
    d. Sales promotion

22. Which one of the following statements is not good advice for a salesperson?
    a. Salespeople should remember that they are employed to serve the customer.
    b. Salespeople should try to understand customers' objections.
    c. Salespeople should not pressure customers into buying merchandise they do not want.
    d. If salespeople sell good products to customers, there is no need for follow-up.

23. Salespeople who sell products for a number of small manufacturers are called
    a. manufacturer's representatives.
    b. advertising representatives.
    c. road agents.
    d. sales managers.

24. Which one of the following statements is sound advice for selecting an advertising agency?
    a. It does not matter if the agency understands the business, as long as the advertising work they produce is inexpensive.
    b. The people working in the agency are not important, as long as the work they produce is adequate.

c. The agency's advertisements should reflect creativity.
d. If the first agency you look at meets your criteria, select that agency.

25. The organization that provides the advertiser with prepared illustrations for advertisements is called
    a. a wholesale agency.
    b. a vendor.
    c. a medium.
    d. a mat service.

UNIT 10

PERSONNEL MANAGEMENT

OBJECTIVES

After studying this unit, you will be able to

- Describe at least four responsibilities business owners have to their employees.
- Perform the seven steps in effective and accurate cashiering and teach how to correctly perform this operation.
- State and briefly explain the main labor laws that affect a small business.
- Explain three of the methods used to settle labor disputes.
- Write at least five personnel policies for your business.
- Define the Terms to Know.

Whether or not owners of small businesses act as their own personnel managers, it is important that they understand the duties of this function. A number of points about personnel relations have already been discussed in this text. This unit focuses on personnel managers and their relationships with individual employees and with labor unions.

MANAGING PEOPLE

Frequently in a small business, the owner is also the personnel manager. The main objective of the personnel manager is to maintain an efficient work force. This calls for the effective use of people, ensuring good relationships between people, and fostering opportunities for individual development.

To get and maintain an efficient work force, the personnel manager has certain specific responsibilities, Figure 10-1. A personnel manager is responsible for the following:

- Selection and hiring of employees
- Training and upgrading of employees
- The health and welfare needs of employees
- Personnel actions, such as the transfer, promotion, and discharge of employees.

FIGURE 10-1
The responsibilities of a personnel manager are great. Sometimes in a small business, the owner must perform the duties of the personnel manager.

_____ **RESPONSIBILITIES OF THE PERSONNEL MANAGER**

Selecting and Hiring Employees

As a small business owner, you should aim to hire those individuals who are best qualified to fill the job requirements. The education, experience, and personality of each candidate must be carefully considered. The selection of effective personnel is essential if a business is to grow and prosper. Before selecting an employee, the following points need to be considered:

- A description of the job to be filled
- A source of applicants
- A basis for selecting the best candidate
- A training program for the individual after hiring

Job Description. It is difficult to think of a contractor building an apartment house without blueprints and specifications. Yet some employers hire a person without knowing what that person is able to do. One way of avoiding this is to write a job description for each position. A job description is prepared by considering all tasks which are a part of the job, and the skills and knowledge required to perform them. This information is kept on file and should be revised as jobs change.

Sources of Employees. It is better to seek out applicants for employment rather than wait for them to come to your business. *Recruiting* is the practice of actively seeking workers rather than waiting for them to come to you. A number of sources of possible workers are listed here.

- Suppliers are a good source of possible applicants.
- Private and public employment agencies, usually for a fee, can help you find the right applicant. The United States Employment Service has over 3,800 offices throughout the United States, and this service is free.
- High schools, vocational and technical schools, business schools, and colleges offer assistance to employers.
- Trade associations and unions offer employment services for their members. These are particularly helpful for the employer seeking a person with a certain skill.
- "Help Wanted" advertisements for applicants in the classified section of newspapers are beneficial, but they must be specific about the job requirements. Most states require that ads such as these must not be discriminatory regarding race, creed, color, sex, or age.

- Additional sources of personnel include radio and television announcements, signs placed in the front of your store, and referrals from your employees, your friends, business associates, and customers.

Selecting the Best Employee

The Application Form. Application forms should fit the needs of the company and conform to the law. Their purpose is to furnish the personnel manager with enough information about applicants so that a judgment as to their qualifications for a job can be made. Applicants can volunteer information about education, experience and skills, and their address and telephone number. Most states restrict questions on applications concerning race, religion, military service, and marital status. Questions about criminal record, drug abuse, driving violations, and sexual preferences are also restricted. Only questions referring to a person's ability to perform a job are permissible.

The Employment Interview. Before conducting an interview, the interviewer should become familiar with the application. Then, in comfortable surroundings and without distraction, the applicant should be put at ease and encouraged to discuss items on the application which need to be clarified. The interviewer should take enough time to obtain information on which to base a decision.

Testing the Applicant. Many forms of tests are used to determine an applicant's aptitudes, attitudes, skills, and suitability for employment. The nature of the work to be performed determines the type of test to be used. If psychological testing is required, a professional psychologist should be employed. For a certain fee, professional testing firms can perform any needed testing.

References. Before deciding to hire an individual, the references which have been provided should be checked. References are persons who have known the applicant for some time and their information may be helpful. They can provide information about the applicant not available from other sources.

Legal Regulations. There are a number of federal and state laws that influence the personnel selection process. The Civil Rights Act of 1964 was passed to prevent discrimination against applicants because of race, color, religion, sex, or national origin. In 1965, the Equal Employment Opportunity Commission (EEOC) was established. This commission hears and investigates complaints against employers concerning employment discrimination. Other laws influencing the employee selection process are the Age Discrimination in Employment Act of 1967 and the Rehabilitation in Employment Act of 1973.

When a new employee has been selected, the employer should allow enough time for training and provide close supervision under actual working conditions. Employers should be patient and not expect too much at first.

To introduce new employees to the business, some companies give booklets welcoming them. The history and policies of the company are reviewed in the booklet. Figure 10-2 is an excerpt from National Cash Register's *Instructions to Checker-Cashiers*. This excerpt illustrates some of the material that might be included in a booklet to new employees working in a supermarket.

Equal Opportunity Employment. Companies doing business with the federal government or with any agency using federal monies must state that they are an *equal opportunity employer*. This phrase simply means that companies will not discriminate in hiring practices because of race, age, sexual preference, religious belief, or national origin of any applicant. In cases where it is possible, companies

---

THE CHECKER-CASHIER AND TODAY'S STORE

As a checker-cashier in one of today's modern self-serve stores, *You* play an important role in the success story of that business. On many occasions you will be the only employee whom the customer comes in contact with during her entire shopping tour. Your ability to satisfactorily serve that customer at the check-out counter — quickly, accurately, and efficiently — may often determine if she will again patronize the store.

To render the best service possible, a new checker-cashier should know the policies and function of the check-out system used in the business where you are employed.

This booklet, combined with personal comment by your employer, will assist you in becoming familiar with the fundamentals of your store's check-out and self-service operation.

STORE POLICIES

Each store has its own rules, regulations, and policies which the management considers im-

portant to the success of the business. They will cover such things as:

Work hours — lunch periods, rest periods, etc.
Dress, conversation, etc., while working.
Explanation of duties.
Store merchandise promotions.
Employee purchases.
Personal grievances.
And other policies characteristic of the store in which you work.

Familiarize yourself with the policies in your store. By observing them faithfully and endeavoring to do your best, a harmonious relationship will exist between you, your fellow employees, and with the management. Equally important, you will enjoy your association with the store.

FIGURE 10-2 A small booklet which provides an introduction to the company is an excellent device for welcoming and training new employees. This is an excerpt from one such booklet.

also will not discriminate against handicapped persons if they are capable of doing the work. Employers are subject to fines and court action if it can be proven that they discriminated against a person during an interview or employment. An applicant cannot be refused the opportunity to fill out an application form without a valid reason. Applicants must also be given an interview within a reasonable period of time. An applicant should be selected for a job because that applicant is, in the interviewer's opinion, the best person available to do the job.

Training Employees

On-the-job Training. On-the-job training includes instruction to employees as they perform their work. A careful plan of teaching should be followed. Instructors should explain to trainees what they are going to show them. It is important that new employees understand exactly what they are going to learn. Instructors should then demonstrate how to do the job, Figure 10-3. They should proceed slowly and, by questioning, find out if trainees are learning each step. Trainees should then perform the operation. Instructors should encourage trainees, and if they make mistakes, should repeat the demonstration until they do it correctly. The trainee's work should be inspected and satisfactory progress should be praised. If progress is not satisfactory, trainees should be assigned easier work or retrained.

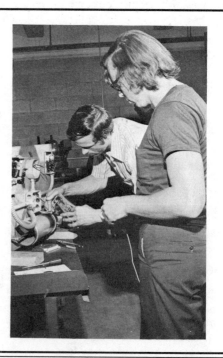

FIGURE 10-3
On-the-job training should always be carefully supervised by an experienced employee or an instructor.

Formal Training. *Formal training* refers to organized instruction in a workshop or classroom situation. One of the best sources of training for the small business employer can be found in adult education programs. These programs are usually offered at a local high school or vocational school. Adult education programs benefit both the employer and trainee as they are of high quality and are usually free. Other formal education, such as special or technical university courses, are sometimes useful in upgrading specific employees. Private trade schools also offer courses at night which may fit the needs of new employees.

The employer may want to pay for this special training. This builds employee morale, and the increased efficiency of the employee more than offsets the cost.

Larger stores and businesses conduct regular training classes for the old and new employees. They have classrooms and training facilities equipped for this purpose. Some stores employ a training director who may also be the personnel manager. The classes combine lectures on theory and information about the store's policies with practical work on the sales floor under the supervision of experienced employees. In a retail store, many subjects are covered in training sessions. These subjects include rules and regulations, cash register operation, sales checks and other procedures, and bagging and wrapping of packages. Workers are shown price tickets and how to mark merchandise. Stock persons are trained to fill out invoices, shipping orders, and other warehouse forms.

Cashiering. Small business implies a small number of employees. Most employees should be familiar with the operation of a cash register and the correct methods of making change, Figure 10-4. A serious error that a business can make is to overcharge a customer and leave itself open to accusations of cheating the public. This mistake will not happen if steps are taken to prevent cash register errors.

The following are common errors that even experienced cashiers make. It is important to guard against losses to either the business or the customer that can occur from these cashier errors:

- Decimal error. Overring or underring caused by placing the fingers on the wrong digits. Example: ringing up 18¢ or $18.00 instead of $1.80.

- Price error. Ringing up the wrong price; guessing at unmarked merchandise instead of asking for the correct price.

- Special price error. Charging the customer the regular price of an item "on special."

- Multiple-price error. Charging the incorrect unit price. Example: ringing up 17¢ or 18¢ for one item marked 2/39¢.

- Tax omission. Failing to ring up tax on taxable items.

- Chart error. Consulting a multiple price chart or tax chart and reading it incorrectly.

1. Call out the total amount of the order.

2. Receive amount tendered from customer and place it on the slab of the cash register.

3. Count the change back aloud to the customer. Always add backwards. Example: $20.00 offered for order of $18.79. Say aloud: $18.79; $18.80 (while giving 1 penny); $19.00 (while giving 2 dimes); $20.00 (while giving 1 dollar).

4. Place amount tendered in the appropriate bins of the cash drawer. Close the cash drawer immediately.

5. Redeem coupons and bottle deposit slips after completing transaction.

6. Issue trading stamps if the store gives them.

7. Make sure that customers have their change, sales slip and trading stamps. Smile and say thank you to let them know their patronage is appreciated.

FIGURE 10-4
Tips on making change. Most employees will work with a cash register at one time or another. They should understand how the register operates and the correct methods of making change.

- Department error. An item is rung up at the correct price, but on the wrong department key.
- Omitting items. Overlooking an item so that it is not paid for. This is the most common error.
- Double ring. Ringing up the same item twice.

Early cash registers rang up the sale and provided a place to put the money. Now, cash registers can record size, color, and other data in addition to price, and this information can be transmitted instantly to a computer. Registers can dispense change automatically, compute change from the amount tendered, and compute the sales tax due. Some registers can even "read" the prices on packages. (See Unit 12 for more information on automation.)

Meeting Employee Needs: Compensation and Financial Incentives

Direct Compensation. The term *compensate* means to balance. When an employer refers to compensating an employee, the idea is to balance employee pay with employee work. Sometimes employers attempt to pay employees less than competitors in the hopes of keeping costs down. This practice often contributes to

FIGURE 10-5
Modern cash registers are able to perform several functions.

low employee morale. On the other hand, employees who cannot produce work equal to their pay cannot be carried by a business for long.

Compensation depends on factors such as the law, regulation of wages, working hours, and conditions of employment. Federal laws apply if the employer transacts business in more than one state. Small business owners should be informed about state and federal regulations which affect them.

Compensation includes wages, bonuses, premiums, salaries, and commissions. *Wages* are compensation paid on an hourly basis. The employee who is paid $4.50 an hour is working for wages. *Salaries* refer to compensation paid to an employee for a period of time, usually one week. Executives and supervisors are usually paid weekly or monthly salaries. *Commissions* are compensation paid an employee as a percentage of a sales. Sales personnel often work on commission, their pay depending upon the amount of sales produced. *Bonuses* are special payments for exceptional work. *Premiums* are incentive payments for producing more of something than usual.

Since commissions are based on the amount of sales, they are appropriate for employees involved in direct selling. The advantage of this is its incentive to the employee to produce at top capacity. For the owner, the advantage is knowing that selling costs will be a percentage of sales. There are also disadvantages: compensations vary during high and low selling periods, supervision is generally not good, and employees may neglect service in order to make a sale.

To lessen the objections of straight commission, employees are sometimes paid both a salary and a commission. This provides the desired incentive toward high production and also allows for steady pay when sales are low. For example, a salesperson in a men's clothing store has a salary of $100 a week and a commission of 3% on sales. If the person sells $1,000 worth of merchandise in a week, that salesperson will receive $100.00 in salary and $30 (3% of $1,000) in commissions.

The salary plus bonus method is similar to the salary and commission plan. The bonus is based on the employee exceeding the given sales quota in any given period. The bonus may be a set amount on a percentage of sales. Bonuses are given to those who are not involved with direct selling. It would be difficult to compensate a receptionist by commission. But if the company is prospering and the receptionist has helped, a bonus can be given to show the employer's appreciation.

The method of payment used in most small businesses is based on time worked. Wages are paid on an hourly basis. The advantages of wages are that they require less clerical work to determine the amount paid and employees usually know how much they will receive. Some disadvantages of wages also exist. There is little incentive for extra effort, and the good worker gets the same pay as the poor worker doing the same work. These objections can be overcome by providing an increase in pay to employees who merit it.

Whatever compensation plan small business owners choose, the objective is to give a fair day's pay for a day's work. When this is out of balance, employee morale is weakened and the business suffers. The nature of the business and experience will determine the best plan for a company.

Fringe Benefits. Financial incentives, also called *fringe benefits*, are nearly as important as direct compensation in attracting and keeping employees. Some of the types of financial incentives are explained here.

- Profit-sharing plans. The purpose of profit sharing is to keep good employees and to encourage them to work toward greater company profits. Employees may contribute a part of their pay which the company matches, or employees make no contribution. Plans are based upon employee salary and length of service. Employees with the highest pay and longest period of service receive a larger share of the profits. The advantage of profit sharing is that employees get extra compensation and the employer may classify the contributions as a business expense. Any profit-sharing plan, however, must be approved by the Internal Revenue Service. Profit-sharing plans can be especially helpful for small businesses.

- Pension plans. The purpose of a pension plan is to provide an income for an employee after retirement. Some plans include death-benefit provisions. Funds for a company pension plan are accumulated by a combination of insurance and investments. Pension plans are subject to approval by the Internal Revenue Service since they represent a business expense. There are a number of private pension plans available, both for companies and for self-employed individuals. The entrepreneur can get information about pension plans from local banks and financial institutions.

- Health and life insurance. Many businesses carry health and life insurance for their employees. Plans may cover hospitalization, surgery, accidents, illness, and dental costs. Insurance companies or such nonprofit groups as Blue Cross-Blue Shield provide such programs. Business owners should compare several plans before choosing. They may assume the entire cost or share the cost with the employee.

- Worker's compensation. This is a form of insurance required by law. It provides benefits for employees and their families who suffer an accident, illness, or death as a result of their jobs. Employers should check with state Departments of Labor and Commerce to find out what the requirements are in their state.

- Leaves of absence. Companies can grant employee leaves of absence for any worthwhile purpose, with the understanding that the person will return to work for the firm when the leave has ended. Such leaves of absence are granted for military reserve programs and for maternity and education purposes, usually without pay.

- Tuition refund. Some firms feel that it is important for employees to continue their education. As an incentive, many companies refund all or part of the cost of college courses taken by employees on their own time, provided a satisfactory grade is received and the course relates in some way to their work.

- Employee discounts. Some retail establishments give their employees a discount on certain purchases. There are some restrictions, and the employee must promise not to resell the merchandise.

- Social activities. Employees who can socialize with each other generally work better together. Employers have at least one or two parties, usually around holidays. All or some of the cost is paid by the company. Gifts, favors, and bonuses are sometimes presented at these affairs. For instance, a firm may sponsor a bowling team for its employees and provide prizes at the end of the season. Trips, outings, and company picnics are frequently organized for the employees.

- Paid vacations, sick leave, paid holidays. Most businesses offer these benefits based on length of service of the employee. If your employees belong to a union, benefits may be an item of negotiation.

The topic of employee benefits is constantly changing. As employers strive to become more competitive, they seek better methods of attracting and keeping good employees. Labor unions are concerned with improving employee benefits as well as increasing employee pay. The successful small business in the future must pay increasing attention to this method of keeping good employees.

Communicating with Employees

Good labor relations are based on good communications between labor and management. Employers should make an extra effort to make sure their employees are informed about company policies, social events, and day-to-day events affecting them. One way to do this is to maintain an up-to-date bulletin board in the employees' lounge or lunch area. A monthly newsletter or company newspaper can be produced with personal items about the workers. Such publications are good morale builders. They are also an excellent means to communicate.

In dealing with personnel matters, employees must know exactly what you intend to do in a given situation. You must make a statement, in writing, stating what will happen in a given set of circumstances. Such a statement is called a *policy*. For example, "If anyone is caught stealing company property, that person will be fired." This is a statement of a condition (stealing) and the action that will result (dismissal).

The company should develop a policy manual in which all policies and procedures are written down. Employees are then informed of all company policies and they will know what action will be taken in various cases. This manual should be given to each new employee. In this way, the company cannot be accused of making up policies as they go along.

Personnel Actions

Evaluation of Employees. Most small business owners agree that the work performance of each employee should be evaluated periodically. This is done not as a basis for a raise but to indicate ways in which the employee can improve. Employee evaluation forms are available, or the small business owner can design a rating sheet for the particular business. Normal salary or wage reviews are conducted at the end of three months for new employees, and then every six months or annually, depending on company policy.

Transfer of Employees. A large amount of money is involved in training employees and making them feel part of a business. It is costly and poor business to let employees go unnecessarily. Every effort should be made to keep employees, if for morale's sake alone. It is better to transfer employees or retrain them if necessary than to lose them entirely. Employees may be terminated for many reasons not of their own doing, such as department closings or lack of work. In these cases, if the company resumes operations, employees should be given the first chance to return if they wish. If a transfer is involved, moving expenses are some-times paid or shared by the company. Employees with long service are interested in protecting their seniority and other benefits. They should be given an oppor-tunity to do so.

Discharge. Termination of employees should always be for just cause. The com-pany policy manual should explain reasons for termination. Most people agree that such violations of company trust as theft, arson, bad conduct, absenteeism or tardiness, and dishonesty are sufficient grounds for dismissal. Employees are usual-ly given a hearing, and the company is responsible for proving the charges against them. Discharges may be at the employee's request for such reasons as maternity or continued education. In cases similar to these, a leave of absence should be considered instead of termination.

Layoff is the term used to describe the suspension of an employee for a cer-tain period of time. Layoffs may be due to lack of business, damage to company facilities, interruption of production, or strike. The layoff is usually not the com-pany's fault, and the employee only makes it a 'discharge' if he or she does not return to work when called back. Companies must faithfully call back all em-ployees who have been laid off before offering jobs to new employees.

A. In one text on human relations in small business, the author lists the following six factors as contributing to employee satisfaction: (1) recognition, (2) means of obtaining recognition, (3) good environ-ment, (4) managerial competence, (5) job security, and (6) justice, equitable treatment. Discuss these needs, describing the methods a small business owner might use to meet them.

B. Suggest some qualifications which a good personnel administrator must have.

MANAGEMENT RESPONSIBILITIES IN COLLECTIVE BARGAINING

An attempt by workers 100 years ago to organize a union to improve work-ing conditions was, according to law, a conspiracy and could result in imprisonment. Injunctions were often used to prevent workers from doing things which would help their union or win a strike. Those who violated the injunction were jailed.

Labor organizations proceeded to get laws passed which recognized their right to organize, strike, and picket. In recent years, laws have given labor not only these rights but many others. By guaranteeing these rights, the laws have helped to bring industrial peace. There are some laws, however, that protect the employer from unions.

MEDIATION

EMPLOYER AND WORKER DISAGREE

MEDIATOR TALKS WITH BOTH

MEDIATOR ADVISES WITH WORKER
AND EMPLOYER

EMPLOYER AND WORKER SATISFIED

MEDIATOR HELPS PEOPLE TO DECIDE FOR THEMSELVES BUT DOES NOT IMPOSE BINDING DECISION

ARBITRATION

EMPLOYER AND WORKER FAIL TO
AGREE

WORKER AND EMPLOYER SUBMIT TO
ARBITRATION

ARBITRATOR STUDIES CASE AND
PREPARES DECISION

BOTH LISTEN TO DECISION OF
ABITRATOR AND ARE BOUND BY IT

THE ARBITRATOR RENDERS A DECISION BY HELPING TO INTERPRET AGREEMENT OR CONTRACT

FIGURE 10-6 Mediation and arbitration

Small business owners must deal not only with individual employees but with groups of employees who have joined together to improve working conditions. Differences of opinion between management and labor do occur. State and federal laws concerning collective bargaining aim to protect the rights of both labor and management so that fair solutions to disputes can be found.

Settling Labor Disputes

Collective Bargaining. The National Labor Relations Act (also known as the *Wagner Act*) became law in 1945. The law required that workers have the right to choose freely those whom they wish to represent them in good faith in collective bargaining with management. It was necessary for employers and employees to meet to discuss disputes which could lead to strikes. In collective bargaining, a group of representatives of the union chosen by the workers meet with representatives of management to make an agreement. When collective bargaining does not lead to an agreement, mediation and arbitration are used.

Mediation and Arbitration. In both mediation and arbitration, a third party is brought in to help settle the dispute. The *mediator* is a peacemaker who listens to both sides, brings the two parties together, and tries to reconcile their differences. Eventually, through the mediator's efforts, terms of agreement may be established. The mediator makes no decision alone, but assists the two sides in reaching a compromise themselves.

Arbitration is quite different than mediation because the third party makes the decision. An *arbitrator* is agreed upon by both parties who each present their case. The arbitrator eventually hands down a decision which both parties have agreed beforehand to accept. This is called *binding arbitration.*

Strikes. When collective bargaining, mediation, or arbitration sessions cannot settle a problem, other methods may be used. *Strikes* are work stoppages ordered by a labor union in an attempt to demonstrate its power to management. Union members, by refusing to work, stop business production and profits. Customers may be lost while business expenses continue. Workers also lose their income and security. Society, in turn, loses the production or services provided. Strikes are the result of emotion rather than sense, and neither party listens to or considers the position of the other. Questions of justice and prestige are involved in strikes. When labor and management are able to calmly talk over problems, there have been few strikes.

Labor Legislation

Federal Labor Laws. Federal labor laws apply only to businesses engaged in interstate commerce. These laws, therefore, do not affect some small businesses carrying on activities within a state. Nevertheless, they usually have exerted an influence on legislation. Probably the most important laws were the Wagner Act, the Social Security Act, and the Minimum Wage and Hour Act. The Minimum Wage and Hour Act provided for a minimum wage in industry with extra pay for overtime work. The Norris-LaGuardia Act restricted the use of injunctions in labor disputes. The unions regarded this act as a landmark decision. Earlier laws guaranteed the right of workers to strike, to peaceful picketing, and to boycott.

State Labor Laws. State regulations on the employment of women and children, wages and hours, and on safety and sanitation required in factories and stores should concern all business owners. Business owners are obligated to find out from their state Department of Labor just how these laws apply to them.

Economic life is based on competition. Federal and state legislation has modified this competition in the following positive ways: by prohibiting unsafe working conditions, employment of young children, substandard conditions, and abnormally low wages. These limitations do not hamper free enterprise. Fair competition is promoted by the legislation which protects all businesses from dishonest competitors who attempt to lower costs unfairly through unethical business practices.

A. Review in sequence the federal laws since 1935 which have affected employers and employees.
B. What state laws presently affect employer-employee disputes?
C. Discuss the differences between mediation and arbitration.
D. What is the present minimum wage required by federal law for companies engaged in interstate commerce? What is the minimum wage required by state law for companies engaged in interstate commerce? (Check state Departments of Labor and Commerce.)

A business which has unhappy employees is not likely to be successful. When employee morale is high, efficiency is usually high also. Achieving good morale depends on the needs of each worker being discovered and considered, and whenever possible, the needs met.

All employees have basic needs. They must receive recognition for their work, fair wages, and respect from the people for whom they are working. They must also have job security, an opportunity for advancement, and a sense of belonging to a group. Realistically, it is not always possible to provide for all of these needs for each employee. Needs such as these can be satisfied, to some extent, by a business owner who cares about employees. The following are a few ways in which business owners can provide for employee needs:

- Provide or attempt to provide job security and job satisfaction by expressing appreciation and recognition for work well done.

- Give timely and constructive support when needed.

- Offer fair wages and salaries in return for good work.

- Provide benefits such as health and insurance plans, paid vacations, profit sharing, pension plans, paid holidays, and similar benefits to the degree the business can afford them.

- Involve employees by means of mutual benefit associations, employee credit unions, recreational programs, and programs in which employees participate, such as suggestion programs with awards.

- Respect the rights of unions to exist and be willing to hear reasonable and constructive suggestions.

When employers make a genuine effort to make their workers' needs an important consideration, and when employees recognize these attempts, the relationship becomes one of mutual benefit.

BUSINESS MANUAL ASSIGNMENT

Prepare a personnel booklet for your company. This might be a one-page or two-page brochure or folder that lists your company benefits, policy statements about infractions of your rules, and the goals, aims, and objectives of the company. Choose at least five company benefits and at least five company rules from the lists that follow, and write a short paragraph for each.

Company Benefits

Vacations	Holidays
Leave of absence	Military leave (summer training)
Transfers	Employee discounts
Hospitalization	Insurance
Credit union	Retirement

Company Rules

No smoking	Possession of abusive substances on company premises
Tardiness	
Insubordination	No stealing
Destroying or defacing company property	Absenteeism
	Refusal to work

TERMS TO KNOW

cashiering
cash register
equal opportunity employer
on-the-job training
formal training
compensation
wages
salaries
commissions

bonuses
premiums
Minimum Wage and Hour Act
Wagner Act
strike
negotiate
arbitrate
mediate
collective bargaining

binding arbitration
fringe benefits
policy
layoff
pension plan
sick leave
profit-sharing plan
leave of absence

UNIT QUIZ

In each of the following, select the word or phrase that best completes the statement or answers the question.

1. Which one of the following statements is true?
   a. Personnel management is usually a staff position in most small businesses.
   b. The smaller the business, the less important personnel management is.
   c. The personnel function should be clearly understood in any business.
   d. When a business is small, good working relationships between employees and the employer take care of themselves.

2. The first step in selecting the best employee for a job is
   a. to contact an employment agency.
   b. to place an ad in the newspaper.
   c. to select a test to be given to the applicant.
   d. to write a job description.

3. Most states restrict employers from using job applications that contain questions about
   a. marital status.
   b. race.
   c. military discharge.
   d. all of these.

4. Which one of the following practices contributes to good employee morale?
   a. Raises and promotions given to favorite employees by the owner
   b. Praise for good work when deserved
   c. No explanation to new employees of what is expected of them
   d. Advice from the owner given to employees concerning their personal problems

5. One advantage of the straight hourly wage is that it
   a. requires less clerical work to determine the amount of pay.
   b. provides incentive for extra effort.
   c. is based on the amount of work done.
   d. attracts the employee who wants to work hard.

6. Which one of the following is an advantage of the commission form of compensation?
   a. It increases during high selling periods.
   b. It requires little employee supervision.
   c. It may cause the employee to neglect service.
   d. It is an incentive for the employee to work harder.

7. Which one of the following employee benefits is required by law?
   a. Profit-sharing stock plan   c. Life insurance
   b. Worker's compensation   d. Sick leave

8. In designing fringe benefit packages, the small business owner should consider that
   a. employees are only concerned with making money.
   b. the small business will never have a union.
   c. the area of employee benefits is one that must be constantly reviewed.
   d. benefits are too expensive for the small business.

9. When selecting employees, the small business owner should
   a. hire friends and relatives because they make the best employees.
   b. interview the applicant before looking at the application.
   c. always check the applicant's references before hiring.
   d. never hire a psychologist to do psychological testing because it is very expensive.

10. An employee operating a cash register rings up 36¢ for one item marked 2/79¢. This type of cash register error is knows as
    a. a special price error.   c. a multiple-price error.
    b. a decimal error.   d. a double ring.

11. The settlement of a dispute by a third party who hands down a decision after hearing both sides of the controversy is known as
    a. collective bargaining.   c. mediation.
    b. binding arbitration.   d. negotiation.

12. When elected representatives of employees meet with representatives of management to work out an agreement, they are engaged in
    a. collective bargaining.   c. mediation.
    b. arbitration.   d. negotiation.

13. Settlement of a dispute with the help of a third party who aids the two sides in reaching an agreement, but makes no final decision, is known as
    a. collective bargaining.
    c. mediation.
    b. arbitration.
    d. negotiation.

14. The Wagner Act guaranteed workers the right to
    a. negotiation.
    c. mediation.
    b. arbitration.
    d. collective bargaining.

15. The use of injunctions in labor disputes was restricted by which one of the following?
    a. Wagner Act
    c. National Labor Relations Act
    b. Norris-LaGuardia Act
    d. Taft-Hartley Act

16. Which of the following is not a policy?
    a. Speeders will be fined.
    c. no parking.
    b. No smoking
    d. no littering

17. All workers' needs cannot always be met because
    a. management does not care.
    c. they are unreasonable.
    b. they are too expensive.
    d. all of these reasons.

18. One factor that does not contribute to employee satisfaction at work is
    a. equitable treatment.
    c. job security.
    b. recognition.
    d. managerial incompetence.

    a. equipment.
    c. employees.
    b. inventory.
    d. cash.

20. Personnel management is actually the proper and intelligent handling of
    a. people.
    c. personal problems.
    b. personnel.
    d. workers.

21. Most people work because they
    a. have to in order to eat.
    b. want to make a contribution and feel recognized and appreciated.
    c. feel they will be punished if they do not work.
    d. all of these reasons apply to some individuals.

22. Personnel management is not an exact science because you are dealing with
    a. people and not objects.
    c. people who do not care.
    b. people who are lazy.
    d. people who feel threatened.

23. A written company statement that states what will happen in a given set of circumstances is known as a
    a. policy.
    c. law.
    b. rule.
    d. requirement.

24. Which one of the following is not a company fringe benefit?
    a. Paid holidays   c. Vacations
    b. Social security   d. Profit sharing

25. Laws that apply only to businesses that engage in interstate commerce are
    a. social security laws.   c. federal labor laws.
    b. state labor laws.   d. compensation laws.

UNIT 11

FRANCHISES

OBJECTIVES

After studying this unit, you will be able to

- Describe the types of franchise arrangements.
- Discuss the advantages and disadvantages of owning a franchise.
- Explain the terms of a franchise contract.
- Name at least twelve kinds of businesses which make good franchises.
- Develop and explain a franchise plan for a business you might want to own.
- Define the Terms to Know.

FIGURE 11-1
McDonald's is one of the many fast-food franchises available today with a proven success record.

In a world where rapid change is an accepted fact, predictions for the future are difficult to make. As world population and technology grow, society deals as best it can in an atmosphere of increasing complexity.

From the beginning of existence, humankind has continually sought to improve the environment. New inventions, discoveries, methods, and ideas occur daily. Despite the rapidity of change, however, some general predictions may be made. In the case of the small business, a number of recent developments will surely affect operation in the future. First, as a way to meet the demands of a growing population, franchises have become very popular. Second, improvements in technology have resulted in widespread automation. Finally, in an attempt to meet growing social needs, federal and state assistance for small business has been extended. New developments will continue to occur. It is important for you to consider the opportunities presented in a modern society for small businesses to grow.

FRANCHISES

Franchise merchandising is the licensing of a local individual to market certain goods and/or services within a specified territory. This license allows the individual to use corporate trademarks, brand names, products, equipment, and methods developed by a parent company.

The franchise idea grew up shortly before World War II, mainly in the soft ice cream and frozen custard industry. A method of providing incentives was sought for the investment of local capital to set up enough outlets to permit economical distribution. The basis of franchising is to provide individuals with their own businesses locally operated and managed, but using standardized methods, central buying, and joint advertising. Car manufacturers and oil companies were pioneers in the franchise movement. Nearly 80% of all petroleum sales take place through franchised outlets. Today, the U.S. Department of Commerce lists over 600 franchisors in this country. The franchisors are further divided into 35 categories according to the type of product or service offered.

The International Franchise Association (IFA) estimates that there are over 500,000 small businesses in the U.S. operating under a franchise arrangement. It is important for anyone looking into a small business opportunity to become familiar with the principles and practices of a franchise.

What Is a Franchise?

Because of the wide variety of franchise terms and conditions, there is no one complete definition of a franchise. In simple terms, however, a *franchise* is a contract to distribute or sell goods and services within a specified area. The *franchisee* is the individual who owns the franchise business. The parent company which grants the license privilege and sets the terms and conditions is known as the *franchisor*.

The basis of a franchising arrangement is the promise that it will be an ongoing relationship from which both parties will benefit. Both must contribute and both must gain. The franchisor offers a "package" which gives real assistance to the franchisee. It includes help in locating a building, designing and construction if necessary, training of staff, and managerial help. The franchisor usually charges the franchisee a fee, which is usually a large cash payment. The franchisee may be required to make additional payments if the business prospers. Hard work is expected in order that the venture be successful.

Advantages of Franchises. What can a prospective franchisee expect to gain from a franchise? The following are some of the advantages outlined by Roger Sherwood, publisher of *National Franchise Reports.*

- A franchised business may be opened with much less cash than is otherwise needed to start a business.

- Because the franchisee is trained by the parent company, little or no previous experience is needed.

- Risk of failure is less because of parent company support.

- The franchisee may expect a higher profit because of the power of combined advertising, purchasing, marketing, and management.

- Less operating capital is needed because it is not necessary to stock as much inventory and financial assistance may be expected from the parent company.

- Benefits are derived from national promotion and publicity, and merchandising assistance in the form of kits is provided.

- The franchisee shares in benefits, such as insurance, offered at a low cost.

- The parent company continues to improve the product or service through research and experiment, which helps the franchisee keep up with competition.

- Assistance is provided for audits, record-keeping systems, and tax problems in order to keep the business operating efficiently and profitably.

- If a problem arises, sympathetic, personal attention from the parent company's staff of experts is always available to the franchise operator.

Disadvantages of Franchises. Some disadvantages of franchises also exist.

- The franchisee can become too dependent on the parent company and therefore lose the initiative to make the business prosper.

- The franchisor may extend too much control over the franchisee.

- The franchised business may have to handle a product or service that is not wanted.

- It may be difficult to profitably terminate the franchise agreement.

- With a certain problem, the parent company may act in its own best interest.

A good franchise with owners who communicate openly may not be that easy to find. Any deal should be investigated carefully.

CHOOSING A FRANCHISE

There are many types of franchise arrangements. The most common type is the *territorial franchise.* This type of franchise provides an area large enough to permit subfranchising. The *operating franchise* is another type of franchise which operates in a smaller protected area and does not allow subfranchising.

The area assigned to a territorial franchisee is usually large enough so that the franchisee can subfranchise if desired. The franchisee gains income by supervising other franchise operators in the area. This type of franchise may cover an area as large as several counties, an entire state, and sometimes more than one state. Because of the size of the area, the income potential, and the responsibility involved, a large initial investment is needed. On the other hand, an operating franchisee can operate only within a limited area. The area assigned to the franchisee is small and the initial investment is considerably less than for the territorial franchise.

FIGURE 11-2
A retail franchise is an excellent choice for a business if an individual is interested in selling goods to the consumer.

KINDS OF FRANCHISES

Retail. If you are interested in selling goods to the consumer, select a retail franchise. This kind of franchise can also include the selling of retail services. Some of the franchises available include laundry and dry-cleaning establishments, upholstery cleaning businesses, car-wash operations, and motels. Such recreational services as swimming pools, miniature golf courses, bowling alleys, miniature car racing, and game rooms may also be franchised.

Whether the franchise is an operating or territorial one, it will most likely be a retail, wholesale, or business service.

Food Operations. Restaurants have been very successful franchise businesses. Excellent examples of this success include Howard Johnson restaurants and motels and Hot Shoppes. White Towers and Dairy Queen Brazier are typical of the fast-food operation. Specialty restaurants, such as Lum's, are typical of recently franchised operations reaching a national scale. Other fast-food operations are listed in the table found near the end of this unit.

Vending Machines. The opportunities in vending machines and automatic amusement devices are almost endless. Companies manufacturing vending machines will assist in setting up a route of machines, provide merchandise, training and repair, and install the equipment. Products sold this way include sandwiches, candy, and hot and cold drinks, just to name a few. A route of 50 candy machines placed in good locations can produce a sizable income for the operator. It is customary to pay a business a small percentage of sales for allowing the vending machine to be on the premises. Vending machines must periodically be emptied of coins,

FIGURE 11-3
This fast-food operation is another example of a very successful franchise business.

checked, and stocked. Vending machine operations are unique because they offer a variety of goods automatically, without salespersons, and at anytime of the day or night. The distribution of milk, ice cubes, postage stamps, and ice cream are other examples of this kind of franchise merchandising.

Coin-operated machines include automatic shoe-polishing machines, identification tag punchers, plastic-coating machines, snapshot photo machines, and key ring machines. Machines have been developed to dispense perfume, cosmetics, paper diapers, and hosiery. Coin-operated television sets and bed massagers are popular in motels. One breakthrough in the vending business has been the invention of the bill changer. An electronic device scans a one dollar bill placed on a special tray, and accepts genuine currency in exchange for coins. Mechanical bill changers for other denominations are being developed.

Rental Services. Rentals of machinery and equipment can form the basis of franchise businesses. The rental of automobiles and trucks became popular just before World War II. This lead to the development of such famous franchise companies as Hertz and Avis. National trailer rental organizations such as U-Haul have successful franchises in service stations and automobile dealerships. The renting of all types of merchandise has formed the basis for many successful franchises. The following is a list of possible merchandise to rent:

- Hospital equipment
- Sporting goods
- Cameras
- Boats
- Airplanes
- Folding chairs and tables
- Housewares
- Mink stoles

Wholesale. You may wish to sell goods to other businesses. If so, you should investigate a wholesale franchise. With this kind of franchise, an individual sells products to retailers. The individual places the products usually on racks and then refills them from time to time. Items that may be sold this way include greeting cards, toys, and health aids. Another type of wholesale franchise is the distribution of tools or parts that are sold to service stations, garages, and manufacturers. There are franchising companies in this field that will provide you with a truck so that you can get to your customers.

Dealerships. A discussion of franchises would be incomplete without mention of dealerships. The right to sell a brand product as a dealer or distributor within a specified area is essentially a franchise. Petroleum companies distribute products and services in this manner, using dealers operating their own stations under the company's name. The oil industry is generally set up as a franchised industry. Some service stations are company owned. But by far the majority of them operate under a franchise agreement. The automobile industry is another example of an industry which uses franchised dealerships. Obviously, greater capital is necessary to establish a Chevrolet dealership, for instance, than to open a hamburger stand. However, the contractual relationship with the parent company is basically the same.

Dealerships selling outboard motors, airplanes, boats, sports equipment, recreational vehicles, mobile homes, and camping trailers have become very successful franchised businesses. Such national brands as General Tire, Evinrude Motors, and Cesna Aircraft enjoy good reputations and almost assured success to the fortunate local franchisee.

Education. Schools, usually of a short-term nature, have made fine franchise businesses. Many people have learned to dance at Arthur Murray's or how to build muscles or lose weight at Jack LaLanne's. Many business schools, model agencies, charm courses, and beauty schools are franchised. Franchised businesses also include shorthand systems, such as Speedwriting and Stenoscript. The famous Dale Carnegie Program, a personality development course, is also franchised.

Suppliers of Business Services. The business service field is also worthy of investigation as a possible business. In this type of business, services are sold to other businesses. Some of the franchises available in this field are tax, accounting, and bookkeeping services, advertising and sales promotion services, and personnel and employment services. The franchisee is not required to have experience in a specific field since the parent company usually gives its franchisees adequate training.

One of the most successful types of franchised services is music. In addition to the coin-operated juke box, piped-in music systems have become quite popular. Music systems are either self-contained using records or tapes, or the sound is piped in through telephone lines or broadcast on high frequency radio receivers. The music is heard throughout the store or office through a series of speakers located in the walls and ceilings. High-quality systems have been developed with attention to tone, stereo, and quality selections. The business providing the location of the juke box shares in the commission. The franchisee operator, working with a record distributing organization or a manufacturer of sound equipment, services the machines, changes the selection according to popularity studies, and makes repairs.

The following are several sources of information about franchises:

- Franchising industry publications
- Franchisor directories
- Consumer magazines and newspapers
- Trade publications
- Franchisor exhibitions
- Franchise marketing agencies

TERMS AND CONTRACTS

Legal Considerations and the Franchise Agreement

There are laws that specifically deal with franchising. The Federal Disclosure Act is one of these laws. The law states that the franchise must provide the potential franchisee with a basic disclosure document at specified times before the

SUBJECT	QUESTIONS
Franchise Fee	How much is it? What is it used for? Can the individual afford it? Can any or all of it be recovered? Must it be paid more than once?
Trade Area	How large is it? Is it protected? Is it exclusive or selective? For how long is it protected?
Quota	How much is the quota? What is it based on? Does it change? What happens when the quota is not met?
Termination of Business	What happens to the investment in the event of the owner's death? Under what conditions can the franchise company cancel the agreement? Can the franchise be sold? Can the franchise be sold at a profit? Under what conditions can the owner voluntarily cancel the franchise agreement?
Promotional Program	Does the company have a promotional program? Is the owner required to pay for part of this promotional program? If so, how much will it cost?
The Return of Merchandise	Under what conditions is the owner allowed to return merchandise to the parent company?
Company Standards	Does the company require the owner to employ a minimum number of employees? What other personnel requirements does the company have?
Business Records	What are the requirements of the parent company so far as business records are concerned?
Factors	Does the owner have to turn in reports to the parent company? Will the company check books periodically?
Pricing	Does the company have any requirements as to the price at which goods or services are sold?
Other Requirements	What other requirements does the company have?

FIGURE 11-4 Many questions should be answered before a franchise contract is signed.

final sale. The document must provide certain information about the franchise organization and the franchise contract.

An "average" franchise contract does not exist because there are almost as many different franchise contracts as there are franchises. Every franchise contract deals with a few common factors. These factors include the franchise fee, the trading area, the sales quota, the right to sell the franchise, and the termination of the contract.

The Franchise Fee. Upon entering into a franchise agreement, the franchisee must pay a franchise fee to the parent company. Such fees vary from $1,000 to $250,000, depending upon the type of franchise. Some fees simply permit the use of the franchisor's name. Other fees include the entire cost of putting the franchisee in business, covering equipment, inventory, training, and promotional materials.

Some fees are paid only once, when the contract is executed. Others are on a yearly payment basis. Fees are sometimes figured as a percentage of net or gross revenue. Franchisees should know exactly what they are receiving for their payment, and whether it is a one-time or an annual fee.

The Trading Area. The *trading area* is the territory assigned by the parent company. It must be clearly defined and mapped, and is a legal part of the agreement.

FIGURE 11-5 A real estate franchise

Trading areas are exclusive or selective. An *exclusive area* is protected from any other franchises within the area. In a *selective area*, this guarantee is not given and there may be other franchises granted within the area. Additional franchises in the same area sometimes increase the business of each franchisee. One of the reasons for this is that the increased exposure of the parent company's name has the same effect as increased advertising and promotion.

The Sales Quota. A *quota,* or minimum, is a standard set by the parent company stating the smallest sales volume expected. It is usually based on the average sales volume of units already established, the expected selling power of the area, and projected yearly sales.

It is essential that the franchisee clearly understand what the quota is and how it must be met. In some contracts, it is not merely a minimum to be met once but is a continuing yearly requirement.

The Right to Sell the Franchise. Once entering a franchise contract, does a person have the right to sell the franchise? The answer to this question is yes. The person cannot be an independent owner without having such a right. However, most franchisors will require some control over the sale. Since it is their name, product, or service which is being transferred, they may buy back the franchise. They may then reissue it to another buyer, which the first owner may have found, who meets their requirements. In any case, the conditions under which the franchisee may sell should be clearly understood before the original franchise contract is signed.

Termination of the Contract. What happens if either the franchisee or the parent company decides to terminate the agreement? The franchise contract should define the conditions under which the agreement can be terminated by either party. Before signing any franchise agreement, the matter of how either party may end it must be understood. An attorney should be consulted before entering into a franchise agreement.

BUSINESS MANUAL ASSIGNMENT

In two or three paragraphs, discuss franchises as they might apply to your business. Give a list of at least ten types of franchise businesses which you might consider. Research the *Franchise Handbook* and other sources in your local library to see if there are any franchise companies operating in the same field as a business that you own or would like to own. Write to the franchise company and ask for any information they are willing to send you. Evaluate their proposition, and give at least two advantages and two disadvantages of franchising your business. Include this franchise material in your manual.

SELECTED FRANCHISE INFORMATION*

Name of Parent Company and Address	Offering	Year Founded	Number of Franchises	Number of Company Units	Franchise Fee	Capital Required
AAMCO Transmissions, Inc., 408 E. 4th St., Bridgeport, PA 19405	Complete transmission repair package — Does not include building	1958	615			$ 26,000
A & W International, Inc., 922 Broadway Santa Monica, CA 90406	Root beer and fast-food operation	1919	1827			$ 50,000
Arby's Inc., 4944 Belmont Ave. Youngstown, OH 44505	Roast beef sandwiches and fast-food operation	1964	113			$275,000
Arthur Treacher's Fish & Chips, Inc. 1328 Dublin Rd., Columbus, OH 43215	Fish (fried) fast-food operation	1969	261	196		$ 50,000
Bubble-up Company, 2800 No. Talman Ave. Chicago, IL 60618	Concentrate for bottling product lemon/lime flavor	1939	155		No fee; must be a bottler	
Burger Chef Systems Inc. College Park Pyramids, P.O. Box 927 Indianapolis, IN 96206	Hamburger/fast-food operation	1958	750			$ 75,000
Burger King Corporation, P.O. Box 520783 Miami, FL 33152	Hamburger/fast-food operation	1954	2,100			$ 85,000
Cock 'n Bull, Ltd., 5664 West Raymond St. Indianapolis, IN 46241	Concentrate for bottlers Tonic water and other flavors	1945	8		No fee; must be a bottler	
Country Style Donuts, Inc., 837 Woodbine Ave. Gormley, ONT-LOH 1 G O Canada	Complete donut baking operation — Does not include building	1962	59 (in US and Canada)			$ 75,000
Dad's Root Beer Company 2800 No. Talman Ave., Chicago, IL 60618	Root beer flavor concentrate for bottlers	1939	155		No fee; must be bottler	
Donutland Inc., Box 409 Miami, FL 52302	Donut baking operation Does not include building	1945	30			$ 15,000
Double-Cola Company Chattanooga, TN	Concentrate (cola flavor) for bottlers	1922	150		Must be a bottler	

Company	Type of operation	Year established	No. franchised	No. company-owned	Franchise fee	Total investment
Dunkin' Donuts of America, Inc. Box 317 Randolph, MA 02368	Complete donut baking operation — Some financial help w/building	1950	901		$27,000	$ 11,000
Firestone Tire & Rubber Company 1200 Forrester Pkwy. Akron, OH 44317	Tire and auto accessories Must have own building	1900	14,000			$ 50,000 (for inventory)
Goodrich, B.F. Tire Company 500 So. Main St., Akron, OH 44318	Tire and auto accessories Must have own building	1870	Thousands			Unknown
Goodyear Tire & Rubber Company 1144 E. Market St. Akron, OH 44316	Tire and auto accessories Must have own building	1896	6,000			$ 35,000
Kentucky Fried Chicken Corporation Box 13331 Louisville, KY	Fried chicken fast-food operation — 20-year lease for building	1934	12,501		$ 4,000	40% of total
Hardee's Food Systems, Inc. P.O. Box 1619, 1233 No. Church St. Rocky Mount, NC 27801	Hamburger/fast-food operation — Building can be financed for 20 years	1962	1,035			$100,000
Howard Johnson Company 220 Forbes Rd. Braintree, MA 02184	Full-service restaurant (including seafood) franchise	1925	250 (6 Ground Rounds/9 Red Coach)			Varies
International Dairy Queen, Inc. Box 33286, Minneapolis, MN 53435	Soft ice cream, hamburgers— Includes building	1938	4,790		$20,000	$ 13,000
Long John Silver's Inc. / Jerrico Inc. Lexington, KY 40379	Fried fish and seafood franchise	1929	528	440	$ 25,000-$ 30,000	$ 50,000
Lum's Restaurant Corporation 8410 Northwest 53rd Terrace Suite 200, Miami, FL 33166	Full-service restaurant Hot dogs cooked in beer	1954	331			$ 50,000
McDonald's Corporation 1 McDonald's Plaza Oak Brook, IL 60521	Hamburger/fast-food operation	1955	4,586		$90,000	$100,000
Midas International Corporation 222 So. Riverside Plaza Chicago, IL 60606	Auto parts repair/ mufflers, brakes, shock absorbers	1956	975			$ 90,000
Mission of California, 197 Chatham St. New Haven, CN	Orange flavor concentrate for bottlers	1920	185			Must be bottler or canner

*Data is subject to change.

329

Name of Parent Company and Address	Offering	Year Founded	Number of Franchises	Number of Company Units	Franchise Fee	Capital Required
Mister Donut of America, Inc. [Int. Multi-foods Inc.], 1200 Multi-foods Bldg., Minneapolis, MN 53435	Donut baking operation Assistance with building	1955	662		$ 6,000	$ 5,000
Mountain Valley Spring Company, 150 Central Ave., Hot Springs, AR	Complete spring water bottling operation, plus importing	1871	112			$ 10,000
Orange Julius of America, Inc. 3219 Wilshire Blvd. Santa Monica, CA 90403	Orange phosphate drink stand, other flavors also	1926	410			$ 30,000–$ 50,000
Ponderosa System Inc., P.O. Box 578 Dayton, OH 45401	Cafeteria-style steak house	1965	207	384		$ 80,000
Shakey's Inc., 5565 First International Bldg. Dallas, TX 75202	Pizza restaurant	1954	514			$100,000+
Spudnuts, Inc., 450 W. 1700th St., So. Salt Lake City, UT 84115	Donut baking operation	1937	130		$15,000	$ 10,000
Southern Maid Donut Flour Company, Inc. 3615 Cavalier Drive, Garland, TX 75042	Complete donut baking operation	1937	225		$12,000	$ 50,000
Stuckey's, Inc., Post Office Box 370 Eastman, GA 31023	Restaurant, gas station, gift shop, pecan candy specialties, snacks	1931	160	168	Negotiable	
Tastee Donuts Inc., Post Office Box 2708 Rocky Mount, NC 27801	Donut baking operation (complete package)	1965	50		$33,800	
Tuffy Service Centers, Inc. 21700 Greenfield Rd. Oak Park, MI 48237	Muffler shops, also brakes and shock absorbers	1970	85			$ 90,000
Wendy's Old Fashioned Hamburgers [Wendy's Inc.], Box 256 4288 W. Dublin-Granville Rd. Dublin, OH 43017	Hamburger/fast-food restaurants—(Complete package including building)	1969	400			$200,000
Western Auto Stores, Inc. 2107 Grand Ave., Kansas City, MO	Automobile accessories and hardware merchandise Must have own building	1909	4,000+			$ 20,000 (for inventory)

*Data is subject to change.

TERMS TO KNOW

franchise	trading area
franchisee	exclusive
franchisor	selective
parent company	franchise merchandising
territorial franchise	Federal Disclosure Act
operating franchise	quota
franchise fee	

UNIT QUIZ

In each of the following select the word or phrase which best completes the statement or answers the question.

1. One of the disadvantages of owning a franchise business is that
   a. the parent companies have standardized products and procedures.
   b. a franchise business requires less cash to start.
   c. the franchise may have a better chance of succeeding.
   d. the owner cannot sell other companies' products.

2. A territorial franchise usually
   a. requires a larger initial investment.
   b. covers a smaller area.
   c. has the least income potential.
   d. requires less responsibility.

3. A franchised business is owned by the
   a. government.   c. stockholders.
   b. franchisor.   d. franchisee.

4. The licensing of a local individual to market certain goods and/or services within a specified territory is known as
   a. territorial franchising.   c. exclusive merchandising.
   b. franchise merchandising.   d. selective franchising.

5. One advantage of owning a franchise is that the franchisee
   a. has a protected territory.
   b. can sell products other than the franchised ones.
   c. is certain to succeed.
   d. has to participate in parent company advertising and sales promotion projects.

6. A franchise is a good idea for someone who
   a. has previously operated his or her own business of the same kind.
   b. is a complete novice with no business experience of any kind.
   c. has a little business experience and sufficient capital.
   d. has none of the above.

7. A franchise business does not have to be
   a. large.
   c. expensive.
   b. a fast-food operation.
   d. all of these.

8. A stipend paid by the franchisee to the franchisor is called a franchise
   a. binder.
   c. deposit.
   b. fee.
   d. expense.

9. One of the main advantages of owning a fast-food franchise is which one of the following?
   a. A low individual cost to you for national advertising
   b. A choice of products from various manufacturers
   c. Freedom to change your prices anytime depending on local conditions
   d. Almost certain success because of the size of the franchise

10. A franchise is a good way for a person to
    a. get business experience.
    b. get started in business with limited capital.
    c. get rich.
    d. meet competition.

11. Franchises include all of the following kinds of businesses except
    a. retailing.
    c. government services.
    b. wholesaling.
    d. manufacturing.

12. One of the problems facing franchises is that franchise areas
    a. are not always protected by the parent company.
    b. are not large enough for successful operations.
    c. are weakened by company-operated units.
    d. have all of these problems.

13. Which one of the following is a source of reliable information about franchises?
    a. *Franchise Handbook*
    c. Small Business Administration
    b. Chamber of commerce
    d. Local merchants

14. Franchises will probably
    a. increase in number.
    c. remain the same.
    b. decrease in number.
    d. be made illegal.

15. Which one of the following would not be a franchised business?
    a. Radio station
    c. Gas and electric company
    b. Auto dealership
    d. Gas station

16. Which one of the following would not be a franchised business?
    a. Television broadcasting station
    c. Candy store
    b. Gasoline service station
    d. Police station

17. Which one of the following is a franchise organization?
    a. Kraft foods
    c. McDonald's
    b. Sears, Roebuck, & Co.
    d. All of these

18. The number of small businesses that are franchises is
    a. increasing.   c. likely to remain the same.
    b. decreasing.   d. unknown.

19. Which one of the following would not be a franchised business?
    a. Motor home dealership
    b. Factory authorized sales and service
    c. Fast-food licensee
    d. Telephone company

20. The right to grant a franchise agreement is reserved to the
    a. parent company.   c. vendor.
    b. franchisee.   d. licensee.

21. There are franchises that sell
    a. hamburgers.   c. transmission repair services.
    b. ice cream.   d. all of these.

22. A law that specifically deals with franchising is
    a. the Disclosure Act.   c. the Equal Employment Act.
    b. the Labor Relations Act.   d. the Wagner Act.

23. Franchise fees are
    a. paid to the franchisor.   c. based on the size of the territory.
    b. based on sales volume.   d. could be any or all of these.

24. Which one of the following is not a franchise organization?
    a. McDonald's   c. J.C. Penny's
    b. Century 21   d. all of these are not franchises.

25. There are franchise agreements that have clauses covering
    a. sales quotas.   c. purchasing and use of products.
    b. termination agreements.   d. all of these topics.

UNIT 12

THE FUTURE OF SMALL BUSINESS

OBJECTIVES

After studying this unit, you will be able to

- Describe new inventions and technological developments that are likely to occur in the future.
- Write a future business plan for your business.
- Explain automation and give examples of the use of automation as it applies to your business.
- Define the Terms to Know.

The question, "Will the teacher, the stenographer, or the cashier ever be replaced by machines?" is often asked. This is an interesting question because some amazing devices have been developed which perform many of the duties related to these occupations.

Teaching machines, program learning devices, and computer-assisted instruction have been around a long time. Even so, the number of professional teachers continues to grow. What happens is that when these devices come on the market, there is a period of adjustment. At first, they usually have many "bugs" in them and it takes a while for public acceptance. Teaching machines have their use, but it appears now that they will never replace the teacher. The personal contact of the teacher is too important. Besides, who would fix the machines when they break down?

Even further in the future is a mechanical secretary. Bell Laboratories, Western Electric, and other companies have been experimenting with voice simulators, voice print machines, and vocabulary computers. A voice actuated typewriter (VAT) does actually exist. However, it makes a lot of mistakes. The words *pare*, *pair*, or *pear* all sound alike to this device, and it has a hard time getting the correct spelling. Most of these devices also are too large and heavy to place on a person's lap for dictation. So, it will be a long time before the secretary will be replaced.

Another device available on the market scans a person's eyes while looking at a standard typewriter keyboard. The machine can tell just what key the person is looking at, and then prints it accordingly.

The electronic cash register is already being used. There is a device that actually *reads* prices on goods and correctly enters them with the aid of a computer into a cash register and memory unit. These scanning devices are commercially available. A number of supermarket chains are currently field-testing these scanners. They are not only expensive, but there are some problems with them. The merchandise must be "fed" to the device or a "wand" moved over the goods so that the device can read the group of black parallel lines printed on the container. This group of lines is known as the Uniform Product Code (UPC). For many years, the Federal Trade Commission (FTC) has required most manufacturers to print this code on the containers of goods (mainly food).

The scanner contains a small laser. This laser puts out enough controlled light so that it can "read" the reflections from the varying light and dark areas caused by the various widths of black lines. The scanner transmits the information from the "wand" as it is moved across the code "patch" to a control unit. This control unit is usually placed under the counter. The impulses are interpreted as digital information, and together with data such as price already fed into the computer, the device is able to determine the exact item and its price. The device then records this information on a sales slip (cash register tape), on a master tape (detail tape), and on a memory disc or punched tape, for future use in inventory control.

There are problems, however, with the equipment at present. Not all products carry the UPC, and for some that do, the code is difficult for the scanner to sense. For instance, since the surface of frozen foods is likely to be coated with frost, the code has a tendency to be distorted. The scanner therefore picks up a fuzzy image which is sometimes incorrect. In this case, the cashier must manually enter the price in a digital keyboard located near the conveyor belt. The digital keyboard then transmits the correct data to the control unit under the counter.

Actually, this device has not caused any cashier to be fired. Most people that use the device would say it is fine when it works. The scanning wand reads prices very fast. All the clerk must do is move the goods along the conveyor belt and wave the wand over each price code. Most times, the device enters the correct amount into the system. But, cashiers must be alert to correct any errors. They must also watch for unmarked goods and enter prices manually on such items as meat, produce, and any product that does not have a code. The equipment speeds up the checking out of goods and increases cashier productivity. Instead of increasing unemployment, perhaps this device will just be another tool like the manual cash register was for so many years.

AUTOMATION

Automatic data processing (ADP) is not a recent development, but it plays a major role in world business. Today's business, because of its size and complexity, requires more and more information in less time so that managers can make accurate decisions.

Automation is the delegating of work to machines. Just as the home has many automatic servants such as washers, dryers, and dishwashers, so the business has machines to remove the drudgery from daily tasks. *Automation* is the systematic use of machines and methods to simplify and speed up almost any task or job. Although the small business may not be able to own an expensive computer, this does not mean that automation cannot improve the business. Today, there are all kinds of machines, methods, and systems available. These systems are made for use by small business owners by reducing their size, sharing their use, and simplifying methods. Every small business owner can make use of ADP equipment in some way. Many owners are taking advantage of new developments to save money, improve accuracy, and increase productivity.

Automation in the Office: Basic Office Machines

Since 1950, when automatic data processing systems came of age, better machines and methods have been introduced each year. One disadvantage of such a vastly changing field is quite obvious. As companies learn more about machines and computers and the amazing things they can do, older machines become outdated. It almost seems that as soon as one machine is developed, another one comes along which will do the job faster and more accurately. Business owners must carefully examine all of the types of machines available. They must make sure that the machines will be useful for several years to justify the cost. This is one reason why many business owners prefer to lease rather than buy automatic data processing machines.

Mechanical office machines are usually less expensive and easier to operate than electronic equipment. Many of these office machines may already be familiar since they are quite common in small offices. However, some basic office machines are being replaced by types of ADP equipment as ways are found to make computers inexpensive and simpler to use.

The Typewriter. The typewriter is a common fixture in every office, and typing is a basic skill required of office workers. Yet there are many versions of the typewriter which have increased its speed and ability to do various jobs. The electric typewriter has reduced operator fatigue. It has also increased the number of carbon copies that can be produced at one typing. Some electric typewriters have easily interchangeable type. This feature permits a variety of type styles from the same machine. Some typewriters also have automatic correction features.

One version of the typewriter includes a magnetic card machine. It memorizes letters from information stored in a memory unit or retypes manuscript material with an even right-hand margin (justified copy). The Varityper and IBM Composer produce copy that looks like printed material. Other unique adaptations of the typewriter have virtually assured it and its descendants a permanent place in the office.

Adding Machine. Machines that add figures have come a long way from the abacus of ancient China. Calculators do far more than just add. They perform most arithmetical processes. Generally, these types of machines include rotary, key-driven, and electronic calculators. Some calculators register the totals in figures that appear on a screen and require the operator to copy down the answer. Other types may record the figures on a paper tape similar to a cash register tape. Some machines have both a screen and paper tape.

Bookkeeping Machine. Various clerical processes in bookkeeping and accounting can be performed electronically by machine. These machines vary in size and capabilities. But almost every function from posting to billing can be performed automatically by one or more of these machines. Special machines have been developed for various types of businesses. For instance, the bank accounting machine was developed for use by tellers in banks and savings and loan institutions.

Special machines have also been adapted for motels and hotels, service stations, department stores, and many other types of businesses.

Copy Equipment. Much time and money have been wasted in copying over letters and documents. Today many good copy systems, several at low cost, are available to make dry, accurate, legible copies of most any document. There are several types of copy equipment. These types include photochemical (wet copy), photoheat (dry copy), and electrostatic (similar to Xerox). Copy machines are available at reasonable cost. They can save hours of unnecessary typing by secretaries and clerical personnel who could be doing other more important tasks.

Reproduction Equipment. When more than a few copies of a document are needed, the small office should have a method for making a quantity of good copies. Sending out small jobs frequently for commercial printing can be very expensive. Depending on the number needed and the type of work to be copied, many types of machines are available at moderate cost. These types include mimeograph, spirit duplication, and photo-offset. Most clerical personnel are trained in the operation of these machines and they are common in most offices. Certain types of copy equipment (just mentioned) can make masters for duplicating machines, making it unnecessary to type the master over again by hand.

Transcribing Equipment. When a letter is dictated to a stenographer, both the stenographer and the dictator are engaged in the same activity. Sometimes this is not the best use of either person's time. By using a machine that is basically a tape recorder, an individual can dictate letters which can be transcribed at a more convenient time by a typist wearing earphones, Figure 12-1. Transcribing equipment records the sound on plastic tapes, discs, belts, wire, or a wax cylinder. Salespeople who travel can dictate sales reports and then mail them into a central office to be transcribed.

Filing Equipment. One of the problems facing most business owners is the storage of records. Some information must be kept on hand only a few days, while other information must be available for years. There are a lot of ways to store information. Original documents are usually stored in metal file drawers arranged in numerical, chronological, or alphabetical order. Motorized file machines, which look like ferris wheels, can greatly speed up the finding of ledger cards, for instance. Documents that are too large or flimsy to be stored for the required time can be copied on microfilm and stored on reels in metal cans. Information may also be stored on punched cards, magnetic tape, film, or electronically on computer chips. In fact, a number of electronics firms are developing electronic filing systems.

FIGURE 12-1
Transcribing equipment greatly facilitates basic office work.

Telephone. Even the telephone has become automatic. New electronic dialing machines (using tones in place of digits) make possible the memorizing of numbers on a console. All that the busy executive has to do is key the electronic secretary with any one of the most often called numbers, and then the desired number is dialed by the machine. The desk phone is not buzzed until the party answers, so that a busy signal or a wrong number will not waste the executive's time.

Various applications of the telephone have greatly expanded its uses, from carrying computer data from a center to the local subscriber, to automatically answering the business phone after normal work hours and recording the caller's message.

OFFICE MACHINES	
Advantages	**Disadvantages**
Low in initial cost	Limited in storage capacity
Grow obsolete slowly	Can perform only one operation
Easily repaired	at a time
Require little training	Limited in types of computations
Usually portable and easy to use	possible
Require no special installation	Slow
Easily adaptable to many jobs	May require manual operation

Automation in the Office: The Computer

Over the last few years the electronics industry has made such advances that many small businesses are able to afford a computer. Within the near future most small businesses will be using computers.

The computers being used by most small businesses are called *microcomputers.* They are also known as *personal computers* or *small business computers.* A computer system is a combination of hardware and software. *Hardware* is the equipment people see when they look at a computer. *Software* consists of the programs that tell the computer what function to perform. Programs are written in *languages* (symbols) that computers can read.

FIGURE 12-2
So many advances in the electronics industry have made it possible for the small business to afford a computer.

Why buy a computer? A computer can save you time, and time is worth money. This is especially true if you own and operate a small business. Computers are used for such activities as bookkeeping, filing, typing of mailing lists, and storage of information. These are all considered time-consuming activities.

If you decide that a computer is needed to complete work for your business, two choices are possible. A computer can be bought or a computer service bureau can be used. There are a number of firms that sell computer time to small businesses.

Questions to Ask When Buying a Computer

If you decide to buy a computer for your business, where can one be bought and what do you need to know about them? Your first step should be to talk to more than one seller of computers. There are stores that sell personal computers in most average size and large communities today. Some of the questions you need answers to before buying a computer include the following:

- What functions can the computer perform?
- Will this computer system meet my present business needs?
- Can the computer system be expanded to meet my future needs?
- Will the computer fit into the space I have available?
- What is the price of the hardware?
- What is the price of the software?
- What software (programs) will this computer use?
- How much training will be needed in order to use the computer system?
- Is the video screen easy to read?
- What is the service agreement for this computer system?

Once these questions are answered, you should be ready to decide on the computer you want to buy. Before the final purchase is made, you should talk with a small business person who owns and uses the computer you are considering. Remember, this is an important and substantial purchase.

Word Processing. Recent advances in office technology have resulted in new methods of handling business communications. The new automated methods and procedures are known as *word processing*. Word processing consists of recording, storing, composing, and text-editing. Although the cost of this equipment is relatively expensive, new developments in the field are reducing the cost each year. Before long, most small businesses will be using word processing systems.

Automation in the Store

Office work and store work are usually differentiated. However, there are many operations, such as totaling daily sales, accounting for cash, and making out payrolls, which are performed in the store and are essentially clerical or office operations. Therefore, quite a few office machines, such as adding machines, calculators, and typewriters, are used in stores. In addition, there are some machines which are thought of as labor-saving devices in the store or shop. The following is a list of these devices:

- Automatic doors
- Cash registers
- Change makers
- Check-recording equipment
- Checkstand and parcel pickup equipment
- Floor cleaning equipment
- Processing equipment
- Security equipment
- Stamp dispensers
- Stock handling equipment

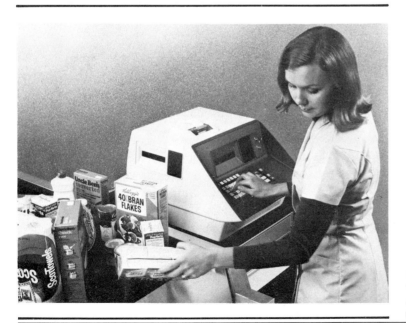

FIGURE 12-3
Today's cash registers are capable of complex computations and record-keeping procedures.

Many tasks must be performed to keep a store clean, attractive, and well stocked. Several of these tasks can be done efficiently and inexpensively by machine. Machines can either replace an employee, make it unnecessary to hire additional employees, or increase the efficiency, productivity, and morale of existing employees. The material that follows describes some of these machines.

Automatic Doors. The automatic-treadle-operated door has become almost a fixture in American supermarkets. Other types include electric-eye-operated doors and touch-operated doors, popular in banks and office buildings. Less well-known to the public are automatic doors on freight and passenger elevators, and on loading docks. Doors to walk-in refrigerators and frozen-food storage areas can be automated so that employees can enter when they are using their hands to transport stock. Stockroom doors can be operated electrically to save wear and tear when struck open by carts and other objects.

Cash Registers. As mentioned in Unit 10, cash registers have advanced from simple adding machines and storage places to rather complex computations. Specific data about purchased merchandise may be recorded and transferred to a computer for inventory purposes.

Change Makers. Automatic change makers are available on the market and used widely in supermarkets and in banks, Figure 12-4. Change-handling equipment saves many hours of labor in businesses where a large volume of coins must be handled, such as stores, offices, and banks. A change-sorting machine will separate various denominations of coins and feed them into hoppers for use in a dispenser or a change-wrapping machine. Some machines can wrap coins in standard amounts by denominations: pennies — 50¢, nickels — $2, dimes — $5, quarters — $10, and halves — $10. Wrappers are colored to indicate the denomination. The wrapped coins may then be stored in the bottom of cash register drawers as a reserve supply of change.

Check-recording Equipment. In supermarkets where many checks are cashed daily, check-copying equipment is desirable. This device photographs on microfilm the check and the person cashing the check at the same time. Monthly reports of the checks and photos of checkpassers are available on request. This type of equipment greatly simplifies the tracing of rubber checks and eases the apprehension of check forgers. A few banks are placing automated terminals in some stores and shopping centers so that customers can cash checks.

Checkstand and Parcel Pickup Equipment. The equipment used to automate the front end of discount and food stores is essentially conveyor equipment adapted for this purpose from conventional stock-handling equipment. Conveyor tracks

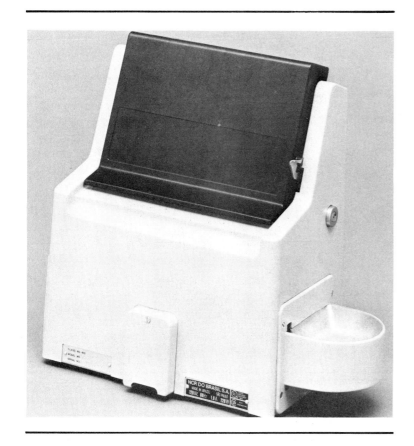

FIGURE 12-4
An automatic change maker

for sending customers' orders out to the pickup area in baskets or in carts are common. The conveyor belts built into the checkstand speed up the cashier's job. The cashier controls the conveyor belts with foot pedals. The use of conveyor belts and checkstand equipment is normally associated with supermarkets and discount houses. However, this equipment is becoming more widespread in self-service retail operations, such as beverage stores, cafeterias, hardware stores, and drugstores.

Floor Cleaning Equipment. As any store owner knows, one of the biggest problems in keeping a store neat is sweeping and cleaning the floors. Any store that has a lot of traffic has a problem keeping floors clean. Automatic floor cleaners are popular in stores such as supermarkets, discount and department stores, and other retail establishments with a great amount of traffic. The machine operates on batteries charged during the day, and is operated at night. The machine cleans a section of floor as it moves along, dispensing water and a cleaning solution,

FIGURE 12-5 This combination of a wrapping machine and an automatic weighing system is designed for high-volume prepackaging. This system will wrap, weigh, price and label meat, fish, poultry, and produce. An attachment is also available for ADP inventory control.

scrubbing the area, and then sucking up the water and drying the area. Some models are equipped to wax the floor.

Processing Equipment. Behind-the-scenes equipment is making the processing of goods of all types faster and making the service for the consumer better. The receiving and pricing of merchandise is greatly speeded up with the use of semi-automatic price ticket machines. These machines prepunch information on the ticket for later use at the point-of-sale. Weighing machines can figure price per pound and automatically print the correct price ticket when processing meat, produce, and other items sold by weight. Electronic counters can verify the count of received goods by weighing packages and scanning them electronically. Goods passing a scanning device can be inspected for flaws. Many routine jobs, previously done by hand, can be adapted to machines in receiving, pricing, weighing, packaging, inspection, and shipping.

Security Equipment. There are many types of machines used by stores to reduce or control shoplifting and stealing. The use of closed-circuit television is expanding.

TV cameras located in various parts of the store make it possible to watch shoppers more carefully than with the use of mirrors. The use of hidden cameras along with burglar alarm systems is widespread in banks and financial institutions. Other security devices include the following:

- ADT (Automatic Direct Telegraph) and other types of burglar alarms with direct connections to local police, fire stations, and the owner's home
- Safety glass which, when broken, will set off an alarm
- Automatic sprinkler systems

The use of sensitive microphones and electric eyes to detect night prowlers is also increasing. Infrared sensing devices can detect potential safecrackers. X-ray and magnetic scanners can detect stolen articles in shoplifters' clothing. One-way glass is used to survey customers, and security personnel can be summoned quickly with the aid of in-store shortwave radio devices.

Stamp Dispensers. Mechanical and electric stamp dispensers are making the checkout process faster in stores where stamps are given. Some cash registers have built-in, stamp-issuing machines. The stamps in these machines are dispensed automatically according to the total sale. Stamp machines can save time in stores doing a large sales volume. The use of stamp dispensers in service stations, dry-cleaning and laundry establishments, and cafeterias continues to grow.

Stock-Handling Equipment. Various kinds of dollies, trucks, and handcarts have been developed to move stock and goods from place to place. Large or heavy stock can be placed on skids or pallets which can be easily picked up by electrically or gasoline powered fork trucks. Conveyor belts and gravity roller tracks greatly speed up the moving of stock from tractor trailers to storage areas. In warehouses, overhead cranes and electric dollies can pick stock from marked bins automatically. Some department stores have stock delivery systems. By simply dialing the desired siding on a computer, stock conveyors on overhead tracks or monorails can be sent automatically to any designated department or place in the store. Adjustable loading docks have also been developed which rise or fall to conform to the height of the tailgate of a truck. Such loading docks make the movement of carts and dollies from the loading area easier.

Automation in Service Businesses

The use of machines in service businesses is varied and so involved that space does not permit a full discussion here. However, if a person is thinking about operating a service business, that person must know about the various types of labor-saving machines available in the specific industry. They vary from all kinds of testing equipment used by the radio and television service people to automatic tools and equipment used by a modern mechanic. The machines and devices available in a particular field should be investigated. Reading trade journals and manuals, which have current listings of equipment, will keep you informed. A great deal may also be learned about new machines and methods from visiting established tradespeople and operators.

As new technological discoveries are made daily, their application to business operation will be investigated, experimented with, and finally applied. The possibilities are many, and the ability of machines to ease human burdens is great. The particular field that the small business owner is involved in will determine just what machinery should be used. Some equipment will be purchased, some rented, or the services of a special firm purchased. Whatever the case, up-to-date knowledge is essential; this, ultimately, is the responsibility of the business owner.

Uniform Product Code. As mentioned earlier in this unit, manufactures are required to print on one side of all packaging materials a particular code. The code is then translated by electronic equipment into price and inventory data. The scanning device reads the black parallel lines on the code in much the same manner as a sensor scans the magnetic ink on an electrographic check, now in popular use. The width and spacing of the parallel lines signifies digits from 0 to 9. The scanner reads and then sends the digital information to the cash register for recording on tapes. If desired, the scanner can also send the information to a coding device which can store the information either on discs or on punched tape. A sample UPC label from a typical product is shown in Figure 12-6. Eventually, most products will be required to have a UPC label displayed on the package, if possible.

FIGURE 12-6
Some sample UPC codes. The parallel lines are "read" by the scanner and translated into useful information.

ENERGY CONSERVATION FOR THE SMALL BUSINESS

In these days of various energy resource shortages, most people have become more energy conscious as consumers. Small businesses are not an exception.

The solar collector shown in Figure 12-7 was used to furnish a local restaurant with hot water for their dishwasher. The collector circulated hot water in insulated underground pipes from the parking lot, where the equipment was located, to the restaurant. The heated water was retained in an insulated storage tank until it was needed. The experiment was conducted for a six-month period by the Atmospheric Sciences Research Center of the State University of New York. The equipment was installed at no cost to the restaurant. Of course, not all small businesses get such a break. In this case, the state paid out tax dollars to prove that solar collectors can work and that they are a viable alternate source of energy. The savings to the restaurant was small. But, the experiment indicates that there is a great deal of potential for solar energy, even for the small business in the future. It is important to realize that small businesses have a stake in the search for alternate energy sources, just as much as individuals do.

As technology continues to develop, we may in the future be using thermonuclear energy to a greater extent, geothermal energy from out of the ground, solar energy, and even hydroelectric power. A local college campus, though not a small business, saves on its energy costs by generating hydroelectric power for the

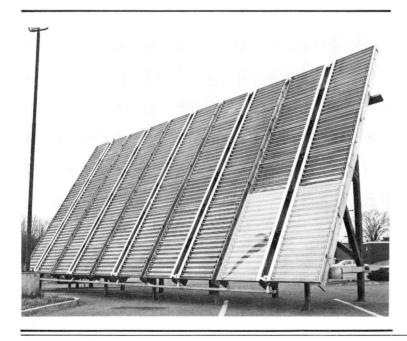

FIGURE 12-7
A solar collector is capable of saving considerably on energy. This collector was located in the parking lot of a restaurant and was used to heat the water for the dishwashing equipment in the restaurant.

dormitories. This project is the work of the electrical engineering department of the college. It is estimated that about 16% of the power needs of the college are supplied by the power of falling water.

You should consult with architects and energy conservation experts when building or renovating any structure. It is a good idea to make sure you have done all you can to make the structure as energy efficient as possible. Adequate insulation, proper use of materials, and the proper placement of the building in terms of prevailing winds can save more energy and money than you may think. Local public utilities have engineering departments that will assist you with your energy needs and planning. They will even help you with the building design. State Departments of Conservation have a great deal of valuable free information about energy conservation. They can give you the latest research on such topics as energy from recycled garbage and energy from the wind. They will also provide you with a list of vendors of these new and experimental devices and equipment, and it may be worthwhile for you to look into their use in your business.

MANAGEMENT ASSISTANCE

Poor management is the most frequent reason for business failure. Incompetence and lack of experience show up quickly in business losses. In starting a business, a person needs all the help possible. There are many experienced people and generous organizations willing to offer advice. With some services, such as management consulting, advertising, and accounting, a fee must be paid. These types of services are good investments because they result in better decisions. Other services, especially those provided by state and federal governments, are free. All a business owner needs to do is ask for aid.

It is very important to the success of any business to find out what aids are available in the local community. Important decisions should not be made alone. Until a great deal of experience has been built up, owners need the advice of trained people. And after setting up a successful business, they must keep up to date with legal, financial, industrial, and scientific developments in their field. They must find out where to get help and then put it to good use.

Public Assistance

Usually when government-business relations are discussed, the subject concerns government regulation of business. Federal, state, and local agencies can be very helpful to the manager of a small business. Information agencies and legal regulations are often one means by which the government helps small businesses to survive and prosper.

Small Business Administration. The Small Business Administration (SBA) is a federal agency which was established in 1953. Its major purposes are to advise, assist, and protect small businesses. The SBA has 10 regional offices and over 90 district and branch offices located in larger cities in each of the 50 states. When planning a business, it is wise to find the nearest SBA office in your area and to make use of its resources. The SBA provides assistance in three major areas:

- Financial advice and backing
- Procurement of markets
- Consultation services in management and technical problems

The SBA makes regular direct business loans on a participation or guarantee basis or loans that are guaranteed through local commercial banks. The Small Business Investment Act of 1958 was passed to help finance small businesses. Under this act as amended, the SBA licenses and supervises privately owned and operated loan agencies. These loaning units are called *Small Business Investment Companies* (SBIC) and provide long-term funds only to small businesses. They are organized by local citizens and chartered under the corporation laws of the state in which they are located.

The SBA is very involved in helping small businesses find a market for their products. They try to bring the small businesses in contact with government agencies which buy the products they sell. Some government orders are set aside for bidding only from small businesses. A large or costly government order may be too much to be handled independently. To handle such orders, production pools are organized among small businesses.

The SBIC may purchase stock in small businesses which have been incorporated or it may make direct loans. The most common type of loan is in the form of convertible debentures. *Debentures* are a type of bond which obligates the business to pay interest and principal when due according to agreed-upon terms. Convertible debentures are purchased from the businesses by the SBIC at a relatively low interest charge. These debentures may be converted to common stock in the business if the investment company wishes.

Perhaps the most important way in which SBA can help a business is in giving advice. It prints many series of management and technical publications, which are available from the Superintendent of Documents, U.S. Government Printing Office, Washington, D.C. A business reference library is also available at the nearest SBA office.

The SBA cooperates with colleges and universities to set up small business research studies. SBA sponsors a Small Business Institute Program with 450 Schools of Business Administration. It also offers evening courses at many local colleges. These evening courses are usually six to eight weeks in length.

Staff specialists in regional SBA offices are able to help individual business owners with the problems of operating their businesses. The SBA has also organized a service group of retired business executives in many sections of the country. Members of *SCORE* (Service Core of Retired Executives) offer their advice free to small business owners with special problems.

The SBA is authorized, under Section 502 of the Small Business Administration Act of 1958, as amended, to lend funds to local development companies in amounts of up to $500,000. The local development companies use the funds to finance projects for small firms. Some of the ways funds are used include:

- Economic opportunity loans to help socially or economically disadvantaged persons to own and operate a business
- Local development company loans
- A variety of loans designed to offset the hardships of economic emergencies

The U.S. Department of Commerce. The U.S. Department of Commerce is an important source of statistical data. This data is helpful in finding a good location for a business, appraising future customers, planning advertising, sizing up competition, and locating sources of supply. Available information includes the following:

- Employment and unemployment rates
- Agricultural data on county basis
- Population count and characteristics
- Estimates on population movements
- Regional trends in U.S. economy
- Business statistics and business indicators
- Development and maintenance of markets
- Distribution channels, facilities, etc.
- Distribution costs
- Research sources for market potentials

The U.S. Department of Commerce, like the SBA, has regional offices. The business reference library in each office contains publications from both governmental and private agencies. The offices stock a wide range of official government publications and employ trained persons to explain the proper uses of the information and to assist in specific problems.

Pollution Control Financing and Incentives. Pollution control standards, and a concern for efficient use of energy resources, require even greater attention to the environmental impacts of industrial processes. Most states have already set up programs to aid industry in the construction of pollution control facilities. These programs include granting tax credits and exemptions for such projects, and providing low-cost financing to ease the burden of meeting environmental standards.

Air- and water-pollution control facilities are eligible for the investment tax credit. This credit can be applied against local and state corporate franchise taxes and unincorporated business taxes.

Industrial waste treatment and air-pollution control facilities are granted certain exemptions. They are exempt from local real property taxes and ad valorem levies against any resultant increase in value when they build or rebuild their facility to comply with the state environmental conservation laws, codes, and regulations.

The U.S. Department of Agriculture. This federal department can supply information on the marketing of agricultural goods and services, consumer buying habits, and trends in retail food marketing.

The Federal Reserve Board. The Federal Reserve Banks put out publications which have information on banking and finance. Owners can find out about trends in interest rates, economic conditions, and consumer-spending behavior through the Federal Reserve Bulletins. These bulletins may be obtained through the U.S. Printing Office.

Your State Department of Commerce. Under the commerce department programs in most states, help is given to manufacturers and other people in business who need trained workers. The programs give aid in the form of training allowances for up to as much as half of an employee's wages. The trainee can be aided for as long as 26 weeks, or 130 working days. The amount of time depends on the worker, how hard the job to be learned is, and the availability of funds. Since the worker is trained while actually working, the program is known as the *on-the-job training (OJT) program.* It is based on the theory that one of the best places to learn a certain job is by actually doing the job until you get it right.

Economic Development Administration (EDA). The Economic Development Administration is an agency of the U.S. Department of Commerce. It offers many kinds of programs aimed at restoring the economic well-being of areas that have high unemployment and low income families.

Under the Special Economic Development and Adjustment Assistance Program, the EDA is authorized to assist states and local areas in redressing actual or threatened economic adjustment problems due to the following situations:

- Action of the federal government, such as closing down a military installation.
- Compliance with environmental requirements which remove economic activities from a locality.
- Severe changes in economic conditions, such as technological changes, resource depletion, or boom-town conditions, created by new economic activity in an area.

The EDA gives grants to qualified applicants (usually the smallest governmental units capable of dealing effectively with the problem) to develop and implement plans for handling the economic dislocation.

Your State Department of Labor. In many states the Departments of Labor and Commerce work closely together. The Department of Labor in any state will assist you in finding suitable trainees for commerce OJT programs, and in preparing the required training schedule for each applicant. Departments of Labor in most states also operate their own OJT programs supplemented with federal funds. These programs are operated under the federal Comprehensive Employment and Training Act (CETA), which has been in existence since 1973. In these programs, employers can be reimbursed for training costs of new workers, provided the labor department refers the worker and gets "credit" for placing that worker.

Another Department of Labor program is the WIN-OJT program (WIN stands for Work IN-centive). Trainees who are getting public assistance or aid to families with dependent children are eligible to be hired under this program. But, they must be referred by the department of labor in your state.

Some of the advantages of these programs to a business owner include the reimbursement of partial wages (every three months) and considerable tax credits for many years. One disadvantage is that an owner cannot select the workers. Persons referred by the department must be taken or you do not get the subsidy. Another disadvantage includes your moral obligation, at least, to pay full wages to the worker upon completion of the program.

Other State and Local Programs. In addition to wage subsidies for trainees, many states and communities have Job Development Corporations. These corporations receive monies from the state's Job Development Authority to make low-cost loans directly to businesses for any of the following reasons:

- Acquisition of buildings and equipment
- Rehabilitation or expansion of existing facilities (especially in urban areas)
- Necessary demolition of old structures
- Land fill and improvement
- Installation of utilities

The business must show that it will create new jobs and can be any type of business except a retail store or a motel, hotel, or restaurant.

Many states through their education departments offer all types of occupational education for workers. These programs include apprenticeship training programs, evening division instruction, and even degree programs. The state will assume all or part of the cost so that workers can become upgraded, retrained, or made more efficient.

Tax Credits. States are always competing with each other to attract businesses. The reason is obvious. Businesses make good neighbors because they provide jobs, increase economic activity, and promote the use of the goods and services they make or offer. When planning to locate or relocate in a given state, find out (from local chambers of commerce, etc.) what kind of tax incentives are offered for coming into the area. Tax credits can include reductions in federal and state business income tax, property tax credits, and investment credits. The Internal Revenue Service and state tax authorities will give small business assistance in tax planning.

Your State Department of Education. State education departments have special services available to the business owner. This department puts out educational publications, some of which may be helpful in a specific business field. The Distributive Education Division, for example, provides instruction for owners and employees in special areas and collects, sorts, and supplies useful marketing information within the state.

Private Assistance

A number of specialized private agencies and organizations have developed to keep pace with the complexities of modern business. When owners have special problems which they cannot solve alone, they should know where to go for help.

Trade Associations. A *trade association* is an organization of people and companies who are in the same business. The organization can be used by the members as a central clearinghouse for information. Activities include trade publications, trade meetings, and training courses. Some associations, like the National Small Business Men's Association, represent their members in working for favorable legislation and helping them in their business dealings with governmental agencies. Additional services provided by trade associations include the following:

- Credit reporting services
- Statistics about local industry or business
- Technical research
- Conventions and meetings
- Publicity and public relations programs
- Better record-keeping methods and distributing methods
- Technical information, especially to small businesses and labor relations services.

Dues are required for membership in a trade association. The amount is determined by the size of the association and the number and quality of the services it offers. Dues may also be partially based on the annual sales volume of the business. National and state associations usually collect dues once each year, but monthly collections may be made for local organizations. It is a good idea for small business owners to join the trade association appropriate to their business and to subscribe to more than one trade publication in their field.

Management Consultants. A *management consultant* is a person with special technical ability, experience, and education who provides professional advice in recognizing and solving management problems. Such problems may arise in the planning, direction, organization, or operations of a business. Owners pay for the consultant's suggestions. It is therefore important that they get their money's worth. Owners must be sure that they are choosing the right consultant for their problems. They must then decide if and how to implement the suggested changes. A management consultant advises, but owners must be able and willing to act upon the offered advice.

Accountants. Adequate accounting records are essential to the success of any business. Studies have shown that about one-third of small business bankrupts keep no records and less than one-fourth keep adequate records. Without good accounting records, it is difficult to know when a business is failing. Good records, on the other hand, can report losses before they become too large.

The services of a *certified public accountant* (CPA) are as important to the owner of a small business as those of a lawyer. An accountant can set up a record-keeping system tailored to specific needs, trace business losses, and provide invaluable service at tax time.

Accounting systems should not be set up without the advice of a CPA. Business owners should collect what information they can on systems, standards, and guides from the U.S. Department of Commerce, their trade associations, and their suppliers. The business should then be thoroughly explained to its CPA. Owners should work closely with their accountants in setting up the system. Certified public accountants should, in turn, check books once a year and prepare statements.

When owners cannot solve financial problems themselves, a CPA should be contacted. Where there is a good accounting system to begin with, the CPA can usually find those areas causing losses and suggest policies to remedy the problem. For example, a business owner who rarely uses out-of-town suppliers may, for expediency, put freight charges under the general overhead cost. When the profit margin slips and the owner calls the CPA, it may be found that out-of-town shipments have gradually increased. The problem could be solved by allocating freight bills to the cost of goods sold.

It is a widely accepted belief that tax returns are confusing. The more complicated business operations are, the more difficult it is to prepare an accurate return. Owners may pay more taxes than they actually owe because they do not take advantage of all their allowed exemptions or deductions. On the other hand, owners may not be setting aside funds for extra tax liabilities because they do not know about them. If a CPA audits a business' books and completes the tax return, a good deal of money and trouble may be saved.

Collection Agencies. For a service charge, agencies will take over the task of collecting delinquent accounts for a business. Collection agencies usually charge at least 25% of the amount they are able to collect. Some retailers feel the service is worth the cost.

Advertising Agencies. In most areas, business owners will be able to find small businesses to help with their advertising. Services such as copywriting, layout, commercial illustration, photography, direct mail, research, and display work are all available. Owners should use these services as needed to make sure their advertising is effective. After all, they are paying for advertising time or space (according to the medium chosen). Ineffective, unskilled advertising is a waste of money. Advertising media usually pay advertising agencies 15% commission on the space or time the agency buys so that, in effect, owners are paying 15% more for services they are not using.

Better Business Bureaus. The *better business bureau* is a local organization formed by business owners to protect themselves against unfair competition. The bureau investigates complaints from both customers and businesses. If the bureau finds that unethical practices are being used, it tries to persuade the business owner to change. If the practices persist, the bureau warns the public through newspapers, radio, or television of the unethical practices used by the business owner.

Chamber of Commerce. A chamber of commerce is a group of local business owners organized to improve and increase business in the community, Figure 12-8. This group encourages new businesses, tries to improve the business community, and works for better public relations. One of the main advantages of belonging to the local chamber of commerce is the personal contact with other business owners. The chamber of commerce offers many of the same services to its members as a trade association.

Colleges and Universities. It is important to find out how the colleges and universities in local areas help businesses in the community. Faculty members may practice as management consultants on a part-time basis. The school may sponsor executive development and management courses or be engaged in research studies and product development of interest to business. And, of course, college

FIGURE 12-8 A chamber of commerce is established to improve and increase business in a community.

placement offices are a good source for finding qualified personnel. Some schools offer apprenticeships or tuition programs providing that the trainees are interested in a career in your type of business.

Manufacturers and Distributors. Manufacturers and distributors provide valuable services in their attempts to satisfy their customers. One way for them to increase their business is to increase the business of their customers.

The sales representatives of manufacturers and distributors can offer advice on matters of advertising, display, buying, stock control, and sales promotion. The suppliers of office equipment may be able to help with office operations such as billing and filing. It is wise to remember, though, that the aid offered by suppliers is sometimes biased in favor of their products and services.

YOUR POLICIES FOR THE FUTURE

Business ethics are principles of conduct which should guide all business dealings. These principles should help determine major and minor policies in all areas: finance, personnel, buying, and customer relations, just to name a few. They should also guide day-to-day decisions. An ethical business owner treats customers with courteous service and suppliers with integrity. They also treat employees with fairness and consideration. An unethical business owner not only harms other people in his or her dealings, but also gets a bad reputation and forms enemies by such actions.

There are a number of situations in which business owners can do nothing legally wrong but must decide between practicing good or bad ethics. For example, suppose Ms. Robertson, the owner of a clothing store, ordered merchandise from a supplier who in turn offered her a cash discount. Cash discounts are often used as an incentive for prompt payment. If she took advantage of the discount by paying the invoice before the amount was due, both Ms. Robertson and the supplier would benefit. This is an ethical transaction. Suppose, on the other hand, that the supplier's representative, Mr. Berne, offered her a kickback, or cash payment, for placing the order through him. Either Ms. Robertson is cheated because the representative must increase prices to cover kickback or Mr. Berne is cheating the company to increase his commissions. This is an unethical business transaction.

To a great extent, the future of any small business rests on the ethical reputation it creates. As advanced technology becomes available to small business owners, competition becomes more keen. Modern and efficient service, as a means of attracting and holding customers, is giving way more and more to a reputation for integrity. In other words, the public is attracted to businesses whose owners are known for their honesty. It appears to be simple, but keeping up a reputation for fair and honest work is a hard task. Businesses are judged by hundreds, even thousands, of customers and smaller numbers of employees, suppliers, and regulatory agencies. How does one begin to please them all?

Workers depend upon the business owners who hire them. Following a good code of ethics means business owners must give good pay for reasonable hours of work. They must listen to reasonable complaints and handle them fairly. They must make working conditions pleasant and safe. Workers, on their part, must do their jobs with interest and enthusiasm, thus earning the money, conditions, and good treatment given them.

Suppliers, wholesalers, and manufacturers should be fairly treated. Owners should not try to cut corners. They should be fair about returns, discounts, and cancelled orders. They should also treat sales representatives with courtesy. Suppliers show their appreciation by giving better service and treatment when owners call upon them. Many business owners who treated salespeople badly before World War II when many representatives were trying to sell the same goods, paid for it dearly when they could not get goods during the war. When sugar was difficult to get, salespeople who had some to sell remembered who treated them well earlier and offered it to those people first.

Customers and the public are the most important consideration. Business owners must give good service, be honest and trustworthy, give full value in price and quality, and advertise in a manner that is sincere, accurate, and useful to the customers. The business will then be rewarded with satisfied customers.

Potential business owners should begin setting up operating policies as soon as they start planning their businesses. A *policy* is a pattern in decision making which results in the reputation or image of a business. All business activities should be based on policies which have been carefully thought out. Following a given policy has the advantage of conserving energy and resources by directing them toward an established goal. Without policy, time and money are wasted away thoughtlessly.

Constantly changing policies are as bad as no policies at all. Once a practice has been set, people expect the owner to abide by it. The routines of suppliers, employees, and customers are determined by specific policies. When these are modified, all affected parties should be notified.

It should now be obvious that ethical practices alone do not determine business success. Unethical practices can, however, cause business failure. No matter how perfect the organization, location, and advertising might be, business success requires sincere purpose and determination. Policy guidelines which are carefully thought out, evaluated, and modified when necessary, are an invaluable tool in achieving this end.

BUSINESS MANUAL ASSIGNMENT

With this assignment, your manual will be complete. Write two or three paragraphs explaining your views on the future of the business you chose. Support your conclusions with facts and statistics, and give examples of future plans you have for the business. Make out a list of equipment you would buy for your business, if the capital was available, to simplify and improve work, data processing, product quality, or any business operations. You might consider a scanning register, a minicomputer, or other items. Call local suppliers for prices and make up a tentative budget.

Conclude your manual with the following items:

- A bibliography
- An appendix (include any additional explanatory material you wish)
- Acknowledgments and references

When you have completed your business manual, you may want to submit it for your instructor's comments and suggestions. The instructor may want to review your manual for grading purposes. It is hoped you will keep the manual as a useful tool in future planning of your business. Good Luck!

TERMS TO KNOW

Uniform Product Code	computer	SBA
scanner	memory chip	on-the-job training
electronic	ADP	management consultants
voice print	hardware	debenture
policy	software	trade associations
automation	word processing	CPA
programming	solar collector	

UNIT QUIZ

In each of the following, select the word or phrase that best completes the statement or answers the question.

1. Which of the following is not an unwise business policy?
   a. Seek help in business when you need it.
   b. Do not bother other people with your business problems.
   c. Asking for assistance with business matters is a sign of weakness.
   d. Do not let on that your business is in trouble by asking for help.

2. Which one of the following statements is true about advertising agencies?
   a. They are expensive.
   b. They can serve a useful purpose.
   c. They do professional work, usually better than you can do.
   d. All of these statements are true.

3. Which one of the following statements is the best advice about legal aid for your business?
   a. Retain a lawyer so you will always have one when you need one.
   b. Get legal advice only when you need it.
   c. Do not worry about legal problems until they arise.
   d. Develop a sound legal policy with the aid of a lawyer.

4. Which one of the following is a good policy regarding machines, automation, and new equipment?
   a. Get the latest devices and equipment so that you will stay ahead of your competition.
   b. Keep track of all developments in your field and maintain an information file.
   c. Do not take a chance on anything new until it has been thoroughly tested and proven.
   d. Develop a sound automation policy with the aid of engineers and scientists.

5. Which one of the following statements is a good reason for joining a trade association?
   a. Because the dues are high, people will think you are successful if you join.
   b. It is a status symbol, and you can proudly display their plaque in your office.
   c. You get up-to-date information about business trends and legislation.
   d. It is always comforting to belong to a group.

6. The future for small business looks good because
   a. it is always good to have an optimistic opinion of the future.
   b. things cannot get worse, so they must get better.
   c. population will probably continue to grow, and with it a need for more businesses.
   d. the government will probably place fewer controls and restrictions on small businesses in the future.

7. The systematic use of machines and methods to simplify work and speed up any task is known as
   a. machine accounting.   c. serendipity.
   b. automation.   d. systomation.

8. A small business belongs to a trade association because
   a. they can provide credit reporting services.
   b. they provide conferences and conventions and product shows.
   c. they can assist with better record-keeping and accounting systems.
   d. they provide all of these services.

9. According to the text,
   a. the small business owner does not have to be concerned with automation.
   b. automation only applies to large computers.
   c. automation is feasible for small businesses.
   d. automation is only used in offices.

10. Automated equipment will be used in the future by
    a. service businesses.   c. manufacturing businesses.
    b. retail businesses.   d. all of these.

11. One disadvantage for the small business that has a computer is that it
    a. is expensive if not utilized fully.
    b. can process large quantities of data.
    c. can summarize data quickly.
    d. can find stored data quickly.

12. Which one of the following groups consists of retired business executives who offer their help to small businesses having difficulty?
    a. SBIC   c. SBA
    b. NARP   d. SCORE

13. Which one of the following is not a function of the Small Business Administration?
    a. To give financial advice and assist in obtaining loans
    b. To regulate small businesses
    c. To help small businesses sell products and services
    d. To give management and technical advice

14. A local organization formed by business owners to protect themselves against unfair competition is the
    a. Small Business Administration.
    b. Department of Commerce.
    c. chamber of commerce.
    d. better business bureau.

15. An organization used by individuals and companies in the same business as a center for information and services is known as a(n)
    a. chamber of commerce.   c. investment corporation.
    b. trade association.   d. parent company.

16. A source of information on energy conservation for the small business is
    a. a local university.
    b. a local public utility.
    c. a State Department of Conservation.
    d. all of these.

17. The computers being used by small businesses are known as
    a. office machines.   c. word computers.
    b. microcomputers.   d. calculators.

18. One caution about using company representatives as sources of assistance is that they
    a. usually know their field.
    b. act as consultants in many situations.
    c. usually help solve a problem.
    d. favor their own products and services.

19. Some sound advice concerning business policies is that
    a. they should be changed frequently.
    b. they should be tested.
    c. they should be based on personal feelings.
    d. they are not really needed by small businesses.

20. An organization used by individuals and companies in the same locality as a center for information and services is known as a(n)
    a. chamber of commerce.   c. trade association.
    b. investment corporation.   d. better business bureau.

21. Small businesses can obtain low-cost loans from any of the following organizations except
    a. the Job Development Authority.
    b. the Industrial Development Agency.
    c. the Small Business Administration.
    d. the Economic Development Administration.

22. Machines that record, store, compose, and text-edit business communications are known as
    a. calculators.   c. computers.
    b. copy equipment.   d. word processors.

23. One of the advantages of using office machines is that they are
    a. slow.
    b. limited in types of computations.
    c. easily repaired.
    d. limited in storage capacity.

24. Which one of the following is an organization that provides long-term funds only to small businesses?
    a. Small business investment companies
    b. Insurance companies
    c. State government
    d. Personal loan companies

25. A federal agency that offers programs aimed at restoring the economic well-being of areas that have high unemployment is the
    a. U.S. Department of Agriculture.
    b. Federal Reserve Board.
    c. Economic Development Administration.
    d. Service Core of Retired Executives.

GLOSSARY

ABA numbers — Numbers appearing on a check issued by the Federal Reserve System and the American Banker's Association. They are used for the purpose of identification and the fast routing of checks through the clearinghouse system.

account — (1) An accounting device used to sort out and summarize changes caused by daily business transactions. An account is the record of amounts classified by the title of the account on a ledger card. (2) Also means to keep track of, for example, account for money, expenses

account number — A number given to an account to show its location in the ledger

account title — A name given to an account, usually arranged in alphabetical order. In the accounts payable and receivable ledgers, the titles of the accounts are the names and addresses of customers and vendors.

accountant — A professional who plans, summarizes, analyzes, and audits financial records

accounting — The process of planning, summarizing, and interpreting financial records

accounting clerk — A person who records the financial activities of a business, for example, a bookkeeper

accounting cycle — The complete series of activities involved in the double-entry bookkeeping system from the beginning of one fiscal period to the beginning of the next

accounting department — The section of a business where the bookkeeping, payroll, and audit functions are carried out

accounting equation — The statement of equality — assets = liabilities + net worth

accounting records — An orderly series of notations of all the financial activities of an individual or a business which are kept in journals and ledgers

accounts payable — The accounts of all the vendors or suppliers to whom a business owes money. The accounts are kept in a ledger called the *accounts payable ledger* and filed in alphabetical order.

accounts receivable — The accounts of all the customers a business has who owe that business money. The accounts are kept in a ledger called the *accounts receivable ledger* and filed in alphabetical order.

accrual basis — An accounting term describing a method of accumulating total income or expense on a periodic basis, even if the income has not yet been received or the expense has not yet been paid, to be sure that there is money set aside to pay them, for example, accruing income tax from employees so that the taxes can be paid to the federal government every quarter

Act of God — A term usually used in connection with an insurance contract. It refers to those occurrences which are not preventable, such as earthquakes, floods, wars, etc., and are the cause of losses for which the insurance company normally is not responsible.

adjusting entries — Notations made in the general journal, usually at the end of an accounting period, to bring ledger accounts up to date

adjustments — (1) Changes made in the ledger accounts at the end of a fiscal period in order to bring the records up to date and in line with correct account balances; (2) Refunds and/or allowances made to a purchaser in a retail establishment for defective merchandise, either returned for refund or exchange

ad valorem — In proportion to the value, a phrase applied to certain duties levied on imports according to their invoiced value, and on real estate taxes where property has been improved and its value has been added on (in Latin, term means *added value*)

advertising — Any paid form of nonpersonal presentation or promotion of ideas, goods, and services by an identified sponsor

advertising agency — A professional organization rendering advertising services to clients for a fee

agency — (1) A business, firm, or person who is empowered to act for another and usually the office of such a firm or person; (2) A form of government organization that administers tax dollars for the benefit of people to provide programs and services which benefit or protect all people. Examples of agencies include the FBI, CIA, FAA, FCC, FTC, and FDA.

agency shop — A place of work where there is a contract between the employer and the union representing the majority of the employees, that requires those who do want to join the union to pay the union an agency fee instead of union dues in exchange for the representation service the union provides. It replaces the *closed shop* which is illegal under the Taft-Hartley Act.

agent — A person or firm empowered to act for another, or a person representing a business (often an insurance company) or firm, such as a business agent or a manufacturer's representative

air check — A video recording or an audio tape of a radio or TV broadcast that serves as a file copy of an actual broadcast or program so that the sponsor can evaluate talent, production quality, and overall performance

aisle — A space between counters in a store or shop that is created by the arrangement of the counters. A standard aisle should be at least three feet wide.

aisle display — A display place in an aisle or at the end of an aisle that forces customers to view a display as they move around the store, because the display is physically in their way

alienate — (1) To offend or so antagonize customers or employees as to remove all trust. For example, employees may be alienated by management because of lack of good faith in bargaining, or customers may be alienated by salespersons because they are rude or impolite (2) To transfer the ownership of property

allocation — (1) The assignment by the Federal Communications Commission (FCC) of the frequency and power (wattage) that radio or television stations may use; (2) The allotting of space in a store for the display of various products

alternate sponsor — If a radio or television program is expensive to sponsor, the cost can be shared with another person, called an *alternate sponsor*, who pays for the program every other week, thus reducing the cost to each sponsor.

amplitude modulation (AM) — A method of broadcasting by using a radio signal that varies the amplitude (the size of the wave) instead of the frequency (the number of waves). The effective range of an AM station can be as far away as 1,000 miles.

announcement — A radio or television commercial that varies in length from ten seconds to one minute

announcer — One who reads the audio (voice) part of advertisements

annuity — An investment usually in a bank or trust account yielding a fixed sum of money periodically for a lifetime or a stated period of time, or in perpetuity for heirs of an estate

apiarist — One who keeps an apiary, that is, a beekeeper, one who helps to produce honey

appeal — A motive toward which an advertisement is directed and which is designed to stir a person to take action that may eventually lead to purchasing the product or service

appreciation — (1) Grateful recognition for doing a job well or for a favor, or a sensitive awareness of the value of something, such as fine music or art; (2) The rise in the value or price of property due to scarcity, or the reduction in the supply of the item, or land, especially, in real estate

apprentice — The term applies to any person who is acquiring a skill, trade, or craft ability, usually as a member of a labor union and under specified conditions requiring classroom instruction as well as on-the-job training.

apprenticeship — The length of time it takes to complete an apprentice program. The length varies with the complexity of the trade, and may be as short as three years or as long as six years.

arbitrate — To settle or judge a dispute between labor and management. When the parties agree to the decision of the arbitrator, this is known as *binding arbitration.*

arbitrator — One who arbitrates, settles a dispute; an outsider who is brought in to bring the parties to a settlement, that is, an unbiased third party

arson — The crime of deliberately setting a fire, usually to commercial property, and sometimes in an attempt to collect on an insurance policy

arsonist — One who commits arson

articles of copartnership — A contract forming the basis of a partnership, stating the rights and privileges of the partners and the terms of the partnership. The contract makes one partner responsible for the debts of the others, unless stated otherwise.

asset — Any property which has value and which can be exchanged or converted into cash

assets — The entire resources of a person or business, tangible and intangible, such as accounts and notes receivable, cash, inventory, equipment, real estate, good will, etc.

association test — A test to determine how well persons can identify a product by its brand name, slogan, logo, trademark, or layout. A panel is asked what product brand comes to mind when each product is named. It is a test of the effectiveness of advertising.

audience — All the people who listen to or see advertising of all kinds, including on radio and television, in printed matter, on billboards, buses and trolleys, and posters

audience share — The number or proportion of receiving sets (radio or television) that are in use and are tuned to a particular program or channel

audio — The sound portion of a telecast

audit — The checking of records or a set of books by a qualified accountant, usually a certified public accountant, for errors and any possibility of fraud or dishonesty

auditor — One who conducts an audit, for example, an accountant

author's corrections — Notes and corrected errors written on a galley proof by the author to show corrections before copy is retyped

automation — A system or method in which many or all of the processes of production, movement, and inspection of parts and materials are automatically performed or controlled by self-operating equipment, electronic devices, etc., to replace human beings in performing routine or repetitive jobs

baccalaureate degree — A four-year college degree: bachelor of arts or bachelor of science

background — (1) A record of a person's activities, sometimes from birth (that is, a security or background check); used to establish national loyalty and for granting industrial and military security clearances. (2) Music piped into a store to relax customers and get them to shop longer; also, music in the background of an advertisement or commercial, and the music or sound effects used behind the dialogue in a broadcast program or announcement used for realistic or emotional effect

back-to-back — Scheduling two different commercials directly following each other

balance — (1) The amount of money in an account; that is, the difference between the debit and credit sides of an account. Used as a verb, it means to balance an account or to determine the amount of the balance. (2) The art of distributing the elements of an advertising layout so that they are in harmony and offset one another; (3) An instrument used in a drugstore to measure small amounts, usually in grams, and also used to weigh precious metals

balance sheet — A financial report listing the amounts of a company's assets, liabilities and net worth, so as to show their relationship to each other, and the totals which balance according to the formula: assets = liabilities + net worth

balloons — Small line drawings in the shape of "balloons" projecting from a cartoon character in a comic strip that imply what the character is saying. When closed, the balloon implies audible speech. When drawn with bubbles, the balloon implies thoughts.

bank — A financial institution; a place where depositors keep their money in accounts which pay interest. There are several kinds, such as commercial banks and savings banks.

bank balance — The ending balance in a bank account, usually at the end of a fiscal period, according to the bank records. It does not show deposits made after the date issued or outstanding checks that have not yet reached the bank.

bank discount — Interest collected by a bank in advance on a note or loan submitted before its maturity date, that is, discounting a note

bank interest — Money earned on a savings account (and on special checking accounts) for letting a bank have the use of the money. The interest is usually paid quarterly.

bank service charge — A fee deducted from the balance of a bank account by the bank to cover the cost of administering the account.

bank statement — A report issued to a depositor by the bank, usually monthly, showing all transactions affecting the account, together with all paid checks drawn on the account within the period

bankrupt — The state of a business or person when insolvent; insufficient assets to equal liabilities. The insolvent person is allowed to pay less than the full amount due to each creditor by dividing all remaining assets equally among them under the supervision of an administrator.

bar — (1) An association of attorneys, within any state, which conducts bar examinations for eligible individuals to be admitted to the practice of law, and working with the state, issues licenses to practice in the courts of the state; (2) A business principally selling wine, beer, and liquor, and when required in some states, food

bargaining — Negotiating between parties to settle contracts and/or disputes, oftentimes dealing with labor relations and usually involving unions (labor) and management (owners). See *collective bargaining.*

bargaining agent — A labor or union representative elected or appointed by a union to represent the union and its members in negotiations with management

BASIC — A computer language; a system of instructions to a computer which programs it and tells it what to do

basic network — The number of stations which national or regional advertisers must agree to have carry their announcements, if buying network advertising. It is frequently less than all of the stations in the network.

bear — A stock market speculator who believes that stock prices are going to go down, and is therefore selling stock

bear market — A condition in the stock market where the trend is for prices to descend

bearer — Anyone who carries (or bears) a negotiable instrument which can be cashed by anyone; for example, cash is bearer paper.

bilk — To cheat or defraud, that is, to get away without paying a bill or debt

bill of lading — A document accompanying a shipment stating the terms of its delivery, the nature of the contents of the shipment, its destination, and rates, etc.

billboard — A term describing a poster sign that is put up outdoors and faces a highway to display various advertising

bills — Invoices or statements, that is, requests for payment

binder — A memo issued by an insurance broker or agency stating that certain insurance coverage exists and is in force; temporary proof of insurance

blank check — A check which has been signed by the drawer with the amount left blank so that anyone can fill in the amount

blank endorsement — A type of endorsement consisting of only the signature on the back of a check, thus permitting anyone to cash it

bleed — A typographical term used in advertising layouts which means to permit an offset photograph (halftone) to run to the edges of the paper, that is, bleed to the edge leaving no margin

blisterpack — A packaging term referring to the practice of mounting small items of merchandise on a card with a bubble or plastic cover to protect the item; also called a *bubble pack*

blowup — An enlargement of a photograph used in advertising layouts

blueprint — A copy of a drawing, used mainly for copying plans, designs, and drawings; used often in the construction and manufacturing fields

board — A group of citizens or members of a firm who form a committee to conduct business, for example, a town board, a school board, a board of directors

board of directors — The governing body of a corporation. A board of directors consists of the officers of the corporation, the directors of the corporation, and a chairperson, elected by the board members.

board of governors — The governing body of a cooperative and other nonprofit corporations, such as educational trusts, foundations, and charitable organizations

board of trade — Another name in some communities for the chamber of commerce. A board of trade represents local business people in affairs which affect the economy of the community.

body — The written text or copy of an advertisement

body type — The type normally used for copy, usually 14 points or smaller

bold — Heavier than normal typefaces which set off words and phrases from the remaining text. The terms in this glossary are set in **boldface** type.

bona fide — In good faith, that is, genuine, real

book of original entry — A bookkeeping term referring to the journal(s) in which the daily transactions of a business are recorded

book of secondary entry — A bookkeeping term referring to the ledgers

bookkeeper — An individual who records the daily transactions of a business in a journal and then posts or transfers the transactions to ledgers. See *accounting clerk*.

bookkeeping — The process of keeping records for a business

box-top offer — An invitation to a customer to send in the top of a box, container, or package, a product seal, a proof of purchase, or a label to receive a premium or gift

boycott — To avoid patronizing a business, that is, to refuse to trade with or buy from a person or a business in protest

brand name — The spoken trademark, a word, as opposed to the pictorial part of the trademark

brochure — A printed leaflet, usually one page and folded, advertising a product or a service

broker — An agent who usually represents more than one principal

budget — A budget is a plan for spending money.

budget accounts — Special accounts, usually in department and retail stores, that permit the customer to pay for a purchase over a period of time. See *installment sales* and *layaway*.

bull — A stock market speculator who believes that the stock prices are going to rise, and is therefore buying stock

bull market — A condition in the stock market where the trend is for prices to rise; also referred to as *bullish market*

bulldog edition — An edition of a morning newspaper that is printed early the preceding evening and sent out of town on night trains and planes

buried ad — An advertisement surrounded by other advertisements, or found at the bottom corner of a page with advertisements alongside and above it

buried offer — An offer for a booklet sample or information, made by means of a statement within the text of an advertisement without the use of a coupon or typographical emphasis. This is sometimes called a *hidden offer.*

business — An economic activity more or less intended to make a profit

business agent — An official of a union who usually is responsible for the records and cash and for increasing the number of members. The business agent may also represent the union in negotiations.

buy — To acquire goods or services as a consumer, usually purchased with cash or with the promise to pay at a later time

buyer — An executive in a department store who is responsible for ordering merchandise for sale to customers. A buyer usually specializes in one line of merchandise, for example, women's ready-to-wear clothing.

buying group — An organization which purchases merchandise for the members of the group in larger quantities and at better prices than would be possible individually. Some of the common group-buying businesses are hardware stores, pharmacies, and toy stores.

cable — A wire within a wire, especially designed to carry high-frequency television signals for long distances without interference; usually means coaxial cable

cable company — A local television service which provides, for a monthly fee, signals to the subscriber's home by means of cables connected to television sets so that the subscriber can pick up additonal television stations

call sign — Letters, usually identifying a radio or television station assigned by the FCC, for example, WABC in New York

campaign — A completely planned advertising program, covering a period of several months, with a specific objective and a theme; usually planned to introduce a product or for a store opening. It uses several media.

capacity — The ability to pay, that is, the relationship between one's earnings and the amount of a loan

capital — (1) Money used in a business (that is, working capital — money set aside for operating expenses; fixed capital — money invested in merchandise, fixtures, and equipment); (2) Also means net worth

capital goods — Goods used to manufacture or produce goods

capital statement — A report showing the amount of capital in a business; a version of the balance sheet used to support a request for a loan from a bank

capitalism — A form of economic activity which places the ownership of the tools of production in the hands of private persons who accumulate sufficient capital to acquire them, and are thus called *capitalists.*

caption — A written statement usually located under a photograph which explains the photograph

car cards — Posters placed in subway cars, buses and trolleys, and commuter trains between the top of the windows and the ceiling where passengers can look at them; commonly called *transit advertising*

cash — Money or any liquid asset, such as checks, drafts, bonds, securities, precious metals, old coins, stamps, or substitutes for money, that can be quickly converted into cash

cash-and-carry — A business which does not grant credit to its customers, and does not deliver merchandise. See *cash basis.*

cash basis — (1) A business that neither grants nor seeks credit; all transactions are for cash. See *cash-and-carry.* (2) To accountants, an accounting term which means that all income and expense is received or charged in the same fiscal period, with no accruals going over into the next period

cash book — A simplified journal in which a cash business records all daily receipts (and sometimes payments) of cash. See *cash journal.*

cash drawer — A drawer set aside for the storage of cash used for making change; used when a cash register is not available and for short-term sales

cash journal — Sometimes called a *combined cash journal.* A record of all payments and receipts in cash for a business is made on a daily basis as each transaction occurs. See *cash book.*

cash over/short slip — (1) An expression meaning that the count of the cash in the drawer is more than the amount indicated on the totals or tape of the cash register; (2) A slip of paper placed in the cash drawer of a register after it has been cashed up to show that the cash amount in the drawer did not agree with the amount of the cash register total or detail tape

cash receipt — (1) A slip of paper given to a customer as proof of payment in cash for an item or a service; (2) Sometimes refers to the cash register tape which comes out of the register after each total sale has been completed

cash refund slip — A slip of paper given by a customer to the store in exchange for the refunding of money for returned goods

cash register — A mechanical or electronic device used to quickly record sales transactions

cash register tape — A piece of paper issued by a cash register which has a copy of the itemized transactions printed on it; frequently given to the customer instead of a receipt

cash short — An expression which means that the total of the cash in the cash drawer of a cash register is less than the amount on the cash register tape

cashier — An employee, usually of a store, whose main duties include handling money, making change, cashing checks, and keeping a record of cash transactions; in a bank, usually called a *teller*

cashier-checker — A cashier in a supermarket who also has the responsibility of packing groceries in paper bags

cashier's check — A bank money order usually issued by a cashier and drawn on funds guaranteed by the bank

cash-up — An expression as in "to cash-up a drawer," which means to check out a cash drawer from a register, counting all cash, coupons, and checks, and to compare totals with the amounts on the register tapes

casualty — A loss (i.e., damage to humans or property) usually covered by insurance

Certificate of Incorporation — A document issued by the secretary of state (in your state) showing that a business has been incorporated and can conduct business. See *charter.*

certified check — A personal check drawn on a commercial bank, presented to the bank, before it is given to the payee so that the bank can guarantee payment by placing funds to cover the check in a separate account

Certified Public Accountant (CPA) — An accountant who has passed an examination and served an apprentice or training period as an accounting clerk for a CPA firm, and now has the privilege of certifying that a set of books that he or she examines is correct, as required by law for most corporations and some other types of businesses

channel — A band of radio frequencies assigned to a given radio or television station by the Federal Communications Commission (FCC) on which it may broadcast

character — One of the 4 C's of credit — a person's moral strength, integrity, self-discipline, and fortitude, among other traits, which make that person honest and a good business loan risk

characteristic — A trait of one's personality or character, such as honesty

charge — To purchase something on credit, as a charge sales

charge account — A customer's account, that is, a record of the amounts owed to a firm

charge cards — Credit cards; usually refers only to independent cards issued by local stores

charge slip — A sales slip or other type of record of a credit sale

chart of accounts — An index or list of the account titles in a set of books, usually in alphabetical order

charter — A document issued by a state agency, usually the secretary of state, authorizing a corporation, and in some cases other organizations, to operate an economic activity within that state for the purposes explained in the charter. See *Certificate of Incorporation.*

Chartered Accountant (CA) — In Canada, the equivalent of a certified public accountant

check — Any of a group of negotiable instruments or money orders drawn on a bank or other financial institution from funds on deposit. See *cashier's check* and *traveler's checks.*

check writer — A device which perforates a personal or business check with the correct amount in such a way as to make forgery or raising the amount of the check almost impossible

checking account — An account, either business or personal, at a bank in which money has been deposited for the purpose of payment on checks drawn by the depositor against that account

checkoff — The practice among some employers, according to union agreements, of withholding union dues from earned wages as a convenience to the union

cheque — The British spelling of the word *check*

Christmas club — A savings club in a bank, which usually matures about two months before Christmas

city directory — A business directory which gives the names, addresses, and other information about certain business persons in an area, and also gives public information about businesses, professional persons, and firms, etc.; an expensive reference book used by persons who use direct-mail advertising methods to select prospects

clear — (1) To obtain legal permission from a responsible source to use a photograph or quotation in an advertisement or to use a musical selection in a broadcast; (2) To obtain

time for a commercial — to clear time is to arrange for a station to provide air time for a commercial program

clear channel station — A radio or television station with considerable power (50,000 watts) which can broadcast on a frequency no other station has been assigned by the FCC

clearinghouse — An organization operated by member banks operating as sort of a "bank post office," to collect, classify, cancel, and return checks and other negotiable instruments to their home bank so they can clear and be paid

clip — A short piece of motion picture film inserted in a program or commercial

closed account — A bank account that has no money in it, or a zero balance; an account that has been officially closed by the bank or the depositor

closed circuit — Live television transmitted by cable for private viewing; used in hospitals, colleges, schools, and universities for instruction

closed corporation — A corporation which does not sell its stock to the public; also referred to as a *private corporation*

closed display — A showcase that has glass or transparent plastic protecting the display so that it can be viewed, but not touched by customers; used in jewelry stores and other locations where the merchandise should be locked

closed shop — An organized business (by a union), illegal under the Taft-Hartley Act, which forces all new employees to join the union before being employed. Also, under a closed shop rule, no employee may work who is not a union member. See *agency shop.*

closing an account — A bookkeeping activity referring to the process of totaling both sides (debit and credit) of an account and transferring the balance to another account for summarizing purposes

closing entries — A bookkeeping term referring to closing all accounts at the end of a fiscal period for the purpose of summarizing the accounts and preparing financial statements

COBOL — A computer language, which stands for *Common Business Oriented Language*

code — (1) A group of laws or ordinances, usually dealing with a particular subject, such as the Uniform Commercial Code or a building code; (2) A symbol used by a retailer to record the cost of an article on the price ticket in such a way that the customer cannot figure the cost; also used for concealing dates of manufacture, etc. See *price code* and *UPC*. (3) An abbreviation or group of symbols used in providing information for a computer in order to save space. The information is said to be encoded.

coined word — An original and arbitrary combination of syllables forming a word, used in trademarks such as *Acrilan, Gro-Pup, Zerone,* and *Kodak*

coins — Cash (that is, silver, change), meaning minted money; usually of laminated metal and ranging in denominations from 1¢ to $1.

coinsurance — Refers to a clause in an insurance policy which requires that the insured carry a face value of property insurance of at least 80% of the property's market value to get full protection, in order to discourage anyone from deliberately destroying the property for insurance gain

collective — An organization, commonly found in communist countries, which is similar to a co-operative but is owned by the state

collective bargaining — A process whereby workers elect unions to represent them in negotiations with management instead of bargaining individually with management

college — (1) A post-secondary institution of higher learning which charges tuition (that is, a community college, a private college, usually a two-year or four-year, degree-granting institution); (2) A professional group of persons who have in common the achievement of certain academic goals; an honorary society to which members are elected if they meet certain requirements, such as the American College of Surgeons

collision — An automobile insurance term which refers to a vehicle that strikes another vehicle, a person, or a fixed object

column — (1) A ruled section of many bookkeeping forms, with vertical lines printed to assist the bookkeeper in keeping figures in the proper decimal relationship; (2) An arrangement of copy in a newspaper or newsletter with even right-hand and left-hand margins to make the copy easier to read; columns vary in width

column inch — Advertising space — a unit of measure meaning an area of one inch in vertical distance and the width (whatever it may be) of the column; used to determine charges for advertising.

comic strip — A series of cartoon or caricature drawings which tell a story or present a message; can be used as an advertisement

commercial — An advertisement usually spoken on radio, and accompanied by music and video on television

commercial bank — A bank that makes loans, grants interest on savings accounts, and may have a trust and mortgage department; offers banking services such as safe deposit boxes, checking accounts, and various other services

commercial paper — Bank drafts and other negotiable instruments used in business transactions

commercial program — A sponsored program from which broadcasting stations derive revenue on the basis of the time consumed in broadcasting the program

commission — An amount of money paid to an agent or other person in exchange for selling goods or for performing a service; usually expressed as a percentage. For example, a real estate agent/broker's commission is usually 6%.

commission agent — A middleman who sells units of merchandise for a manufacturer or jobber and receives a commission from the seller

common stock — Shares of ownership in a corporation which are paid dividends only after the shareholders of preferred stock are paid

commonwealth — In a loose sense of the term, any state; in a strict sense of the term, Kentucky, Massachusetts, Pennsylvania, and Virginia, which were designated as commonwealths in their first constitutions; any state that is self-governed and where the wealth is held in common for the general welfare of the people

commune — A community living facility

communism — A system of economic and political government which places the tools of production in the hands of the government (state) in the name of the people

Community Antenna Television (CATV) — A method whereby one antenna is placed in a good location, at a high elevation, and can receive television stations better than regular household antennas. From this antenna, programs are transmitted by coaxial cable to the sets of subscribers who pay for the service.

community shopping center — A shopping center located in the suburbs, usually with plenty of off-street parking, and having approximately 11 to 30 different stores

comparison shopper — A person who buys or price checks merchandise in competitors' stores so that the merchandise can be undersold

competition — In business, the act of trying to vie for customers or markets; the effective opposition in a contest for customers, sales, or a share of the market for a product

competitive stage — The advertising stage of a product when it is in general use and is recognized, but its individual superiority over similar brands has to be established so that it secures the preference of shoppers

competitor — A business rival; a merchant or business person who sells or makes the same goods or offers the same services as another merchant

composition — Assembling and arranging type for printing; also known as *typesetting*

comptroller — A senior fiscal officer in a company (also spelled *controller*)

computer — An electronic machine, which by means of stored instructions and information, performs rapid and often complex calculations and/or compiles, correlates and selects data, and prints or in other ways renders this information useful for business and scientific purposes

computer language — Instructions to a computer

conditional — Depending on an event or other happening; a restriction

conditional endorsement — A signature on the back of a check with the words *when* or *depending* written above the signature stipulating that a condition or event take place. For example, "Pay to the Order of John Jones when he finishes painting my garage"

conditional sales contract — A contract to sell merchandise "on time" under specified conditions, such as when all or part of the full price is paid. See *installment sales*.

conditions — In business, usually refers to economic conditions. For example, Is the stock market going up or down? See *market conditions*.

consignment — Goods shipped to a retailer or vendor to which title does not yet pass. The retailer has the opportunity to sell the merchandise before payment is required. At the end of a prescribed period of time, the display is counted by a representative of the shipper, wholesaler, jobber, and the retailer is billed for the missing (presumably sold) merchandise.

consumer — An eventual user of a product or service

consumer advertising — Advertising directed to those people who will personally use the product, as opposed to trade advertising, business advertising or professional advertising

consumer advocate — A person or organization dedicated to protecting and informing consumers about inferior quality or unsafe manufactured products

consumer affairs — A department in many businesses which deals with customer complaints; also, any group of agencies established by government to handle consumer complaints

consumer goods — Products that directly satisfy human wants or desires, such as food and clothing, and products sold to an individual or family for use without further processing, as distinguished from industrial goods

consumer movement — In recent years, a business trend in which consumers are complaining about the quality of manufactured goods. As a result, many organizations have been formed to lobby for better consumer protection laws

consumer's cooperative — A cooperative that is organized, owned, and operated by its customers, providing service or providing goods, usually at a savings because the members volunteer to perform much of the labor. See *cooperative.*

consumer's union — An organization which tests products and publishes the results of the tests as a guide for consumers; not to be confused with the organization which uses that name — Consumer's Union and publishes *Consumer Reports*

consumption — The act of consuming or using goods and services. See *mass consumption.*

continuity — Script material (teleplay, etc.) for a television program or radio program

contract — An agreement between two or more parties that can be enforced in the courts if the agreement meets certain requirements; must usually be in writing

contractor — Literally one who contracts, but usually refers to a building or construction business person who contracts to erect structures of all kinds or performs construction work under the terms of a written contract

controlled circulation — Circulation of free suburban shopping newspapers to prescribed areas or homes

controlling account — A bookkeeping term which refers to an account in the general ledger that summarizes all transactions of that type in the accounts of the subsidiary ledgers, such as accounts payable

controlling interest — An individual is said to have a controlling interest in a corporation if one more than half (a majority) of all the issued capital stock is owned.

convenience goods — Those consumer products that are bought frequently at nearby stores usually on short notice, when a person runs out of needed goods

cooperative — A business organization owned and operated by persons who can benefit from its goods and services; known as a co-op. See *consumer's cooperative*

cooperative advertising — Advertising in which the cost is shared by both the manufacturer and the retailer who sells the product

copier — An office machine which makes quick copies of any document by any one of several processes: electrostatic, thermofax, or chemical

copy — An advertising term which means the written, descriptive material about a product or service that accompanies an ad

copyright — (1) The title and legal right to written works including novels, poems, songs, lyrics, and any other type of written creative work that is new and exclusive with the author; includes the rights of publication, production, and sale of literary, dramatic, musical, or artistic work and the rights to the use of a commercial print, logo, trademark or label, granted by law for a specified period of time to the author, the composer, artist, or distributor; (2) The legal right to own an original intellectual effort

copywriter — An individual who writes ad copy

corporation — A type of business organization; an association of stockholders, formed with government consent, which has the power to transact business in the same manner as if it were one person

correcting entry — A bookkeeping term for an entry in the general journal that has been made to correct an error or mistake

cost — (1) The price one pays for an article — to the consumer, the selling price; (2) The price a retailer pays for goods at wholesale; (3) In manufacturing, the total expense in making a product, up until the point of shipment

cost accounting — A branch of accounting which specializes in the computing of expenses in operating any business, making any product, offering any service, for the purpose of informing management in order to assist in decision making

cost of goods sold — The total cost of goods and services sold, including all expenses. In retailing, it is the total of all expenses, including purchases, in connection with the sale of goods and services to customers.

cost of merchandise — The actual amount a business pays for the goods or services it intends to sell, that is, the wholesale price

coupon — (1) A discount certificate issued by manufacturers of food products or other products, or by supermarket chains, distributors, and some jobbers, giving the purchaser a small discount on the marked price of the product. They are especially effective in introducing new products to the market. (2) An addenda to a bond certificate which permits the bondholder to send in each coupon after its maturity date for collection of interest. Also, frequently used with bonds, called *coupon bonds.*

cover — The front cover of a publication is known as the *first cover;* the inside of the front cover is the *second cover;* the inside of the back cover is the *third cover;* and the outside of the back cover is the *fourth cover.* It costs more to run advertisements in cover positions.

cow catcher — An advertising term used to refer to a radio or television ad (commercial) which is squeezed in during a station's break period, just before the beginning of a regularly scheduled program

credit — A bookkeeping term describing a notation which can decrease asset accounts and increase liability and capital accounts accordingly, so as to always equal an offsetting debit; also, the practice of granting credit to customers

credit balance — An excess in an account on the credit side, that is, the sum of the credits exceeds the sum of the debits, yielding a credit balance; normal balance for liability and capital accounts

credit bureau — An association of merchants in a community organized to investigate credit of potential customers. A small fee is charged for each credit profile requested.

credit card — An embossed plastic card issued by a firm which permits persons to whom the cards are given to charge purchases and be billed at a later date. There are two major kinds: bank credit cards and commercial credit cards.

credit entry — A double entry bookkeeping term which is the other half of the debit entry. It is made on the right-hand side in either a journal or ledger and offsets (keeps in balance) the debit entry.

credit memo — Short for *credit memorandum;* a slip issuing credit to a customer for an error, overcharge, return, or mistake, removing an amount from the customer's account

credit rating — A report from a credit bureau or other credit reporting organization describing the record of payment of a credit applicant who has been investigated. The rating is sometimes quoted in code or in an abbreviated style.

credit reporting — Credit investigation by credit bureaus or by businesses which prefer to check their own credit applicants. Some consumer finance companies do their own credit reporting.

credit sales slip — A sales slip with space on it to record charge purchases. There are several copies: one for the customer, one for the credit department, one for the cash register, and one for the department file.

credit side — The right-hand side of an account

credit union — A sort of cooperative bank, organized by its depositors who perform services for one another at reduced costs. Credit unions offer good service, high interest rates, and liberal loans to their members.

creditor — A term used to describe a person or a business that is owed money. The firms who are listed as accounts payable (to be paid) are known as the creditors of a business.

cropping — Trimming part of a photograph so that it fits in a specific space, or so that unwanted detail is removed from the photograph

customer — A debtor. A customer is one who buys goods and services from a business.

customer profile — An estimate of the demographic characteristics of the people who are buying any given brand of product at a certain time

cut — A photoengraving of a picture used in letterpress printing

cutout — A printed advertisement with a design literally cut out of it and used in floor displays; sometimes the size of a person

date of note — The date on which a promissory note is issued and the time from which interest is computed

dealer — A retailer who sells exclusive merchandise or products from one manufacturer or distributor and may perform service on the products

dealer imprint — The name and address of a local dealer either printed or pasted on (with a label) national advertising, such as catalogs and brochures

debenture — A bond issued against the general assets and reputation of a corporation; an unsecured bond. The government can issue debentures.

debit — In bookkeeping, a term describing a notation which increases asset accounts and decreases liability and capital accounts accordingly, so as to always equal an offsetting credit

debit balance — An excess on the debit side of an account, and the normal balance for asset accounts; always found on the left side of an account

debit entry — A bookkeeping notation in which an amount is placed as a debit in the left-hand column of a journal or ledger; one of the two elements in a double-entry system

debit memo — Short for *debit memorandum;* a slip issued by a bookkeeper showing that a debit has been made on a customer's account

debit side — In bookkeeping, the left-hand side of a journal or ledger in which debits are recorded

debitor — One who owes a person or business money; not an often-used term

deductible — (1) An expense that can be claimed either on an expense account or on an income tax return as a legitimate business expense; (2) An amount that is subtracted from the claim in a property insurance settlement to reduce rates and provide coinsurance

deductions — In payroll accounting, a term describing all the amounts taken from a worker's gross wages, including such items as taxes, social security, and hospitalization

delayed broadcast — A radio or television program that is recorded on tape for broadcast over a station at a later time, as opposed to a live broadcast

delivery ticket — A slip which serves as a receipt for merchandise delivered to a customer

demand — A need for or a desire for a commodity, together with the ability to pay for it, as in the law of supply and demand

demand deposits — Money kept in a bank which can be drawn out at any time during normal business hours at the immediate request of the depositor; the opposite of time deposits

demographic characteristics — The vital statistics about a group of people or a neighborhood

demurrage — The delaying of delivery of a shipment by rail or ship, due to the carrier's failure to leave, arrive, or unload on time. A charge is made for this delay.

deposit — An amount of money placed in a commercial or savings bank by an individual or a business

deposit box — Usually meaning *safe deposit box;* a depository in a bank vault used by individuals to keep their valuable belongings safe

deposit slip — A receipt for a deposit made in a bank

depositor — One who makes a deposit

detailed audit tape — A cash register tape that records all transactions on a register for a period of time; also called a detail tape

diorama — A three-dimensional model display, usually of a store window; uses actual miniature figures. A diorama is used by owners to see how a store window or show design will look before actually constructing it.

direct advertising — Any advertisement that is given directly to prospects by a salesperson, by canvassers at the point-of-sale, or by mail

direct mail — Advertising sent through the mail

direct sales — Door-to-door selling, route selling, and selling directly from the manufacturer; distribution without a middleman

disaster — A major catastrophic event which causes great damage to property and loss of life, including floods, earthquakes, tornadoes, and hurricanes. See *Act of God*.

discount — An amount deducted from the total of a bill for any of several reasons. See *quantity discounts*.

discount slip — A document that entitles the bearer (customer) to a reduction in the total amount of a bill

discount store — A general merchandise retailer that sells merchandise at less than its fair traded price

discounted note — A promissory note which is surrendered to a bank in advance of the maturity date to claim the proceeds. A portion of the interest is forfeited.

discrimination — (1) The act of selecting quality goods over inferior ones; (2) Deliberately or unintentionally treating any individual or minority group member unfairly in hiring practices, employment, or in human relations because of race, color, religion, ethnic origin, or sex; considered illegal by federal and state laws

dishonored check — A bad check, or one that is said to have bounced. It is a check that has been returned from the bank for a reason, sometimes for insufficient funds or because a stop payment order was issued against the check.

dishonored note — A promissory note that is not paid on maturity; can result in a lawsuit

display — Any exposing of goods to customers in a window display, an aisle display, a counter display, or in a display case, in order to attract customers into a store, or to a counter, with the intention of allowing them to examine or view the merchandise and eventually buy goods

display advertising — Print advertisements in any section of the newspaper except the classified section; sold in units of at least 14 column lines and may have a rule around it. This type of advertising is a little more expensive than classified advertising.

displaying — The art of arranging merchandise, flowers, mannequins, or any props in an attractive manner

dissolve — A camera technique in which the picture gradually gets smaller in the center of the screen until it eventually disappears

distribution — The process of getting goods from the producer to the consumer; may involve transportation, packaging, and storage

distribution paper — A bookkeeping term meaning 12-column (or more) worksheet paper used for the distributing of costs or other classification in columns, for the purpose of analyzing records and preparing reports

distributive business — Any business which assists in the distribution process (that is, channels of distribution), including middlemen of all kinds, wholesalers, agents, brokers, distributors, jobbers, manufacturers' representatives, drop shippers, commission agents, rack wholesalers, route sellers, vending wholesalers, direct sellers, and retailers

distributor — A middleman who usually has a guaranteed territory allocated by the manufacturer and an exclusive right to sell the line or group of products within that area

dividend — A payment made, usually at the end of a quarter, representing earnings on a share of common or preferred stock of a corporation. Dividends must be declared, that is, voted on by a majority of the directors each quarter.

dock — (1) A loading platform at the end of or beside a storage area or warehouse where goods are assembled before being loaded onto boxcars or freight trucks; (2) A slang expression meaning to fine or take away, as in to dock pay from an employee's wages

dolly — A cart with wheels used to move a television camera around on a sound stage without making any noise

door-to-door — Direct selling, selling products directly to the customer in the home. See *route sales* and *direct sales.*

double coupons — A promotional activity in which a retailer grants a customer double the amount of the coupon on a purchased product as an incentive to patronize the store and buy the product

double decker — Outdoor advertising (billboards) erected one above the other

double-entry bookkeeping — The system of bookkeeping which involves making two entries to record a transaction, thus keeping a balance or equality continuing throughout a set of books. This system creates a method of checking the accuracy of the recording of transactions by checking at anytime to see if everything balances.

Dow-Jones averages — Refers to stock market quotations of selected stocks from different industries which are thought to be indicators of stock market trends. The quotations are reported daily by a financial reporting firm known as Dow-Jones (publishers of the *Wall Street Journal*, a financial newspaper). See *economic indicators.*

draft — (1) A check drawn on a bank; usually drawn on funds of the bank, not an individual, and therefore guaranteed by the bank; (2) To write a rough outline or first copy of anything, as in a rough draft, for example, to draft a proposal

draw — To make out a check; to order payment of a sum from deposited funds, that is, to make payment by check

drawee — The bank or other establishment (savings association, credit union, etc.) on which a check is drawn, that is, the place where the funds are deposited

drawer — (1) One who draws a check, the person whose funds are used, and the person who signs the check; (2) A cash container, usually in a cash register, which is divided into compartments for bills and coins; also means a cash drawer, an unlocked container for cash used on a temporary basis

drawing account — (1) A bookkeeping term which means an account especially set aside for each salesperson who may be paid by commission, or paid by salary plus commission. The account serves to accumulate earned commission, and permits the salesperson to draw amounts from the account, in lieu of salary, against earned or prospective commissions. (2) An account used for the owner or partners of a company so that they may draw funds from the firm, that is, a capital drawing account

drive-in — Any business where its goods or services are available directly to the driver and/or occupants of an automobile, such as a drive-in, fast-food restaurant

drive-in teller — A bank window located on the side of a branch bank office that permits a depositor to make a bank transaction without getting out of the car. See *pneumatic tubes.*

drive-in theater — An outdoor theater which permits patrons to view motion pictures from their vehicles

drop — A slang expression for a night depository; a secure door or slot in a bank, that can be opened only by key, for use in making after-hours deposits

drop shipper — A middleman who does not take title to goods he or she sells, but instructs the wholesaler, distributor, or manufacturer about where to ship the goods. The drop shipper is paid a commission by either the buyer or the seller, or both. See *commission agent.*

dubbing — Making a voice-over or audio signal for any program, commercial, or visual presentation after the video portion has already been recorded. See *lip-sync.*

dummy — (1) A paste-up or rough copy of a brochure, pamphlet, booklet, or any printed materials in advertising, which involves more than a single page. A paste-up or rough copy is done so that the printer and layout people can plan the copy and illustrations, and arrange the numbering of the pages. (2) A slang expression for a mannequin — a model of a human form for displaying clothes

economic indicators — Facts and statistics which are supposed to show a trend in the stock market and in the general economy of the nation. See *Dow-Jones averages*.

economic system — Any system in a country which attempts to provide for its people the goods and services necessary to life. There are several economic systems: agrarian, capitalism, communism, and socialism.

economics — The study of a human's ability to survive in an environment: to obtain, grow or produce food, clothing, shelter, and that which a human needs to survive

economy — Any system of producing, distributing, and consuming wealth

effective circulation — (1) An outdoor advertising term meaning the number of people who have a reasonable chance of seeing a poster. The term is defined as one-half of the pedestrians, one-half of the automobiles, and one-fourth of the surface public transportation passengers who pass the poster in a given time period. (2) Newspapers and magazines; the estimated number of people who have an opportunity to read and/or look at any periodical, including those to whom it was sent, who purchased it, and those in the immediate family who could have seen it

elective — An alternate choice or solution; in college, a course that is not required for a specific curriculum, but one that can be taken in addition to required courses

electric — Produced or operated by electricity and mechanical machines operated by electricity, as opposed to electronic

electric spectacular — An immense electric sign which advertises a product. This type of sign uses a great deal of electricity and is very expensive. It is illuminated with hundreds of light bulbs and neon tubes and may have motorized, moving parts.

electrician — A tradesperson who works with residential or industrial electrical circuits, electric motors, and power distribution systems

electronic — Of and pertaining to the electron, systems using electron tubes, semiconductors, transistors, and all kinds of electronic components in radio, television, sound, and space travel and communications

eleemosynary — A charity or a nonprofit organization supported entirely by donations

em — Short for *pica em;* the square of the body of any typeface; named after the letter *M*, which is as high as it is wide

employee — An individual who works for (is employed by) others and is paid wages, commissions, or other compensation in exchange for labor, talent, or a service

employee discount — A discount or reduction in the selling price of an article extended as a courtesy to an employee

employee discount slip — A document that entitles an employee to a discount on merchandise sold by a store, and that is signed by an authorized store official

employee earnings record — A personnel form used to record all wages, deductions, and bonuses, etc., an employee is paid during a period. Used by the employer to prepare W-4 forms and used by the employee to prepare income tax returns

employer — One who employs, engages others for the purpose of performing labor

employment — (1) The act of hiring an individual to work for or labor for another; (2) The name of the department in a business that interviews and may hire workers

employment manager — An official in a business who has the authority to hire personnel; not to be confused with the personnel manager who keeps records of persons who are employed

employment office — An office in a business where applicants for employment are interviewed, tested, and given an opportunity to complete an employment application; not to be confused with the personnel office

endorsement — A signature written on the back of a check for the purpose of cashing the check

endorsement in full — The signature of a payee on the back of a check, followed by the words "pay to the order of" and the name of a new payee

engraving — actually meaning *photoengraving*; a process of etching metal to make a plate in offset printing or letterpress printing using chemicals or acid. See *cut.*

enterprise — Any business activity in the free enterprise system

entity — One; in corporate law, the concept that a group of people who incorporate is seen as one person in the eyes of the law

entrepreneur — Anyone who undertakes an enterprise, that is, one who undertakes to operate a business

entry — In bookkeeping, a notation in either a journal or a ledger

equity — Ownership; in effect, that portion of a business that the owner would actually have if he or she were to convert all assets into cash and pay off all debts, that is, the owner's net worth

ethical advertising — (1) Advertising of a drug or product addressed to physicians only; (2) Advertising that attempts to be honest about the claims it makes for the sponsor's product

ethical drugs — Substances that can be obtained only from a doctor's prescription

exclusive — (1) Selective, special, not available to all, and therefore usually more expensive; (2) The right to sell a product or service in a protected territory with no other person having that same right

exempt — Released or excused from, as in exempt from paying taxes. Clergy and charitable and nonprofit organizations are tax exempt.

exemption — Short for *withholding exemption;* the number of dependents claimed by a worker for the purposes of figuring income tax withholding

expense — Any cost of doing business

expense account — A special account set up to record the expenses of a sales person working outside of a business. With this type of account, expenses are recorded, and money is advanced or reimbursed as needed.

expense voucher — Any source document which shows proof of a cash expenditure for an expense

experience — An activity that may include training, practice, observation, and participation, and the presumed knowledge and skill derived from such activity. Presumed to be a qualification for employment if the experience is related to a prospective or similar job vacancy.

expert — A person who is highly skilled or specifically trained in a special field

expertise — The knowledge, skills, and information of an expert

face — The amount of a life insurance policy, that is, the amount that a company would be forced to pay under the law in the event of a loss

fade — A camera technique, similar to dissolve, in which the picture either gradually appears (fades in) or gradually disappears (fades out)

fair market value (FMV) — In an automobile insurance property policy, this term refers to the value of an insured vehicle at the time of loss.

Farm Credit Bureau (FCB) — A government agency which grants loans to farmers to finance the production of crops

Federal Aviation Authority (FAA) — Formerly the Civil Aeronautics Authority; a government agency that supervises the aviation industry and sets safety standards for all aircraft

Federal Communications Commission (FCC) — A government agency which regulates the broadcast communications industry

Federal Deposit Insurance Corporation (FDIC) — A government agency that insures the deposits of all member commercial banks and trust companies

Federal Housing Authority (FHA) — A government agency which makes loans to develop the housing industry and provides shelter for the elderly and low income citizens

Federal Insurance Contribution Act (FICA) — Also known as *social security;* refers to the legislation which founded the Social Security Administration, and requires contribution from employers and employees for old age pensions and survivors' benefits

Federal Reserve System — A system of government banks, assigned to areas in the U.S., serving banks in their areas as depositories. The Federal Reserve System also distributes money, government bonds, and provides other banking services to banks.

Federal Savings and Loan Insurance Corporation (FSLIC) — A government agency which insures the deposits in savings and loan associations

Federal Trade Commission (FTC) — A government agency which regulates trade and advertising practices, and attempts to prevent businesses from operating in restraint of trade or using unfair trade practices

Federal Unemployment Insurance Tax — A tax imposed on employers to provide for a fund to pay workers who are laid off for a certain period of time

field intensity map — A map which shows the quality of reception possible with radio and television stations on the basis of the signal strength

FIFO — Means *first in, first out;* a system of rotation of inventory where the most recently purchased merchandise is sold after the current stock is sold

15 and 2 — The terms on which recognized advertising agencies secure space from publishers — 15% commission from the publisher on the gross amount and 2% for the client on the net cash payment

fill-in — The salutation and any other information that must be inserted in a form (preprinted) advertising letter sent by direct mail

finance company — Meaning a consumer finance — a lending institution that specializes in short term loans to families for household goods, appliances, etc., on installment sales contracts; also called a *sales finance company.*

financier — One who finances a venture, that is, a capitalist, also a philanthropist

fine — (1) An amount assessed by a municipality for violation of an ordinance, such as a parking fine. (2) To penalize an individual for infraction of the rules, that is, to dock an employee an amount from wages for breaking a rule

fire — (1) Slang expression meaning to dismiss an employee from work for cause; (2) A conflagration, a burning of matter, that is, the destruction of property by fire

fire insurance — Property insurance that covers risks of fire, arson (except one with an insurable interest involved), and damage from smoke, water, etc.

firm — A company or business partnership of two or more persons, but not legally a corporation. In a loose sense, the term means any company.

firm order — A commitment for advertising space that cannot be cancelled after a certain date. This date is known as the *firm order date.*

fiscal period — An accounting period, that is, a month, a quarter, a year

fixed capital — Money invested in tools, machinery, real estate, equipment, fixtures, and supplies, that cannot be easily liquidated

fixtures — Store furniture, showcases, tables, counters, etc., usually movable, in order to permit changes in the layout

flood — A catastrophe or disaster not covered by normal insurance

flood insurance — Insurance issued especially to cover the risk of damage due to flooding. There are deductible amounts for flood insurance

font — An assortment of type characters of one size and one typeface containing all the letters of the alphabet, both uppercase (capital) and lowercase (small letters) and marks of punctuation

footings — Usually means *pencil footings;* totals of columns in a journal or ledger written in pencil until their accuracy is proven, and then they are erased

foreign advertising — Local newspaper advertising that is paid for by a manufacturer or distributor, as opposed to local advertising that is paid for by local merchants

foreign exchange rate — The rate at which U.S. dollars are traded for currency of another country. The rate fluctuates daily.

forgery — The illegal writing of another person's name on any legal document or negotiable instrument with intent to defraud, the raising of an already written amount on a check, or the altering of any legal document for personal profit or gain

fork truck — A gasoline, propane or electric-powered industrial lift truck used to move merchandise on pallets around a warehouse

format — The size, shape, style, and appearance of a book or publication

FORTRAN — A computer language which stands for: *for*mula *tran*slation; used in computer applications where scientific computations are common

4 C's of credit — Characteristics considered favorable to an individual applying for a loan. They are *character, capacity, capital,* and *conditions*

franchise — A company which grants the right to an individual(s) to use its name, methods, benefit from its national advertising, and sometimes use its capital to operate a privately owned or leased local business

franchise contract — An agreement between a franchisee and a franchisor permitting the use of a franchise

franchise fee — Consideration (payment) for the right to make a franchise contract

franchise territory — In a franchise contract, the specified geographic area (counties, states, etc.) in which the franchisee can operate exclusively in exchange for the franchise fee. The franchisor agrees to grant no other franchises in the area, either indefinitely or for a specified period of time.

franchisee — The party purchasing the franchise, that is, the local franchise operator

franchisor — The parent company, the party granting the franchise agreement

franking — The privilege of sending mail free by writing your signature in the upper right-hand corner of the envelope where the stamp is usually placed; reserved for officials, legislators, etc., for official use only. This practice has generally been replaced by tax-exempt printed envelopes and mailing permits.

fraud — Criminal intent to deceive, to cheat, or to commit a crime involving cheating, forgery, or deception

free lance — Artists, photographers, authors, or any other creative people who sell their work on the open market or accept commissions for specified work; generally self-employed

freezer plan — An agreement whereby a meat packer or wholesaler, or any food broker, will supply meats, frozen foods, and other items on a contract basis at reduced prices, provided a certain minimum is purchased each week or month, depending on the contract; also can include the purchase of a freezer on installments.

frequency modulation (FM) — A method of transmitting a radio signal by varying the frequency of the radio waves, instead of their size (amplitude), which gives better reception but limits the effective broadcast area to about a 40-mile radius. The audio portion of all television broadcast uses the FM method.

fringe benefits — Any of a group of benefits or paid-for services provided by a company for its employees on a fully paid or shared-cost basis. Fringe benefits include hospitalization, paid vacation, paid holidays, pension plans, profit-sharing plans, etc.

fringe time — In television, the hour directly adjacent to prime time, that is, just before or after 8 PM to 11 PM

full showing — An outdoor advertising term meaning full coverage of an area with posters or car cards. The number of posters or car cards required to do this varies from market to market.

function — A specific area of responsibility in an internal organization, that is, a job

functional organization — A company organized by task, as opposed to direct authority from top to bottom

galley proof — A rough copy of printed matter made from the letter-press process of printing so that the accuracy of the typesetting can be checked

garbage — A slang expression in computer terminology which refers to unintelligible or scrambled information either going into a computer or coming from a printout

general journal — A bookkeeping term which identifies a section of the journal where special entries, correcting entries, and adjusting and closing entries are recorded

general ledger — The ledger containing all general and controlling accounts, as opposed to the subsidiary ledgers which contain accounts receivable and accounts payable

ghost — In television, a shadow of the main image, shown on the viewing screen, that is caused by a delayed signal or reflected one; can be eliminated by adjusting the tuning of the set or the antenna

ghost writer — A person who assists another in writing copy, but does not claim credit for his or her work

GIGO — Means garbage in, garbage out; a slang expression in computer terminology which points out the importance of accuracy in preparing input to computer systems

Good Housekeeping Institute — A highly respected consumer testing agency which gives a seal of approval to various products that meet its high standards; an activity of the magazine *Good Housekeeping*

goods — Product, manufactured items; usually refers to consumer goods, as opposed to industrial or capital goods

grace period — A period of time during which an insurance company will continue an insurance policy in force even though the premium due date has passed. A grace period is usually about 10 to 15 days.

gross profit — A surplus that remains after cost of goods sold is subtracted from total receipts

gross profit on sales — The same as gross profit, except that only sales are considered income

gross wages — Total pay before deductions are made

gross weight — The total weight of a vehicle including its load, as opposed to its axle weight, meaning its unloaded weight

group buyer — An organization which buys merchandise for independent merchants who belong to the buying group. The organization buys considerably larger quantities than the individual merchants could afford, thus providing savings because of quantity discounts.

guarantee — A warranty or a statement of fact about a product on which the buyer can rely

guild — A trade union, or a craft union, dating back to the 18th and 19th century trade associations in Central Europe; a group of craftspeople

gutter — In a publication, the white space that is formed by the inside margin of two pages that face each other

half run — In transit advertising, a car card placed in every other car of the line, as opposed to a full showing (or full run) in which a car card is placed in each car

half showing — Half of a full showing; in outdoor advertising, half coverage of an area with posters or car cards

handbook — A manual describing how to perform a service or accomplish a task, or a product instruction booklet accompanying the product which tells the user how to operate and care for the product, etc.

head — Short for *headline* in an advertisement

headline — A phrase or expression that is set in type larger than body type, usually set in **boldface,** and often in CAPITAL LETTERS

headquarters — The main offices of a chain or the corporate office of a corporation; the place where the principal officers of a company are located

hiatus — A short cessation of activities, for example, a temporary stoppage of an advertising campaign during months designated by the sponsor

hierarchy — A listing or arrangement of items by rank, for example, the arrangement of skills from simple to difficult, or the ranking of employees in an organization

hitch-hike — Or hitchhiker; an advertising term meaning an ad or commercial on television or radio which is run at the end of a program. The commercial advertises a product sponsored by a different company than the one sponsoring the program. See *inherited audience.*

horizontal publications — A term used in industrial advertising meaning those publications which seek readers from the management level, as opposed to vertical publications, which are aimed at an entire industry

house account — A charge account which is extended to a preferred customer, usually in a large chain store, etc., where there is no commission paid to the salespeople

house organ — A newsletter or publication produced by a company exclusively for its employees; includes news about the company and the employees and their activities

house unit — An operating unit in a franchise company, not franchised to an individual, but operated by the parent company with paid managers; not part of the franchise unit, but rather a company store

housing cooperative — A popular form of cooperative which provides low-cost housing for its members by operating condominiums or apartment houses on a cost basis; the members voluntarily provide all of the services and repairs needed

I.D. — A very short spot commercial on television used to identify a product and may include a slogan; usually ten seconds in length

I.D. card — Short for identification card; a wallet-size card that identifies an employee of a company, and may have on it a photograph of the employee, the employee's fingerprints, and other important information

impulse merchandise — Goods, frequently small items, such as candy, placed at the check-out counters or near the cash register in a full-service or self-service store to remind customers of items they may need

income — (1) A bookkeeping term meaning money coming into a business, money received, and therefore a debit to cash, and if in cash, usually recorded in the cash receipts journal; (2) Money taken in by a business — gross receipts, revenue, sales, etc. — in either cash (cash income) or in the form of debts owned

income account — A controlling account in the general ledger used to summarize all sources of income in order to determine whether a business took in more than it paid out

income statement — A financial statement issued periodically showing income made as a result of business operations; formerly called a *profit and loss statement*

income tax — Literally a tax on an individual's income. Income tax is levied on personal income and on business income.

income tax return — For an individual, a form which must be filed with the Internal Revenue Service each year before April 15th for income earned the preceding year; tax due is sent with the form

individual retirement account (IRA) — A private account in a bank set up by self-employed individuals to establish a pension fund for themselves. See *Keogh plan.*

industrial goods — Capital goods, tools, equipment, and machinery that are needed to make a product, process raw materials, or carry on a business

inherited audience — The listeners of a radio show or television program that remain tuned to the same channel or station, at least for a few moments, after a program changes

inserts — (1) Brochures and other types of advertising material placed in the same envelope with a customer's monthly bill, in the hope of producing additional sales; (2) Whole pages or groups of pages printed, usually on heavy, color stock, for inclusion in a regular edition of a newspaper; printed for an advertiser

insolvent — Unable to pay one's debts, that is, bankrupt; a condition where the liabilities of a business exceed its assets

installment — A partial payment for merchandise that is purchased "on time"

installment sales — A sale made in a retail store on which a down payment is made, and the remainder of the purchase price is paid to the store in equal monthly payments, usually including an interest and finance charge, until the full amount is paid

installment sales contract — An agreement whereby a store will sell merchandise to a customer for partial payment, and the remainder is to be paid for in installments. When the last payment is received, the ownership (title) of the merchandise is transferred to the purchaser.

insurable interest — An actual ownership in a business or enterprise or a relationship with an individual (such as a family member), where in the event of loss or death of a person, a loss could result. An individual must have an interest, other than personal, in another person's life or in property in order to insure it.

insurance — In business, the cost of protecting against the possible loss of business property in return for the periodic payment of a small amount of money called a *premium.* Some of the risks that can be insured against include loss from fire, theft, flood, robbery, and burglary, etc.

intaglio — An expensive printing process which produces engraving-like printed images. The ink is applied to a hollowed out impression on a printing plate; the ink accumulates on the paper in a slightly raised amount. This process is used on expensive stationery and business cards.

intangible — Something you cannot see or touch, for example, a person's reputation

intensity — An advertising term meaning the degree to which an advertising message is repeated in the medium; that is, the number of posters or car cards in an area or the number of times in one day a message is repeated on radio or television

interest — A financial investment or equity in a business or other enterprise. A person is said to have a 50% interest in a business if that person owns half of the business.

interest (compound) — Interest that is computed on accumulated savings plus the interest that is earned on the savings each fiscal period, added on each time (compounded)

interest (simple) — Money charged for the use of money; a percentage of the amount borrowed is the interest rate, and is usually quoted per annum (yearly)

interest rate — The amount of money the loaner charges the borrower for the use of money. The amount borrowed is called the *principal,* and the rate is expressed as a percent for one year.

Internal Revenue Service (IRS) — A government agency that is responsible for collecting the nation's income taxes

International Business Machines Corporation (IBM) — A company that makes computers and several different types of office machines, including electric typewriters

inventory — A list of all the merchandise in a business that is available for sale

inventory counting forms — Slips used to count items in a warehouse or storeroom when taking a physical (actually counting) inventory

inventory tickets — A ticket attached to an item of inventory to show that it has already been counted; used to prevent an item from being counted twice

invest — To put one's money in a business, etc., in the hope of earning a profit or return

investment — Money placed in such property as securities, bonds, stock, or other property for the purpose of earning income, as a result of the property appreciating in value or because of the ability of the property to earn income because it is a capital good or will increase in value

investor — One who places his or her money with a broker to purchase shares of stock, bonds, or securities, or other income-earning property

invoice — A bill, or request for payment from a creditor

ISF — Means *insufficient funds;* a notation on a check indicating that it has been returned because there was not enough money on deposit in the account to cover the amount of the check

island display — A display that is freestanding on a table; separate from any counter or gondola, and usually in the middle of an aisle where it is noticeable

italics — In a family of type, a typeface in which the letters are slightly slanted upwards and to the right, to distinguish them from medium or regular type. *This is an italic typeface.*

jargon — Special terminology that is used in a particular trade or business, etc., by those employed in the trade or business

job application — An application for employment

job description — A written explanation of a particular task, operation, or work position; explains in detail all the operations that must be performed by the employee, and may state required experience and training. A job description may also include the rate of pay.

jobber — A middleman who performs a distribution service by stocking a wide variety of merchandise from many different suppliers, thus providing a single source to a retailer or vendor, instead of requiring the retailer to purchase from many different sources. A jobber may also ship some items on consignment.

jogger — A device in a printing shop or office which vibrates a ream of paper to make the sheets fall into place

joiner — A machine in a woodworking plant which shaves pieces of wood at right angles or cuts grooves in the pieces of wood so that they can be joined together and glued

joint account — A bank account which is in the names of more than one person

joint apprenticeship council — A group of individuals, including union representatives, state labor department officials, state education personnel, vocational counselors and school guidance personnel, and other interested persons, who serve on the board to determine vacancies in the union trades. The council also publishes announcements, tests applicants, and sets up and supervises apprentice training programs.

journal — In bookkeeping, a record of daily transactions. There are several kinds of journals: the cash receipts journal, the cash payments journal, the general journal, the purchases journal, and the sales journal.

journeyman — A term which indicates that an individual has completed an apprenticeship program of several years, which leads to full qualification in a trade or craft

justification of type — Setting type in such a manner that the **right**-hand margin and the left-hand margin are even

Keogh plan — An individual retirement account set up by self-employed persons in a savings or commercial bank, which can legally be tax exempt up to a maximum of 15% of one's gross income or $15,000 per year, depending on which is less

keying an ad — The practice in advertising of tie-ins or connecting an ad in one medium with an ad in another. For example, a life-size cutout picture of a celebrity in a store next to a display of a popular beer, in the same format as an ad appearing on national television with the actual celebrity standing in a characteristic position introducing customers to the product. The presumption of this practice is that customers will make the necessary product identification and will buy the beer.

kind — In this text, a term referring to the business classification determined by the goods and services a business offers, and the purpose of the business — producer, distributor, retailer, personal trade or technical or professional service, and business services and communications

king size — A term used in merchandising to indicate that the size of merchandise is larger than average size, for example, a king-size bed

klieg light — A high powered search light usually mounted on a trailer with its own generator; used at openings of stores and for sales promotions

landfill — A dump operated by a city or town for the sanitary disposal of garbage and trash; usually supported by taxes, but sometimes a fee is charged for use.

landlord — The owner of rented property

Lanham Act of 1946 — Established a register in the U.S. Patent Office for trademarks

Law of Supply and Demand — An economic principle which explains the relationship between supply, price, and demand for goods and services

layaway — A plan in a retail store for a customer to request that an item of merchandise be set aside from regular stock and not sold until the customer pays the full purchase price of the item, in exchange for the payment of a small deposit

layaway ticket — A document given to the customer which is proof of an item being held on layaway and that a deposit has been paid; shows location of an item in a storeroom

layout — (1) The arrangement in a retail store of the counters, tables, and displays so that customers can view them and select merchandise. There are two general types of layouts: self-service, which permits customers to help themselves to goods, and full-service, in which customers are served by salespeople. (2) An advertising term which refers to the arrangement of the elements of an advertisement on a page

l.c. — Abbreviation for *lowercase;* means small letters in a type font

lead — (1) Pronounced *led;* to increase the space between lines of type; (2) Pronounced *leed;* refers to the first paragraph of a news article which states the important facts of the article

lead-in — A voice-over or an announcement at the end of one program urging listeners to stay tuned to the same channel or station for the next program

lease — A long-term rental agreement

leave — Short for leave of absence; an absence from employment for any cogent reason, such as military service or maternity. A leave can be with or without pay, and usually for a period of time not longer than a year.

ledge — The small shelf on a cash register just in front of the cash drawer. When making change, bills should be placed on this ledge before they are put in the drawer, just in case there is a question about their denomination.

ledger — A book of secondary entry; the book of accounts in bookkeeping where journal transactions are recorded by topic or subject (classified), called *posting*

ledger cards — Ledger pages, usually of stiff paper, which can be filed in order, and may be kept in a ring binder or in a file with divider cards

Ledgers - Boston ledger — A style of ledger in which there are three columns on the account page, the right-hand column provided for a balance so that the account balance is computed each time an entry is made. This is called a *running balance.*

Ledgers - T Account — A style of ledger page in which there are two distinct sides separated by double-ruled lines in the shape of the letter *T*. The left side is the *debit* side, and the right side is the credit side.

letterpress — A method of printing using typefaces which actually press against the paper after being coated with ink, and thereby transfer the impression to the paper; good method to use when a large number of copies is needed

liabilities — (1) Insurance risks, such as damage to others. Liability insurance covers damage you do to others accidentally. (2) Debts owed by the business, that is, a bookkeeping term referring to the accounts and notes payable and other obligations owed by the firm

license — Long-term permission, usually given in the form of a document, permitting an individual to operate equipment, perform an act, etc., with the approval of a state agency. An examination is usually required before the license is granted to determine competency, especially if the act to be performed could cause damage to individuals or to property.

life — (1) The term of a contract, that is, how long the contract lasts; (2) The length of time a business stays in operation; (3) The age of merchandise; (4) Short for life insurance

life insurance — An insurance policy on a person's term of existence, in which the insurance company hopes that it will collect enough premiums from an individual before an individual dies so that the premiums will at least equal if not exceed the face amount of the policy. Life insurance is designed to insure against early death, so that the dependents of a person will collect the face amount of the policy as a form of compensation for that person's death.

life policy — An insurance policy or contract on one's life. It is not uncommon for partners to insure each other's lives for the obvious reason that each partner would suffer a loss from the other's death.

LIFO — Means *last in, first out;* a system of rotation of inventory in which the most recent merchandise that comes into a store is placed in front of older merchandise, and is sold first

limited — Short for *limited liability;* used extensively in England and Canada after the names of firms which have limited liability (for example, Jones & Jones, Ltd.) and may refer to either partnerships or corporations

limited life — An insurance policy which states the number of years the policy must run before it becomes paidup, that is, before premiums are no longer necessary to keep the policy in force

limited time station — Usually a radio station (some television stations) which is licensed by the FCC to operate during certain hours of the day, for example, from sunrise to sunset, because another station uses that same frequency during the remaining hours of the day; actually a shared frequency station

line — (1) A term referring to a form of internal organization which has direct line authority from the top to the bottom; (2) A line of merchandise; a group of products of the same general kind, such as a hardware line or a line of women's dresses, often from the same manufacturer or from the same buying group or chain; (3) An open amount of credit, that is, a line of credit; established by a bank or some other financial institution that permits amounts of money to be added to an account, which presumably will be paid off at a later date

line organization — A form of internal organization which has direct authority from top to bottom

line and staff — A form of internal organization which combines the authority of a line form of organization with the specialists that can be provided by a staff method of organization

lip sync — A television term meaning the synchronization of lip movement on the screen with the audio (voice) portion

liquid — The state of being easily converted into cash, that is, assets which are liquid are those such as bonds and negotiable securities, etc., which can be cashed quickly

liquidate — To sell everything, that is, to convert all assets into cash

list broker — A middleman who sells lists of the names and addresses of prospective customers and any individuals classified by occupation, area, or any other demographic characteristic for use in direct-mail campaigns

lithography — Actually *offset lithography;* a printing process based on the principle that oil and water do not mix. This process uses photographically developed plates which reproduce the image by picking up the ink and transferring it to the paper by means of a blanket roller which does not make contact with the wet areas. The result is the inked image, which is set off from the rest of the roller and printed.

live — At the same time; an instant telecast, as opposed to a taped or recorded broadcast

loan — An amount of money that is borrowed and that must be paid back by a certain date or on demand; usually interest is charged on the money borrowed

local ad — An advertisement paid for by a local sponsor, as opposed to national advertising

local channel station — A radio station that is allowed just enough power to be heard locally on a frequency assigned to other low-power stations

local program — A radio or television program originating from a local station and produced locally, as opposed to a network program which comes from the national network. Most local stations produce their own newscasts.

local rate — A lower advertising charge for advertisements aired during local programs than the higher national rates charged for national programs

logo — Short for *logotype;* choice type styles and typefaces in a distinctive arrangement that can be copyrighted as a trademark

long bed — A term used to describe a pickup truck that has a bed longer than normal, and therefore has greater carrying capacity

long term — An expression referring to a loan or credit that is usually extended for longer than one year, or a contract that is more than one year in duration; must be in writing

long wave — A radio term used to describe normal broadcast AM wavelengths; the commercial broadcast range

loss leader — An item that is advertised to persuade customers to come into a store. The item is actually priced lower than what it costs at wholesale, and the loss is charged to advertising.

Magnetic Ink Character Reader (MICR) — An electronic device which senses figures printed on a check and translates them into information for sorting

magnetic ink characters — Figures printed along the lower edge of a check or draft which can be read (sensed) by an electronic scanner and translated into useful information to assist in sorting and processing checks, etc.

Magnuson-Moss Warranty Act — This act requires that the manufacturer or distributor of any manufactured product must either repair or replace any product that can be shown to be defective as a result of normal use, or refund the purchase price at the individual's option. The act does not apply to insurance, real estate, automobiles, camping equipment and vehicles, travel facilities, catalogs and merchandise portfolios, mail-order items, premiums, advertisements for schools, hotels, summer camps, or similar institutional advertising.

mail order — Any business which contacts its customers through the mail for the exchange of goods and services. Initial contact is usually made by advertisements in the print media.

mail-order ad — An advertisement in a periodical or newspaper directed at a customer who will send in by mail for an advertised item using a coupon or order form printed in the ad

majority stockholder — A person who owns one more than half of the total of all stock issued by a corporation. See *controlling interest.*

make good — A free rerun of an advertisement by the publisher or the network, because there has been a serious error in the reproduction or the transmission.

maker — The person who signs a personal check, that is, the drawer

maker of a note — The individual who signs the note; the borrower, who promises to pay the note (loan) back usually with interest

making a deposit — The process of placing money and checks (endorsed) in an account of the bank using a deposit slip, a passbook, or a night-depository envelope

malicious mischief — Damage to property resulting from pranks of juveniles; can be covered by insurance under an extended coverage rider

mall — An enclosed shopping center

malpractice — An error or mistake in a personal or professional service rendered to an individual causing bodily harm or physical injury, embarrassment, or suffering

malpractice insurance — Insurance that covers a practitioner to the limits of the face amount of the policy from loss due to malpractice

market — (1) Any group of people who are able to buy a product if they know about it and if they should desire it; (2) A store, usually self-service, that sells food and food-related items

market conditions — Usually refers to the stock market. Is the trend upwards (bull market)? or is it downward (bear market)?

market profile — Demographic information about the people or the households of a product's market and may also include economic and retailing information about the territory

market research — (1) Gathering of information about a product's market to determine the best approach in making merchandising decisions; (2) A tool used in market research to determine the needs and wants of potential customers and their preferences; conducted by telephone or in person

marketing — All those activities which are intended to get a product from the manufacturer to the eventual consumer, that is, distribution

mass consumption — The ability of an economy to use very large quantities of goods and services, making production and distribution practical on a larger scale

mass distribution — A very large transportation network and storage system which enables large quantities of goods to flow from producer to consumer

mass media — An advertising method which is directed toward a wide range of people, a sort of shotgun approach

mass production — A method of manufacture using automatic methods and machinery, assembly lines, and other labor-saving technology which produces large numbers of items all exactly alike, thereby tremendously reducing the individual cost per item compared to the cost of a similar handmade item. The mass production system in this country depends on mass distribution and mass consumption in order for it to work.

master — (1) A level of proficiency in a trade or craft more skilled than a journeyman, and achieved only after many years of practice in the occupation; (2) A paper or aluminum sheet sensitized with an image that can then be placed on an offset press to print copies, that is, an offset master; (3) In the recording business, a prototype copy of a recording in special material so that wax or plastic copies can be molded from it, that is, a record master

mat — Short for *matrix*

maternity leave — A leave of absence granted to an employee for the purpose of having a baby

matrix — A mold of pulp paper that is made with movable type pressed into it; hot metal is poured into the mold to form an impression of the original type, which can then be placed on a press for printing. The molded metal is called a *stereotype.*

maturity date — The date on which a note becomes due, or matures; usually expressed in a number of days, for instance, a 60-day note matures 60 days from the date it was signed

mechanical — For an advertisement, a layout of photographs and set copy that is mounted on a sheet, from which a negative is made with a camera; the negative can then be printed on a plate for printing

median — In statistics, the middle number in a series

mediator — A professional reconciliator who attempts to bring management and labor bargainers together in order to settle a dispute

Medicaid — A federal program of outpatient services for the aged

Medicare — A federal program of health insurance for the aged

medium — (1) The vehicle that carries an advertisement, such as a radio wave, a poster, or a newspaper page; (2) The method or process used by an artist, such as oils, charcoal, pencil, water colors, pen and ink, wash, or crayon

memo — (1) Short for *memorandum;* a form on which a brief interoffice message or communication is written; (2) In bookkeeping, advice or a notice given of a credit or a debit to an account, that is, a credit or debit memorandum

memorandum entry — (1) A bookkeeping entry or notation that is used to record information, usually that is not posted, in the journals; (2) An entry to record a credit or debit memorandum

memory — A term used to describe the ability of a computer or similar device to store information on magnetic tapes, drums, banks, etc., for reference

merchandise — A term which refers to the goods a business buys for the purpose of resale to its customers, and also the goods the business has on hand

merchandise business — A business that buys and sells goods and/ or services at wholesale or retail presumably for a profit; the customer is charged more than the goods cost in exchange for the convenience of allowing the customer to buy in small quantities and from a wide selection

merchandise inventory — In bookkeeping, the name of the controlling account in the general ledger which is used to accumulate and summarize changes in the amount of inventory a business has at the end of a fiscal period, and as a result of the sales recorded and the purchases made, during the period

merchandising — (1) The practical science of selling more goods and services based on the correct interpretation of the trends in buying habits of customers as indicated by an analysis of accurate market data; (2) "The planning involved in getting the right merchandise or service at the right place, at the right time, in the right quantities, and at the right price" (definition given by the American Marketing Association)

misdemeanor — A violation or criminal act, less serious than a felony, but punishable by fine or imprisonment or both

money order — A bank check which can be purchased at a bank or any financial institution, and even at some stores, which is universally accepted because it is backed by the issuing company's funds

mutual — A term referring to an insurance company which returns any surplus to its policyholders in the form of dividends, or premium refunds, or bonuses, which amounts to reducing the cost of the next year's insurance if applied to the premium

national advertising — Advertising of any trademarked product, or of any advertising with nationwide circulation, or sponsored by a manufacturer or producer

National Association of Retired Persons (NARP) — A nonprofit organization which helps small businesses, among other things; members have many years of experience and are willing to help

national brand — A product name that has wide (national) acceptance as the result of major advertising in all the media

neglect — Ignoring a business or depriving it of care; a cause of business failure

negotiable instruments — Checks, drafts, and any other kind of commercial paper which can be used to transfer funds and which are endorsed on the back

negotiate — To bargain; the process of collective bargaining in which disputes are settled between labor and management by discussions, arbitration, and mediation

neighborhood shopping center — The smallest of the shopping centers, having no more than six stores and usually fewer; features those stores which carry convenience goods or offer consumer services and are usually within walking distance of the customer's home

neighborhood showing — In outdoor advertising, a term referring to a very small selection of posters, covering a small area or neighborhood, with a number of posters advertising a locally offered product or service; banks, restaurants, and department stores find this a good method of advertising

nemo — A broadcasting term meaning any program not originating from a local station

net income — Income from sales or services after all expenses have been paid, including such items as freight, allowances, discounts, and sales taxes, but excluding operating expenses

net loss — A financial condition which occurs when the income of a business is not sufficient to pay all the expenses during a period. The difference between the total expenses and the total income is known as the net loss.

net profit — A surplus after all the expenses have been paid, including operating expenses such as heat, light, rent, and wages, but excluding taxes

net sales — Actual receipts from sales, less returns and allowances

net wages — The amount of wages left after deductions, that is, the take-home pay

net weight — The weight of the contents of a container or vehicle after the weight of the container or vehicle has been subtracted, that is, the actual weight of the contents or load

net worth — The capital investment an individual or partners have in a business after the liabilities have been subtracted from the assets, that is, the capital value of the business

network — A group of radio or television stations connected together by radio, microwave relays, or coaxial cable to form a system capable of locally broadcasting programs emanating from one location

Nielson Television Index (NTI) — The name given to a television rating service, that is, the *Nielson ratings;* a measure of the audience of a television show at a given time

no fault — A principle in automobile insurance in which there is no effort to fix the cause or blame in small property damages cases, since the time spent in court for litigation is waived and the insurance company for each insured person pays the damages instead of the person whose fault the damage was; saves on claims settlement costs and court costs, and is supposed to reduce premiums

no loss — A clause in a contract in which a party is guaranteed to at least break-even

noninterest bearing note — A promissory note which does not require the payment of interest

nonstore retailing — Any means of getting goods and services to the consumer without the customer coming to the store; includes route selling and direct selling, vending machines, and mail order

note — Short for *promissory note;* a written promise to pay a fixed or determined sum of money at a future date with or without interest, or on demand

notes payable — Promissory notes a business owes and which are payable

notes receivable — Promissory notes which are owed to a business and which are collectible

O and O — A radio or television station owned and operated by a network, as opposed to one that is independently owned

odd lot — A number of shares less than 100 purchased from a broker. The commission is higher.

off camera — A television term for an actor or announcer whose voice is heard, but who does not appear in the commercial or on the screen; get paid less than if the actor or announcer actually appeared "on camera"

office machines — Any of a group of electric and electronic calculators, adders, and other machines including typewriters, etc., designed to print, type, or process information; generally portable

offset — A printing process that uses an image placed on a photographically or chemically developed master or a plate so that parts of the plate will pick up ink and transfer the ink to paper. See *lithography*.

Old English — A style of type with fancy serifs and and wavy lines, making the design very ornate and decorative; often used for trademarks and heads

one-time rate — A charge made for advertising that is placed only once, as opposed to a time rate or a rate that is discounted

open account — A bookkeeping term meaning an account (customer) that has a current balance, and if the customer has good credit, can therefore charge additional amounts to the account

open end — In television or radio, a broadcast or program in which the commercials are locally added at the end of the program

opening an account — A bookkeeping term meaning to set up an account in any ledger, and to write in the account title, page number, and other heading information, including the initial or opening balance

opening entry — In bookkeeping, the first entry made in starting a set of books, in which the balance sheet is recorded in the general journal

operating expenses — Those costs which are incurred in the course of operating a business such as rent, utilities, and labor

operating funds — Money set aside in a special account, if necessary, to pay for operating expenses for a period of time when a business is first opened

operating statement — A report which shows the income and expense of the operations of a bus for a fiscal period and the profit or loss for that period; prepared at the end of a fiscal period

operations — Those economic activities undertaken by a business.

operations manager — An individual who has local authority to supervise the activities of a unit of a company, or of all the company's activities; usually reports to the general manager

operations manual — A booklet prepared by the company giving its operating policies and rules and regulations for the operation of the company's activities

order of merit — Testing a trademark, slogan, logo, or any item of advertising; a panel of individuals who are asked to rank or rate several samples and then arrange each of the choices in order according to the ones which receive the most votes

ordinance — A local law usually issued at the county or town level

organization — (1) Any business of several people, but usually a company or corporation, that is, any group of duly constituted people banded together for a common purpose; (2) Internal organization refers to how a group is arranged in terms of relationships and authority. See *organization chart*. (3) External organization refers to the legal method in which a business operates under control or charter of a government agency, that is, sole proprietorship, partnership, corporation, cooperative, nonprofit corporation, agency, or controlled corporation

organization chart — A diagram showing the arrangement of the various persons in an organization and the relationships that exist in terms of duties and authority among them

outstanding checks — In a checking account, those checks not returned with the monthly statement by the bank; checks not yet cleared by the bank

outstanding deposits — Deposits that have been mailed or sent to the bank which do not yet show on the bank statement, but which have been entered in an individual's checkbook

package — (1) A container for a product, frequently a food product, that is designed to hold, protect, and present the contents in a desirable and attractive manner so that the prospective shopper will select the product; (2) A deal or a combination offer, usually a contract, including several items at a price lower than the total of the items individually; frequently used in real estate, advertising, and wholesaling

packaging — The distributive business of putting goods in containers, and the art and science of their design.

packing slip — A document inserted in a shipment that lists the contents and their quantity; used to make sure an order is complete

panel — A group of persons selected at random for product testing and commercial reaction, that is, a consumer panel

panel truck — A delivery vehicle with no windows

paraprofessional — An assistant to a professional such as a dental technician or a surgeon's assistant; has at least four years of college-level training

parent company — In the case of a franchise, the organizer of the franchise; also known as the *franchisor*

parties — Persons who enter into a contract

partnership — A business owned by two or more people

passbook — A booklet issued by a savings bank, which is actually a copy of the account ledger for a person's account; shows all deposits and withdrawals

patent — A statement and description of an invention, device, idea, or an original process that has been filed with the U.S. Patent Office; shows the date and number of the patent, and protects the inventor from infringement by providing exclusive rights to the invention for a period of at least 17 years

pay — Usually wages; as a verb, to give someone cash or the equivalent of cash

pay-as-you-go — A policy, sometimes applied to government, which suggests that programs are not instituted until there is a source of revenue to pay for them, that is, a business that operates on a cash basis

payee — The person on a check or draft to whom the instrument it made payable, that is, pay to the order of: the person who endorses the check and who can cash the check

payor — The bank or financial institution on which a draft or check is drawn

payroll — A list of employees who are paid periodically by a firm, along with other information; also includes the money to pay employees

payroll number — A number or symbol assigned to each employee for payroll purposes

payroll register — A document, or worksheet, used to record the wages and deductions paid each pay period for each employee

payroll savings plan — A system used in many companies whereby deductions can be made from an employee's weekly wages for the purpose of purchasing U.S. savings bonds. A small amount is accumulated each time an employee is paid until the purchase price is reached, and then the bond is issued to the employee.

peddler — A salesperson who travels to different areas selling goods from a pushcart, packbag, or a truck; usually requires a license, and can be prohibited in some towns. See *direct sales* and *route sales*.

penalty — A fine, or forfeiture of something of value, as punishment for failure to conform to a regulation or for violating a rule or ordinance. For example, if personal income taxes are paid late, there is an interest penalty.

pension — A retirement income, either from social security plans, from a private annuity or retirement fund established by an employer, or from an individual retirement account established by the individual. After retirement, payments are made monthly, either until death, to a spouse, or for a term.

performance — One's work, that is, the quality and quantity of a worker's labor measured over a period of time, usually by a supervisor

performance review sheet — A document on which a supervisor writes an evaluation of a worker's labor record for a given period of time; used frequently as a basis for granting or refusing a raise or promotion

performance test — A test in which the person being tested performs or accomplishes a specific task or activity, usually observed and timed. The purpose of the test is to determine the person's degree of competency in performing a specific task.

performing arts — Creative entertainment involving a person performing a physical act, such as singing, dancing, acting, or twirling a baton, etc.; one of the creative businesses

permit — A document granting permission for someone to perform a specified act, usually for a limited period of time. The time period a permit would cover is not long as the time period a license would cover; subject to many restrictions

perpetual inventory — A system of merchandise records which keeps a record on a continual basis of all increases and decreases in the number of each item of inventory, using cards or computers to assist. The data can be recorded manually, or from the output of a cash register or other similar device.

personal data sheet — Sometimes called a *resume;* a document showing personal and career information about an individual; usually a person sends a personal data sheet when applying for a job with a company

personality — Characteristics which make up a person's total being, that is, their character

personnel — A collective term for a group of people, usually with something in common, that is, all of the people (personnel) who work at a certain plant or in a certain office

personnel manager — An official of a company who is responsible for keeping records on the workers who are employed at that company, and for dealing with their needs and problems. In small businesses, this person may also act as the employment manager

personnel manual — A handbook, often issued to new employees of a company, explaining facts about the company, and its rules, regulations and policies. See *policy handbook.*

personnel office — In a company, the office where employee records are kept

petty-cash fund — A small amount of cash usually kept in the office safe to pay small bills instead of issuing a check

petty-cash journal — A booklet in which small payments of cash for various purposes are recorded

petty cash voucher — A receipt for the payment of a bill from petty cash funds

physical inventory — The actual counting, one by one, of each item of inventory to see how many of each specific item is actually in the store or warehouse

PI — Means *per inquiry;* an especially inexpensive advertising rate, for radio stations and some TV stations, in which the advertiser offers a product for sale (frequently records) and pays the station so much for each record or item actually sold

pica — (1) A unit for measuring the width of a column in printing, that is, 1 pica = 1/6 inch, or there are 6 picas in one inch; (2) Also means *pica em,* a term meaning a space 1/6 inch square; (3) Refers also to the height (1/6 inch) of a letter

piggyback — A transportation term which refers to the practice of placing two motor transport trailers on flat cars and hauling them long distances by rail to destinations where they are unloaded and hauled to final destinations by tractor-trailer motor trucks; saves on gasoline or diesel fuel, and the use of tractor units

planning — (1) Preparing a project beforehand, that is, laying out in advance on paper an ad, a store layout, or an arrangement of merchandise so that the finished job will be successful

plant — A shop or factory where manufacturing takes place

plant operator — In outdoor advertising, the person who arranges to lease, erect, and maintain outdoor signs and to sell the advertising space thereon

playback — The playing of a recording for audition purposes

pneumatic tubes — In a department or retail store, the compressed air powered tubes which propel canisters containing money and receipts from one station to another at a high speed; saves time and makes possible a central location for receiving cash

point (pt) — A unit of type measure, that is, 1 point = 1/72 of an inch; used to specify headline type size

point-of-purchase — The location in a store where money is exchanged for goods and/or services, that is, the check-out counter or the place where the cash register is located

point-of-sale advertising — Advertising placed at or near the point of purchase in the hope it will remind customers at the last minute of items they need. See *impulse merchandise.*

point-of-sale display — Displays placed at the check-out counter in the hope of increasing sales by suggesting items that the customer may have forgotten while shopping

policy — (1) A written insurance contract between the insured and the company which agrees to indemnify the insured against loss of property, etc. In the case of property insurance, the policy is usually written for one year. (2) A statement of intent concerning rules and regulations in a company, indicating what action the company plans to take under a given set of circumstances

policy handbook — A booklet published by a company, stating all of the company's policies; given to new employees so that they are informed about the policies

post closing trial balance — In bookkeeping, a check to see if all the debits equal all the credits after the books have been closed for the fiscal period

postal money order — A post office draft, similar to a money order, which can be sent safely through the mails ordering payment to a specified individual

poster — A large outdoor structure approximately 12 feet high by 25 feet long used for the purpose of displaying an advertiser's message which is pasted on the display surface. The poster is shown for an agreed upon period of time, it can be lighted at night for an additional charge.

posting — A bookkeeping term meaning to transfer information (entries) from the journal to the ledger so that the information can be cross-referenced and later summarized

preempt — To remove one program from the air so that another may be shown in its place

preferred stock — Stock that is granted preference in the distribution of dividends over common stock

premium — (1) A charge paid monthly or yearly, usually for an insurance policy, which keeps the policy in force; (2) A promotional offer; merchandise offered free of charge (except postage and handling) in exchange for a box top or proof of purchase certificate from a product; used to establish mailing lists and to promote products

prepaid insurance — A bookkeeping term which refers to an account in which payments for insurance are recorded from time to time as the insurance period expires

primary — Within a political party, when two or more candidates for the same office and from the same party are running for election

primary circulation — The residents of households who receive a publication

primary service area — The area to which a radio or television station can deliver a signal of sufficient strength to override noise levels day and night and during all seasons of the year with unfailing steadiness

prime time — (1) In television, the period when there are the most listeners tuned in, usually the period from 7 PM to 11 PM, for which the station charges the most money; (2) In radio, prime listener time is usually from 7 AM to 8:30 AM and from 4:30 PM to 6:30 PM

principal — (1) The chief official of an educational institution, such as a high school; (2) The amount of a loan or the face amount of an insurance policy; (3) In a contract with an agent, the principal is the originator and responsible party, as the agent is only acting for the principal

principal register — The main list of recorded trademarks, service marks, collective marks, and certification marks under the Lanham Act

principal stockholder — A stockholder of a corporation with more shares than anyone else, but not a majority stockholder

principle — A fundamental belief or statement of fact or truth, which may help in planning a course of action

private brand — The trademark of a distributor of products which the distributor alone sells

private corporation — A corporation which chooses not to sell its stock to the public, but is reserving all stock for members of the family or the original founders. See *closed corporation.*

proceeds — The net amount realized when a promissory note is discounted or prepaid. The proceeds is the amount remaining when the interest and other charges are subtracted from the principal.

produce — Agricultural products such as fruits and vegetables

producer — (1) Any business which makes or processes a product, that is, a manufacturer; (2) In radio and television, one who originates, finances, and presents a program

product — Any item made or fabricated by man

product liability — The risk of injury, loss, or damage to a person or to property as a result of using a specific product or service according to the instructions

product protection — In television, the guarantee that an advertiser's ad will not be aired closer than 15 minutes (air time) to a commercial that is sponsored by a competitor

production — (1) The manufacturing or assembly of large quantities of goods in a plant or factory, using machines, materials, and labor. See *mass production.* (2) The planning, organizing, filming, taping, editing, and dubbing of a movie, documentary, or television program of any kind

professional — A highly skilled practitioner of an art or science who usually has had at least four years of college-level training, may have qualified on a performance test, and may have a license to practice the profession

professional association/society — Actually a trade association for professionals; an organization that represents and protects the working conditions of its members, its ethics, and examines and licenses or recommends licensing of new members (for example, the American Medical Association and the American Bar Association)

profit — A surplus remaining after expenses and costs have been paid. See *net profit* and *gross profit*

profit margin — A planned percentage markup on cost to cover overhead

profit motive — The desire to make a profit which encourages individuals to become entrepreneurs

profit sharing — A system whereby excess profits of a company are distributed to employees as an incentive or reward for good workmanship or loyalty, rather than declare the profits as surplus and therefore pay tax on them

promissory note — A written promise by the maker of the note to pay a stated sum of money, with or without interest, to the payee at some future or determinable date, or on demand

promo — Short for *promotional;* any sales promotion activity

promotional consideration — A commercial message or mention of a sponsor's product in exchange for goods or services, such as hotel rooms, transportation, etc.

proof — An inked impression of set type for the purpose of checking for errors

proofreader — A person who checks copy for errors

proprietor — The owner of a business

proprietorship — The equity or amount of ownership an individual has in a business, that is, the value of the net worth

proving cash — The process of adding up all the cash, checks, and coins in a cash register drawer and then comparing the total with the amount that is supposed to be in the cash drawer according to the detail record tape on the register or in the register totals

public corporation — A corporation which sells its stock to the public; also known as an *open corporation*

public interest — For the benefit of all, that is, nonprofit and any business activity or company which exists to serve the public, such as foundations, trusts, charities, and philanthropic organizations

public interest corporation — Any corporation, sometimes organized by and for the government, which exists to service the public or provide a service for the public that cannot be provided under other circumstances; examples include authorities, commissions, and administrations

public relations — A department in a company assigned the responsibility of dealing with the public on an individual basis, handling complaints, correspondence, conducting plant tours, and trying to obtain and maintain a "good press." Public relations agencies contract with companies to promote their so-called public image, but they are really advertising agencies.

public service corporation — A privately owned corporation which is a controlled monopoly or which has special permission to offer a service to the public in an area on an exclusive basis to avoid confusion, such as a telephone, telegraph, broadcast, or power company. Some of these public service companies are called *public utilities.*

public utility — A controlled monopoly offering service to the public, but it is privately owned

publicity — Favorable information, usually in the media, about a company or a product that is free because it has news value

purchase — An item bought and paid for

purchase on account — To buy merchandise for resale from a vendor on an open account

purchase order — A document, prepared with several copies, authorizing a vendor to supply a company with goods or services described in the order, and binding the company to pay for the goods or services

purchase requisition — An internal form requesting that a purchase order be issued by an authorized person, so that merchandise or supplies described on the form can be ordered

purchases — (1) Goods and services required by a company for resale, or as raw materials, or as supplies, in order to conduct business; (2) Merchandise bought from vendors and wholesalers for resale, usually on account, and recorded in the purchases journal

purchases journal — A record of all purchases or orders on credit from vendors and suppliers, that is, a record of credit orders

purchasing — The activity of buying merchandise and supplies for a business at the lowest possible price, consistent with specifications and having reasonable quality, and maintaining accurate records of these purchases; also includes planning of the purchases and the preparation of a budget, and may include inventory control

purchasing agent — An official of a company whose primary responsibility is to buy merchandise and supplies for the company

quantity discounts — Discounts (trade) given to retailers, etc., who purchase larger than normal amounts of merchandise from wholesalers, and who thereby get additional discounts because they bought large quantities. Quantity discounts are given for carload lots.

quasi-public corporation — A business, usually a corporation, which is owned and operated by the government but for the good of and for the benefit of the public. Private citizens serve on the board of a quasi-public corporation. It is not permitted by law to make a profit.

quota — (1) A minimum, an amount below which commissions are reduced, or a goal for salespeople; (2) A set goal for sales or another effort such as fund raising, in terms of dollars, units, or a percentage of the total goal

rate — (1) A discount or charge quoted as a percent, for example, 10%; (2) A charge made for something, such as insurance rates or freight rates

rate card — A document issued by a publisher or broadcasting station listing its charges (rates) for various amounts of advertising time

rated policy — An insurance policy that has been issued by the company, but at a higher premium than usual because of an excessive risk, or in the case of life insurance, because of a health condition such as high blood pressure

rating — A number of points a given program receives at any one time in either radio or television based on the share of the possible listening audience, that is, the percentage of the audience that watched that program as compared with the total audience

reach — The total audience a medium actually covers

ream — A measure of paper, usually a package containing 500 sheets

rebroadcast — A radio or television program repeated at a later time to reach parts of the country that are in a different time zone

receiving — The activity in a retail store or in any business which receives merchandise, materials or supplies, and includes checking incoming goods to see if they conform to the purchase order, a packing slip, a purchase requisition, or any other source document as to size, color, number, quantity, etc., of the goods, and may include testing to see if the goods meet certain specifications

receiving department — A department in a business where goods are received, tested, and counted, and if certain specifications are met, the goods are accepted

receiving ticket — A document showing that goods have been received, the date on which they were received, and that they conform to specifications

recognized agency — An advertising agency which is recognized by publishers and broadcasters and is granted commission of the space it sells to advertisers

regional channel station — In radio, a station that is licensed to use more power than a local station, but less than a clear-channel station, and is assigned a frequency reserved for regional stations, giving it greater reception area

regional shopping center — A shopping center, which serves several counties, with about 50 to 100 stores and 2 or 3 well-known stores serving as traffic magnets. The regional shopping center is larger than the suburban shopping center, yet smaller than the super mall

register — (1) A metal box containing printed slips for recording sales. The slips can be torn out of the register when completed. A copy of the slip is given to the customer as a receipt. (2) Short for *cash register;* (3) A printed form on which checks are recorded, etc., issued for payroll or for other purposes. See *payroll register.* (4) A list of professional persons who have been granted licenses to practice a profession, such as registered pharmacists, etc. The register is maintained by a government agency (usually the state secretary of state) and monitored by the appropriate professional society or association.

registered nurse (RN) — A professional nurse who has passed state board examination and has been admitted to the profession and is duly entered in the RN Register for the state

registering a trademark — The act of recording a trademark with the U.S. Commissioner of Patents

registration — In printing, the degree to which colors in a multicolored press coincide with each other

regulation — A law, ordinance, or other statement issued by competent authority requiring that an activity or certain behavior be abided by. For example, it is a regulation in certain states that you wear a helmet when operating a motorcycle.

release — A written and signed statement giving permission for a person or business to permit the use, reproduction, or dissemination of a photograph, statement, endorsement, or quotation, in advertising or in any form of printed or broadcast matter, for example, a release for the use of a photograph of a fashion model

report — A printed statement, usually prepared at the end of each fiscal period, showing summaries of financial data about a business, for example, financial reports

report form of the balance sheet — In bookkeeping, a term referring to the balance sheet which has the assets, liabilities, and net worth arranged vertically in a column

residuals — Payments to an actor, or an author, or a firm holding a copyright for material used in a program, advertisement, or any other publically shown work, as royalties for the use or showing of the material for as long as the material is copyrighted or repeated

respondent — A person who answers a questionnaire in a market survey

restrictive endorsement — A phrase written on the back of a check restricting the conditions or purpose under or for which a negotiable instrument can be cashed, followed by an individual's signature (e.g., "for deposit only . . . John White")

retailer — A business person who sells goods directly to the consumer in a store or shop; the last link in the distribution chain

retailing — The act of operating a retail business

retentive stage — The stage of the advertising spiral in which a product is widely recognized and relies on the strength of its reputation

retouching — The process of correcting or improving by hand any artwork or photographs in the darkroom or elsewhere before printing

returned check — A check that has been returned to the payee by the bank, because the bank refused it for a reason, such as insufficient funds in the account, or a stop payment, etc.

revolving charge — A monthly charge account, most often used in a retail store, which bills the customer according to a given day in the month, usually determined by the initial letter of the person's last name. For example, the G's are all billed on the seventh day of the month.

right of contract — In this country, the freedom to make legal agreements

right of free enterprise — The freedom to enter into any business activity that is legal and does not infringe on the rights of other people

right of profit — The freedom to try to make a profit in an honest manner

right of property — The freedom to own, buy, sell, and use property

round lot — A purchase of 100 shares or more (in multiples) from a broker. The commission for round lots is less than that given for odd lots

route — The delivery stops made periodically by a vendor or delivery truck in a given area. See *route sales.*

route sales — Selling goods and/or services to customers on a periodic basis and delivering directly to their homes or stores, and making deliveries according to an established or prearranged schedule. The customers pay for goods by check usually at the end of the month.

route seller — A wagon vendor or delivery retailer who delivers goods to an ordered list of customers each day or less often, for example, a milk route or a bakery route

route vendor — A wagon vendor who visits customers less often than weekly, but usually at least once a month. The visits are usually unscheduled. Customers pay for purchases on delivery.

route wholesaler — A route seller who sells to retailers on a periodic basis, but not to consumers, for example, a wholesale bread route

rule — A stipulation, law, ordinance, etc., forbidding or banning an action

running balance — A bookkeeping term referring to a Boston-style ledger which gives a balance after each transaction instead of requiring that debits be subtracted from credits to get a balance each time

salary — A fixed amount of money paid to an employee for labor performed periodically, usually in two-week periods

sale — (1) An exchange of money for an item of merchandise, that is, a transaction; (2) A method of promotion in which certain items of merchandise in a store are reduced in price and advertised in order to attract customers

sale on account — A bookkeeping term which refers to selling merchandise to a customer (account receivable) on "account" to be paid for at a future date, that is, a credit sale

sales — A bookkeeping term referring to the amount of income derived from the sale of merchandise or services, both for cash and on account, less taxes, returns, and allowances

sales finance company — A consumer finance company specializing in the financing of the sales of expensive merchandise, such as furniture, appliances, and television sets. A sales finance company issues an installment sales or conditional sales contract to the buyer and pays the seller (retailer) the proceeds of the note so that the credit (loan) is carried by the finance company and not the retailer.

sales invoice — A business form which acts as a bill (invoice) to the customer and becomes the basis for billing and collecting

sales journal — A bookkeeping record in which only credit sales are recorded

sales promotion — Any activity or group of activities designed to increase the sales of merchandise or services

sales returns and allowances — A bookkeeping term referring to deductions from gross sales for refunds to customers for returned or defective merchandise

savings account — A depositor's account in a savings bank which pays a slightly higher rate of interest than a regular account, but restricts the time and method of withdrawal

savings and loan association — Not really a bank, but a financial institution which specializes in savings accounts and limits its loans primarily to mortgages and other long term loans; often uses a commercial bank to handle its money

savings banks — Banks which specialize in savings accounts, as opposed to commercial banks

savings club — An account in a bank which allows the depositor to save a certain amount of money each week for a specific goal, for example, a vacation club or a Christmas club

scab — A slang expression referring to a strike-breaker or a nonunion worker brought in by management to replace striking workers

scale — (1) A metal ruler, usually steel, used in making layouts; (2) A ratio of dimensions in a drawing or sketch to the actual length that each line represents; for example, *Scale: 1" = 1'* means that a line on a drawing one inch long actually represents a line one foot long; (3) An expression meaning agreed upon union wages, that is, the union approved the hourly rate for a particular job. To pay scale is to pay union wages.

scan — (1) To view rapidly, that is, to scan copy; (2) To view electronically with a laser or with a video camera

scanner — (1) An electronic device which scans, for example, an MICR or a UPC scanner; (2) A closed-circuit television camera in a bank or retail store which moves back and forth across a predetermined area in order to provide surveillance in the event of robbery or shoplifting

schedule — A business form listing a group of accounts, usually for some specific purpose, for example, a schedule of accounts

schedule of accounts — A list of accounts along with their current balances

schedule of accounts payable — A list of creditors and amounts owed to them

schedule of accounts receivable — A list of customer's accounts and the amounts owed by the customers

scrambler — A device on a television cable network which mixes the signal so that only those subscribers with an "unscrambler" can receive the signal. There is a monthly charge for using a scrambler.

securities — Collectively, stocks and bonds, that is, ownership or loan certificates, either negotiable or nonnegotiable, in business or government

Securities and Exchange Commission (SEC) — The government agency which oversees the transactions of stocks, etc., in the various stock exchanges and requires certain regulations of companies trading in securities in order to prevent fraud

security — (1) That department of a business responsible for the safekeeping of company machinery, inventory, equipment, and tools. The term may refer to a guard force or personnel who perform surveillance and security checks when looking for stolen merchandise or illegal substances. (2) An item of value, such as a gold ring, which is pledged as collateral for a loan

selective — Choosing something or someone with a criteria in mind rather than at random

self-analysis — The act of examining one's self

self-mailer — A direct mail piece that can be used for a reply by simply folding the piece in reverse, sealing, and mailing it again to the address thus exposed by reversing the piece

self-service — A retail store that is arranged in order to permit customers to wait on themselves to a great extent. Merchandise is put in easy-to-reach places and packaged in convenient quantities.

semi-skilled — A worker who is partially trained, usually half-way through a training program

serendipity — A term meaning an apparent ability to make fortunate discoveries by accident

service — An act performed by one person for another, usually requiring special skill, equipment, training, knowledge, or practice

service agreement — A contract sold by a retail store at the same time a large appliance or another item is sold, extending the warranty period and guaranteeing service at no additional cost for the period of the agreement

service order — A work request for the repair or service of an item, either within an organization or from a service organization performing such service, that is, a work order

service record — (1) A record or written account of repairs and service performed on a customer's property, such as a car, plane, or boat; (2) A personnel form showing worker's employment history, indicating all important facts about the worker, a record of promotions, and work assignments, etc.

services — A group of activities, usually of a related nature, and in an organization chart, usually controlled or supervised by one individual, for example, Director of Administrative Services

signature — A legal writing by hand of a person's name, which when placed on a contract or business document implies agreement or consent, or when written on the back of a check, constitutes an endorsement

signature card — A card that is maintained by a bank, bearing an example of the signature of an individual(s) authorized to draw checks on an account

signature facsimile — A copy of one's signature, either on a steel engraved plate used for authenticating large numbers of payroll checks, etc., or transmitted by telephone or radio signal for use in another location. In some states, facsimile signatures are considered legal.

single entry bookkeeping — A method of recording business transactions that is not totally accurate because it lacks the safety factor of a trial usually called balance; usually referred to as *record keeping*

social security — A mandatory system of old-age and disability insurance provided by the federal government through a system of taxation of both employee wages and matching employer contributions; otherwise known as Federal Insurance Contributions Act (FICA)

social security taxes — The employee's and the employer's contribution to social security which must be withheld from wages and forwarded to the Internal Revenue Service through the Federal Reserve System every three months (quarterly)

source document — In bookkeeping, any piece of paper with information on it about a transaction, etc., serving as the basis for making an entry in a set of books. A source document is considered any one of the following: an invoice, bill, receipt, voucher, draft, check, or note, from which a journal entry is made.

special journal — In bookkeeping, a journal in which only certain types of transactions are recorded, for example, purchases on account would be recorded in the purchases journal

state disability tax — Depending on the business, either a state or federal disability contribution must be withheld from employees' wages and accrued for future payment.

state income tax — Most states have income tax withholding from earned wages, as does the federal government. Employers withhold state taxes from employee's wages generally in the same manner as they do federal income taxes.

state unemployment insurance tax — Depending on the business and on past experience with layoffs and work stoppages, an amount of money must be accumulated and paid out by an employer for each employee who works, in order to provide funds for unemployment insurance in the event the worker is no longer employed.

statement — A summary of an account sent periodically (usually once a month) to the account holder, listing all transactions and the balance due. It is not an invoice.

statement of account — In bookkeeping, a form that shows the changes in a customer's account, all transactions, and is a duplicate of a ledger card for that account; most times, sent on request

stop payment order — A written form authorizing a bank to dishonor or refuse to pay funds on a check when presented for payment, and to return the check to the last endorser

subsidiary ledger — A ledger that is summarized in a single account in the general ledger

supplies — Goods bought by a business that are necessary for its operation, not to be confused with merchandise or purchases which are goods intended for resale. Supplies are of several types, including office supplies, shop supplies, factory supplies, etc.

supporting schedules — A list of accounts, etc. attached to a financial report as part of it, and used to show additional information not contained in the original report (e.g., tables, charts, etc.), which support the authenticity of the report

T account — The arrangement of a ledger page account in such a way as to show the debit and credit columns side by side with the rulings separating the sides, roughly in the shape of a letter *T*.

take-home pay — Net wages; the amount of money left after deductions have been made from a worker's gross wages

time of a note — The term or length of time a note runs, from the date of the note (date when signed) to the maturity date or the date when it is called

total — A sum

total earnings — Gross wages; the amount of earnings a worker accumulates in any given pay period before any deductions have been made

transactions — Usually any business or financial activity in which the ownership of goods or services, and/or financial interest, changes

traveler's check — A type of money order guaranteed by a bank or financial institution requiring two signatures of the maker to the negotiated — one at the time of issuance and one at the time of transfer

trial balance — A totaling of all accounts in an attempt to bring them into balance

trust companies — Financial institutions which administer people's estates

underwriter — An individual or a company that secures or protects another's interest in something from loss or damage in exchange for payment of cash, called a premium, over a term, that is, an insurer

voiding a check — Destroying or in some way defacing a check so that it cannot be cashed

voucher — A receipt

voucher check — A check which has a receipt attached to it

worksheet — A page of distribution paper used to summarize accounts at the end of a fiscal period in order to attempt a trial balance, and then to prepare financial reports

INDEX